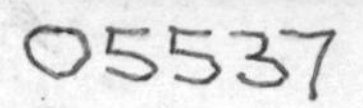

Essays Catholic and Radical

ESSAYS CATHOLIC AND RADICAL

A Jubilee Group Symposium for the 150th Anniversary of the beginning of the Oxford Movement 1833-1983

Edited by Kenneth Leech and Rowan Williams

THE BOWERDEAN PRESS 1983

First published in 1983 by
The Bowerdean Press
55 Bowerdean Street
London SW6 3TN

Cover designed by Douglas Martin

Printed and bound by
Stantonbury Parish Print
Milton Keynes, MK14 7PL

ISBN 0 906097 10 X

Contents

Note

Many people have helped to make this symposium possible by their support and financial help. We are particularly grateful to the Christendom Trust and to the United Society for the Propagation of the Gospel for grants which they gave towards its production.

Introduction

Kenneth Leech and Rowan Williams

Towards the end of 1974 a letter was circulated among a number of priests, mainly in the East End of London. It was concerned with the renewal of the social conscience of Anglican Catholics. Part of this letter ran as follows:

> 'A number of us are very disturbed at the trend in the Catholic movement towards a sickly pietism and a right-wing reactionary stance in social and political issues. This trend represents a serious betrayal of the social tradition of Anglo-Catholicism and it may spell the death of the movement as such. Whether the present organs of Anglo-Catholic opinion are reformable remains to be seen: it is hardly likely that any of them will be transformed into organs of revolutionary zeal. They seem to be more concerned with changes in the liturgy than with changes in the world, and one fears that for too many within the Catholic movement, religion has become a substitute for life.'

However, the letter went on to propose a coming together of a number of people who shared the outlook of the writers, and suggested that it would be useful to produce a broadsheet which might begin, in a modest way, to reverse some of the unhealthy trends. It was out of this letter and the subsequent discussions that the Jubilee Group came into being. And it was from the movement initiated by Jubilee that the present volume came into being. Although the contributors represent a wide spectrum of outlook, they all share a concern for the renewal of the social conscience of Catholic Christianity.

The emergence of the Jubilee Group antedated the setting up of the wider movement of Catholic Renewal in the Church of England, but, while there was no official connection, the parallels are close in some respects. From its inception the Jubilee Group movement was concerned with the renewal of the Catholic movement in the Church of England. An early leaflet from 1975 explained:

> 'The Group came into being as a result of a series of discussions on the current state of Catholicism in the Church of England. While there were, and are, some important differences among us, we found that we were united in (i) a commitment to the Catholic movement, and a strong sense of standing within the tradition of Catholic Orthodoxy; (ii) a sense of alarm and frustration at the present decayed and demoralised state of the movement; and (iii) a concern for the resurrection of the unity of contemplation and politics. In addition, within the wider framework of Christianity, we shared (iv) a concern at the woolly liberalism of much current social action in the church, and in particular at the state of the 'Christian Left' with its lack of clear theological thought.'

So arose the 'Jubilee tendency' within Anglican Catholicism, a tendency more than an organisation. There were few rigid lines on specifics, rather certain trends and directions, and, most of all, a discernible theological style. Jubilee was characterised from its inception by two particular concerns.

The first was a concern for Catholic orthodoxy and an insistence on the importance of revealed truth. Thus Jubilee has naturally been critical of reductionist trends in the theology of the past decade, but it is also struggling against the temptation to take refuge from hard theological questioning in the security of a traditionalism which is complacent and static (and which sometimes prides itself on its deeper 'spirituality'). Several of our essays in this volume attempt to show what might be involved in a vigorous dialogue with tradition rather than a mere repetition of it. We are worried about the survival of orthodoxy; we are not specially concerned about the maintenance of an *uncritical* orthodoxy. The second concern – deeply related to this – was, and is, for the development of a *theological* critique of capitalism. Jubilee remains dissatisfied with any kind of social comment resting on unquestioned assumptions; and this means that we look for a political voice which is both a renewal of, and renewed by, Catholic theological tradition. This above all is a unifying theme in the present volume – the search for a 'revolutionary orthodoxy', to retrieve a term used in some of our early literature.

It was over two years after the emergence of Jubilee, in January 1977, that the Bishop of Chichester wrote a letter which was sent to a number of people who were concerned about the state of the Catholic movement in the Church of England, and this letter was followed by an initial meeting in February. At this meeting a number of people spoke of the dangers of a false triumphalism and of a return to the past. In the early writing which helped to launch the movement for Catholic Renewal, there was a stress on the wholeness of the faith and on the need for a social critique. The first circular which was issued by the Bishop of Chichester and others at Ascensiontide 1977 referred to the need to 'recover the wholeness of its faith' and to 'challenge the false values, both spiritual and material, which confront society'.

It was out of the long period of discussion and thought which followed these early soundings that the Loughborough Conference 'Proclaiming the Risen Christ' took place at Eastertide 1978. While there were genuine and widespread fears about Loughborough, there were also optimism and hope that the movement might help to bring about a renewal of social vision. An 'Open Letter to the Loughborough Conference' from the Parish of St. Mark, Swindon, expressed their hope thus:

> We hope that there will emerge from Loughborough a renewed sense of corporate social concern (like that which characterised the Catholic Movement so illustriously in the past) as a basis for sound social teaching in the spirit of *Populorum Progressio*, *Pacem in Terris* and *Mater et Magistra*. The weighty matters of love, justice and mercy must again be at the heart of our discipleship.

In all honesty it cannot be said that this has happened.

Certainly there was a sense of wholesomeness and a lack of fanaticism at the Conference. The 'lunatic fringe' of the Catholic movement, while not entirely absent, was pretty quiescent.

But the years following 'Loughborough 1' have seen a steady retreat towards preoccupations of a mainly ecclesiastical nature. Not that these are trivial or silly; but it is hard to avoid the impression of a degree of insulation from the wider world in a lot of Catholic activity in recent years.

The contributors to this volume are highly critical of certain trends and developments within Anglican Catholicism. Some of the essays will meet with hostility and anger from many sources. Not all the contributors would agree on every issue. Nevertheless we believe that these essays raise issues of critical importance, not only for the Catholic movement in Anglicanism but also for the future of Christianity in the modern world.

In 1933, the centenary year of the beginning of the Oxford Movement, the notable and remarkable Catholic thinker Maurice Reckitt said this:

> 'Men may celebrate no second centenary of our movement if we do not determine now to stand in social or in doctrinal issues plainly upon our own ground, with a message and a philosophy for the

whole range of human life, and a true order of ends and values, which men may reject indeed, but the distinctive character of which they can no longer mistake.'

His words abide.

RETURNING TO PRINCIPLES

1 What is Catholic Orthodoxy?

Rowan Williams

1 The obvious answer to the question in my title is that 'Catholic orthodoxy' – whether in the Anglican Communion or in the Christian Church at large – is the system of belief characterising those who describe themselves as 'Catholics', a group distinguishable by certain common modes of behaviour and organisation. 'Protestant' or 'Reformed' or 'Evangelical' orthodoxy would likewise be the system of another group or groups with rather different patterns. And in such a description lies the embryo of the familiar and dull – if not actually repellent – understanding of 'orthodoxy'. 'Monetarist orthodoxy', 'Marxist orthodoxy', 'liberal orthodoxy', scientific, medical, psychoanalytic, whatever: almost always an expression favoured by people who do not share the views so described, an expression suggesting a strongly and clearly determined set of ideas and responses, a comprehensive ideology. 'Orthodoxy' is the sort of system that minimises conflict or dialectic, and is programmed to resist fundamental challenges.

And so people not unnaturally come to think that opposition to 'orthodoxy' is of itself a praiseworthy thing. They hesitate to join political parties or churches or any other structured associations out of a fear of being captured by an 'orthodoxy' – having their intellectual and moral options foreclosed, losing the right of critical exploration. Their ideal, not always very fully or articulately expressed, perhaps, is one of rational enquiry and flexibility of response. The trouble with such an approach, though, is that it is, in important ways, naive about how things are known. 'Rational enquiry' is not a completely homogeneous thing: different sorts of rationality may be appropriate in different areas, and no one scheme of coming-to-know will work equally well in all fields of thinking and engagement. Sharp debates are carried on between different disciplines: therapeutically oriented psychology battles in many hospitals for independence from organic or behaviourist psychology, and the philosophy of science continues to puzzle over the questions of 'reductionism' – whether the behaviour of complex systems or organisms can be fully described in terms of the behaviour of simpler component systems ('a chicken is only an egg's way of making another egg'). The notion of an independent judgment, a lighthouse beam, falling dispassionately across the phenomena of the world is seductive but hopelessly inadequate (and, as Professor Donald MacKinnon remarked, in a seminar on knowledge and agnosticism, it is an image of secure detachment and superior position, which raises some moral and spiritual, as well as more narrowly philosophical, questions).

We come to know because we have some idea of 'how to know' in diverse situations – or, in other words, we learn by learning what might be appropriate questions. And this involves an ability to discriminate between different sorts of enquiry, different areas of questioning: a discrimination which is never simply invented out of nothing but depends on traditions, ways of seeing and of speaking about the world. Traditions or languages in this sense are essentially communal matters, processes of sharing and transmission. And so we end up with the irreducibly social nature of knowing and learning, the bond between knowledge and communities and their life. There is no need instantly to draw the drastic conclusion that therefore all we claim to know is absolutely determined by what our community allows us to know; full-scale relativism of this kind is actually quite difficult to state with any precision and coherence. But the basic point is unavoidable: knowing, discriminating, is learned by participating in a communal life. And the converse implication is equally important: communal life is a life of shared speech and shared symbols. What makes a community a community is a tradition of discriminating, imaging and symbolising – an ideology, if you like, or an 'orthodoxy'. 'A social group without ideology and utopia would be without a plan, without a distance from itself, without a self-representation, consigned to a history fragmented into events which are all equal and insignificant'.[1]

Only tradition makes thinking possible – an engagement, even a struggle, with what is given, rather than a passive and meaningless observation. Paradoxically, it is only 'orthodoxies' that make us critical, that enable us to ask questions. How is it, then, that ideology or orthodoxy is seen as repressive, or, worst of all, as actively distorting reality in order to preserve certain social (class) interests, as it is understood in many forms of Marxism? There can be no doubt that this kind of perception is pretty accurate in a wide range of contexts, What is seen to have happened is that a certain dimension of indeterminateness and candid self-appraisal has vanished from the group's life – 'indeterminateness' in the sense of grasping that the group's symbolic life and speech do not provide an absolutely comprehensive map of reality. The goal of the group has become a matter of internal adjustment, rather than fidelity to structures or constraints coming from beyond its language and mythology. You could say that such a group has lost the sense of being answerable to anything, it judges – and justifies – itself; or that its 'orthodoxy' has ceased to be a method for creation, discovery and a flexible and developing self-understanding. It no longer equips you to see, to discriminate for yourself. It expects you not to take part in a conversation but to repeat what is delivered to you by authoritative guardians of the tradition. In short, ideology, the self-representation of a group, has become a phenomenon of power, the sign of the dominance of an interest group. While there are inevitably issues about power involved in the development of any orthodoxy (how are symbols authoritatively determined, and by whom?), the crucial shift seems to occur when, in a complex society, ideology is used to justify, ground or explain existing relations of power, and so is used, consciously or not, as an instrument by one section of society for determining the destiny and the identity of those without power.

That is no doubt why the quotation above speaks of 'ideology and utopia', not only of a 'grid' for mapping reality, but a proposal for remoulding it. The ideological map, the structure of understanding, can be a response not simply to everyday reality, but to some sense, variously generated or informed, of deeper connections and patterns; and so it can be a means to discover or, indeed, actively uncover and restore the working of such patterns. And when it operates in this way, ideology/orthodoxy is not and cannot be static and uncritical. It should be prepared to question and test the working of its own power structures. Unless it has become rigidified, it should represent a self-limitation of present authority, allowing the possibility of error or distortion in transmission and exercise. It may indicate the nature of appropriate questions, but will not regard itself as a system of final and satisfactory answers.

What I have said so far suggests that we may need to develop an understanding of 'orthodoxy' as a tool rather than as an end in itself, a tool for discovery rather than control. Like any language, it is unintelligible without some idea of grammar – necessary rules and regularities. But it is there essentially as something both functional to the life of a community, and necessarily bound up with – grounding, perhaps – the identity of a community. It is there so that the community can explore as fully as possible the reality or realities which it exists in relation to. We learn to discriminate in a community; but the community comes into being in the first place out of some embryonic move towards new kinds of discrimination. Old styles come under increasing strain, new speech needs to be generated; and as it is generated, so is the new community, which then transmits a tradition across the generations, a tradition of enquiry nourished and enabled by the community's style of speech and act. This is the inevitable 'circularity' of community tradition – vicious only when it loses awareness of the relation to reality which generates it in the first place.

It is that awareness which gives 'orthodoxy' its critical edge. If we think of tradition as a means of access to the generative, creative events at the source of a community's life, an 'orthodox' tradition is one which keeps a community authentically attentive to and thus – in the sense already suggested – answerable to something above and beyond its own present life: to its source. Thus its present life and experience is always liable to be brought into question by the abiding possibility of retrieving the original points of novelty, distinctiveness and discrimination which brought it to birth. Not that the source event is repeatable: that would be nonsense. The whole meaning of a tradition is that transmission and re-presentation in history has been accepted, the reality of time and change has been grasped. But the source event is 'available', and because it is available it is not possessed by and swallowed up in the community but interacts with it and (potentially) extends it. It is not just a highly-organised set of memories, but an agenda, a project.

So in this perspective what 'orthodoxy' and the idea of orthodox tradition are for is to guarantee that the language and image-making and image-contemplating of a group retain an element of dialogue with the past and of self-critical adaptability. If orthodoxy is understood as inseparable from the continuing life of some human group, it ought not to be a purely static principle. And much depends here, of course, on how seriously we take history and development. It has been easy enough at times to see history as essentially a matter of decline and alienation from primitive purity or unity; and when that happens, orthodoxy readily becomes a principle only of conservation, a tool for reproducing the past rather than recognising its strangeness and distance and engaging on a mutual questioning, challenging and being challenged – not to overcome or abolish the distance, but to cross and re-cross it, enlarging both the relevance of the past and the scope of one's own hopes and capacities of action or understanding. We ought to be able to avoid seeing history simply as alienation without falling into the trap of supposing there is no gap, no strangeness, to be overcome. Orthodoxy, in other words, is not there to make the past instantly intelligible and relevant, but to preserve some possibility of really encountering that past in its very oddity and pastness. That is where fruitful dialogue emerges.

But it is quite true that, in the history of ideas and of communities, alienation does take place: the past becomes a burden or just a puzzle – ie, more and more aspects of current exploration and questioning simply raise impossible and intolerable paradoxes when considered in the light of existing traditional orthodoxy. The strains are resolved only by some kind of breakthrough, a new 'generative event': philosophers of science speak of 'paradigm shifts', writers may think in terms of the creation of a new metaphor. But here we come up against an obvious problem when we turn to the question of religious orthodoxies. It is possible – in theory, anyway – to recognise the conditioned, provisional character of ideologies and the need for revolutions in understanding and new images; but what about the claims of systems which see their area of enquiry as the entire human self and the world of selves, decisively illuminated by some central image or myth? Systems of this sort do not take easily to any suggestion that there could be points of intolerable paradox or any running-out of significant dialogue. For them the past is always a resource: orthodoxy remains a tool for uncovering truth. History, so far from being a fragmented and discontinuous experience, is ultimately one, a continuity, a system of participation; present and past can communicate.

Claims like this are certainly problematic; yet they are not obviously nonsensical. The question of relativism is much too complex to be discussed in full here, but we can at least note that there is a clear connection between the idea that there is a continuous human history and the conviction of a single human destiny. To believe that all men and women have one goal, not several, that there are not different degrees of hope and fulfilment for different human beings in different ages and places, this is a belief which assumes some abiding truth about the human condition, inaccessible to modification by sectional interest or political convenience. The unity of the human story is, in this context, a critical and liberating idea; and the relativism which assumes different and mutually incommunicable human worlds runs the risk of exposing all humanistic projects to the manipulation of changeable will and uncertain circumstance. There is no ground for resistance or for 'utopian' hope and transforming action. Of course this does not make relativism untrue; but it places the onus on a relativistic view of mental and imaginative life to justify any enterprise of translation and interpretation on the one hand and of criticism and transformation on the other. Speech and meaningful action continue, it seems, to revolt against thoroughgoing relativism, against any idea of the absolute untranslatability and inaccessibility of what is culturally or historically strange. The claim to some kind of access to reality is more than a piece of straightforward intellectual arrogance or naiveté, but is rooted in the whole human effort at 'living significantly', constructing and communicating significant modes of action (purposive, shareable, discussable modes of action). And if this is so, the idea of an abiding, continuous 'orthodoxy' is still a viable one.

At least so long as we remain aware of what purpose it serves. To talk of some kind of ultimate or universal orthodoxy as if it meant possessing a theoretical perspective from which the entire human world could be viewed and decisively understood, a system with pigeon-holes for every person and situation we might ever encounter – this is in fact the ultimate ideological sclerosis – orthodoxy as a power mechanism; and it is this which produces the sharpest revolts against traditional paradigms. All that a religious orthodoxy ought to claim is that it is a way of access to certain patterns of human living and dying that are –irrespective of even the most far-reaching shifts in historical understanding – 'fundamental' in concern and orientation. And that is itself a maddeningly difficult word to interpret. I suppose that it refers to aspects of human stories which all men and women attempting to explore and understand their historical experience fully and 'fulfilledly' have to come to terms with. Thus they are patterns of living with or living out finitude, historicity and memory, relation and dependence, death. And an orthodoxy of a religious or (in the old-fashioned sense) metaphysical kind identifies certain patterns or families of patterns as classically appropriate responses, 'appropriate' normally because of a conviction about the underlying realities to which they respond.

The test of an orthodoxy, then, is something to do with its potential for authentic comprehensiveness. Can it continue to show the appropriateness of its classical models by continuing to nourish patterns of life and speech and transformative action that are not obviously regressive, evasive, exclusivist and defensively self-conscious in a contemporary setting? And can it show that it offers a fresh and deeper context of meaning or purpose for other and related patterns without instantly imposing on them predetermined behavioural constraints of its own? Can it interpret them without just attempting to 'colonise' them?

The understanding (not to say the defence) of orthodoxy in the religious context depends a great deal on the manifestation of its power to illuminate and enlarge – or, at the very least, to ask significant questions. It may not need to conquer its rivals and challengers in the ideological field so much as to demonstrate that it is resourceful enough both to question and to be questioned by them. And our judgment as between rival ideologies has, I think, something to do with the depth and scale of the questions with which they engage: how much of the human world do they find problematic? How much of it do they refuse to see as unclear, tormenting, resistant to glib solution? How many questions do they ignore or trivialise?

The same sorts of issue arise too in assessing the internal variation in a world-picture of this kind. 'Orthodoxy' carries with it its counter-image of 'heresy', a mutation of its basic concerns which radically distorts the available patterns. And in the light of the foregoing discussion, it makes some sense to view 'heresy' as a major reduction in the range of available resources of meaning: it is the decision to disallow certain kinds of question, perhaps for the sake of greater coherence. Its error may thus be a misreading of the job which the symbol-system of 'orthodoxy' seeks to perform; it will see the system as a defective kind of explanatory/descriptive account, in which coherence is a matter of conceptual economy and precision, rather than as a set of symbolic resources offered as a means of access to truth, policies for unillusioned but hopeful living, in which coherence at the level of conceptual economy may be less important than variety, resilience, imaginative comprehensiveness. The coherence involved here is far more the coherence of lived fidelity, a life held together by continuing engagement with the system, bearing out in the flesh its capacity for nurturing and transforming and directing the whole of a variegated experience.

A life lived in this kind of engagement may show us that the symbol-system does not easily 'run out': its resources are not exhausted. On the contrary, the testimony of each life so lived becomes part of the resource that is now transmitted to others; it 'enters the tradition'. So we can say that a religious and symbolic orthodoxy is 'cumulative': its coherence is shown in a constantly expanding network of narratives, biographies. The more such narratives are seen as illustrations, subordinate to a governing theoretical structure, the more the tradition closes in on itself, offering self-justifying projections rather than the risks of incarnation. The more these stories are seen as fresh statements (new metaphors?) in a common tongue, the more the tradition shows itself to be a living – and therefore an incomplete – thing. To some extent, new classics displace old, new statements make older ones problematic: perhaps we really cannot 'talk' like that now. Yet the language remains, carrying with it a history of expressive extension and increasing distinctiveness. There is no blandly (organically) straight line of development, but there is a background of continuity – not simply the continuity of corresponding ideas, but the continuity of common life, shared behaviour. And the idea of 'orthodoxy' is what evolves as the common life gropes for a sense of the criteria for continuity – what I have already called the 'grammar' by which we can discern that even wildly divergent utterances are being made in one and the same language.

2. So far, so (very) abstract. But it seemed worth trying to sketch in very general terms the sort of relation existing between any community and its 'orthodoxy' as an inevitable feature of its identity, and more particularly, any religious community and its symbolic system – meaning by 'religious' any group that sees its field of enquiry as the fundamental and inclusive context of human life. The picture emerging is one that is, I think, applicable to a wide assortment of groups: an 'orthodoxy' is the way a group pictures itself, its past, and its present and future task; but also, and especially in the religious sphere, the way in which it guarantees access for itself, across generations, to a set of generative and decisive

events, insights, actions, which began to make it a distinctive body. It pictures itself in relation to a determining source, a point of judgment; and as it evolves in history, it employs the notion of orthodoxy not only to restrict possibilities (though that is often how it is used), but also to keep open a set of options and policies, ways of 'truthful' living, embodying and interpreting its normative source event, or vision, or whatever it may be. It provides the symbols needed to live in a way 'appropriate' to the realities uncovered in its sources. And as a communal enterprise, it also makes possible the discipline of testing the individual's conceptions and projections against a wider critical background; it provides at least some means for avoiding merely consoling or self-indulgent, self-oriented, interpretations of the inherited deposit, because that deposit is now a more-than-individual matter. It is still community speech or it is nothing. And so the problem of heresy is a real one: orthodoxy does exclude viewpoints which narrow and distort the range of its language. Athanasius battled against Arianism partly because he saw it as limiting the possibilities of transformation ('deification') opened up for humanity through Christ. More immediately, perhaps, Barth rejected the German Christian doctrine of 'orders of creation' as restricting in advance the radical universalism of the gospel and providing a tacit apologia for anti-semitism. If orthodoxy is an aspect of a life-giving tradition, it will have limits: not everything and anything can be said in this language. Above all, it cannot be a language for the systematic degrading of the human or for the particularism of power groups – though no one will deny that this is exactly how the rhetoric of orthodoxy has regularly been used in the Church's history. But in fact, orthodoxy's challenge to the individual or to the local and specific group need not be seen as a threat to some sort of absolute spiritual independence: it is rather a challenge to the shrinking of a tradition to the dimension of one person's or one group's need, for comfort or for control.

I do not intend in this essay to consider in detail just why the Christian 'orthodoxy' should be preferred to any other: such a judgment would have to do with those questions already raised of comprehensiveness of application, breadth of questioning, and so on. It would be a judgment of the 'ultimacy' of what is grasped in the story of Jesus' death and resurrection. In the words of Margaret Masterman – both a scientist and a Christian philosopher – 'it is not just a question of defending a particular religion: let alone of defending any one variant of it: it is the question of exploring a possibly universal and fundamental type of human action and state and determining the implications of both of these to our view of the ultimate nature of the Universe'.[2] But, if we have once made such a judgment, in however inarticulate or inchoate a way, 'orthodox tradition' becomes the indispensably necessary condition for the possibility of this 'type of human action and state' being transmitted, nurtured and matured from one generation to the next. If we have realised what kind of work it is that ideology is meant to do; if we have stood outside it sufficiently to see that it is not meant to be (however often uncritically thought to be) a supra-historical, 'God's-eye' account of the structure of reality; if, in short, we have taken a critical stance towards it, we need not instantly assume that it has nothing to do with truth or reality, that it is a deliberately constructed fiction to guide our policy-making. There may be areas where it is increasingly hard to treat certain 'orthodox' doctrinal statements as recording matters of fact – look at the emerging consensus among a great many Catholic theologians (Karl Rahner among them) about the significance of the dogma of Our Lady's Assumption. But this does not leave us in the position of having to say either that no dogmatic statements have any real truth conditions (eg in historical fact) or that a contemporary 'orthodoxy' must discard any doctrinal tradition or image that fails to meet the condition of simple reporting. In the centre stands the concrete event of generation and transformation; around it a cluster of several different kinds of reflection – narrative, pictorial, or abstract. In so far as all attempt to mediate and serve the central transformation, they belong in a single family, a self-continuous tradition.

It is the fact that this tradition has a centre that stops it being just a pluralist mess. The shape or form of the central story is constantly interacting with the reflective, mediating stories and systems which transmit it, and 'orthodoxy' lies in the continuing making possible of that interaction. We habitually oppose orthodoxy to conflict, doubt, or provisionality; but if I am right in my reading so far, there is an aspect of Christian orthodoxy which is precisely a negative moment. At its heart is the confrontation with an event, an image, which is permanently disturbing, an image of loss: meaning, hope, and communication ('*Logos*') rejected by the world; but also an image of consummation: the 'ascension' of a human life and death into a level of reality and speech beyond historical limitation. The Word becomes final and free communication, universal hope and meaning, only as it is lost and abandoned and buried. Jesus is risen and glorified only in and through the cross.

'Orthodoxy' sets out to realise that Easter transaction, the death and birth of meaning, in each generation. It is the human co-operation with God's disclosing act, the clearing of a space in history and imagination, 'shepherding' the paschal event. Its paradox is that in this way it always subverts its own finality – as a system of words or pictures. The creed, for instance, in its proper setting as a baptismal profession, is not a simple description of how matters are in a 'religious' world; it is part of a lived process of submission to and sharing in the form of cross and resurrection. It commits the person uttering it to the very risk of loss which it expresses at its own heart in speaking of the Word in hell. It is saying, in effect, 'If you do believe in and commit yourself to this frame of reference, this point of judgement, you may expect to live with a continuing breaking and recovery of this same frame of reference, at deeper and deeper levels'.

All this because the 'type of human action and state' with which orthodoxy is concerned is what is narrated in the history of Jesus' cross and resurrection. The human destiny, for the Christian, is to be God's child as Jesus was and is: to act freely and compassionately, to assume the 'divine' right to bless, pardon and accept oneself and the world, without this liberty being destroyed or this authority undermined by the historical victories of violence and rejection. The more apparently total the victory of the unloving world, the deeper the real liberty of the son or daughter of God who refuses to collaborate with its programmatic violence; and to believe this is part of believing that Jesus expresses and embodies the unchanging pattern of God's creativity.[3] God makes the world because he is not a God of exclusions, proud individuality, isolation and purity; because he is a God who will 'lose' himself to share himself, so that he is only (and barely) to be perceived in the realisation that the world is fundamentally a world of share, exchange, interconnection, materially no less than spiritually. Thus loss-and-recovery is identified as the pattern of creativity itself, as 'Logos'. And faith in this, trust in its reality and endurance, takes in the potential negation, the risk of meaninglessness. 'Faith without this underlying lostness is no faith. And asserted lostness is a form of assertion which faith has renounced. It is the flight before doubt has become part of the terror of war and threat from all sides. . . But the source is fear; not thought leading to doubt.'[4] Words from the writings of a wholly remarkable Greek Orthodox nun, Mother Maria Gysi, whose own passionate commitment to the life of the mind as a real Christian discipleship left her in no doubt that the 'asserted lostness' of fashionable relativism or subjectivism was a flight from the cost of real doubt, that openness to the negation and staying with the question which for her was the only authentic apprehension of truth.

Here, I should argue, is the life-blood of any Christian orthodoxy. It is a training, a path, a world to inhabit, by which the historical reality of Christ's death and resurrection are constituted the focus, the governing interpretation, of human lives; and it carries with it the conviction of a universal accessibility and a universal pertinence. This, and no other story so decisively and exhaustively, is the story of God's creating Word. In relation to this, the tradition of belief is a perpetually self-critical one, and in relation to this it holds out both challenge and promise to the crucifying world.

But it is self-critical not just at the level of intellectual dialogue. Orthodoxy is, as we have said, corporate or it is nothing; and the orthodox

Christian community identifies itself not simply and absolutely by some mode of organisation, but by gathering to do certain things. Orthodoxy is inseparable from sacramental practice. The community gathers for those acts which put it in the presence of its source, gathers to recover Easter; it comes to be both fed and judged by the source event. In short, it is identified by meeting to pursue just that dialogue, that drama, which is the dynamic of orthodoxy. As Nicholas Lash has said, in an unpublished paper, the Church does not read the Bible merely, but 'performs' it. The reading of Scripture in worship is not for the edification or instruction of a congregation; it is part of an occurrence in which lives are 'dramatically' caught up into a classical narrative that is now being enacted, and re-formed through that participation. This is true obviously at the great junctures of the Christian year, Holy Week above all; it is the structure implicit in Baptism; but every Mass too is a Holy Week, an entry into Easter, in which we have our mundane identities shattered, stretched, turned on their heads. And every rite of penance is a Holy Week, a meeting with and an exchange of identity with the paschal Christ. The immense importance given in Catholic tradition to the sacrament of penance (and in sore need of consistent and forceful restatement in contemporary Anglican Catholic understanding) depends on this faith. As Christians, we cannot pretend that our sins are part of a private memory detached from the shared symbolic life we have entered; we need to bring our failings and betrayals into the drama of the betrayal and vindication of Jesus, so that we 'find' ourselves both as the faithless disciples of Maundy Thursday and as the newly-called disciples of Easter Sunday. From being scattered to our corners and shelters on Thursday, we are gathered again, ready for communion and thanksgiving. 'Sacrament', for the Christian, is, then, a process in which we find that level of identity where we are sinners, God-less, murderers of truth, wilfully blind and rejecting, and, deeper still, the level where we are still the brothers and sisters of God's first-born, Jesus; because beyond our rejection God continues to hold out a hope and a calling, and is working to finish in us the image of Christ.

'Christian believing also is founded on an event or events which make possible the offer and acceptance of a given status and the ascription of appropriate roles. For all this to be meaningful, however, there *must* be a relatively stable background of repetition, habituation or 'expected' belief and conduct. Language which identifies appropriate roles (forgiven sinner, obedient son) now functions as a firm semantic marker for identifying what we mean when we talk about being a Christian'.[5] My only addition or qualification to this excellent statement would be to insist that symbolic action is the central form of Christian language for identifying appropriate roles. Orthodoxy (any orthodoxy) involves shared ritual enactments, crystallisations of the kind of life the ideology serves: the

Christian sacraments, above all the Eucharist, show the believer engaged with and challenged by the source event of faith, engaging in 'cross and resurrection', and so making the paradigm his or her own, making the life lived from that sacrament a reflection, a kind of translation of the paradigm. And so – as remarked earlier – every believing life becomes, in some measure, part of 'orthodox tradition'.

3 Perhaps this is where Catholic orthodoxy does take on a rather more specific colouring within the Christian spectrum. If Christian orthodoxy is the constant renewal of dialogue with Christ crucified and risen, each place where that dialogue is committedly undertaken may show us more of the other partner in our own dialogue. When I now attempt to open myself to the challenge of the cross, I can be helped to hear it by seeing how it is 'translated' into the lives of Polycarp, Augustine, Wesley, Edith Stein, Janani Luwum. I shall not see Christ as John the Baptist did, but only with and in the faces of his saints. He is not any one of them; he is what they share, yet without losing his own, obscure but sharply-outlined, historical individuality – no mere abstract 'family resemblance', but an area where they all meet. In conventional theological parlance, I meet Christ not alone, but in the communion of saints. And this sense of 'tradition' of human biographies as a means of enlarged access to truth, of an 'orthodoxy' of narratives, a grammar of sanctity, is something which still identifies Catholic Christianity. Granted that it perennially risks a loss of focus, a remoteness from the centre; it is also true that it underlines most powerfully the nature of the tradition as concerned with the possibilities of life and action, and serves to do precisely what a sound orthodoxy should, in preserving a spaciousness of perspective, the endless imitability (though that is a weak and misleading word) of God's Word fleshed out in the lives of those who have answered that Word.

Catholic orthodoxy, then, is Christian orthodoxy at its fullest awareness of living in a shared world, of language, symbol, communion and communication. It should be aware of the risks mentioned in the last paragraph, but equally aware that turning away from symbol and story carries its own risks of weakening the conviction that God's redeeming creativity is to be looked for in history, in the concrete biographies of men and women attempting to live 'truthfully'. If Catholics live in a heavily-populated imaginative world, it is partly because the world is one of participations, overlap, diversity and interlocking at once. But what makes a life decisively part of the tradition is precisely its exposure to – and so its pointing to – Christ (that is why martyrs are most immediately part of this tradition and why, from the earliest days of the Church, people have spoken of sharing and embodying Christ's passion in their martyrdom). And thus there is not and cannot be any appropriate way of remembering and celebrating the saints apart from the Eucharist. The Eucharist is celebrated with 'the whole company of heaven', never in historical any more than in geographical isolation; and it is the Eucharist alone which shows the 'order' of love in revelation. In the Eucharist, we renew our encounter with the paschal Jesus, and in a Eucharist commemorating the saints, we celebrate their encounter with the same Jesus, and allow ourselves to encounter Jesus in them, in their Golgothas and their transformations.

Likewise the Eucharist celebrated in connection with any special purpose or for any person brings that purpose or person into this encounter, to be judged and changed. Always in this act there is the classical symbol of our return to the centre and our dependence upon it. The Eucharist is the paradigm of that dialogue which is 'orthodoxy'; so long as it is celebrated in obedience to Jesus' words, the Church has not surrendered to the great blasphemy of believing in itself. The eucharistic Church is the orthodox church. And lest that dialogue should become private, interior and individual, apolitical or abstract, Catholic Christianity adds that a properly self-aware eucharistic Church is one conscious of historical links and continuities, communion across time and space and conventional limits, the obligation to attend to the witness and the gift of other ages and cultures and the baffling diversities of Christian thought and styles of living. Which is why Catholics speak of ministry in the Church as also sacramental, the effective present symbol of continuities: once again, a theological interest in apostolicity of ministry ought to be something which guarantees a concern for keeping questions open, a sensitivity to the varieties of Christian experience in history – and which thus regularly unsettles uncritically hierarchical models of leadership in the Church, since the symbol it serves involves a story of the inversion of normal authority patterns. Here again, Christian and Catholic orthodoxy should be systematically self-questioning in the light of the very nature of its focal paradigm. It is sad that – like 'orthodoxy' itself – this whole issue has been distorted into questions about power, purity and exclusion. People talk largely about the danger of betraying Catholic faith by compromising Catholic order, as if order were something on which faith depended rather than being a symbol of a continuity and faithfulness which may in fact be present in any number of ways at any number of levels. It is one thing to say that articulate, sacramental self-awareness in this area is good, or even is God's will for the Church; another to make it a decisive test of orthodoxy in itself. (And how many Anglicans would have to admit that 'Catholic orthodoxy' in their ears speaks instantly of squabbles over covenanting and women's ordination? How many have been dismissed as un-Catholic because they take the 'wrong' side in these questions?)

Let me try to sum up. I have suggested that the idea of an 'orthodox tradition' is how communities or societies give themselves the possibility both of clarifying and reflecting on their distinctive vision of things and of criticising and changing present versions of it. Orthodoxy is in part 'access to the source', and so can carry an invitation to a measure of debate and provisionality within a group's language. Religious orthodoxies claim abiding value and unlimited relevance (unlimited 'translatability') for their vision, because they deal with humanity as such and its universal and non-negotiable capacity and destiny; and we noted in passing the threat posed by relativism in this area to any critical convictions about what is and is not properly human – the threat of some kind of apologia for power-groups rewriting the definition of the human. Christian orthodoxy is committed in a very particular way to a self-critical process, because of the nature of its central story; it has to accept an internal 'lostness', a negative dimension, a crucifixion. It is suspicious of its own images, yet, because it connects loss and sharing, death and love, it is never simply iconoclastic (here, perhaps, Don Cupitt's passionate espousal of the negative way within Christianity[6] fails to put it in its proper context, turning suspicion into 'asserted lostness' only). And because the risk and loss of the Easter encounter are possible only within a language and a community, Catholic orthodoxy insists on the centrality of shared symbols, on the essential importance of multiform narratives to interpret the focal event, and on signs of living continuity in time and space – sacraments, saints, apostolic ministry, all of the means of freeing us from the prison of a 'given' social perspective.

Catholic orthodoxy lives in the continuing interplay between an ever-increasing web of image and story and a persistent critical negation. Its task is simply to preserve the seriousness of both symbol and silence. 'Theologies of story' on their own risk self-indulgence, the mere accumulation of detail; 'theologies of negation' alone reduce the Christian enterprise to a private struggle towards self-transcendence. A shared world, a communicating world, that is also a world capable of self-awareness and change, requires the interaction of the two, and a genuine Catholic radicalism will be loyal above all to this. It will be creative and imaginative, capable of offering a widening of human horizons, a constructive questioning and deepening of social goals, in its conviction that God has shared His liberty, and His resources of compassion with the human world: He has made His Word flesh, and so made 'flesh' a language in which love, mutuality, and freedom can be manifested. And it will be contemplative, in the most far-reaching Christian sense: dissatisfied with its words and images, even its loves and its freedoms, ready to be 'lost' for the sake of a truth too manifold and comprehensive for the limited mind; aware of the tragic – the gulfs between the vision and fact, project and realisation, the pervasiveness of the destructive longing for final clarity, totality of vision, which brings forth the monsters of religious and political idolatry.

That may be an odd way of approaching orthodoxy; but if orthodoxy really is a tool, not a goal, the goal must be something like that. If that is where orthodoxy has led and kept the saints, the contemplatives and the radicals, the poets or scientists or revolutionaries, of the Catholic Church, it may do no harm to see it in the light of that end; so that 'orthodoxy' can also, finally, be something to do with discovering what are the conditions for hope.

References

1 Paul Ricoeur, 'Science and ideology' in *Hermeneutics and the Social Sciences* (ed and trans John Thompson, Cambridge, 1981), p 241.

2 Margaret Masterman, 'Integrity in the Religious Quest', Pt 1, *The Modern Churchman*, 20:4 (summer 1977), pp 149–50.

3 I have tried to give a slightly fuller account of this in *Resurrection: Interpreting the Easter Gospel* (Darton, Longman and Todd, London, 1982).

4 *Mother Maria: Her Life in Letters* (ed Sister Thekla, Darton, Longman and Todd, London, 1979), pp 14–15.

5 Anthony Thiselton, 'Knowledge, myth and corporate memory' in *Believing in the Church: The Corporate Nature of Faith*. Doctrine Commission of the Church of England (SPCK, 1981), pp 65–6.

6 See *Taking Leave of God* (SCM, 1980) and *The World to Come* (SCM, 1982).

2 Orthodoxy in Practice

Michael Langford

The rediscovery of orthodoxy

In 1830 John Henry Newman responded to an invitation to write a book on the Council of Nicea, which was to form part of a series on the Councils of the Church. His study was published in 1833, the year the Oxford Movement began, as the *Arians of the Fourth Century*. In his *Apologia*, Newman was to recall that the project launched him on an ocean with innumerable currents. Very little of the book was about the Council itself, the major part of it being concerned with the issues which had been raised in his own mind during the course of his research. The more Newman moved out of the 'shadow of liberalism' which was affecting both Church and society, the deeper he found himself in the Church of the Fathers, of men like Athanasius, which was to become the main source of his religious opinions, and which finally led him in 1845 from fourth-century Alexandria to nineteenth-century Rome.

This last point is of considerable importance. It was the rediscovery of the existence and importance of Christian orthodoxy which Newman always regarded as the main concern of the Oxford Movement, before it became identified with ritual and social questions in subsequent generations. But the Oxford Fathers had not discovered an obscure refuge in the Church of the past in order to hide from the onslaughts of the contemporary world. Newman had rediscovered the undivided Church of the Fathers as a living tradition, as an infinite resource in which to live in the contemporary world. Newman was never frightened of liberalism, nor did he, like so many of his contemporaries, become fascinated by it. There was a patristic dimension to the Church, for the Fathers were his colleagues and fellow-travellers in the modern world and their counsel demanded action.

The purpose of this essay is to sail a little of this ocean on which Newman had been launched and to follow the two main currents which had been raised in the minds of the Oxford Fathers, and which are still of pressing concern in the Church a century and a half later. The first is to do with the relationship between the Church and its intellectual grasp of its faith, and the contemporary intellectual climate in which it seeks to bear witness to Christ. Later, in his *Apologia*, Newman noted that his rediscovery of Christian orthodoxy did not happen in a vacuum. It was shaped by his response to liberalism, to the changing European culture of which he was so much a part and of which he spoke so prophetically. Newman foresaw the secularisation of European values, education, trade and commerce. He recognised the emerging privatisation of religion where one creed is as good as another, with the implication that no creed is of any value. Since religion was no more than another private possession it was excluded from human relationships and from society, and it had become as impertinent to enquire into a man's religion as into his source of income. This is the European mind which the present-day Church has inherited.

The second current on which we shall sail concerns the event from which Newman himself dated the beginnings of the Oxford Movement. Whatever John Keble actually said in his Oxford civic sermon on national apostasy on 14 July 1833, the sermon was widely interpreted as a protest against secular interference in the Church, as the government proposed the suppression of certain Irish sees and the sequestration of their income. Orthodoxy was responding to its historical context, to a concordat between the Church and the world which had remained unchanged in substance since Constantine and the Council of Nicea.

The contradictions inherent in this desire for a genuinely Christian culture, and a protest against putting trust in the princes of this world, converge in the central issue which was brought into the Church's consciousness during the Arian controversy and the Council of Nicea. How does man conceive of God's relationship to this world in Christ, and how is this relationship grasped and realised in practice in both individual and ecclesial terms? What is orthodoxy in practice? We shall follow these two currents by a return to the sources of Newman's own thought in the Council of Nicea, when Christian orthodoxy was born and the Church was coming to terms with its new-found acceptance in the world, with the hope of proposing a model of orthodoxy in practice. This model will have three interrelated components: the transformation of ideas, of wisdom itself, the transformation of man, and the transformation of human society. The underlying emphasis will be that orthodoxy can be grasped and understood only in practice, that orthodoxy and orthopraxis indwell each other.

The transformation of wisdom

The writings of Athanasius of Alexandria (c 296-373 AD) are almost entirely concerned with theological controversy. He arose to meet the emergency of the Arian controversy, which surrounded and followed the Council of Nicea, and the emergency lasted for 35 years. One neglected aspect of this most violent of theological disputes is the relationship between Athanasius, the archbishop of the great city of Alexandria, and Anthony of Egypt, the hero of the new monastic experiment in the deserts of Egypt which involved the withdrawal from society of many thousands of individuals. Until comparatively recently much doubt was cast upon this relationship, to the extent that what is still the standard study of Arianism (Gwatkin 1882) assumes that Anthony did not even exist. The result has been that the role of the monastic life in the struggle for orthodoxy in this period has either been undervalued or ignored altogether. It is enough to say that the authenticity of Athanasius' biography of Anthony, which had so much immediate influence, including the conversion of St Augustine in the West, has been generally established and appreciated for its innovative hagiographical style. In addition, we have the teachings of Anthony in the *Apophthegmata Patrium* (the *Sayings of the Desert Fathers),* and thanks to the patient lifetime's work of an Oxfordshire country parish priest, seven authentic letters of Anthony.

What is at stake here is not any direct and tactical collaboration between Athanasius and the monks in the Arian controversy, although such co-operation did occur. But few of the Coptic peasant monks would have been able to grasp the arguments. What is important here is the mutual admiration of Anthony and Athanasius and their unity of vision and purpose. In this shared vision and purpose it is possible to distinguish three dimensions of the orthodox strategy in relation to the intellectual struggle of the Arian controversy. For the birth of orthodoxy was a response to the intellectual pressure that was being placed on the Church as it was coming of age in the world.

The first element in the orthodox strategy is the preservation of the relationship between theory and practice. Athanasius' motivation in writing the *Life of Anthony* was clearly to make Anthony the monk a champion of orthodoxy. The *Life* is a case study of orthodoxy in practice, a model of the Christian life, and its value lies precisely in what independent observers would call Athanasius' hidden polemical interests. Here, Athanasius tells us, is a concrete example of what it is to be orthodox.

During a bad period of depression in the inner desert, a condition which is well-known among solitaries, Anthony was beset by many sinful thoughts. Near to despair, he cried out to God to be saved.[1] It was such experiences which dominated the life of the monk and for which he was expected to provide answers and encouragement for his many visitors. But it was also this practical question which determined Athanasius' theological method, his use *ad libitum* of the soteriological argument. Athanasius never allowed himself to be led by theoretical and speculative approaches to the incarnation; rather orthodoxy is the reply of the Church's teaching magisterium to Anthony's practical and desperate plea: how can a man be saved? Athanasius' concern, in his dispute with the Arians, was to maintain the reality and fullness of Christ's divinity and humanity, in opposition to the Arian Christ who was no more than a deified creature, albeit the most exalted of all creatures. It was Newman who later noted that the honour paid to Christ's humanity by the Arians was properly due to Mary. Unless the fullness of the divine nature dwelt bodily in Christ, a man could not be saved. In the *Life*, Anthony's victory over the demons which enslave the world is always the victory of Christ in Anthony, the conquest of God in man through the incarnate Word, and occasionally Athanasius has to check his own deep admiration for the Father of monks by reminding his readers that this in fact is the case. Arianism had allowed itself to be led by philosophical considerations, and in order to fit the prevailing categories Christ could be no more than a creature. The Arian Christ was little more than an object of speculation, and Arian salvation no more than imputed, forensic and theoretical. Athanasius the theologian and Anthony the monk replied by witnessing to the relationship between theology and practice, to the hominisation of God and the deification of man in Christ. Already in the Arian controversy, at a critical period in the Church's development, we see the beginnings of two divergent forms of Christianity which have dominated subsequent history down to the present day, and which have their roots in christology, in how man conceives of God's relationship to man in Christ.

The second element in orthodoxy's response to the intellectual pressure being placed upon it is the transformation of philosophy. Attempts by scholars to relate Arianism to a neoplatonic background, and to both Athiochene and Alexandrian christology, have proved inconclusive. Whilst this is in part due to the lack of evidence, a much more fruitful approach has emerged recently, which is to view the Arian controversy as a crisis in the relationship between Christian theology and Greek philosophy.[2] This relationship was already beginning to be explored by the apologists and by Clement and Origen at Alexandria, and as the Church began to emerge in the world certain questions were beginning to appear in its consciousness. What then was the orthodox response in this crisis between theology and philosophy?

The Arian controversy was to bring much of both its heat and light to bear on the introduction of the unscriptural term *homoousios* (of one Being) at Nicea to describe the relationship between the Father and the Son. The international academic community has spent much effort in discussing the background and meaning of this term.[3] Whilst such discussion cannot be lightly ignored, it suffers by seeking to demonstrate a dependency of the term on certain philosophical backgrounds, as though this was the intention of the Council Fathers. Athanasius, who attended the Council as a deacon and secretary to his predecessor in Alexandria, confirms and expounds the use of the term in his letter *de Decretis*, which is also one of the primary sources of the proceedings of the Council. At no time, either in this letter or elsewhere, does Athanasius feel constrained by language or by a fixed conceptual framework. On the contrary, his language is relaxed, uncomplicated and independent of technicalities, whereas it is the Arians who resorted to rigid systems of thought, to slogans and ballads, and to 'borrowing from the Greeks'. For Athanasius, *homoousios* is not a concept but a symbol to preserve the meaning of scripture against the influence of philosophy, and not a means of reinterpreting the gospel for the spirit of the age. To meet this requirement, *homoousios* had to be shorn of its materialistic and philosophical background. Orthodoxy is not an alternative ideology, a philosophy competing amongst other philosophies, but the transformation of human thought itself.

In seeking to demonstrate the faith of Nicea as the faith of the prophets and apostles, Athanasius assumes that there is an orthodoxy, a right-thinking, a meaning to scripture, which has been preserved in the inner life of the Church, and transmitted from the apostles by the Church's normal activities of worship and prayer and by catechesis. For Athanasius the incarnation which energises the Church, and even the Church herself, are data of his experience, and he likes to refer to the Church's vitality and superabundant life as evidence to support his assertions that the divine life itself is bestowed upon man in Christ. As Hilary of Poitiers, the Athanasius of the West, was to say, defending the development of doctrine, it was because this inner life of the Church was being threatened by the world from within, that the Fathers were being forced to entrust the deep silence of adoration of the Church's interior life to the perils of human thought.

The third element in the intellectual struggle for orthodoxy is the transformation of wisdom itself as a possession. Anthony's attitude to learning is well-known: with creation all around him as his encyclopaedia, and his own remarkable memory for scripture, he had no need for books. But it would be wrong to attribute to Anthony a naive anti-intellectualism and simplicity. The *Life* shows Anthony perfectly capable of mastering the current crisis for Christian platonism. Also, in his letters, Anthony is appealing to the rational and intelligent, and to the rational use of freedom, but the intelligent man is not the man who can handle intellectual arguments. He is the man who has come to know God and come to know himself, the man who has learnt by bitter experience to discern the spirits and distinguish good from evil. Knowledge for Anthony is lived wisdom and not an abstract possession, and Arian theology, along with Greek philosophy, was alien to this way of life.[4] To give Athanasius the last word, Christ had been able to persuade whole churches of men to despise death itself by the use of ordinary language and unlettered men, and the philosophers with their sophisticated arguments had scarcely been able to convert their own neighbourhood. The fact of the incarnation had immediately discredited the perspectives of Greek philosophy.[5]

The transformation of man and society

The Arian controversy began as a theological problem and entered the arena of politics. But it was the orthodox who suffered at the hands of an Arian majority who enjoyed imperial patronage, Athanasius himself enduring exile five times. The Arian Christ became the patron of imperial religion when the empire already suffered internal weaknesses. The stability of the empire was further threatened by the controversy itself and by increasing guerrilla attacks from the emerging surrounding nations. Christianity was to emerge in the Roman Empire during its final period of decadence and decline.

It has become customary to speak of Athanasius *contra mundum* during this period, but what was the character of this stance against the world? A number of studies in the 1950s and 1960s have highlighted a relationship between heretical movements within the Church, and national and social movements of discontent and rebellion in the later Roman empire.[6] Could the birth of orthodoxy, along with the monastic life, be a reaction to the recognition and acceptance of Christianity in the immediate post-Constantinian era, and if so, what was this reaction?

Prior to Constantine, those who had experienced the call of the gospel most acutely had remained within the Christian community, living the 'religious life' on the edge of their villages, or they had become martyrs. Anthony's innovation was to help pioneer and organise the life of the *monachos*, in the strict sense of one who lived in solitude with God, for no one as yet knew the inner desert. Even allowing for exaggeration in contemporary accounts, out of a population of seven and a half million in Egypt tens of thousands left society to pursue the new life in the desert. Part of this exodus was associated with Pachomius, a young Roman conscript who had been converted by Christian charity, and who began organising the coenobitic life, the monastic life lived in community. Many had left to escape the increasing burden of taxation and conscription and the injustices of the magistrates. The monasteries became self-contained economic units or traded with each other along the caravan routes. Some of the monks also provided casual labour at harvest time. Whilst there were scholars and aristocrats among the monks, most of them were Coptic peasants who were culturally distinct from their middle-class, Greek-speaking counterparts in the city of Alexandria. Even amongst the monks themselves there was conflict arising from their different social backgrounds.[7] It was Athanasius who was the first Greek Father to preach in Coptic, the language of the majority of people in Egypt.

Gibbon, in his classic *Decline and Fall*, was to blame the collapse of the Roman Empire on Christianity, which had weakened the political unity of the empire by one theological dispute after another, and undermined Roman culture by importing into it values and ideas proper to the uneducated masses. For him, monasticism in particular was inhuman and irrational, and motivated by a hatred of the world. Yet this extraordinary phenomenon of *anachoresis* cannot be understood simply as rebellion, as anarchy, as a counter-culture, or as the alternative society of the later Roman empire. Although there is much evidence that Egypt was ripe for such a rebellion, the monks had taken the struggle into a different continuum. It was not so much that they wanted to overcome Rome, rather that they wanted to overcome the world. In any case it was the barbarian nations who actually succeeded in replacing the Roman oppressor. Athanasius seems to have had some time for Constantine, whilst objecting to his interference in the Church. He despised the Arian Constantius but was content to settle down later in life as the elder statesman. Anthony was quite indifferent to an invitation to meet the emperor, and in his desert retreat must have wondered much of the time which empire was ruling the world.

In a society which had been dominated for centuries by the thought of death, and in which the old Egyptian religion was still alive, the monks went to live in the tombs and caves of the desert, the place of the demons. When Anthony withdrew to the inner desert, it was popularly believed that the experience would do irreparable damage to the human mind and body, which explains the general astonishment at his state of health when he returned. As Rome had colonised the world, and as the Church entered that world, the monks colonised the wilderness, the fringes of the known civilised world and of human experience. The lasting value of Athanasius' *Life of Anthony* lies in its exaggerations, in its grotesque demonology. For they are based on Christian orthodoxy, on the victory of the incarnate Word and on the life of God in man. The monastic life was the continuation of the life of the apostles, and of the primitive Church in Jerusalem in which self-interest was subordinate to the common interest, for the new age of the Church's life. Anthony showed that this transformation could be achieved without the destruction of humanity.

He lived to the age of a hundred and five, still possessing all his teeth, yet owning little more than the clothes he wore. Or, as Athanasius expressed it, it was not that the divine nature was diminished and extinguished by human nature in the incarnation, rather that human nature itself was deified and rendered immortal.[8] But even Anthony suffered no illusions about himself. When he returned from the desert he found one who was his equal living in the city of Alexandria.[9]

Anthony and Athanasius shared an estimation of man which was both near to despair and almost utopian. Man's moral condition was symptomatic of his pathological state, his ever-deepening condition of loss of vision and ignorance of God, his confusion and deep despair at himself. In his search for God, his mind fell on creatures rather than the Creator, on one invention after another. The human condition was essentially one of blindness and disease, of enslavement to idolatry. The human race needed a teacher and a healer rather than a professor of religion and ethics.[10] This, for Athanasius and Anthony, is almost the only reason for the incarnation. God's descent into man in Christ was not to impress people, otherwise he would have appeared as a great king or a star. Christ came to teach and to heal, to restore man's vision of God,[11] and the continuation of this divine purpose was the raising up of a great physician for Egypt in Anthony.[12] Athanasius in his theological disputes, and Anthony in his teaching on the discernment of spirits, were helping the human race to distinguish the true God and Father of our Lord Jesus Christ from the idols, from the projections of the human mind and condition whose power enslaved the world. Satan, the great deceiver of mankind, used man's enormous capacity to deceive himself, but now in Christ, in the monks, he had been beaten back by being detected and unmasked by the distinguishing and naming of the demons, by the discerning of the spirits. Moreover, this monastic task was the continuation of the essential mission of Christ typified in the temptations and exorcisms in the gospels. But since Christ had conquered the demons, and the Church had burst into life all over the world, converting even the gentiles, the Fathers saw that Satan had stumbled on a new deceit. By using the Christian name itself they had destroyed the unity of the Church by introducing into it heresy and schism. Orthodoxy and monasticism were essential to each other as the Church entered the world, and the world began to enter the Church.

A generation after the collapse of Rome, Egypt went Monophysite, rejecting the Council of Chalcedon, and the monks were already beginning to live off endowments as wealth poured into the Church. Perhaps Egyptian nationalism had found a new lease of life. But as community life was re-established, the monk found a new place in his society as the stranger on the edge of civilisation and the friend of God, the ambiguities of whose life might lead him to be framed for murder or held responsible for unaccountable pregnancies in his village. Their holiness and their spectacular feats, such as sailing down the Nile on the back of a crocodile, made them the most loved and most despised men in their society.[13] The monk's complete dissociation from the influences of society and his close friendship with God made a distant God near. Consulted by bishops, priests, magistrates, aristocracy, and ordinary people, he was confessor, therapist, mediator in disputes, a man who had power over demons, who could work miracles, and who could encourage those who doubted that a man could be saved at all. As the *Historica Monachorum* testifies, as citizens of heaven whilst living in this world, through the monks the Saviour performed miracles, and through them the world itself was kept in being and human life was preserved.[14]

The monks were the brothers of the martyrs, the replacing of red martyrdom by white, the continuation of the life of the apostles and the primitive Church for new circumstances. They were the living witness that God had descended into man in the incarnation to overcome the world. As the Church risked becoming conformed to the world, they were the transformation of man, his ideas, and his society, in Christ. The paradox which Christians faced in this age of orthodoxy, monastic withdrawal and uncertainty can be seen by comparing and contrasting the attitudes of Christians a couple of generations apart. At the turn of the fourth century, Anthony entered Alexandria to encourage Christians to defy the state and the emperor Diocletian. At the turn of the fifth century, Jerome in his monastery in Bethlehem lamented the invasion of Rome as though the whole world had collapsed in a single day. Had not Diocletian himself attempted reforms, including the persecution of Christians, in order to save the empire? Perhaps Athanasius hoped for the transformation of Roman civilisation and its Greek heritage, by replacing its pagan values and ideas with those of the Christians. Athanasius never ceased to spurn Arianism as atheism and idolatry, for Christianity was beginning to accommodate itself to the culture it was being called to transform. It was Athanasius and the monks, and not the Arians, who were willing to face the ambiguities that this raised.

Orthodoxy and dissent

Nicene orthodoxy was a response to a philosophical, social and political context, but it was not determined by that context by accommodation or reaction. Whilst Athanasius and the monks lived in an anxious age, neither were conditioned by fear or necessity. Athanasius and Anthony proclaimed and preserved the possibility of authentic knowledge of God by man. It was not that God had become subject to man and his thoughts in the incarnation, but that man himself in his total existence had been transformed by it. Orthodoxy is the man freed from necessity and fear, and yet intimately bound up with practice, with the harsh realities of living in the desert. Monasticism is the Church's laboratory, the testing and living out of the mystery of Christ, who is himself the Church's interior life and purpose, and who is dimly grasped and apprehended by dogmatic formularies.

Orthodoxy is not a compromise solution between different 'points of view', nor is Christian doctrine an alternative ideology, a fixed system of ideas competing amongst other such systems. Christian doctrine developed (and continues to develop) in emergencies, and yet it is the life of the Holy Spirit in the Church, integral to the life of the Church in history. As Newman saw, the model of the development of Christian doctrine is Mary pondering the significance of all that Christ said and did, of all he was and is. Or as Leo the Great perceived, after the ascension and the outpouring of the Holy Spirit, Christ's earthly, physical life passed over into the sacraments and Christian doctrine.[15]

These considerations raise two major questions for the Catholic movement a century and a half on, which were already present in the minds of the Oxford Fathers. The first concerns the authority of Christianity in a world of individuals and private opinions, of deterministic views of human thought and action, and of individualistic and democratic models of authority – a world where religion, as Newman foresaw, has become just another private opinion and possession.

The nineteenth-century Russian theologian Aleksei Khomyakov had this to say about Western European culture, as that culture began to enter and influence Russia:

> 'Every belief, every discerning faith, is an act of *freedom* and must stem from previous free investigation, to which a man has submitted the phenomenon of the external world, the inner phenomenon of his soul, the events of transitory time, and the testimonies of his contemporaries. The Protestant world is by no means the world of free investigation.'[16]

Perhaps a century and a half after the original Tractarian alert against liberalism it may at last be emerging in the Western European mind that Western views of individual freedom are open to serious criticism, and that belief in the infallibility of the individual is just another one of those illusions and cul-de-sacs into which we have manoeuvred ourselves to avoid certain issues. At the same time, words like 'dogma' and 'doctrine', and even 'theology', need to be redeemed from their popular usage and from their detractors on both sides – both those who reject them, and those who seem to imagine that Christian doctrine is some kind of abstract framework to be possessed at all costs, and in which to dissent from all responsibility towards the contemporary alien world. Orthodoxy must be lived, since orthodoxy is bound up with integrity, with orthopraxis; it is not an ideology to insulate people from the real world and even from life itself.

The second major question in need of exploration is the place given to Constantine in the Church, which has remained unchanged in substance since his day, although the relationship exists in a variety of forms. The ambiguities of accommodation and withdrawal, the positive and negative aspects of this relationship, need both to be taken seriously. The reassertion of the traditional Western European values of freedom and individuality which is taking place may conceal not only material poverty and decay, but also the decadence and decline of a culture in which the Church has been much more of an ally than a critic, and whose outlook contains the seeds of its own moral and spiritual decline. To what extent is this association in conflict with the Church's interior life and mission, and what is the character of this conflict? The resource to meet this is that rediscovered by the Oxford Movement itself, the infinite resource of Christian orthodoxy, which is the mystery of Christ the incarnate Word indwelling his Church in the contemporary world.

References

1 *The Sayings of the Desert Fathers*, trans Benedicta Ward, SLG (Mowbrays, 1975) p 1, saying 1.

2 A Louth, *The Origins of the Christian Mystical Tradition* (Oxford, 1981). See chapter V for a discussion of the main issue.

3 C Stead, *Divine Substance* (Oxford, 1977), chapter IX, especially pp 242–66, contains a summary of this discussion.

4 *The Letters of Anthony of Egypt*, trans Derwas J Chitty (Fairacres Publications, SLG Press, Oxford). The conclusion of letter 4 for Anthony's attitude to the Arians, and the *Life of Anthony* pp 72–80 (see *The Nicene and post-Nicene Fathers*, Eerdmans, 1975) for his approach to philosophy.

5 *de Incarnatione*, 46, 47.

6 See especially A H M Jones, 'Were ancient heresies national or social movements in disguise?' in the *Journal of Theological Studies* 1959, pp 280–98; W H C Frend, *Martyrdom and Persecution in the Early Church* (Blackwell, 1965); and R MacMullen, *Enemies of the Roman Order* (Oxford, 1967). There are also a number of articles in the journal *Past and Present* for the 1950s and 1960s, on the early Church and the later empire, which explore various aspects of this relationship.

7 *Sayings*, op cit, p 31.

8 *de Decretis*, 14.

9 *Sayings*, op cit, p 5, *Sayings* 24.

10 E Mersch, *The Whole Christ*, trans J R Kelly, (Dennis Dobson, 1949), chapter IV, points out that Athanasius was a bishop and not a professor. He also shows Athanasius' reluctance to remain within the constraints of philosophy, and discusses Athanasius' doctrine of the divinisation of the Church as the whole humanity of Christ.

11 *de Incarnatione*, 43.
12 *Vita Antoni*, 87.
13 See P Brown, 'The Rise and Function of the Holy Man in Late Antiquity', *Journal of Roman Studies*, lxi (1971), pp 80–101, for an illuminating social perspective on the monks.
14 *The Lives of the Desert Fathers*, trans Norman Russell (Mowbrays, 1980), p 50, Prologue 9.
15 *Sermon 2* on the Ascension, 1–4.
16 In *Ultimate Questions* (ed Alexander Schemann, Mowbrays, 1977), pp 40–1.

3 Stepping out of Babylon: Sin, Salvation and Social Transformation in Christian Tradition

David Nicholls

On no aspect of Christian belief has there been more fundamental disagreement than on salvation. Even if we set aside the Reformation controversies on justification, when opposed answers to the question 'What must I do to be saved?' led to bitter conflicts, there remains the central issue of the 'content' of salvation – in what does salvation consist?

Some theologians have taught that salvation is concerned essentially with the future, while others have insisted that it is a present reality. Much theological and devotional literature has pictured salvation as having to do with another life and has consigned this earth to the devil, while another tradition has insisted that salvation must be seen as involving a transformation of this earth. By considering the answers that have been given to two questions, it is possible to outline four basic positions on salvation. These questions are:

a Is salvation to be thought of as here or not here?
b Is salvation to be thought of as now or not yet?

It will, however, be necessary to make further distinctions in these four basic positions. Also, we shall see that few theologians fit neatly into a single category. It is possible, for example, to speak of salvation as a state enjoyed by the individual after death in another world (ie not here and not yet) and also to adhere to a belief in the 'Second Coming' of Christ when salvation would be manifested on this earth. The important question to ask would be what is the governing conception of salvation, to which other ideas of salvation are subordinated?

For John Henry Newman and most of the Tractarian writers, salvation was essentially concerned with the fate of the soul after death. The 'great and solemn doctrine which gave the Gospel a claim to be heard when first preached' was the immortality of the soul. Heaven, Newman insisted, is above the sky, 'a certain fixed place, and not a mere state'. Although he allowed that God's Kingdom should also be seen, in a subordinate sense, as 'here and now', the governing conception of salvation in Newman's writings is 'not here and not yet'. Christ came not to transform or sanctify this evil world, 'not to turn the whole earth into a heaven, but to bring down a heaven on earth'. This heaven Newman identified with the Church which, in his Anglican days, he pictured as a 'regal body', a 'great corporation', an 'imperial power'. This Church exerts an 'absolute and almost despotic power' over its members, and incidentally exercises a beneficient effect upon civil institutions, tending to make men contented subjects. 'It keeps the lower orders from outbreaks', it opposes rebellion and is 'the best guarantee for private property'.

Among the Tractarian writers there is little idea that Christians should attempt to play any part in the transformation of this earth. In so far as salvation is concerned with such a transformation it is seen as effected solely by God in the Second Coming of Christ; as with Bultmann, the importance of this idea is to be sought in its effects upon the believer in the present. 'We should be able to await the fulfilment of the promise', wrote the author of Tract 16, 'in the spirit of calm confidence and joy'. It was left to a later generation of Anglo-Catholics to question these assumptions about salvation and to outline a more satisfactory position.

Sin and Salvation

Before continuing with our critical analysis of concepts of salvation it is important that we look briefly at the question 'Salvation from what?'. The answer which Christians have generally given is that we need to be saved from sin and its consequences. Following Tillich, we may see salvation as properly addressing itself to three types of human anxiety: death, guilt and meaninglessness. These, however, are all problems that in their classic form afflict the individual. However, from earliest times, following the prophets of the Old Testament, Christians have also seen the results of sin in such social phenomena as plague, famine, war, oppression, hunger and destitution. How far and in what way does the Christian Gospel promise salvation from these evils? Or is salvation properly applied only to the state of the individual soul?

Sin has traditionally been thought to involve both 'actual' and 'original' sin. The former is seen as action taken by morally responsible individuals (or possibly by groups) which contravenes a moral law and which constitutes in some way an offence against God. The popular view of sin as essentially disobedience or rebellion needs to be examined critically, because it is clearly related to the idea of God as an arbitrary monarch to whose will all men must bow. As one United States writer put it, 'When theological definitions speak of rebellion against God as the common characteristic of all sin, it reminds one of the readiness of despotic governments to treat every offence as treason'. The New Testament idea of sin as lawlessness may in fact be more satisfactory than talk of sin as rebellion.

Whether groups, as distinct from their members, can commit sin is a contentious question. The answer partly depends upon whether we can properly think of a group as possessing a personality and a will, enabling it to take actions for which, as an entity, it can be said to be responsible. The law, in certain contexts, recognises group personality and is prepared to acknowledge the responsibility of a company, corporation or other group, which is distinct from the responsibility of its directors, trustees or members. I believe that the law on this matter, which has evolved considerably since the beginning of the century, has gradually been compelled to come to terms with social realities and that this legal recognition reflects something which is true about the nature of human groups.

If we wish to say that groups as such can act and can act wrongly we should also be ready to say that they can be guilty and in need of forgiveness and salvation. I am not at all sure, however, that groups can feel guilt, though individual members can, of course, feel guilty as members of groups which have done evil. At times this feeling of guilt may be misplaced (as is true with respect to individual sins) but there are undoubtedly occasions when the individual members of a group rightly feel guilty for the activities of the group. The guilt feelings of such an individual would seem to be appropriate only in those situations in which he or she has in some way contributed, by commission or omission, to the evil actions of the group. Germans born after 1945 ought not to feel guilty for Auschwitz and Buchenwald. Nevertheless they may rightly feel that they are members of a nation which is in need of salvation. When children of parents (or later members of any group) benefit from the evil actions of the group in a previous generation they may, I suppose, be said to share in some way in the guilt. The sins of the fathers are frequently visited upon the children in the form of legacies or other benefits. Does not the enjoyment of these involve some degree of participation in the guilt of the original act?

What is certain is that individuals find themselves thrown into situations in which the opportunity of doing good is severely restricted by institutional factors and by precedents set in the past. A new president of the United States is elected, but however saintly he may be, he will find that the actions of his predecessors (among other things) will have limited his own freedom of action. He finds himself in the position where even the best possible choice is the lesser of several evils. It will also be the case that the new president's ability to do harm is limited by institutional factors; structural limitations are not always bad. In so far as the new president contributes by his own actions to reinforce an evil situation, putting his successor in even more evil circumstances than he faced himself, he is individually guilty. But however good and well-intentioned he may be, the solution is a change in the institutional arrangements, in the web of relationships, rather than the adoption of an improved moral code on his part. Financial corruption may, in some countries, become so essential to the running of government that any attempt to remove it would be like starving a motor-car of oil; it will grind to a halt. Only a revolutionary change in the form of government is likely to eradicate the need for this lubricant; the cost of success or the risk of failure may, however, make such a revolution unjustifiable.

This discussion of corporate guilt and sin has in fact brought us on to the subject of original sin. It is sometimes suggested that one of the principal and irreconcilable differences between Christians and Marxists is that, while the latter believe in the perfectibility of human nature, the Christian doctrine of original sin implies an ineradicable tendency towards wickedness from which every individual (with the exception of Jesus and Mary) suffers. Marxists, it is said, believe that the selfish tendencies which are characteristic of human nature in a class society will disappear with the advent of a classless society. Christians, on the other hand, take what they claim to be a more 'realistic' view of the human predicament. They recognise, in the words of that great devotee of original sin, Reinhold Niebuhr, a 'bias towards evil', a 'defect of the will'. within each individual which stands in the path of perfection.

The idea of original sin as some kind of individual defect, 'an inherited psychological malady', (N P Williams), which is passed on at birth or conception, and the corresponding notion of baptism as an 'original sinectomy', preferably performed at an early age, constitute a serious misunderstanding of the Christian faith. The doctrine of original sin, as I understand it, involves our being born into a whole set of relationships as members of various groups and institutions. These relationships are organised apart from God and reflect that disordered love which Augustine saw to be the distinguishing feature of the earthly city. Even the youngest child is involved in this web of sinful relationships; it is born into a particular family, class, nation and race. By this very fact it inherits all the ambiguous aspects of these relationships. Even the 'holy family' which has been idolised in western Christianity is a much more ambiguous institution seen from the perspective of New Testament writers – than popes, archbishops of Canterbury and popular preachers and moralists would recognise. The fact is that the family, like other institutions which we find in the world, shares in that selfishness which characterises 'the world'.

For the Christian it is not by hard work, nor by clean living, that men are delivered from the power of individual and corporate egoism, but it is by Baptism. In Baptism we enter into a new set of relationships, becoming nevertheless members of a new society, the Church, which recognises

God as its centre and sees all other human beings in the relationships to him. Whatever differences there are between Christianity and Marxism, they are not to be sought at this point. Christians believe in the perfectibility of man (and woman). 'Be perfect', said Jesus, 'as your father in heaven is perfect'. What stands in the way of perfection is the set of warped relationships into which we are born and to which we ourselves contribute. We must be born again.

Salvation, if it means anything at all, means deliverance from some or all of these evils which we have been considering. When and where is this deliverance to be sought? Is salvation a future hope or may it be a present reality? Is it concerned with a transformation of this earth or is this earth to be abandoned for a home in the heavens? These are the questions to which we must now turn.

A holy nation

We shall first consider the position of those who believe salvation to be essentially here and now. How is it manifested? A number of quite distinct positions may be detected in answer to this question. Some see salvation as embodied in institutions: in the Church, the nation, the empire or in 'Christendom'. To erect the church into an object of ultimate concern (to use Tillich's expression) is characteristic of certain theologians in the Catholic tradition who have lost sight of the future dimension of the Christian hope. There are, as we have seen, traces of this 'ecclesiolatry' in Newman's Anglican writings. Later, however, he was rather more guarded about identifying the Church and the Kingdom of God. In his *Apologia* he warned that 'the Church will remain, even till the end of the world, only a symbol of those heavenly facts which fill eternity'. In an earlier age Augustine at times seems to identify the church and the heavenly kingdom; in his *De civitate dei* he demythologised the apocalyptic idea of Christ's millennial reign, representing it as the era of the Church. I was recently criticised by a Roman Catholic theologian for stating that the Church shares in responsibility for unjust situations in parts of the world. We must not say 'the Church', he claimed, but 'Christians', for the Church is holy, and cannot be guilty of sin. I insisted that I was speaking of the Church as a hierarchically organised society, not simple of Christians in their individual capacity. My position was, he maintained, 'Protestant'. Quite the reverse, I argued; it was his separation between the visible, institutional Church, composed of sinful members, and an immaculate invisible Church, which is 'Protestant' (and futhermore idealist). Fortunately I could call on Karl Rahner's writings for support! The Church indeed symbolises and points to salvation and to the heavenly Kingdom, but should never be identified with it.

Perhaps even more dangerous is the tendency to identify salvation with life in the theocratically conceived nation or empire. Again it is possible to find seeds of this idea in the writings of Augustine and in much of the political ideology of Byzantium. A later example would be the propensity in nineteenth-century Britain to equate God's rule with the British empire. Prayers for 'the extension of Christ's kingdom throughout the world' were clearly assumed to involve an enlargement of the empire:

> 'Go to the conquest of all lands,
> All must at length be his.'

The 'German Christians' of the 1930s were also in danger of accepting a similar idea of salvation, while in recent years the campaign known as 'Christians for Europe' has manifested traces of this form of 'henotheism' (as Richard Niebuhr termed it). Europe, they declare, must discover its 'historic vision'. 'A Europe', they continue, 'united to meet the threats that face it today will also help to restore that Christendom which broke apart in the sixteenth century'. It is sad to find seven Anglican bishops, joining with a well-known Jesuit, the Duke of Norfolk, Mrs Shirley Williams and Lord Longford to distribute such rubbish. Fortunately, however, it is so out of touch with reality that it is unlikely to do much harm. At times this identification of salvation with sacred political institutions has triumphed but there have always been, in the Church or outside, prophetic and other-worldly voices to challenge this form of idolatry. The social groups from which the advocates of henotheism are drawn tend to be the bureaucratic classes of Church and State, and the political consequences of the theological position they assume are generally conservative (though, as we have seen, in the case of 'Christians for Europe' the perceived consequences are in the most literal sense reactionary).

Moral life or authentic response

We now turn to those who see salvation as here and now, but as manifested not in institutions but in the life of the individual. It is possible to distinguish two distinct emphases here, the moralistic and the existential. The more individualistic Liberal Protestant thinkers of the late nineteenth century, like Adolf Harnack and some other followers of Albrecht Ritschl, saw salvation as revealing itself gradually and silently in the heart of the individual believer; the Kingdom of God is within. Some of the more clear-sighted of these men acknowledged that Jesus' own idea of the Kingdom was radically different from this. Jesus preached an eschatological and apocalyptic message. 'The real difference,' wrote Johannes Weiss, 'between our modern Protestant world view and that of primitive Christianity is that we do not share the eschatological attitude. We pass our lives in the joyful confidence that this world will evermore become the showplace of the people of God'. These men believed that it is possible to leave behind the indigestible fragments of apocalypse and distil from Jesus' message of salvation something of value for our time. Salvation, they insisted, may be enjoyed here and now in this present order of things in so far as we 'co-operate with his wish in the strengthening and extension of the rule of God within ourselves and others'. Those among the Liberal Protestants who believed that salvation is possible only with a major transformation of the social order will be considered later, when we discuss ideas of salvation as here and not yet.

The existentialist interpretation of salvation differs from the moralistic in that the proponents of the former claim to take seriously the eschatological aspect of Jesus' message; we cannot, they claim, legitimately set aside the catastrophic emphasis in the New Testament revelation. Yet this cannot be taken literally; it must be seen as symbolic. The future becomes present and the cosmological becomes existential. It is in the conflicts and choices of the individual in the present that salvation is to be found. Each of us must live as though the present world is passing away. This eschatological perspective is, according to Albert Schweitzer, what makes the message of Jesus relevant to every historical epoch, by raising men above the world of their time and making them 'inwardly free'. Salvation, in Bultmann's view, is to be experienced inwardly by a life of calm confidence lived in a world of conflict and cares. We should never look for Christ's Kingdom to be demonstrated in the visible sphere. 'The true victory over our distresses,' he declared in 1945, 'is an inner victory but an effectively present one. The point is not how we are to remove our trials, but how we are to bear them steadfastly not how happy we shall be when they are passed, but how in the very midst of them we may have the peace which passes understanding'. This seems to be the notion of salvation entertained by Enoch Powell, who rejects the idea that Christ's Kingdom involves the transformation of the earthly condition. The prisoners remain in prison, the poor remain poor, but 'everything would be different for them because of what Christ came to do'.

This existentialist understanding of salvation as here and now has been particularly evident in the Lutheran tradition, going back through Schleiermacher to German eighteenth-century pietism, and it is reflected in Luther's own writings and hymns:

'And though they take our life,
Goods, honour, children, wife,
Yet is their profit small;
These things shall vanish all:
The city of God remaineth'.

It is this idea of salvation which allowed many German churchmen to gaze sadly but helplessly at the rise of Nazism, and which inspired the noble but ineffective suffering which many of them endured in Hitler's concentration camps.

While Bultmann recognised that Jesus' idea of the Kingdom was basically apocalyptic and cosmological and must therefore be demythologised for twentieth-century consumption, C H Dodd attempted to argue that the message of Jesus, and of the New Testament generally, was in need of no such radical reinterpretation. Although some of Jesus' pronouncements were in the form of predictions, his central message, Dodd maintained, was that the eschatological hope was already being fulfilled. The Kingdom of God is not something yet to come; it came with Jesus. 'The future is not our concern', he announced. This perverse interpretation of the New Testament attained a certain popularity among British theologians of an earlier generation but today finds few defenders.

The existentialist interpretation of salvation becomes accepted in times of great crisis when Christians feel helpless to affect the course of events; it is generally evident in Protestant, particularly Lutheran, countries. The political consequence of this view of salvation is to assert the irrelevance of Christianity to politics, either by a quietist attitude or by emphasising the autonomy of the political.

Mystical paths

It is important to distinguish a mystical interpretation of salvation which, in contrast to the existential and moralistic definitions, sees salvation as now but not here. Men are saved by being raised above the conditions of this present world to a realm of mystical experience, from a world of shadows and appearances to an invisible world of realities. Mystical experience involves the possibility of a direct encounter between God and the individual, between 'the soul' and its maker. Although Christian mysticism must recognise the universe as a creation of God and the physical body as the temple of the Holy Spirit, there is a propensity, inherited from Neoplatonism, to see the body as in some way imprisoning the soul. Mystics frequently write of a divine 'spark' in all men which needs to be liberated from the confines of the physical world. Jakob Boehme, writing in the early seventeenth century, declared: 'The third and most abominable chain by which the poor soul is bound, is the corrupted and completely vain earthly, mortal flesh and blood, full of evil desires and inclinations'. He insisted that heaven is to be thought of as within us.

Mystical ideas of salvation are normally to be found among elite groups, though there have been cases of popular mystical movements, particularly in the Middle Ages. The social consequences are usually quietist. 'Problems of secular morality', wrote Ernst Troeltsch, 'are regarded as unimportant'. Yet the insight of the mystic sometimes provides inspiration for action. William Blake's mystical vision led him to urge the building of Jerusalem in England's green and pleasant land, while the inner light of the Quakers not only indicated when a change from brewing to banking was called for, but has guided them into such social movements as the Campaign for Nuclear Disarmament and OXFAM.

Bright mansions above

We must now turn to ideas of salvation as future. In the first place there are those who see salvation as not here and not yet. Men are saved after death, when they are able to enjoy perpetual peace and have eternal light shining on them (the nearest analogy in human experience being a dentist's chair!). In popular Victorian religion, both Catholic and Protestant, this idea of salvation was dominant:

> 'Nothing is worth a thought beneath,
> Save how I may escape the death,
> that never never dies;
> How to make my own election sure,
> And, when I fail on earth, secure
> A mansion in the skies.'

While Catholics have tended to see heaven as bringing eternal rest, Protestants have often seen it as a glorious opportunity for perpetual employment, which is (alas) impossible on this earth owing to time necessarily wasted in sleep! Popular writers from both traditions have frequently emphasised that heaven is a place of family reunions: one Victorian author devoted seven chapters of *Heaven our Home* to the vexed question of the recognition of friends in heaven. The writer of the well-known hymn 'Ten thousand times ten thousand' saw heaven as a place of

> ' knitting severed friendships up
> Where partings are no more.'

This particular notion of salvation is clearly a religious response to the obsession with personal relationships which has been a feature of European culture over the past century and a half. The concept of salvation as not here and not yet has at all times played some part in Christian thinking, and this is not surprising when we remember that death has been seen as a problem in many different cultures. The vision of heaven, however, has varied considerably. The mediaeval heaven was certainly a place of milk and honey, but it was characterised above all by order, hierarchy and the splendour of court. Slave religion in the Americas pictured heaven as a place of great activity, of feasting, of walking up and down in a city of golden streets, pearly gates and bright mansions.

While it is clearly the case that a view of salvation as not here and not yet if often associated with deprived groups who see little hope of changing their earthly conditions and who look for compensation and comfort in a heavenly mansion, it would be wrong to conclude with Feuerbach that the political consequences of such conceptions of heaven are always quietist. As with mystical experience, so with the picture of heaven above the skies – the earthly order may be judged by the criteria derived from these visions. In his book on *Slave Religion*, Raboteau reminds us that the other-worldly emphasis did not always result in indifference towards injustice in this world, while Peter Brown, writing of an earlier period, states that conceptions of heaven in late antiquity 'enabled the Christian communities, by projecting a structure of clearly defined relationships on to the unseen world, to ask questions about the quality of relationships in their own society'. 'Why may we not have our heaven here,' demanded the Digger, Gerrard Winstanley, 'and heaven hereafter?'

Millennial hopes

Finally we shall consider the ideas of those who think of salvation as here but not yet. We must immediately distinguish between the millennial conception of a purely divine intervention, openly and dramatically bringing this present age to an end by inaugurating the reign of Christ, and those conceptions of salvation as a transformation, gradual or sudden, in which men may play a part.

The concept of the 'millennium' is taken from the Revelation of St John the Divine (20:1-5), where the author refers to a thousand-year reign of Christ on earth. In this chapter, however, we shall use the term more widely to include all ideas of salvation which see God's kingdom coming on this earth, by his own agency and without significant human co-operation. Millenarian movements have, in recent years, become a fascination of sociologists, anthropologists and social historians, and much has been published on the subject. Millenarian understandings of salvation were important in the early Church, but with the spread of Christianity and its establishment as the official religion of the empire, less emphasis was place upon a future apocalyptic transformation of this earth. In the later Middle Ages, however, popular millenarian movements again emerged as a significant feature of religious life and they were influential in post-Reformation Europe. Millenarian hopes have been entertained most frequently by the poor and the oppressed, and, according to Norman Cohn, were particularly lively in times of severe famine, plague and social disruption. There are, nevertheless, several instances of middle-

or upper-class millenarian movements, either within the historic churches (as with Isaac Newton and his contemporaries) or in sects such as the Catholic Apostolic Church in Victorian Britain.

With respect to political action, millenarians have generally fallen into two categories. On the one hand there have been those who believed that Christians must separate themselves from the evil world and prepare for the coming of the Lord. In some cases this has resulted in the formation of religious communes having as little to do with the world as possible. Mennonite and Hutterian communities in the USA would be examples of this attitude. On the other hand there have been millenarians who have believed that they were called to purify the social order and, by thus preparing the ground, hasten the birth pangs of the coming Kingdom. Some of the Anabaptists of sixteenth-century Germany and the Fifth Monarchy Men in seventeenth-century England would fall into this category. Apocalyptic expectation has often led to a violent struggle against the forces of evil, as occurred with the Taborite movement in fifteenth-century Bohemia. They believed that they were called to rid the world of sinners: 'accursed be the man who withholds his sword from shedding the blood of the enemies of Christ,' they declared, 'every believer must wash his hands in that blood'. Sometimes the dynamic of millenarian movements has been such that their militant members have moved from the notion of a preparation for the coming of Christ to a belief that they can themselves build the heavenly kingdom on earth, under the power and inspiration of the Holy Spirit. When this happens they cease to fall into my category of millenarians, for I stipulated that this would include only those groups who believe that God's Kingdom would be established by God alone. The ideas of those who assert the possibility of man's co-operation in this enterprise will not be considered.

Working together with Him

The Second Vatican Council of the Roman Catholic Church addressed itself to the question of the relationship between salvation and human history, but its conclusions are by no means unambiguous. While it was clearly recognised that Christ died and rose again to break the power of evil forces, 'so that this world might be fashioned anew according to God's design and reach its fulfilment' (*Gaudium et Spes*, section 2), the relationship between this transformation and social action is not clearly stated. 'Earthly progress,' we are told, 'must carefully be distinguished from the growth of Christ's Kingdom. Nevertheless to the extent that the former can contribute to the better ordering of human society, it is of vital concern to the Kingdom of God' (*Ibid*, section 39). The Council fathers clearly wished to reject the idea that by political and social action

Christians can, brick by brick, build God's kingdom on earth. Such a concept was characteristic of some of the Liberal Protestants at the turn of the twentieth century associated with the social gospel movement. But we must be careful here. Walter Rauschenbusch, one of the leading prophets of the movement, was keen to emphasise the divine origin and inspiration of the heavenly Kingdom and recognised that conflict and catastrophe would be a part of this forward march. 'We should estimate the power of sin too lightly', he warned, 'if we forecast a smooth road'. Yet he saw the manifestation of God's Kingdom in terms of a gradual evolution which approaches but never realises its final goal, and he identified too easily the liberal and democratic assumptions of his day with the will of God.

The social gospel writers rightly saw human efforts to remove oppression and injustice as related to the Christian concept of salvation. Because of this they are clearly to be distinguished from even the more socially conscious among the Conservative Evangelicals, who think in terms of the 'social implications' of the gospel. As only one quarter of the healing stories in the synoptic gospels includes the word *soteria*, Ronald Sider concludes that it would be unbiblical to extend the use of the term 'salvation' to include anything other than the relationship between the individual believer and Jesus Christ. Social concern and social action are, however, Christian imperatives, of equal importance to evangelism. Sider, of course, takes this position in conscious opposition, on the one hand, to 'liberation' theologians, like the Peruvian Gustavo Gutierrez, who insist that political liberation is a central feature of salvation and, on the other hand, to fellow-evangelicals who put social action very much in second place. 'Jesus', Sider declares, 'commanded us to feed the hungry and to preach the gospel without adding that the latter was primary'. What is significant about the distinction made by Sider is the very narrow definition of 'salvation', to include only the relationship between the individual soul and God. But the message of Jesus and about Jesus recorded in the New Testament concerns God's Kingdom and the transformation of this earth. Formally Sider is wrong – the primary task of the church is surely to preach and to live the gospel and not to turn itself into a social service agency. As Conrad Noel put it:

> 'We believe, then, in this Catholic Church, a visible Army to be the first-fruits of His Kingdom and to battle for its achievement among men: the very Body of Christ to redeem mankind from the inward tyrannies of sin and the outward tyrannies of cruel systems and cruel men ...We therefore believe that our principal work is not "social reform" not pietistic exercises, but the stirring within the people of the hunger and thirst for that righteousness which shall fill them with eternal things and a due measure of the things that are temporal.'

Those Christians who rightly believe that salvation in its fullest sense involves the transformation of this earth, so that 'the kingdoms of this world become the Kingdom of our God and of His Christ', a transformation in which they are called to participate as workers together with Christ, must however be on their guard against a fanatical utopianism. A failure to recognise that it is 'your Father's good pleasure to give you the Kingdom' will lead to a perfectionism which is both inappropriate and pernicious. They must be willing to settle for the best in the circumstances rather than attempting to impose an unattainable best and must be loth to sacrifice a known and certain good for a chimerical better.

Those who have held ideas of salvation as involving a future transformation of this earth in which men and women may play a part have tended to come from those groups which were not so poor or depressed that they felt unable to affect the course of events. They have frequently been denounced as visionaries and as betrayers of their class or nation. Political consequences of this idea of salvation have, by definition, been radical or at least progressive.

An adequate concept of salvation should include elements of all four basic positions which have been considered above. Yet it is the contention of this chapter that the last position discussed (which sees salvation as here but not yet and insists that it is something to which human action may contribute) should be the one which governs the rest. While it is, then, true that salvation concerns the whole man, in his social as well as in his psychic life, the Church must recognise the legitimate role of other agencies in making a contribution to this end. The Church should not try to become a total society, and its main concern is not social work or 'improving society'. Its central message is other-worldly, without being unearthly. It points to values and priorities which are radically different from those accepted in the world. It challenges the very basis upon which the present social order is built. When a man came to Jesus, asking him to adjudicate in a dispute about property rights, his reply was 'avoid covetousness' (Luke 12 13ff). Many Church pronouncements in the field of social ethics assume the very things that the gospel calls into question. Much of what is said about work and wage rates, for example, assumes – and in assuming gives a certain kind of endorsement to – the whole wage system by which people sell part of themselves to employers. Much of what is said about the duties of government assumes the legitimacy of coercive authority. As our descendants look back to the twentieth century they will surely wonder at the uncritical support given by almost all Christian churches to the growing power and scope of the coercive state and to the tragically mistaken policy of getting the state to do for us things that we should be doing for ourselves. Social action does not necessarily mean state action, and we are disastrously wrong in rendering to Caesar the things that are God's and which he has given to us, being made in his image. Salvation, as the transfiguration and transformation of all things, will not come by legislation, nor by the heaping of power and prestige on the coercive state. Christians should rather be in the vanguard of those who are 'stepping out of Babylon', for 'where the Spirit of the Lord is, there is liberty'.

4 Kingdom Come: the Catholic Faith and Millennial Hopes

Gresham Kirkby

'Will the Catholic Revival go all the way?' This was the sub-title of a tract published by the Catholic Crusade for the Oxford Movement centenary in 1933.[1] The Crusade was a group of Anglican radicals which gathered round Conrad Noel at Thaxted in the period 1918–36. As its name implied, the Crusade stood for an uncompromising, if somewhat esoteric, brand of Catholicism. Nevertheless, it has a significance for today because it anticipated what is now called 'liberation theology'. The Crusade's 'theology' was done in a particular situation, that of the grim years between the two World Wars, and for a particular puropose, namely to explain and justify the new revolutionary socialism manifested in the Russian Revolution of 1917. It sought to recover what it considered 'the whole Catholic Faith', and by this it meant, first and foremost, belief in 'the coming of the Kingdom of God on earth', the fulfilment of the biblical hope. In this it claimed to carry on and develop the tradition derived from F D Maurice who, in the mid-19th century, in response to the challenge of Chartism, declared: 'To me, the Kingdom of Heaven is the great existing reality which is to renew the earth'.[2] Nor were Noel and the Crusade alone in this. From 1922 onwards the League of the Kingdom of God, under the inspiration of Percy Widdrington, was calling no less vigorously for the recovery of the Kingdom of God as 'the regulative principle of theology'.[3] If Anglican Catholics did not readily respond to 'the challenge of the Catholic Crusade', the League was offered recognition as expressing the social outlook of the Catholic movement.

Maurician theology, with its Johannine and incarnational emphasis, had a considerable influence on Anglican thinking, and, through Stewart Headlam and the Guild of St. Matthew, on Anglican Catholicism – Frank Weston, the revered leader of the movement in the 1920s, was a member of the Guild. The weakness of this theology was that it was Platonist and 'idealist', it neglected eschatology, the doctrine of 'the End'. Nevertheless, its understanding of the Kingdom seemed closer to the Bible than the view implied in the Anglican burial rite: 'that it may please Thee shortly to accomplish the number of Thine elect, and to hasten Thy Kingdom'. Some form of socialism was now attracting many Christians, generally on a liberal basis. Some notable Catholic clergy were members of the Church Socialist League (1906–22). Socialism was seen as the modern counterpart to feudalism and as being preferable to *laissez-faire* capitalism. If the Church of England was still, by and large, 'the Tory Party at prayer', a significant part of it looked like becoming 'the socialists at Mass'. However, socialism in this period was developing on collectivist lines, and this did not greatly appeal to the disciples of Headlam. So it was that Noel and Widdrington, in their different ways, looked for a more vigorous and distinctively 'Catholic' socialism, resting on a better theological foundation.

The 'Call to Action by the Servants of the Catholic Crusade' – which was not in fact composed by Noel[4] – presented a rosy picture of the 'Ages of Faith', together with a naive criticism of Protestantism as the major source of social evils. So far it was likely to appeal to Anglican Catholics: not so its apparently uncritical support for the Russian Revolution. However, its main contention was: 'The central belief of the Church of the first three centuries was the coming of the Kingdom of God on earth'.[5] In fact this was a very doubtful claim. A more generally accepted view was that expressed by Dr. Edwyn Bevan: 'The Christians thought the end was very near. They expected any day to see Jesus return on the clouds, and all the imperial strength and splendour of the pagan world melt to nothing at his glance.'[6]

Nevertheless, radical Christians have continued to repeat the Crusade's simplistic view. Further, it is often claimed that the change came with the conversion of Constantine at the beginning of the fourth century when (it is alleged) the church compromised with the world, and the necessary theological adjustment was made by Augustine, who transferred the hope of the Kingdom to the 'next world'. At this stage, then, it will be valuable to look in more detail at these historical questions, before returning to the nineteenth- and twentieth-century developments of the theology of the Kingdom.

The millennial hope

Augustine has been criticised both by millennialists, who look for the return of Christ to the earth to establish his thousand-year reign (as in *Revelation* 20), and by radical Christians, who ascribe a somewhat different belief to the 'first Christians'. We need, however, to ask: who are meant by 'first Christians'? Those of New Testament times, or those belonging to the first three centuries? There is another theory, that the New Testament Christians became disillusioned when the expected *denouement* did not occur, and that the fourth gospel was written to compensate for this. (It has also been suggested that Paul turned towards 'mysticism' for similar reasons.) The theory fails to explain why millennial beliefs were so widely held from the second century onwards. Justin Martyr, Irenaeus, Hippolytus, Tertullian, Lactantius, were all millennialists – even Augustine was at first. Since by the fifth century the expected return had not taken place, Augustine attempted to deal with the problem. He reinterpreted the millennium as the whole interval from the first advent to the last conflict, the 'reign of the saints' representing the church's entire course as the Kingdom of God on earth. He transferred the 'parousia', understood as the (second) 'coming' or 'return', so that it became the prelude to the 'heavenly Kingdom'. Its primary purpose now was judgment. By spiritualising the millennium, Augustine brought it into the present, which meant that the Church became vitally concerned with the world: but its function now was to sacralise the established order. The overall effect was to 'transfer the New Testament emphasis upon a present and future Kingdom of God on earth to a present church on earth and a distinctly remote future Kingdom in heaven'.[7] However, if it is Augustine who is ultimately responsible for the slang expression 'Kingdom come', a contingency too remote to merit consideration, his critics have generally failed to account for the 'deferred and distant parousia'.

Belief in the earthly paradise did not fade out with Augustine's 're-interpretation'. The Donatists of his day, anticipated by the Montanists of the second century, looked for a Third Age of the Spirit. This theme was developed by Joachim of Fiore in the 12th century, whose teaching provided another strand of millennialism of lasting significance. Joachim's visionary mysticism attempted to give history a meaning and a future. It differed from the older millennial beliefs in that it placed the parousia at the end of the 'Third Age' which would be the work of the Holy Spirit. Belief in Christ's imminent return was revived by popular preachers and prophets at a time of great social unrest in the 13th century, and other early doctrines of Byzantine provenance concerning the last World Emperor and the coming of Antichrist began to merge with Joachimism. Norman Cohn's study *The Pursuit of the Millennium*[8] describes the messianic movements which spread through Europe, and which, in secularised forms, are still with us. The various strands of millennialism continued to develop and interweave, one with another, to produce widely differing movements. The Reformation and the 'open Bible' encouraged this, while the works of Joachim and his imitators continued to be read, and the writings of the Silesian mystic Jakob Boehme (1575–1624) nourished Protestant dissent for the next two centuries. In spite of Cranmer's original 42 Articles, which condemned it as 'Jewish dotage', millennialism was the generally held belief of educated people up to at least the late 17th century. The only question was how soon Christ's return would occur, and dates were calculated. 'Nothing was too fatuous for the prevailing taste'.[9] Wesley popularised a wildly millennialist book by the German Bengel which had great influence on the most religious men of the time, so that millennialism existed at least on the fringe of Methodism. The term 'millenarian' is sometimes used to describe the even more bizarre sects which developed in the 18th and early 19th centuries. Reincarnation provided a new mode for Christ's return – and in female form! Similar patterns emerged in all these movements from the 13th century onwards, and in them are found the seedbeds of radicalism. The process of secularisation, the separation of radicalism from strange religious beliefs, was one of the gains of the 19th century, even if it left radicalism with little foundation. Radicalism in England may owe more to Methodism than to Marx, but that is not necessarily to its advantage. Religious revivals in this period aroused false hopes of an immediate return of Christ, which probably weakened belief, yet strange beliefs and cults continued to develop, Of interest to Anglicans is the Guild of Prayer for the Return of Our Lord, founded in 1891, and distinctly 'Catholic' in tone, but holding some strange views. What is significant for our purpose is the persistence of the millennial hope, and its propensity for even further development.

However, the late 17th and early 18th centuries were also affected by the new spirit of 'rationalism', aided by a weariness of Puritan 'enthusiasm'. Millennialism again became a problem for thoughtful people as it had done in Augustine's time, but a more 'liberal' solution was at hand which, in a sense, had been anticipated by Augustine and by Joachim. The millennium, understood as a restored earth, now became the prelude to the parousia, the new form of the belief being generally known as 'post-millennialism'. It is perhaps not surprising that this development owed a lot to an Anglican clergyman in Salisbury, Daniel Whitby (1638–76), who held Unitarian views, and the new outlook is reflected in the hymns of Isaac Watts (1674–1748) and Philip Doddridge (1702–51). Those who adhered to this view held that the Kingdom had come in our Lord's time, and the righteous would enter it – to that extent it was 'realised eschatology' – but they looked for a future earthly manifestation: it would come in a sense not yet present. Theirs was an essentially 'revolutionary' outlook, and it is here that we find the seeds of that 'liberal' progressivism' which was, and is, a constituent element of much 'Christian Socialism'. For liberalism even more than for Catholicism the parousia is an awkward appendage.

The challenge to liberalism

The liberal interpretation of New Testament eschatology (the term came into use in the 19th century) was seriously challenged first by the work of Johannes Weiss, but more especially by the publication in England of Albert Schweitzer's *The Quest for the Historical Jesus* (1910). The importance of Jesus' eschatological teaching was emphasised. According to Schweitzer, Jesus had expected an imminent 'coming in his Kingdom', either in his own lifetime or as a 'return from heaven' in the lifetime of some of his hearers. Since this had proved to be a non-event, the message of Jesus could have only an existentialist value. However exaggerated the theory, it drew attention to a neglected element in the gospels and in the New Testament generally, as well as in its Jewish background: the doctrine of 'the End' and the apocalyptic language in which the doctrine was clothed. Here too was exposed the weakness of the theology of Maurice, of Headlam and the Guild of St Matthew, and of what might be termed the 'Social Gospel' movement. It lay in the problem of the parousia. Seemingly the options were to ignore the matter, as some did, or to discard the whole apocalyptic apparatus.

If the Schweitzerian theory presented a challenge to those Christian radicals who looked for the Kingdom conceived as an earthly millennium, Noel dealt with it in a characteristically daring manner. Taking the idea of an imminent parousia as a 'myth', he reinterpreted the myth as a description of what was happening in the 'last times', and saw the dawning of the Kingdom in the Russian Revolution. Not surprisingly, this was something which Anglican Catholics, however sympathetic to Maurician theology and Fabian socialism, were unable to accept. I want to suggest, however, that Noel's 'heresy' was a step towards discovering the truth of the matter (there is a sense in which every heresy witnesses to neglected truth). It could even be seen as a recovery of the Old Testament idea of God Himself coming to judgment, a conception which lies behind the Battle Hymn of the American Civil War:

'Mine eyes have seen the glory of the coming of the Lord:
He is trampling out the vintage where the grapes of wrath are stored;
He hath loosed the fateful lightning of His terrible swift sword:
Our God is marching on.'

At this point it is important to note the striking parallel between the Christian hope and the Marxist hope as set out by Bertrand Russell in his *History of Western Philosophy* (1946).[10] 'To understand Marx psychologically', Russell says, 'one should use the following dictionary:

Yahweh	=	Dialectical Materialism
The Messiah	=	Marx

The Elect	=	The Proletariat
The Church	=	The Communist Party
The Second Coming	=	The Revolution
Hell	=	Punishment of the Capitalists
The Millennium	=	The Communist Commonwealth.'

'The terms on the left hand [says Russell] give the emotional content of the terms on the right hand, and it is this emotional content, familiar to those with a Christian or Jewish upbringing, which makes Marx's eschatology credible.' There is something exciting about this which Noel would have understood, but it would have been incomprehensible to Anglican Catholics who, for the most part, were content to follow Augustine and identify the Kingdom with the Church. (So the party becomes the substitute for the commonwealth, as in fact has also happened in Marxism.) Now I want to suggest that the terms on the right hand might help us to understand better the terms on the left hand. One might also add to Russell's list:

The Reign of the Saints	=	The Dictatorship of the Proletariat
The Final Consummation	=	The Withering Away of the State

I shall refer again to parts of this dictionary. It would seem that Marx (and Conrad Noel) unconsciously took the Second Coming and the millennium as myths, and reinterpreted them. I shall suggest that there has been a serious misunderstanding of the 'Second Coming' (not a biblical term) and of the millennium. This would indicate both a flaw in the psychological background of Marxism, and also a need to re-examine the Christian terms. However, it seems true to add that Noel was only saying (with less obscurity) what some *avant-garde* Catholics are saying today: that the coming of Christ in his Kingdom needs to be reinterpreted as 'the future of man'. Noel certainly suggested that the Second Coming would be fulfilled in Christ's appearance in 'a glorified humanity of which he was the first-fruits', though he also admits the possibility that 'we shall see him with our bodily eyes among the great company of the redeemed'.[11] Noel was a visionary, but if he was starry-eyed about Marxism-Leninism, he was also too much of a libertarian to stomach Stalinism.

There were certainly differences of outlook between Noel's movement and Widdrington's. The transformation of the Church Socialist League into the League of the Kingdom of God was heralded by the publication of a volume of essays, *The Return of Christendom* (1922). Widdrington contributed the chapter entitled 'The Return of the Kingdom of God', which was intended to establish the essential theological foundation of the new body. He argued that in the Bible and the Fathers, the Kingdom of God was a hope for this world, a hope which was lost in the fifth century, mainly due to the influence of Augustine. 'The abandoning of the Kingdom of God as a hope for this world', he declared, 'was the greatest act of apostasy which a religion has ever known.' This view was quoted from a liberal scholar, Dr. Bethune-Baker. Widdrington argued against the view which regarded the Church as the Kingdom of God on earth – the lie on which medieval Catholicism was founded. He opposed those who would confine its meaning to 'the reign, or sovereignty of God', maintaining that 'although such was the root meaning of the term, everywhere in the Bible it included the sphere in which this reign is actualised'.[12] It is this world which is to be the scene of a 'divine order'. Widdrington's outlook was, and remained, strongly Maurician. Though his essay has been described as 'magisterial', its argument was regarded by some as unconvincing. Critics felt that in some respects it appeared to controvert a more 'rounded' statement of 'The Necessity of Catholic Dogma' by Fr Lionel Thornton, CR.[13] In citing the chiliastic (millennialist) opinions of the Fathers in support of his argument, Widdrington glossed over the point that what they looked for was an imminent return of Christ to inaugurate the millennium. If, unlike Noel, he did not reinterpret the parousia myth, he certainly put it into the background. To this extent, he was unconsciously adopting the more liberal outlook of the post-millennialists, though it was allied with a strong sense of Catholic churchmanship. It was this weakness in its theological foundation which caused the League, and the Christendom Group which grew out of it, to lose the vision of its founder.

Anglican Catholicism

If Schweitzer's theory was a challenge to liberals, it was no less a challenge to Catholics, and they too were unable or unwilling to face it. Some even welcomed it as a blow to liberalism. The period we are looking at, 1918–33, was also the period of Anglican Catholic 'triumphalism'. The movement, long persecuted in the parishes, now went in triumph to the Albert Hall. The Anglo-Catholic Congresses had begun. The opening paper at the first Congress of 1920, by Professor Cuthbert Turner, had as its subject 'The Faith and Modern Criticism'. He alluded briefly to the issues raised in *The Quest for the Historical Jesus*, but, he said, 'We are on holy ground, it is enough to have said so much when fewest words are best'.[14] The time had not yet come when Catholics might suggest either that the disciples had misunderstood the sayings of Jesus (and conceivably attributed to him words derived from their own apocalyptic imaginings) or even that Jesus himself might have been mistaken. Father Thornton contributed a paper on 'The Kingdom of God'. As the Kingdom had been embodied in the old Israel, and in the Church, and, however imperfectly, in the Christian past, so, he maintained, it needed to be born again in a new civilisation. However, he did not move far from the Augustinian position, and ended on a note of uncertainty.[15] Catholics have never taken up a wholly escapist attitude to the world: they have continued to look back to the past, to the 'Christendom' that was, and to hope for a 'New Christendom' which, in Maritain's phrase, would be a 'refraction' of the Kingdom and of the world of grace.[16] It would not be feudalism, but it would be a system which upheld 'Catholic order'. The dominant 'Catholic' view throughout this period was that the Church was the only Kingdom of God one could hope for on earth. Dr N P Williams' final paper at the Second Anglo-Catholic Congress in 1923, on 'The End of Time', could only have confirmed his hearers in what they already believed.[17] Aubrey de Vere's paean 'Who is she that stands trumphant?' sums it up:

'Hers the Kingdom, hers the sceptre,
Fall, ye nations, at her feet!'

This is the logical conclusion of Augustinianism – the deification of the Church. And meanwhile an anti-liberal rival to Marxism, prepared to accommodate a quiescent Church, was already on the horizon in the shape of Fascism.

Bishop Gore, in *Christ and Society* (1927), recognised, but failed to answer, the problems raised by Schweitzer. He too insisted that the Kingdom is not merely the reign of God 'as some moderns have led us to suppose'. 'It is always', he wrote, 'the reign or sovereignty of God as embodied in Israel. It is not an abstract idea, but an embodied ideal.'[18] Yet even for him it is the Church which is the visible organisation of the Kingdom of God on earth. At the same time, Gore held that this earth, purged and regenerated, was to be the scene of the divine order; it was to become part of the eternal Kingdom. He rejected the false distinction between heaven and earth, and the view based on a literal interpretation of one New Testament saying (2 *Peter* 3:10) that this earth would be destroyed. Nevertheless, he maintained that the Christian hope for the world is centred on a future 'end' which is in no real sense either present or imminent. Gore's view was to triumph in Vatican 2. Only Marx and Noel had succeeded in giving some relevance to 'the end', even if it was 'Christian apocalyptic in secular dress'. But meanwhile Adolf Hitler was dreaming of a 'Third Reich', a great synthesis of Teutonic imperialism and 'the twilight of the gods', to last a thousand years.

After the centenary

It is significant that not long after the centenary of the Oxford Movement the Catholic Crusade began to fall apart over the Stalin-Trotsky argument. Some of its keenest members had been driven out in 1932 for refusing to take the 'party line'. The Crusade was disbanded in 1936, though the Order of the Church Militant continued until Noel's death in 1942. Nor did the League of the Kingdom of God fare much better. In the early 1930s it was put into cold storage – from which it never emerged – and was effectively replaced by the Christendom Group. Widdrington's younger disciples rejected his Maurician theology and preferred instead to identify the Kingdom of God with the Church. Today's radical Catholics are nearer in outlook to Noel and the Crusade. Sir Henry Slessor, a founder member of the League, was a prominent Anglican Catholic who, towards the end of his life, transferred his allegiance to the Roman Church. From this position he accused the League of heresy for its refusal to identify the Kingdom with the Church. It would be interesting, were he alive today, to have his thoughts on the new radical Catholicism.

In retrospect, the differences and similarities between the Crusade and the League are of some interest. While the Crusade looked to the Russian Revolution for its inspiration, the League looked back to 'Christendom'. Yet the Crusade also cherished libertarian ideals derived from John Ball through William Morris, and older members of the League acknowledged their attachment to Guild Socialism and their debt to Kropotkin. Both movements made mistakes, and if the mistakes of the Crusade were more obvious to Anglican Catholics, there were those on the fringe of the League who rightly warned of the 'servile state' but failed to recognise it when it appeared in the shape of Fascism. Noel and Widdrington were both unhappy with the attitudes of some of their disciples. It is tempting to ask how far the failure of the Catholic social movement was related to the obvious decline of the Catholic movement itself in the years following the centenary.

Some new thinking

It is my contention that Anglican Catholics have made the most significant contributions to the 'recovery of the Kingdom of God', and that even in their mistakes they have only anticipated the mistakes of those who have come after them. Before turning to two scholars who, in my view, have pointed a way to a solution of the parousia problem – and, by implication, to an understanding of the millennium – I want to look briefly at some interpretations which have developed during the last half-century. First, there was 'realised eschatology', associated particularly with the late C H Dodd. According to this theory, the Kingdom was already present, and had come in the ministry of Jesus. However, this interpretation required a minimising, if not excising, of the apocalyptic sayings attributed to him. It 'saves' Jesus at the expense of the early church. The view that the Kingdom has already come also tends to limit its meaning to the 'rule of God in the hearts of individuals'. This fails to do justice to the Bible as a whole, and robs history of any real significance. On the other hand Bultmann, a decade later, preserved the apocalyptic sayings of Jesus, but reinterpreted them in an existentialist sense. For modern man, the futurist eschatology must be regarded as a 'myth' which needs to be demythologised. 'The meaning of history lies always in the present, in every moment slumbers the possibility of being the eschatological moment.'[19] If Dodd's view might conceivably have some 'implications' for history, Bultmann's is entirely individualistic. Throughout this period there were others, including Anglicans, who sought to explain the parousia as fulfilled in Pentecost. There is undoubtedly an element of truth in this, deriving not only from the fourth gospel. The Old Testament idea of God himself coming in judgment was regarded as a second coming – Sinai being the first. Keble upheld a sound Catholic tradition when he wrote:

> When God of old came down from heaven,
> In power and wrath he came . . .
>
> But when he came *the second time*,
> He came in power and love.

But to suppose that parousia equals Pentecost is Platonism, the 'fudge' in which many Anglicans delight.

A different note, however, was sounded in the early 1950s by John A T Robinson. In his *In the End, God . . .*[20] Robinson argued that the theological issue before the church was as much the problem of 'the End' as, one hundred years earlier, it was the problem of the beginning. Robinson also contributed a brilliant essay on 'The Christian Hope' to a symposium *Christian Faith and Communist Faith* (1953),[21] the result of a series of discussions concerning the Anglican attitude to Communism initiated by Bishop Bell of Chichester. This was a period when a mood of pessimism went hand in hand with a kind of inverted theology, and 'ecumenism' was seen as part of the Cold War against Communism. Robinson wrote: 'For the New Testament writers, the point upon which every hope was concentrated was the restitution of all things in the return and reign of Jesus Christ with all his saints, and the consummation of history in a new heaven and a new earth. The New Testament Gospel without the parousia or (Second) Coming would be as impossible as Marxism without the classless society'. That this hope was replaced by 'a very different expectation fixed on the moment of death and the prospects for the individual beyond it' he attributed to 'the original absorption of the biblical faith to a Hellenistic civilisation whose doctrine of the soul was as individualist as its conception of reality was unhistorical'.[22] This at least was an alternative explanation of what had gone wrong at some stage in the early Church. Yet Robinson leaves the reader with the impression that the parousia is a myth to be interpreted as what is happening all the time – the coming of Christ into everything. Although superficially attractive, it suggests an evolutionary 'coming', and the phrase 'Coming One' suggests an Oxbridge don. Once more it is Anglican Platonism, the Maurician outlook arrived at by a different route, and one less satisfactory than the revolutionary vision of Noel – or of Marx!

The Second Vatican Council led to a new understanding of the relationship of the Church to the world. The Council Fathers were ambiguous, but the sharp distinction between heaven and earth disappeared. Though the Kingdom remained on the further side of the parousia, this earth was seen as being included in the 'restoration of all things'. The Augustinian notion of a spiritualised millennium was apparently abandoned, though the Church was still in some sense the Kingdom ot God in the making. However, some Catholic theologians have adopted a more adventurous approach to the parousia doctrine, and the way was set by the German Protestant theologian Jurgen Moltmann in *The Theology of Hope* (1969).[23] In much of the new Catholic thinking, as in liberation theology, we arrive again at Noel's position, that 'the future of Christ' is revealed in the 'new humanity', and in some sense, though not as clearly as it appeared fifty years ago, this is related to Marxism.

Evangelical writers have also taken up the theme of the Kingdom of God, with careful examination of the Scriptures and an openness to new understandings. The emphasis is on the Kingdom as the 'dynamic reign of God'. It has come in Christ, it can be accepted by individuals, it is a realm into which we may enter now, but it is also a coming Kingdom. George Eldon Ladd, in *The Gospel of the Kingdom* (1958), strongly upheld the millennial reign of Christ, inaugurated by a future parousia, and also a final consummation in a new heaven and a new earth. Strangely, however, in his most recent work *The Presence of the Future* (1974), he does not once mention the millenium.[24] Stephen Travis, in *I Believe in the Second Coming* (1982), [25] explicitly rejects it, but sees the final consummation as including a regenerated earth. What does not seem to be questioned by these writers is the meaning of 'parousia', or the view that Jesus foretold his own second coming. The appeal to the Bible is made with preconceived ideas. Yet the new Evangelical outlook is close to that of Vatican 2. It has acquired a 'high' doctrine of the Church, but it is equally ambiguous.

One of the most informative books to appear in recent years is Rosemary Ruether's *The Radical Kingdom* (1970).[26] This is a study of 'the Western experience of Messianic hope', and the introductory chapter is entitled 'The Theology of Revolution and Social Change: the basic motifs'. In a few lines, she draws attention to the old doctrine of the millennium, which, as she makes clear in subsequent chapters, lies at the root of all movements for social change. The opening chapter contains some interesting observations. Originally the Messianic Kingdom was for this earth: it would be a time of great prosperity, and people would enjoy long life. The Messiah was human and would die like everyone else, and so when belief in the resurrection of the dead first arose it was seen as a temporary resurrection. In the second century BC the apocalyptists developed the idea of a transcendent Kingdom, a new heaven and a new earth, with an eternal resurrection. So, as Ruether puts it, in the first century BC these two alternative models of the New Age were 'stitched together'. Here, she points out, we find the origin of some later complications – two resurrections, two cosmic battles, and two judgments, one at the beginning of the temporal Kingdom, the other at the beginning of the transcendent Kingdom.[27] This is important when we come to consider New Testament eschatology: we should expect to find some confusion, and also the possibility of further development. This is, I suggest, what we do find. What the 'first Christians' really believed is not easy to determine – there were as confused as we are!

Two Anglican scholars

I want now to turn to the two Anglican scholars referred to earlier who belonged to the decade after 1933. I want to draw attention first to some paragraphs on eschatology in Dom Gregory Dix's *The Shape of the Liturgy* (1945) in the chapter on 'The meaning of the Eucharist'.[28] Dix observes that the primitive understanding of the Eucharist

> 'brings us close to a whole habit of mind and thought about the relation of this world and things in this world to the "world to come" which is almost entirely foreign to our ideas, but which is of the very substance of early Christian thinking and of the New Testament documents . . . Its exploration takes us afield, back beyond the Gospels into the Old Testament and the world of Jewish thought from which our Lord and his apostles and the Gospel came.'[29]

Dix acknowledged his indebtedness to the work of C H Dodd, though he adds: 'I do not fully subscribe to his theory of realised eschatology'. He goes on to suggest that the 'Day of the Lord' and the ideas connected with 'the End' are at once within history and beyond it, the consummation of time and its transmutation into what is beyond time, the 'Age to Come'.[30] Thus the prophets both foresaw 'the End' as a definite event, and yet were forced to describe it in the fantastic language of myth. For primitive

Jewish Christianity, says Dix, ' "the End" had come in the life, death and resurrection of Jesus . . . and yet history continued!' However, he adds that 'for pre-Christian Jewish thought, the *eschaton* had a double significance: (1) it manifested the purpose of history, and (2) it also concluded it. But even in Jewish thought these two aspects were not regarded as necessarily coincident in time.'[31] This bare summary is sufficient to indicate the stupendous questions which faced the disciples after the Lord's ascension.

Further, in a lengthy footnote, Dix pays generous tribute to another Anglican Catholic scholar of the period, and because of its importance I quote it in full:

> 'I would like to draw attention to an essay by Dr W K Lowther Clarke on *The Clouds of Heaven* . . . of which unsufficient notice seems to have been taken in England. In his own words his thesis is that "When our Lord said: 'Ye shall see the Son of Man sitting at the right hand of power and coming in the clouds of heaven', he referred to his Ascension, not to a Descent, to his vindication by the Father and only indirectly to a judgment of this world. The true meaning of his words was gradually lost until in the second century they were taken to mean a coming from heaven." So far as I have any means of judging, the materials assembled by Dr Clarke entirely bear out his contention, which seems to me in line with much in the Jewish prehistory of Christian eschatology. But such a view calls for a drastic revision of current theories about primitive Christian messianism and eschatology generally, and in particular of the relation of the 'second coming' (parousia) to the paschal sacrifice of Christ in his death, resurrection and ascension together.'[32]

If Dr Clarke's thesis is substantially correct, and if it does call for 'a drastic revision of current theories'. as Dix suggests, the consequences are considerable, though neither had fully worked them out. We must first, however, look at possible objections. Dr Clarke might seem to imply that parousia equals ascension, though he does also emphasise a 'coming in the Spirit' and, somewhat vaguely, a final coming. Archbishop Temple, in his *Readings in St John's Gospel* (1939), interprets Jesus' references to 'the Coming of the Son of Man' primarily in relation to the Cross and resurrection, in terms which certainly minimise the apocalyptic elements. Dix is more positive in declaring: 'When Jesus passed through death to life, and so by his ascension into the "glory" (*shechinah*) of God, in his person the "Age to come" has been inaugurated.'[33] The crucial saying, in its earliest form, is in *Mark* 14: 62 where, in reply to the high priest's question, Jesus declared: 'You will see the Son of Man seated at the right hand of power and coming with the clouds of heaven'. Here, for the only time, he claimed to be the Davidic King (of Psalm 110) and the Son of Man (cf *Daniel* 7: 13–14). The latter saying describes 'one like a Son of Man coming on the clouds of heaven to the Ancient of Days'. It is neither an ascension nor a descent; the scene is laid entirely in heaven. What Jesus believed about himself and his mission was derived from 'the Prophets and the Psalms', and there was nothing there to suggest a return to this earth. That Jesus was acquainted with sayings from the Book of Enoch (100 BC onwards) we may well suppose. Here the Son of Man judges in heaven on 'the throne of his glory'. and descends to earth only after heaven and earth have been transformed. There is thus a hint of a final coming, or revelation (apocalypse), of the Son of Man in a transcendent Kingdom, but nothing to suggest to Jesus an imminent 'return' to this earth to accomplish what he had failed to do the first time. As Dr Clarke puts it: 'Rather he believed he would fulfil what was written concerning himself – and this was the movement of thought which changed the world – only through suffering culminating in death would he achieve world dominion. Vindication by the Father at his own time and in his own way was the faith which filled the mind of Jesus'.[34]

The meaning of parousia

Now we will turn to the disciples and the New Testament. The word 'parousia' does not occur in the Gospels, except in *Matthew* 24, which is a later version of *Mark* 13. It does not mean 'second coming' (which is not a New Testament term at all) nor 'return': it means 'presence' or 'coming'. The Gospel sayings use the participle of the verb *erchomai*, to come, to go, or to pass by (as in the phrase in Bishop Walsham How's well-known hymn 'The King of Glory passes on his way'). 'Parousia' is used in the earlier New Testament letters to refer to a future coming, but not, it seems, to a return to this earth. When Matthew's Gospel was written, it could have been understood as referring to a future coming, but in the unlikely use of the word by the disciples and Jesus it would have meant the moment when Jesus would assume the Messianic role. If he had ridden into Jerusalem on a war horse, this would have been the sign of his 'parousia'.[35] Already, in Jewish thought, the earthly messiah was being regarded as the heaven-sent deliverer. Two fundamentally irreconcilable views of eschatology were being crudely combined. Strange messianic ideas were held then, as they have been since, and as they are held today.

The ascension was the sign to the disciples of Jesus' entry into glory. This is the meaning of 'the cloud' as at the transfiguration, the sign of God's presence. The notion that Jesus would return to earth 'on the clouds' is based on a misreading of the ascension story, on a misunderstanding of its meaning, and on a confusion of symbols. 'The clouds' are a symbol of judgment and blessing – God 'rides on the clouds' – and such symbolism can be applied to the Coming from the ascension onwards. Bishop Christopher Wordsworth put it thus:

'See the Conqueror mounts in triumph,
See the King in royal state,
Riding on the clouds his chariot
To his heavenly palace gate . . .

See him, who with sound of trumpet
And with his angelic train,
Summoning the world to judgment
On the clouds will come again.

Up the the moment of the ascension, the disciples expected Jesus to fulfil the role of the earthly Messiah and restore the Kingdom to Israel. From that moment he would be regarded as the heavenly Son of Man, and they would expect him to come in glory – a future but imminent parousia – in the sense of a revelation (apocalypse) when they would be caught up to heaven to reign with him in a transcendent Kingdom. This appears to be the earliest view, reflected in 1 *Thessalonians* 4: 16–17, which does not imply a return to this earth. Since the idea of a return from heaven to earth to inaugurate the millennium was firmly established by the middle of the second century, we might expect to find traces of it in the New Testament. The remarkable thing is the absence of such evidence, and even *Revelation* 20 is ambiguous. From Paul's letters we gather that some strange beliefs were current. He had to warn against a forged letter 'to the effect that the Day of the Lord has come' (2 *Thessalonians* 2: 12) – a completely realised eschatology – and against those who held that 'the resurrection is past already' (2 *Timothy* 2: 17) – they held the Greek view of immortality.

Pentecost brought a new understanding, as Peter perceived in his use of Joel's prophecy (*Acts* 2: 17 ff): the gift of the Spirit was a sign that the 'Age to Come' had dawned. The fourth gospel, so far from being a consolation for disappointed hopes (of which there is no real evidence), is a development of what had been there from the beginning. The 'scoffers' of 2 *Peter* 3: 3–4 are more likely to have been ardent 'charismatics', early Montanists who had so exaggerated the Johannine teaching as to see no need for a future coming. There is considerable development within the New Testament, so that the later Paul comes close to John. The sense that 'the End' had come gave meaning to time and history; the Lord was seen as exercising judgment in heaven where his throne was set, and banishing evil from his face (cf 1 *Corinthians* 15: 24–5). The true meaning of the ascension is given in *Ephesians* 4: 10 'he ascended above all heavens to fill all things'. The parousia had come to be understood as presence as well as coming, and this suggested the possibility of a 'restoration of all things' as implicitly in certain passages of Paul. The idea of an earthly millennium seems to underly *Acts* 3: 20–1 and 1 *Corinthians*, and with *Revelation*, in which a new heaven and a new earth precede the final coming of Christ, The likelihood is that these ideas were not completely worked out. So the predominantly Gentile church of the second century took over the view apparently found in *Revelation* 20 because it was unable to understand Jewish apocalyptic. The first Christians certainly developed the conviction of a final coming at the consummation of time and history, an 'epiphany of his presence' (2 *Thessalonians* 2: 8) in the transcendent world of the resurrection. What was insecurely grasped, and eventually lost, was an understanding of parousia as presence – and this was something which Joachim of Fiore did not perceive.

The Coming of Christ in his Kingdom

If the parousia is the consequence of the paschal sacrifice, and Pentecost its first sign, what then do we mean when we say: 'He shall come again in glory to judge the living and the dead, whose Kingdom shall have no end'? Or when we proclaim: 'Christ will come again!'? We affirm that this is happening now, that the parousia is a process which is both present, and also moving towards its final consummation, This consummation is the essential transcendent element without which the process is meangingless. (Marxism also has a sense of transcendence which it has lost sight of – the withering away of the state.) If the parousia is already dynamically present, we can restate the Maurician dictum thus: 'The Coming of Christ in his Kingdom is the great existing reality which is renewing the earth'. And this involves a revolutionary transformation of which the millennium is the powerful symbol. It is this ancient Jewish-Christian conception which the important insights of Dix and Lowther Clarke need to give them substance, and John XXIII's vision of a 'new Pentecost' has its place in it. Conrad Noel caught the vision of the earthly Paradise because he took the apocalyptic dreams seriously, and so the *Manifesto of the Catholic Crusade* (1919) has a message for today. Noel would still be challenging the Catholic Revival to 'go all the way'. Hating what he called 'the safeties of central churchmanship', he would be among those who describe the Church of England today as 'the SDP at the Parish Communion'. Nor should Widdrington's passionate plea for the recovery of the Kingdom of God as the regulative principle of theology go unheeded. It was necessary, he argued, for the defence of the Catholic Faith, to purge it of what was false and to re-establish it on its true foundation. This would 'involve a

Reformation in comparison with which the Reformation of the sixteenth century will seem a small thing.'[36] And if he sounded expansive in claiming that the fate of civilisation depended on its effective proclamation, the time seems only to have proved him right. 'Kingdom Come' sums up the caricature of the gospel and the Lord's Prayer which we have presented in place of the biblical hope for the earth. Is the movement of Catholic Renewal now ready, fifty years on, to respond to the challenge of the past, and to recover the vision of the Coming of Christ in his Kingdom?

> 'Write the vision: make it plain upon tablets, so he may run who reads it.
> For still the vision awaits its time: it hastens to the end – it will not lie.' (*Habakkuk* 2: 2–3)

References

1 *The Oxford Movement. Will the Catholic Revival go all the way?* By Servants of the Catholic Crusade, 1933.
2 cited in M B Reckitt, *P E T Widdrington: a study in vocation and versatility* (SPCK, 1961), p 83.
3 P E T Widdrington in *The Return of Christendom* (George Allen and Unwin, 1922), p 108. See also Reckitt, *op cit*, pp 71–85.
4 According to Reg Groves, *The Catholic Crusade 1918–36* (Archive One, 1970), p 24, the author was Jim Wilson.
5 *The Oxford Movement, op cit*, p 3.
6 cited in W K Lowther Clarke, *Divine Humanity: doctrinal essays on New Testament problems* (SPCK, 1936), p 9.
7 J E Fison, *The Christian Hope* (Longman, 1954), p 40.
8 Mercury Books, 1962 edn.
9 R H Charles, *Studies in the Apocalypse* (Edinburgh, T and T Clark, 1913), p 43.
10 Bertrand Russell, *A History of Western Philosophy* (George Allen and Unwin, 1946), p 383.
11 Conrad Noel, *The Life of Jesus* (Dent, 1937) pp 529–30.
12 P E T Widdrington, 'The return of "the Kingdom of God" ', in *The Return of Christendom, op cit*, pp 91–113.
13 in *ibid*, pp 65–86.
14 *Report of the 1st Anglo-Catholic Congress, London 1920* (SPCK, 1920), p 30. For the whole paper see pp 20–33.
15 *ibid*, pp 53–61.
16 Jacques Maritain, *True Humanism* (Bles, 1938), pp 101, 105. On the Kingdom of God see pp 91–104, on the theme of a 'New Christendom' see pp 205–50.
17 *Report of the Anglo-Catholic Congress, London, July 1923* (Society of SS Peter and Paul, 1923), pp 167–178.
18 Charles Gore, *Christ and Society* (George Allen and Unwin, 1928), p 33.
19 Rudolph Bultmann, *History and Eschatology* (Edinburgh, 1957), p 155.
20 John A T Robinson, *In the End, God . . .* (James Clarke, 1950), pp 15 ff.
21 D M Mackinnon (ed), *Christian Faith and Communist Faith* (Macmillan, 1953).

22 *ibid*, p 210.
23 Jurgen Moltmann, *The Theology of Hope* (SCM Press, 1967).
24 George Eldon Ladd, *The Gospel of the Kingdom* (Paternoster Press, 1977 edn); *The Presence of the Future* (SPCK, 1980 edn).
25 Stephen H Travis, *I believe in the Second Coming of Jesus* (Hodder, 1982).
26 Rosemary Ruether, *The Radical Kingdom* (Harper and Row, 1970).
27 *ibid*, pp 7–80.
28 Gregory Dix, *The Shape of the Liturgy* (Dacre, 1946 edn), pp 256–63).
29 *ibid*, p 256.
30 ibid, pp 256–7.
31 *ibid*, p 261.
32 *ibid*, p 262 n 1. For Lowther Clarke's essay see *Divine Humanity, op cit*, pp 9–40.
33 William Temple, *Readings in St John's Gospel* (Macmillan, 1959 ed).
34 Clarke, *op cit*, p 37.
35 See the interesting suggestion in Dorothy Sayers, *The Man Born to be King* (Gollancz, 1943), p 213.
36 *The Return of Christendom op cit*, pp 108–9. This is where contemporary ecumenical discussion ought to begin.

5 Manhood into God: the Oxford Movement, the Fathers and the Deification of Man

Andrew Louth

The appeal to the Fathers, and perhaps especially to the Greek Fathers, is something traditional in Anglicanism, so it is not surprising that in their appeal to the Fathers, the writers of the Oxford Movement found themselves rediscovering dimensions of the Anglican tradition that had been hidden or forgotten. Why appeal to the Fathers should be so important a part of historical Anglicanism is not difficult to understand, for Anglicans have never felt that they were any other than English Christians: Anglicanism is no confession dreamt up in the sixteenth century – to quote Archbishop Bramhall, 'the Church of England before the Reformation and the Church of England after the Reformation are as much the same Church as a garden, before it is weeded and after it is weeded, is the same garden; or a vine, before it is pruned and after it is pruned and freed from luxuriant branches, is one and the same vine'.[1] So to explain their separation from the rest of the Western Catholic Church Anglicans have looked to the Fathers for a sense of identity, an identity deeper than the rupture of the Reformation period. Especially perhaps they have looked to the Greek Fathers, to a tradition that may not contain the seeds of the division that manifested itself in the sixteenth century. Such an appeal to the past runs the danger of antiquarianism, but it would seem to be the case that where the influence of the Greek Fathers has been felt within Anglicanism we find not academic mustiness, but the seeds of renewal: one might point to the Anglicanism of Richard Hooker who, as a glance at the sources drawn on in his *Of the Laws of Ecclesiastical Polity* shows, was deeply read in the Greek Fathers, or to the influence of Greek patristics on such different groups in the late seventeenth century as the Cambridge Platonists and the Nonjurors, or in the late nineteenth century on the 'Cambridge Triumvirate', Westcott, Lightfoot and Hort, or (and it would be natural to an Anglican to see this as part of the same tradition) to the influence of Greek sources on such figures as Aelred of Rievaulx, or the profound influence of Denys the Areopagite on the author of the *Cloud of Unknowing.* But here we are concerned with a more precise aspect of this influence within Anglicanism: that is, with the influence of the doctrine of deification, so central to the thought of the Greek Fathers especially, on the Fathers of the Oxford Movement. And to set the scene, let us briefly sketch what is involved in the patristic doctrine of deification.

'The Word became man, that we might become god': that famous assertion of St Athanasius' sums up in the simplest and most direct way the heart of the Fathers' understanding of God's dealings with man and man's destiny in God. Man's destiny is to become god, deification. It is customary for scholars to shrink from this doctrine, to regard it as 'dangerous', to point out pagan, and especially Platonic, parallels, thus suggesting that despite the frequent iteration of such language in the Fathers, what we have here is rather echos of their hellenic heritage than the very heart of the Christian faith. (It is a fact, however, that the language of *theosis* and *theopoiesis* is Christian language, newly coined, not borrowed from pagan sources.) But it is important to realise, first of all, that for the Fathers deification does not at all mean that man regains some original divine state (as Plato might have thought of it): deification, as our quotation from St Athanasius suggests, is the counterpart of incarnation – God became man, that we might become God. The language of divinisation is part of a wider concern: it is one side of the *sacrum commercium* that God has established between himself and men; deification is the result of God's ineffable condescension to us in the incarnation of his son. And as that incarnation is, in the words of St Anatolius' hymn, *mega kai paradoxon thauma*, so is our deification such a great and mighty wonder, something outside the bounds of human expectation, a radical and deep change wrought within us by the power and grace of God himself. And it is perhaps here that we see the real reason for the way scholars have of shrinking from this doctrine: for, if true, to respond to the incarnate Lord is to open oneself to change at the deepest level, to a *metanoia* that will not stop short of giving us a share in the divine life itself. And that is cause for alarm, it is frightening: yet such is clearly the consequence of getting entangled with the God who makes himself known to us in the Scriptures. 'For what great nation is there that has a god so near to it as the Lord our God is to us, whenever we call upon him?' (*Deuteronomy* 4: 7): but the consequences of having a god so near to them were not at all comforting to Israel. On the contrary, they were deeply disturbing. And as we probe the patristic doctrine of deification we see that its central concern is to keep us close to a God who disturbs us and transforms us.

One way in which we can see this is to notice how the doctrine of deification relates to the doctrine of the Trinity. To see the mutual implication of deification and incarnation is to begin to see this, for the incarnation is the incarnation of the Son of God. But the lineaments of the doctrine of deification become clearer when we recall how in the theology of the Greek Fathers the doctrine of the Trinity is not at all a consideration of puzzling relationships within the divine substance, but is the doctrine of Father, Son and Holy Spirit: the Father, the source of divinity (*pege theotetos*), manifest in his image, the image of God, the Son, after which image we were originally created and in which image we can be restored by the operation of the Holy Spirit, so that in the phrase of St. Basil's, 'our mind being enlightened by the Spirit looks up to the Son, and in Him as in an image beholds the Father' (Ep 226).

Two quotations from Fathers of the East can be given to illustrate this understanding of our deification as a participation in the life of the Trinity. First from St Cyril of Alexandria (one of the greatest of the Eastern Fathers, who has been deprived of his proper influence on English theology by being denied a place in the *Library of Nicene and Post-Nicene Fathers*, though he was, as we shall see, a profound influence on Pusey, whose son edited many of the works of Cyril):

> 'For the Word became flesh, according to the word of John. He bore our nature, reforming it to his own life. And he himself is in us. For we have all become partakers of him, and have him in ourselves through the Spirit. For this reason too we have become partakers of the divine nature and are called sons, in this way having in ourselves the Father through the Son. And Paul bears witness of this, saying, "Since ye are sons, God has sent the Spirit of His Son into your hearts, crying, Abba, Father".'[2]

And secondly from St Maximus the Confessor, a seventh-century monk, deeply important to the Byzantine tradition, though not (as far as I know) known to the Oxford Fathers:

> 'The Word bestows adoption on us when he grants us that birth and deification which, transcending nature, comes by grace from above through the Spirit. The guarding and preservation of this in God depends on the resolve of those thus born: on their sincere acceptance of the grace bestowed on them and, through the practice of the commandments, on their cultivation of the beauty given to them by grace. Moreover, by emptying themselves of the passions they lay hold of the divine to the same degree as that to which, deliberately emptying himself of his own sublime glory, the Word of God truly became man.'[3]

Both these quotations bring out clearly the trinitarian dimensions of the doctrine of deification: they also bring out how the doctrine of deification is the deepest implication of our taking seriously the doctrine of adoption, the doctrine that we are called in Christ, to be sons in the Son, to find in his vocation of obedience to the Father in the darkness and desolation of a fallen world our own vocation. And Maximus in particular draws out in the passage quoted the radical ascetic implications of deification: that as the Word of God became man by *kenosis*, by emptying himself of his glory, so we are to become God by responding to that *kenosis* with our own *kenosis*, an emptying of our passions, the pursuit of *apatheia*, a detachment and *disponibilite*, through which the divine is manifest within us.

Such a doctrine of the Holy Trinity enables us to see our divinisation as a participation in the mutual relationships, the mutual life, the communion of love, of the Trinity. But more significantly: such a doctrine of the Trinity makes it clear that to respond to Christ, to welcome the Spirit and to work together with him, is to be plunged into the depths of the life of God himself. There is no escape. 'Our God is a consuming fire', as the Epistle to the Hebrews puts it: and we might well shrink from such an encounter. We might well – and it might be suggested that in the history of theology, especially in the West, we can see such a shrinking, we can see an attempt to evade the alarming closeness of a God who deifies, by the development of a doctrine of grace that keeps him 'at arm's length', as it were.

To sketch such a development in a few lines is foolhardy in the extreme, but may perhaps be excused if it is seen as providing a useful background against which we shall be able to appreciate something of the genuinely radical nature of the thought of the Oxford Fathers. But it would certainly be fair to say that in the West the language of deification falls into the background: and it is significant that as the notion of deification recedes so too does the doctrine of the Trinity as something that is known in Christian experience. The doctrine of the Trinity retreats into itself, as it were: it becomes a doctrine of inaccessible relationships within God, a God who is known to his creatures as One. And this one God has to do with his creatures by the medium of grace. To begin with, grace was spoken of as the Holy Spirit (and indeed such language was never wholly lost in the Western tradition, though it receded from its formal theology) – Peter Lombard, in the 12th century, still speaks in these terms – but soon there develops the concept of *gratia creata*, created grace, an intermediary between God and man, which preserves the infinite gulf that separates God and man.[4] Whatever the reasons for this development (and there were good reasons), one cannot avoid the impression that God can now be kept 'at arm's length'. And from such a perspective the Reformation, with its doctrine of imputed righteousness and the idea of man at once righteous and a sinner, *simul justus atque peccator* – though its rejection of 'created grace' was intended as the rejection of some intermediary between God and man in which man has a hand – can be seen as giving a further twist to the screw on the patristic doctrine of deification: God is not only at arm's length, but in responding to God man is not called to holiness, and does not know in his being the beginnings of a change that will lead to radical transformation.

It would be wrong, however, to suggest that the doctrine of deification vanished from the Western scene altogether. There are two exceptions to this that we ought at least to mention: for the language and doctrine of deification is preserved in the doctrine of the Sacraments, especially the Eucharist, and in the writings of those we call the mystics. The case of the mystics is familiar: it was precisely their fondness for the language of deification that drew suspicion upon them (in the case of Ruysbroek, for example). But it is significant that the language of deification, of transformation into God, is so deeply rooted in their thought. It is no eccentricity: it is central to St John of the Cross, for instance, who speaks of souls becoming 'truly gods by participation, equals and companions of God' (*Spiritual Canticle* 39.6), of the soul's transformation into her Beloved: *amada en el Amado transformada*. In the case of the Eucharist, it may be sufficient to quote St Thomas Aquinas, from one of his *opuscula* on the Feast of Corpus Christi: 'The only-begotten Son of God, wishing to make us sharers in his divine nature, assumed our nature, *ut homines deos faceret factus homo* – that made man he might make men gods' (*opusc* 57).

'And that a higher gift than grace
Should flesh and blood refine,
God's presence and his very Self,
And Essence all-divine.'

We are now perhaps in a position to see what Newman was trying to express in that familiar verse, which has caused such puzzlement and distress that it is marked with an asterisk in our hymn books. How could there be a higher gift than grace? one might ask: and the answer is obvious, if grace is created grace, if grace is God's mere acceptance of us. For He could give us Himself, His 'presence and His very Self, and Essence all-divine'. And it is this realisation that God gives us not just His gifts, but Himself, that is the deepest conviction of the Fathers of the Oxford Movement.

'*This* is really and truly our justification, not faith, not holiness, not (much less) a mere imputation; but through God's mercy, the very Presence of Christ' (J167):[5] here, in a sentence which sums up the central theme of his *Lectures on Justification*, Newman gives expression to this central conviction of the Oxford Movement, the conviction that as we respond to God in Christ, God Himself is present to us, in our hearts, drawing us to Himself: a conviction which expresses, as we have seen, the heart of the patristic doctrine of deification. Our engagement with God really affects us, radically changes us: we have to do with 'not a change merely in God's dealings towards us, like the pale and wan sunshine of a winter's day, but (if we may seek it) the possession of Himself, of His substantial grace to touch and heal the root of the evil, the fountain of our misery, our bitter heart and its inbred corruption' (J37). In this we find Keble and Pusey at one with Newman. So, in his work *On Eucharistic Adoration*, Keble speaks of the Eucharist as 'that gift which is God Himself, as well as having God for its giver. "Christ in us", not only Christ offered for us; a "divine nature" set before us, of which we are to be made "partakers" ' (EA8). And Pusey in one of his sermons:

> 'We can only dwell in God by His dwelling in us. To dwell *in* God is not to dwell *on* God only. It is no mere lifting up of our affections to Him, no being enwrapt in the contemplation of Him, no going forth of ourselves to cleave to Him. All this is our seeking Him, not His taking us up; our stretching after Him, not our attaining Him; our knocking, not His opening. To dwell in God, must be by His dwelling in us.' (SP297).

And the notes to that sermon (on 'The Christian's Life in Christ') reveal unmistakably the source of Pusey's inspiration: for they consist of long quotations from the Greek Fathers – from St Athanasius, St Gregory of Nazianzus, and especially St Cyril of Alexandria. Pusey himself makes this explicit when he says a few lines later: 'By dwelling in us, He makes us part of Himself, so that in the Ancient Church they could boldly say, "He deifieth me"; that is, He makes me part of Him, of His Body, who is God' (SP298). This quotation brings out too something deeply important to the Oxford Fathers: that the doctrine of deification is essentially ecclesial, that it is through our life in the Church, through our participation in the sacraments, that we are deified. As Keble puts it, apropos the miracle at Cana in Galilee:

> 'Thus according to the Scriptures, the Sacramental Touch of the Church is the Touch of Christ; and her system is "*deifica disciplina*", a rule which, in some sense, makes men gods, and the human, divine; and all this depends on the verity of the Incarnation, therefore his Mother is especially instrumental in it; besides being, as nearest to him, the most glorious instance of it.'[6]

'All this depends on the verity of the Incarnation': we have already noticed that the patristic doctrine of deification is a reflex of the doctrine of the incarnation, and that both find their deepest meaning in the context of the doctrine of the Trinity. We have also seen that in the West, as the doctrine of deification receded, so too did the doctrine of the Trinity, as a genuinely apprehensible fact of Christian experience. So it is no surprise to find that the recovery of the doctrine of deification in the Oxford Movement goes hand-in-hand with a recovery of the doctrine of the Trinity. Newman makes this connection explicitly when he says:

> 'Since the promise expressly runs that we shall be made one *as* the Father and the Son are One, we are necessarily led either to think highly of the union of the Christian with God, or to disparage that of the Father and the Son; and that such schools of religion as maintain that the former is but figurative, will certainly be led at length to deny the real union of our Lord with his Father, and from avoiding mysticism, will verge and fall upon what is called Unitarianism.' (J162)

The same point is made in what at first sight appears a somewhat paradoxical way in Keble's introduction to his edition of Hooker. There he draws attention to the fact that in the *Christian Letter*, a Puritan attack on Hooker, one of the charges against Hooker is that of subordinationism. The precise phrase cited from the *Ecclesiastical Polity* is this: 'The Father alone is originally that Deity which Christ originally is not' – and at first glance there seems substance in the complaint. But as Keble points out, the background to this is Calvin's innovation in the doctrinal tradition in ascribing to the Son the title *autotheos*, a title used in Greek theology for the Father. The consequence of this Calvinist doctrine is to render nugatory the doctrine of the Trinity in the patristic sense, according to which the Son receives his being from the Father and exists in dependence on Him. It is indeed the final twist of the tendency in the West to swallow up the Trinity into the unity of God: or not the final twist – for the next twist, difficult now to resist, will be some variety of Unitarianism. Against this Hooker firmly set his face and determined, in opposition to the dominant influence of Calvinism, to set forth a doctrine of the Trinity as the triune life in which we can participate in the Son through the Spirit: 'Life as all other gifts and benefits groweth originally from the Father, and cometh not to us but by the Son, nor by the Son to any of us in particular but through the Spirit' (*Eccl Pol* V.lvi.7). Indeed, the passage cited by the *Christian Letter* comes from the long exposition of the doctrine of the incarnation in book V, an exposition which leads into his discussion of the sacraments, which is itself set in the context of the doctrine of the Communion of Saints, within which we are partakers of Christ: 'His Church He frameth out of the very flesh, the very wounded and bleeding side of the Son of man. His body crucified and his blood shed for the life of the world, are the true elements of that heavenly being, which maketh us such as himself of whom we come' (*Ibid*).[7] This faithfulness to a doctrine of the Trinity which is open to, and indeed implies, the doctrine of the deification of man is something found again a century later in Ralph Cudworth who, like Hooker, drew the fire of Calvinists: but it was in Ralph Cudworth that the twentieth-century Orthodox nun, Mother Maria, could find something of a kindred spirit, for in him she found a doctrine of our real participation in God, a 'mysticism' in the sense in which Newman used the word in the passage quoted above.[8]

Pusey too sees this connection between the Trinity and deification, when in the introduction to his *Parochial Sermons* he discusses Hampden's attack on the scholastics, and on Pusey himself, but more deeply on the whole patristic tradition. For Hampden attacked any notion of deification as 'pantheistic', professing it nothing strange to find such 'in a mystic writer of the Church of Rome' (ie Bonaventure), but continuing: 'the strange thing is, that a minister of the Church of England (i e Pusey) should adopt it as his own, and recommend it to others'. Pusey regards such an accusation as damaging, for he (rightly) saw pantheism as a growing danger, and, as he puts it: 'it is directly to prepare the way for error, to represent the truth as involving it'. For Pusey it is precisely the Catholic doctrine of the Trinity, which implies and involves the doctrine that we are to be 'partakers of the Divine Nature', that is the antidote to pantheism. He quotes 'the thoughtful words' of W H Mill, 'one of the most reflective minds of our own time': 'The sacred and mysterious doctrine of the Trinity in Unity has ever been the surest safeguard against Pantheism in the Christian Church' (SP xvi–xix).

Given all this, it is not surprising that we find a simple and direct apprehension of our participation in the life of the Trinity in the writings of the Oxford Movement. So Pusey says:

> 'In each separate Mystery is the operation of the Trinity, although for us the Son alone took flesh, suffered, died, rose again, ascended; the Holy Spirit alone is 'shed abroad in our hearts', although through him, the Father and the Son come and make their abode in the faithful. Each Mystery is, at once, a stooping down of his Unchangeable Majesty, and a raising up of our deep-sunken misery.' (SP438)

And such language is echoed in the writings of Newman and Keble.

We see then, in the Fathers of the Oxford Movement, the recovery of the patristic doctrine of deification which speaks of a real engagement between God and man in the work of redemption and sanctification. We suggested earlier that such a doctrine is alarming in that it is radical: for man faces the prospect of a real change, a true transformation or transfiguration of his very being. And it is just this that lies at the heart of the doctrine of deification as understood by the Oxford Fathers: the real demands of holiness, the alarming nature of our surrender into the hands of God Himself. Pusey's sermon, already referred to, on 'The Christian's Life in Christ' closes with Pusey drawing out the consequences for the Christian's life of the doctrine of deification:

> 'My brethren, there is no middle way. We must be the dwelling-place, though we know it not, of the Good or the evil; of the Spirit of God, or of Satan . . . Our condition is the more aweful on account of the greatness of God's Gifts to us . . . Seek we, then, to rise again in the Spirit, in faith, in hope, in charity, that we may hereafter rise, through It, in the body also . . . Seek we to live less to the world and less like the world, and more like him who hath overcome the world . . . Seek we more to share his lot of poverty by foregoing what we have, to benefit his poor; his obedience, by setting God alway before us and in all things. his humility, by putting others forward and longing to be last ourselves . . . ' (SP322–5).

So Newman in a sermon on fasting sees it not just as an ascetic discipline, but rather contemplates how fasting weakens us, robbing us of self-control and exposing us to temptations, and goes on to comment: 'And, perhaps, this is the truest view of such exercises, that in some wonderful unknown way they open the next world for good or evil upon us, and are an introduction to somewhat of an extraordinary conflict with the powers of evil' (SN7–8). Fasting then is to be viewed 'chiefly as an *approach to God* – an approach to the powers of heaven – yes, and to the powers of hell' (SN9).

But the deepest consideration of deification as surrender to the transfiguring power and presence of God is found in the seventh Lecture on Justification, where Newman considers how the effect of Christ's sacrifice is wrought in us. Protestants, he says, 'consider that Christ's Sacrifice saves by the mind's contemplating it. This is what they call casting themselves upon Christ . . . Surely we ought so to *come* to Christ . . . but the question is, in what form and manner he *gives* himself to us; and it will be found that, when he enters into us, glorious as he is himself, pain and self-denial are his attendants' (J200). To receive the fruits of Christ's sacrifice in ourselves is, then, a costly and painful process: as costly and painful as the transformation of our warped and wounded nature into the purity and power of God. 'Christ's Cross does not justify by being looked at, but by being applied; not by being gazed at in faith, but by being actually set up within us, and that not by our act, but by God's invisible grace'; 'Men say that faith is an apprehending and applying; faith cannot really apply the Atonement; man cannot make the Saviour of the world his own; the Cross must be brought home to us, not in word, but in power, and this is the work of the Spirit. This is justification; but when imparted to the soul it draws blood, it heals, it purifies, it glorifies' (J200–1). Newman spells this out by discussing various passages from the epistles of St Paul, from whom, he says, we shall find 'that the gift of the Justifying Cross as certainly involves an inward crucifixion as a brand or stamp causes sharp pain, or the cure of a bodily ailment consists in a severe operation' (J201); 'The saving Cross crucifies in saving . . . O easy indulgent doctrine, to have the bloody Cross reared within us, and our heart transfixed, and our arms stretched out upon it, and the sin of our nature slaughtered and cast out . . . Our crosses are the lengthened shadow of the Cross on Calvary' (J202). Alarming, then, and costly and painful, this doctrine of the indwelling Christ, this doctrine of deification! But because it is about a real transformation into God it speaks of the releasing into the world of a real power, the power of God to heal and forgive, a power laid hold of in prayer and the sacraments:

> 'This, again, is the very mystery and blessedness of the Sacraments; that, by the one, Christ knit us into himself; by the other, he descendeth to us, that he may become 'One with us, and we with him'. This is the force of prayer, that it is a calling down of God to ourselves, a going forth of ourselves to God . . . Our prayers go up unto the Throne of God, because they are His Voice in us.' (SP428)

In conclusion, we can see that the appeal to the Fathers by the Oxford Movement, particularly as it manifests itself in the recovery of the doctrine of deification, is no antiquarianism: rather it was a realisation of what Yves Congar has in our own day said about the Fathers, that 'their work was blended with prayer, fasting, penitential exercises and the life of divine union. This gives to many of their writings a tone which puts them among "the writings of an eye-witness about the country of his birth". In the Fathers we find an immediacy of contact with spiritual realities . . .'[9] In the Oxford Movement we could indeed say that we find not so much recourse to the Fathers, as a rediscovery of the patristic tradition, in that the lives and writings of those whom we may well call the Oxford Fathers we rediscover that 'immediacy of contact with spiritual realities', which is the hallmark of the Fathers.

References

1 *Works* (Library of Anglo-Catholic Theology, 1842–5), i.113.
2 *Comm. on St John's Gospel*, bk IX (Pusey's edn, II.486).
3 *On the Lord's Prayer.* E T (modified) from *The Philokalia* (ed Palmer, Sherrard, Ware, 1981), II.287.
4 See C Moeller and G Philips, *The Theology of Grace* (1961), 11–23, esp p 18.

5 References to the works of the Oxford Fathers are given in abbreviated forms in the text, the numbers being page numbers. The abbreviations are: J = J H Newman, *Lectures on Justification* (2nd edn, 1840); EA = J Keble, *On Eucharistical Adoration* (2nd edn, 1859): SP = E B Pusey, *Parochial Sermons*, vol I (2nd edn, 1883 reprint); SN = J H Newman, *Parochial and Plain Sermons*, vol VI (1869). (I am indebted to Dr Geoffrey Rowell of Keble College for the help of a connoisseur as to where to look for likely material.)

6 From *Lyra Innocentium*, quoted by A M Allchin in *The Rediscovery of Newman*, ed Coulson and Allchin (1967), p 55.

7 See *Hooker's Works*, ed J Keble (3rd edn, 1845), vol I, pp lxxxiff.

8 See Mother Maria, *Ralph Cudworth: Mystical Thinker* (1973).

9 *Tradition and Traditions* (E T 1966), 449 (quoting Ivan Kireevsky).

6 'Behold I am doing a New Thing': mysticism and politics in contemporary Christianity

Emmett Jarrett

'Remember not the former things,
nor consider the things of old.
Behold, I am doing a new thing,
now it springs forth, do you not
perceive it?
I will make a way in the wilderness
and rivers in the desert.
The wild beast will honour me,
the jackals and the ostriches;
for I give water in the wilderness,
rivers in the desert,
to give drink to my chosen people,
the people whom I formed for myself
that they might declare my praise.' (*Isaiah* 43: 18–21)

Something new is happening in the Anglican Communion, indeed in the contemporary Christian world. There is no use looking for precedents, or digging around for the roots in the distant past. The basis of this 'new thing' is, of course, biblical, and there are no doubt analogous movements of the Spirit in every period of the Church's history, even the Oxford Movement of nineteenth-century England. But it is important to recognise the movement of which I speak as a 'new thing', something surprising which God is doing now in the Church and the world. It is quite as surprising to us as the redemption which Isaiah saw coming to Israel in captivity, something as unexpected as 'a way in the wilderness and rivers in the desert'.

God is acting in the last years of the twentieth century to bring about the convergence of two impulses that Christians have long thought contradictory: the contemplative impulse to prayer, and the impulse to Christian social and political action. Mysticism and politics, things we had thought incompatible in one human soul or one Christian community, are being revealed in the practice of Christians today as aspects of one another, two sides of the same human coin.

What is happening in historical terms is the reversal of the dichotomy of religion and politics. Religion since the Enlightenment has been understood as essentially a private matter, and prayer as the relationship between the individual soul and its God. Politics has been thought of as social, having to do with things public, verifiable, objective. This dichotomy reflects the rise of capitalism as an economic dogma, with political consequences which religion was not permitted to question. It is not that prior to the Enlightenment Christians held prayer and politics, mysticism and religion, to be one in the sense that we are beginning to see them as one. Rather they were related to one another organically in ways and by institutional forms which were appropriate to a pre-Enlightenment frame of reference.

A good example of this older arrangement which survived into the nineteenth century was the old High Church party of the Church of England. At its best, the insistence of this party was that the Church of England, the established Church, was the expression of the Catholic religious experience of the English people. The High Churchmen attempted to preserve a unity which had long since disappeared. At worst, the Erastianism of the Church of England led not only to the subservience of the institutional Church to the State, but of the religious impulse of the people to the prevailing rationalist mentality of the times.

The Oxford Movement of 1833–45 drew on the historical Catholic roots of this older tradition, but even in its infancy it could be distinguished from the High Church position in ways which foreshadow current developments. In 1833 Hurrell Froude

> '. . . realised that Liberalism was not the only enemy. Even more dangerous was the interested friendship of the party [the Tory party] which regarded the Church as a bulwark of the established order . . . Though he regretted the romantic associations of the old order . . . he realised that the Church must be separated from its class associations and that what he calls "the gentleman heresy" must be denounced as such.'[1]

What Froude saw in embryo was, I believe, the potential for a new synthesis of mysticism and politics which the old institutional forms of the established Church and the secular State would not be able to hold.

The relegation of religion to the 'private sector' is most clearly to be observed in the United States. The laudable desire of the founders of the American Republic to avoid State involvement in religious controversy in a society which was from its foundation pluralistic in matters of religious expression has resulted in the privatisation of religion, and with it the trivialisation of religious experience. Religion is a 'personal matter' no doubt, but the personal is defined as individual or 'private', not social or political. Religion has become, in America, 'a matter of opinion', and opinions don't matter.

How far this perspective has departed from the Christian gospel can be seen from a glance at the 'text' of Jesus' first sermon in Nazareth of Galilee:

> 'And [Jesus] came to Nazareth, where he had been brought up; and he went to the synagogue, as his custom was, on the sabbath day. And he stood up to read; and there was given to him the book of the prophet Isaiah. He opened the book and found the place where it was written,
>
> "The Spirit of the Lord is upon me,
> because he has anointed me to
> preach good news to the poor.
> He has sent me to proclaim release
> to the captives
> and recovering of sight to the blind,
> to set at liberty those who are oppressed,
> to proclaim the acceptable year of the Lord."
>
> And he closed the book, and gave it back to the attendant, and sat down; and the eyes of all in the synagogue were fixed on him. And he began to say to them, "Today this scripture has been fulfilled in your hearing".' (*Luke* 4: 16–21)

Christians since the Enlightenment have not understood this gospel as social in its very essence because of the blinders they have worn to the unity of prayer and politics, mysticism and social concern. Froude had at least an inkling of the Church's communal dimension and social rôle from the more distant past. He dared to go further than the High Church party, whose allegiance was to 'Church and King', to the Church of England 'as by law established', and criticise the Tudor settlement itself. If Henry VIII had resisted the encroachments of papal power, the Church of the later Middle Ages had obscured its primitive constitution in accepting civil establishment. In his *Remains* Froude wrote:

> 'The wealth of bishoprics and dignities, which was once regarded as the patrimony of the poor, had by degrees assumed the character of worldly property, was bestowed by patronage, and used for selfish gratification; while the lordly personages who possessed it, with the enjoyment of riches had imbibed the dread of poverty, and shrunk

> from asserting their station as successors of the Apostles for fear of losing their station in society.'[2]

Such ideas, however, were not predominant in the Oxford Movement, or the Anglo-Catholic movement which developed from it. The spirituality of the movement was imitative of French Roman Catholic practice, devoted chiefly to individual spiritual direction with 'alms-giving' as the sole expression of the social dimension of Christian religion. The leaders of the movement made no original contribution to the development of Anglican spirituality. Urban T Holmes III writes in *A History of Christian Spirituality* that

> 'The Tractarians are . . . uninspiring. John Keble is sweet, but limited. Edward Pusey is erudite, arrogant, and boring. John Henry Newman was an original theologian, but as Friedrich von Hugel, himself no mean student of Christian spirituality, once observed, Newman was incapable of ending a sermon, or a poem on anything but a note of gloom.'[3]

This judgment is harsh but accurate, and gives us all the more reason for regarding the current development as a 'new thing' in the Anglo-Catholic movement, as it is in Christian history at large. It is always, of course, possible to detect development. Like the Tractarian leaders, F D Maurice is an 'ancestor' to contemporary Christian concerns. John Oliver notes that 1877 was the year

> '. . . that saw the first explicit fusion of the two dominant streams of theological thinking in the Church of England during the second half of the nineteenth century, the Maurician and the Tractarian – a combination which was to prove particularly valuable in the field of Christian social thought.'[4]

And of course the Anglo-Catholic priests of the East End of London, Stewart Headlam and the Guild of St Matthew, the various Christian socialist groups, and latterly the English and American Jubilee Groups, follow this path. But it is only in recent years that the emphasis has shifted, and prayer and politics have begun to be seen as a unity of thought and action in the Christian life. This indeed is a 'new thing'. Especially in America, where the Anglo-Catholic movement has been mainly a ritualist club – the significant exception being Father Smyth's Society of the Catholic Commonwealth – the development of urban priests and activist congregations of a Catholic complexion committed to political action as well as prayer and spiritual growth is unprecedented. Even the Episcopal Urban Caucus, regarded with distaste by a conservative Presiding Bishop, is committed to spiritual discipline as well as advocacy for the poor, to prayer groups and rules of life as well as community organising and political action.[5]

If the dissociation of prayer and politics occurred as a result of the breakdown of an older, more corporate perspective on Church and society, what does the union of prayer and action, the convergence of the mystical and political impulses in Christian life look like as it overcomes this false dichotomy and moves in the power of the Spirit to transform the Church and the world? What, indeed, is the name of this 'new thing' that God is doing in our midst?

It is not a new denominational division, for which Americans are notorious, but a truly ecumenical movement of Christians of different viewpoints confronting realities which call for common action. It is not a 'movement' in the sense of an organised group seeking to lead the Church down different paths. There are no 'leaders', though many would point to Thomas Merton, the Trappist monk, and Martin Luther King Jr, the black civil rights leader, as 'ancestors'. Evangelicals such as Jim Wallis and the Sojourners would assert that it is simply 'Biblical Christianity'. The Jubilee Anglo-Catholics in England would point to its basis in Scripture and tradition, liturgy and the documents of Vatican II, and call it, perhaps, 'renewed Catholicism'. Many Anglicans on both sides of the Atlantic would see it as a contemporary expression of the perennially Anglican incarnational theology, and others would call it 'Kingdom theology' and the actions consequent upon taking Jesus' proclamation of the Kingdom of God in the New Testament seriously. They would all be right, of course, for it is all of these things.

Those of us who are priests and lay Christians in inner city parish churches see ourselves simply as Christians, worshipping God in the Eucharist, praying daily as the Church has always done, proclaiming the gospel to the poor and oppressed, being advocates for the outcast in imitation of our Saviour Christ. We read the signs of the times, look for the Kingdom of God, that divine society to which we pledged our loyalty in baptism, and work out in community the implications of our baptismal commitment to 'believe in God', Father, Son, and Holy Spirit, and 'strive for justice and peace among all people, and respect the dignity of every human person'.[6]

For the purposes of this essay I will use the term 'radical Catholics' to describe us. I speak chiefly out of Anglican experience, although the same 'new thing' is happening among Methodists and Presbyterians, while Roman Catholic bishops and members of evangelical urban communes stand together in refusing to pay taxes to build yet more nuclear weapons for the American arsenal. And I am also aware that the term 'radical Catholic' is in fact redundant, since to be Catholic is to be rooted – in Scripture, tradition, liturgy, and the common prayer of Christians in all times and places. The fact that Catholics are commonly thought to be politically conservative (and often are!) is an indication of the sea-change taking place in the Christian consciousness. To be Catholic and radical, to be rooted in Scripture, tradition, prayer and action, is to be grounded in God and in history, in the incarnation and the Church, in the material world which is God's good creation, and in our sisters and brothers, who are God's other children. From this rootedness, this commitment to the Kingdom of God which Jesus proclaimed and personified, comes our radical commitment to Christ and to one another, and our radical opposition to the structures of evil which divide person from person, by nationality, race, gender, class, economic status, or even religion. And from this radical Catholic perspective comes the awareness that what divides us politically, socially, economically, as individuals from one another and from our communities, is the same thing that divides prayer from politics, the worship of God from the mutual loving service which is God's will for all persons.

Radical Catholics mean something different by the terms 'mysticism' and 'politics' than the degenerative form of those words mean to the ordinary person. It is not surprising that a civilisation which does not believe in God does not believe in a personal relationship with God. The word 'mysticism' is used to indicate something strange, unreal, not to be taken seriously. F C Happold noted some time ago that

> '. . . the word is . . . used with a number of different meanings and carries different connotations to different minds. To some it is simply a type of confused, irrational thinking. In the popular mind it is associated with spiritualism and clairvoyance, with hypnotism, and even with occultism and magic, with obscure psychological states and happenings, some of which are the result of neurasthenia or other morbid pathological conditions. To some it is bound up with visions and revelations. Others use it as a synonym for other-worldliness, or to describe a nebulous outlook upon the world or a religious attitude which does not care for dogma or the outward forms of religious observance. Some would limit its use to that rare state of consciousness which is found in the contemplative saints.'[7]

The confusion is indeed widespread, and it will not do for contemporary Christians simply to claim the last definition and reject popular opinion. For a radical Catholic, the notion that the 'state of consciousness' of contemplatives is 'rare' represents a fundamental misapprehension of the nature of Christian prayer. Jesus in the New Testament calls all of the disciples to prayer, not just a cadre of spiritual specialists. St Augustine in his *Confessions* refers to all human souls when he says to God, 'you made us for yourself and our hearts find no peace until they rest in you'.[8]

Kenneth Leech, addressing a wide audience of ordinary Christians in *True Prayer*, writes:

> 'Prayer in itself is a human activity, something we all do. At its simplest, prayer is longing, desire, the expression of our deepest aspirations, joys, or sorrows. . . . The prayer of Christians is not something essentially different from this basic human prayer, but it builds upon it and moves beyond it. Julian of Norwich, the fourteenth-century mystic, believed that prayer was a natural experience and should be a common one. "It seems to me", she wrote in her *Revelations of Divine Love* (Chapter 10), "that this should be and is an experience common to us all." But Christian prayer is a specific kind of prayer: it is prayer *in Christ*. And this prayer is rooted in, and arises out of, the Christian understanding of God.'[9]

I suggest that from the radical Catholic perspective, prayer is simply the name for the Christian's relationship with God. It is, therefore, a human relationship as well as a divine one, and has characteristics similar to those we experience in other human relationships. It is personal, a relationship between persons, because God is personal and human beings are personal, because made in God's image. But it is also social because God is social, and the social nature of human beings is what it is because we are made in the image of a social God. Reductionist spirituality speaks of prayer as the flight of 'the alone to the Alone', but Christian theology teaches that God is trinitarian in nature, not Alone, and that human beings made in the divine image are spiritual natures which are not by God's design isolated, alienated, private. Prayer which pulls us into relationship with the social God inevitably pulls us out of our alienation into society with other human beings as well as God. And this is politics.

Politics is commonly thought of as a profession, the art or science of government, statecraft, administration. Some politicians are elected officials and some are career civil servants, but politics is a professional activity, and often an unsavoury one. Because modern society is divided against itself, economic life is thought to be something different from social and political life. Politics is no longer the proper work of men and women who are fellow-members of the *polis*, a recognisable community. It is a special task delegated to specialists. (The overwhelming majority of United States Senators and Representatives are lawyers by profession.) Community is not involved in politics in the modern bureaucratic state. Politics is not the sphere of activity of citizens any longer.

As more and more Western social institutions break down, the absence of 'community' becomes a subject of lament in newspapers and magazines. Families have been reduced to husband, wife, and child, and the stress of putting all emotional weight on this one relationship has resulted in the break-up of nearly half the marriages in society, some of them several times over. Hospitals and schools have become so large and so unrelated to the neighbourhoods and communities they serve that people not only have no control over their medical care and the education of their children, they generally get neither adequate medical care nor quality education. In the Commonwealth of Massachusetts in 1982 over one million citizens who are eligible to vote in local, state, and national elections have not bothered to register. Democratic institutions no longer serve the *demos*, and the people are voting with their feet.

But politics, properly understood, is an aspect of personal life. It is the way people work together to accomplish common tasks. In November of 1981 over half the townships of New Hampshire voted in town meetings to endorse a 'mutual freeze' of nuclear weapons. These votes have no influence on national policy, but they reflect the frustration of people with suicidal policies when they have a local opportunity to talk with one another and express an opinion.

The radical Catholic has no policy for national elections, but is committed to local institutions and community organising. Caring for sisters and brothers is a Christian matter for us. We reject the Reagan policy of robbing the poor to enrich prosperous investors in instant profits, but we do not accept that the human right to food, shelter, society, education and medical care is a 'private sector' responsibility. The radical Catholic begins in the congregation, and sees the movement of the Spirit in building communities first in churches – for churches are the only institutions that have not yet been rendered totally impotent by a rapacious lust for profit. Local churches are places where people pray: they are also the base from which people are beginning to organise to proclaim good news to the poor and release to the captive. The radical Catholic takes seriously the proclamation of the Kingdom of God.

How, then, are prayer and politics the same thing? In practice, the same people who gather on Sunday for the Eucharist, each receiving the same amount of heavenly food from the table of the Lord as every other, are the people who go out into the community to feed the hungry, heal the sick, work for peace, advocate for justice for the poor and oppressed. They do this locally, and they are already organising to do it nationally. It is only a question of time before they will begin to do it on an international level. The day will surely come when gatherings of Christians in international groups will be recognised as subversive by governments who want Christians to remain quiet in the face of economic exploitation, the rape of the earth's resources, and the building of instruments of destruction for the next and last holocaust.

The liturgical basis for this position is clear in most rites promulgated since the Second Vatican Council. The American Prayer Book is but one example of many in which peace is never prayed for except in the context of justice. What was always implicit in the Eucharist as 'foretaste of the Messianic banquet' is now explicit in contemporary liturgical texts. The exhortation to confession, whether generally in the context of the Eucharist, or in the sacrament of reconciliation, is no longer concerned exclusively with individual sins, but recognises the social dimension of sin as well as of salvation. Eucharistic Prayer D, one of six provided in the Book, refers explicitly to the Lord Jesus' proclamation of the Kingdom to the oppressed:

> 'To the poor he proclaimed the good news of salvation; to prisoners, freedom; to the sorrowful, joy. To fulfil Your [the Father's] purpose he gave himself up to death; and rising from the grave, destroyed death, and made the whole creation new.'[10]

But the baptismal rite is perhaps the clearest formulation of the Church's recognition of the social dimensions of a renewed Catholicism. The ancient practice of Easter baptisms is restored for the whole Church, not just for Anglo-Catholics, and the assembled congregation renew their baptismal vows of faith in God, as expressed in the Apostles' Creed, and commitment to justice, peace, and human dignity, at least four times a year on great festivals.

These changes in the public prayer of the Church both reflect a change in the understanding of prayer as social and personal but not private that has been growing all along, and will in turn further deepen this understanding among the people of God as they pray in public and private, using the Book of Common Prayer as their guide. And these changes are scripturally based.

Jesus taught that the Law could be summarised in two commandments, which are the stipulations of the baptismal covenant, as the whole Torah was the stipulation of the Sinai covenant. Love of God and love of neighbour are united in the baptismal summary. They cannot be separated from one another without doing violence to the teaching of the founder of Christianity. The New Testament writers understood this. The Letter of James, so long despised by Protestants, is today being understood as a radical indictment of religion as the handmaid of the state.

> 'My brethren, show no partiality as you hold the faith of our Lord Jesus Christ, the Lord of glory. For if a man with gold rings and in fine clothing comes into your assembly, and a poor man in shabby clothing also comes in, and you pay attention to the one who wears the fine clothing and say, "Have a seat here, please", while you say to the poor man, "Sit at my feet", have you not

made distinctions among yourselves, and become judges with evil thoughts? Listen, my beloved brethren. Has not God chosen those who are poor in the world to be rich in faith and heirs of the kingdom which He has promised to those who love Him? But you have dishonoured the poor man. Is it not the rich who oppress you, is it not they who drag you into court? Is it not they who blaspheme the honourable name which was invoked over you?' (*James* 2:1–7)

'Is it not the rich who oppress you?' These words are being heard by Christians again for the first time in centuries, as they (as we) begin to understand who it is who has called us, and to what purpose, and to take our place with Christ among the outcast and the oppressed.

Johannine theology makes the connection between love of God and love of neighbour even more clear. Love comes in the first instance from God to us, not from us to God. And because God's love comes to us, therefore we love one another. And if we do not love one another, the love of God is not in us, because the evidence of God's love in us is love of the children of God, whom God loves as well as us. The writer of the First Letter of John says it over and over again, but nowhere more clearly than in these words:

'Beloved, let us love one another; for love is of God, and he who loves is born of God and knows God. He who does not love does not know God; for God is love. In this the love of God was made manifest among us; that God sent his only Son into the world, so that we might live through him. In this is love, not that we loved God but that He loved us and sent His Son to be the expiation for our sins. Beloved, if God so loved us, we also ought to love one another. No man has ever seen God; if we love one another, God abides in us and His love is perfected in us.' (1 *John* 4: 7–12)

Individualism in religious practice, and especially in prayer, is an impossibility for Johannine thinking. Radical Catholics are thinking in this way, and acting upon this thought.

Conventional religious leaders, armed with a ghetto-mentality and desiring to preserve what is left of their authority, insist on the priority of prayer, of religious activities, of worship, over what they contemptuously refer to as 'social work'. (Somehow the parish picnic and the altar guild are not 'social' works on the part of these clergy – and they are inevitably clergy – but feeding the poor and organising to provide public services for the elderly are!) The radical Catholic refuses to choose between prayer and action, or to slight one by saying the other is less important. The radical Catholic prays and works. The radical Catholic takes seriously the words of the deacon's dismissal at the end of the Mass:

'Let us go forth into the world, rejoicing in the power of the Spirit'. Don't just sit there waiting for the extinction of the candles; go forth, and go forth into the world! The radical Catholic takes seriously Jesus' promise to Peter that 'the powers of death will not prevail against (the Church)' (*Matthew* 16: 18). This was not a promise of institutional security of success, in Jesus' time or in 1833, when Hurrell Froude had a glimmer of the possibilities open to the Church of Christ if she were faithful to her Lord. It is a promise that 'doing the works of God' is what Christians are called to do, and the institutional supports will be supplied as needed, and perhaps not as we (or our bishops) think they are needed in any particular place or time. The Kingdom of God is for us the 'regulative principle of theology'. Our ecclesiology is that of a community of friends of Jesus, brothers and sisters in faith, daughters and sons of the living God.

Radical Catholicism gives a new perspective on old theological issues, but I can do no more than indicate these issues here, and point, in conclusion, to new developments that hold promise for the future. In trinitarian doctrine, the radical Catholic takes seriously the words of the Athanasian Creed (restored to the American Prayer Book in 1979): 'And in this Trinity none is afore, or after other; none is greater, or less than another; But the whole three Persons are co-eternal together and co-equal'. As prayer is shaped by the nature of the God to whom it is addressed, the prayer of the radical Catholic, addressed to a social God, is social in its implications and social in its outcome. Human nature is made in the image of God, and the radical Catholic doctrine of human nature affirms the social nature of our human being. We reject hierarchy. God is properly at the centre of each human life, and of every human life in community. Domination of one human being over another, whether in the political order or in marriage or in the Church, is sinful. Co-operation is the economic law which expresses our understanding of divine and human nature; competition is sinful, except perhaps in sports. The material world is affirmed as God's good world in the doctrine of creation, and any sort of body-soul dichotomy is rejected. But the riches of the material world are good, and they are God's; therefore they are intended by God to be shared among all God's human children. Eucharistic Prayer D again provides fitting expression of this doctrine: 'You formed us in your own image, giving the whole world into our care, so that, in obedience to you, our Creator, we might rule and serve all your creatures'.[11]

Prayer is relationship with God, and this concept of relationship provides the key for understanding a radical Catholic view of human sin. Sin is not located in the body, or in matter, to be 'escaped' in death or sublimation or by psychic distancing. Sin is a break in relationship, and is therefore social as well as individual. The fundamental break is in the relationship between God and all human creatures. This fundamental break, described in Scripture not only in the Genesis story of the Fall but also in the prophetic indictments of Israel's collective idolatry, manifests itself in societies as well as individuals. A prophetic understanding of spirituality does not try to 'adjust' the errant individual to a value-free human social structure. Human social structures are also broken, sinful, in need of restoration in the Kingdom of God and the new creation which God in Christ wills for all people. Individual sins are not so much causes as symptoms of our broken relationships with God and with each other. Broken relationships in families, communities, in society as a whole, are manifestations of the broken relationship between human society and God. Radical Catholics do not join the new religious Right in condemning various groups of people for their different *mores*, in the hope that the return to the bad old days will make America strong again. We know that God calls all people to repentance, none more loudly than Christians, and we strive to overcome the dividing walls between groups, races, sexes, nationalities.

Prayer includes repentance, and social repentance means work to change the world, to transform the structures of evil into structures which admit the grace of God into human lives and communities. Radical Catholic theology attempts to address the issues which the life of God's people in the world presents to us. We strive to bring the Word of God, which is a word of hope and reconciliation, to bear on issues of racism, sexism, classism, economic justice, imperialism, ecology, and community. We wish to be in the vanguard of theological reflection where ground is being broken by racial minorities, feminists, Third World thinkers, liberation theologians, and others. A Christian theology which does not address, for example, the issues of human relationship raised by feminists, is failing in the mandate of the gospel to proclaim liberty to captives. Radical Catholics in the American Church have embraced the ordination of women to the ministerial priesthood, as we have embraced the ministry of the whole people of God as an expression of Christ's High Priesthood. We believe the ordination of women to be a movement of the Holy Spirit in the Church in our time, and that this movement of the Spirit is renewing the priesthood of the Church, making it less hierarchical, less professional, less a patriarchal tyranny, and more an expression of the ministry of servants to which Christ summoned the Church.

Racism and peace remain the pre-eminent issues for American Christians, and the radical Catholic who lives and works in the inner city's ghettos knows the life and suffering of the poor, and the threat of annihilation which hangs over all of God's creation. From this locus, we take our stand with Jesus and with Isaiah, with Peter and with Francis, with Thomas Merton and with Martin Luther King, as people who pray and work for the coming of the Kingdom. With Jesus, we go away 'to a lonely place apart', a haven of silence in the noise and suffering of the poor of our cities, and come back into the world to feed the hungry with the bread of heaven, and with the bread which we earn with the sweat of our brows, and which some sell to others for a pair of sandals. The prophet Isaiah provides us with our model for the unity of prayer and politics. He was himself of a priestly family, often in the Temple, and God spoke to him in the Temple 'in the year that King Uzziah died'. He saw the vision of God, the goal of contemplative prayer, and he repented not only of his own sins, but of the sins of his people, for he dwelt 'in the midst of a people of unclean lips'. And in the ecstasy of his union with God, he heard a word, a calling, he was healed and sent out to heal:

> 'Go, and say to this people,
> "Hear and hear, but do not understand;
> see and see, but do not perceive." ' (*Isaiah* 6).

The Spirit who is inspiring the Church in the last years of the twentieth century is the Spirit of the living God, the same God who commissioned Isaiah to proclaim good news to Israel, who sent the eternal Son into the world to redeem the world. The leaders of the Oxford Movement might not understand a great deal of what this God is doing with the Church and the world in these years, but perhaps they would follow where the Spirit led today, as they did in their own time. Isaiah spoke of a 'new thing' which the Lord was doing, bringing captive Israel home from Babylon to Jerusalem. He compared it – as he had to, for we have only our past to compare things with, and we are, as Catholics, rooted in our past, which is the history of God's ways with us – to the Exodus from Egypt into Canaan, the movement of God's people from slavery to freedom. We, too, can make comparisons. But the important thing is to see what God is doing. 'Behold, I am doing a *new* thing'.

References

1 Christopher Dawson, *The Spirit of the Oxford Movement* (Sheed and Ward, Inc, New York, 1933), p 67.
2 *Ibid*, p 72.
3 Urban T Holmes III, *A History of Christian Spirituality* (Seabury Press, New York, 1980), p 144.
4 John Oliver, *The Church and Social Order* (Mowbray, London, 1968), p 2.
5 The third Assembly of the Episcopal Urban Caucus, held in New York in February 1982, adopted not only resolutions in favour of a 'freeze' on nuclear weapons and delivery systems and development and economic justice with special reference to the urban poor, it also adopted a 'Rule of Life' based on the Baptismal Covenant of the Book of Common Prayer (1979). This representative group of urban activist priests and lay people of the American Episcopal Church committed itself to the Apostles' Creed, Eucharistic worship, daily prayer and fasting, personal and corporate repentance, as well as to racial, economic, and social justice for all persons. The Assembly's resolution

affirmed that Christian religious commitment and commitment to justice and peace in the modern world were inseparable.

6 The Book of Common Prayer (American, 1979), pp 304–5.
7 F C Happold, *Mysticism* (Penguin Books, London, 1963), p 36.
8 St Augustine, *Confessions*, trans R S Pine-Coffin (Penguin Books, London, 1961), p 21.
9 Kenneth Leech, *True Prayer* (Harper & Row, New York, 1980), p 7.
10 The Book of Common Prayer, *op cit*, p 374.
11 *Ibid*, p 373.

ADDRESSING THE CHURCH

7 Rubric and Spirit: a diagnostic reading of Tractarian worship

Judith Pinnington

Bishop Stephen Neill, in a somewhat partisan symposium on Prayer Book worship,[1] has recently said: 'It was in the nineteenth century that things really began to fall apart'. What he meant by this was that 'for the most part people did what they thought right, or failed to do what had seemed to be otiose'. He seems to fix a great part of the blame for this on the Oxford Movement.

Certainly before the Oxford Movement, and for a considerable time after it began in the Anglican Church at large, worship was a matter of habit, and choice, where it was expressed, was the choice to exclude the unfamiliar and very little else. Ordinary people, said a *Times* leader in 1845, were determined to have 'the Service of the Church as their sires and grandsires had it'. One correspondent in *The Times* on 20 January 1845 equated this with 'decorous observance'. The Tractarian Malcolm McColl suggested that it amounted to a process of 'soothing', the point of worship being seen as a set of 'solemn and impressive decencies' which, while 'affecting', in no way provoked to 'undecorous and unbecoming scenes of excitement'. Liturgy was a bland sandwich for the clergyman's ritual of talking to people 'very pleasantly for half an hour' (*The Times*, 10 February 1881). It was such as to charm small shopkeepers, humble citizens, cooks and housemaids, and to provide the mighty with a feeling of having done their duty.

The quality of this worship cannot be estimated merely from the numbers attending it, not even from the numbers presenting at Communion, which, in the days immediately before the Movement, could cause a Eucharist to last anything up to five hours.[2] McColl found behind such social conformism much slovenliness masquerading as 'simplicity', and Newman declared that it had a 'dreariness that could be felt'. This points to the coarse dullness verging on irreverence which led Isaac Williams to produce his provocative tract on 'Reserve in Communicating Religious

Knowledge'. One did not, he argued, cast pearls before swine. Indeed one must not, for one's soul's sake. There was much in Evangelical practice which simply perpetuated social insensitivity. Hence G W E Russell's memory of an east window with the patron's coat of arms in the centre and 'patriarchs and saints grouped round it in due subordination'. Lord Shaftesbury was once moved to bewail the 'coldness and insincerity' of most of his fellow-Evangelicals which reduced their religion to a political and personal level. When he dared to praise a lecture by Pusey, he felt the full vindictive force of that political religion. High Churchmen, Papists, even infidels, were, he said, more understanding.[3] If a visiting American churchman could find 'honest reality' in this manic solemnness, one wonders how shallow must have been Episcopalian worship in the United States.[4]

Publications in aid of worship before the Oxford Movement probably did more harm than good to the integrity of the liturgical sense. A prayer book which omitted large sections of the real thing was not the way to get through to simple people, thought W J E Bennett, the pioneer of 'ritualism'.[5] There was massive ignorance. 'I have had to deal,' wrote Archdeacon Manning to Bishop Phillpotts of Exeter, 'with men of 20 and 30 years old, who had been confirmed, but did not know the name of our Saviour, the way or cause of his death, or the meaning of the figure on the Cross.'[6] For the illiterate and semi-literate, this was the nemesis of a religion of purely verbal symbol, which inevitably led theological Tractarianism into ritualism. Men and women needed to be brought face to face with the symbols of the gospel. When this was first tried at St Barnabas, Pimlico, rioters carried banners declaring 'No Creed Worship', 'No Forgiveness of Sins'. When given tangible tokens of creed and forgiveness, they found they wanted neither the token nor what it stood for. In the end it came down, as one young man in the embattled parish of St George-in-the-East said to his night-school teacher, to 'a question of beer'. That was the symbol that had meaning: that could rent a mob. And the cultivated stood by, with hands raised in horror at such excitement, and with a sense of religious duty which Newman perceived did not partake of the liberty of the Spirit, but was a kind of easy sleep, remote from the narrow way to holiness, a sleep in which men turned only so long as to deprecate the devotion of those who provoked ritual riots.[7] Such a drowser feared, as Archbishop Benson put it in a eucharistic sermon, to 'know truth somewhat too intimately', to 'allow the sacraments to mean too much'. Such a drowser is like Bishop Collins' old lady who dimly perceives her new parish priest to be wearing something 'at the back of his neck that looks like a shirt button, but they tell me that it's really the thin end of the wedge'.[8]

This huge poverty of the spirit, even among the conventionally devout, was that to which the early Tractarians addressed themselves. This was what brought forth from them Dean Church's short sharp cry of pain. They were not aesthetes. Indeed, as has often been charged to their discredit, they were fierce ascetics, conscious of the need for the Bride to be prepared to meet the Bridegroom, conscious of men's preference for 'orderly initiation and affectionate commemorations' in manageable quantum over a direct confrontation with the living God. They wished to make men and women aware of 'that lovely and mighty energy of God'.[9] Pusey, in an open letter to Bishop Blomfield of London, said that the remedy for secessions from the Church was her own spiritual health, and her consciousness of the presence of God. The Church, said F W Faber, must not be reduced to an abstraction, for it was 'a person . . . his body, who is both God and Man'.[10] In a letter written for transmission to his clergy after his death, Henry Phillpotts, the sole befriender of the Tractarains among the older generation of English bishops, identified the 'one prevalent shortcoming in our ministerial life' as the 'want of diligence and fervour in setting forth to our people the full force, dignity and blessedness of sacramental grace' the object being 'our insertion into Christ's body and our growth in it'.[11]

To achieve this, however, required iconic embodying. Ritualism may not have been the logical, or even originally the consciously intended, outcome of Tractarianism, but it was both spiritually and sociologically inevitable. The cost in peace of mind was tremendous for those church leaders who trod this path. They were open to the most fluid charges of Romanism. Writing of the assertion of Bishop Manton Eastburn of Massachusetts in 1844 that the Church of the Advent, Boston, had a 'Romish altar' (because it bore two gold candlesticks and had a wooden cross set into the wall behind it), Massey Shepherd has mused whether the Bishop found it 'Romish', also that the clergy there looked towards the altar rather than 'into their chairs'.[12] But it was no laughing matter for the early Tractarians: it was an immense pain for those who sought to 'worship God seemly, in body and soul', to have some 'indifferent neighbour lament their Romanism'.[13] It was no laughing matter constantly to have thrown in one's face 'the genius of the English people' for simplicity of worship, which often amounted to little more than a misdirected cult of masculinity in matters of dress.[14]

However, bearing in mind the later liturgical history of the Movement and the legacy it bequeathed to the liturgical renewal of our own day, it is surely permissible to ask whether in some respects it may have lost its way. Have the heirs of Tractarianism anything much to dance about before the Lord in that 'tumultuous round-dance' which the ex-Tractarian Ronald Knox saw as central to the Mass? At the time of the first Lambeth Conference, Bishop Whitehouse of Illinois prayed for a 'holy force and daring' which would enable Anglicanism to stand 'more developed in her Catholic power and adaptive in her Catholic love'.[15] Anglicanism did indeed develop remarkable power and adaptivity as an ecumenical force in this century, and for this the Oxford Movement must bear the greatest responsibility. Yet did Anglicanism really develop Whitehouse's 'holy force and daring', and, if not, what was the deficiency of the worship which Tractarianism inspired within it?

Perhaps there was something too impulsive in the development of ritualism. It made observers not especially prone to hysteria distinctly uneasy. Benjamin Jowett, for instance, saw in the rash of ritualism spreading through the parish churches evidence of its purely aesthetic character.[16] The sheer ferment of it encouraged the worst in journalistic purple prose. One may sympathise up to a point with the leader-writer in *The Times* on 19 October 1866 who wrote of what he say in St Alban's, Holborn, when eucharistic vestments first appeared there:

> 'Three of these personages, bedizened with green and gold and yellow and covered with black stripes and crosses, stand with their backs to the congregation on the elevated steps at the east end of the church. The altar is overladen with gorgeous ornament and illuminated at noon-day with two great lighted candles . . . These gorgeous and flaunting dresses and candles and odours and gesticulations have in them something almost revolting to an English stomach . . . To introduce these gilded adornments would in any other profession be despicable childishness; around the solemn realities of religion it is simply revolting to a reverent mind.'

Considering the state of things from which the Tractarians had to proceed, it may be that such impulsive haste put an impossible strain on a national (rather than a gathered) Church, quite apart from the question as to the judgment of individual clergy, or the movement as a whole, on what was essential to truly 'Catholic' worship.[17]

The Lutheran scholar Dieter Voll is logical in saying that ritualism was not really a liturgical movement at all, because so much of its ceremonial was consciously used as a teaching aid to get over points of theology. It lacked a kind of integrity of vision necessary to a living liturgy.[18] In the earliest stages of ritualism, and especially where the guiding hand had the discretion of a Pusey or a Butler of Wantage, we find an evenness and measuredness of development lacking elsewhere, not least in the early religious communities where a common purpose and sophistication made the teaching-aid aspect of secondary importance, and inward discipline a high priority. Of the Breviary which he prepared for the Park Village sisterhood, Pusey could honestly say that 'there is nothing but what is framed on the service of the Church of England; there is no passage read from a Father which I could not myself preach in a sermon before the Bishop, nor any prayer which the Bishop himself might not use'. Pusey and William Dodsworth felt, rightly, that the detail of Catholic religious life should grow gradually out of a deep spiritual reality, and not be superimposed. Butler, who knew the character of continental Catholicism better than most Tractarians of his generation, eschewed large-scale importation with his sisters at Wantage, who in consequence remained long after his death very moderate in their ritualism. He knew the dangers in forcing the liturgical pace, and acted accordingly even when he had all the powers of a Dean of Lincoln.[19]

That spirit was so easily dissipated in the strenuous round of leading a parish into 'Catholic Truth'. What Dean Church called the 'short, rapid utterances of men in pain' tended to turn into a temper of arrogance. The Presbyterian philosopher H L Stewart found in the 'posturing' of a Hurrell Froude the seed of what was to grow within twenty years into Disraeli's 'exuberant priestliness'.[20] Young Tractarians were often emotionally unstable – as their young successors have continued to be. Faber was immoderately hostile to Rome while he remained in the Church of England, declaring her to scarce retain the 'lineaments of a true Church of Christ'. Whatever she touched, she had marred, he declared; one by one, her lamps had gone out, and now the lines had melted away into the dull, cold evening of the world around her.[21] Within a decade, he was singing an equally extreme but somewhat different song. As early as 1841 we find W F Hook complaining to Pusey of young disciples contemptuously dismissing what they were 'pleased to call *merely* Anglican'.[22] Such arrogance could not but affect the spirit of liturgy which it sought to promote. W J E Bennett, wiser than most, admitted that it was the priest's duty not to force practices on congregations before they had understood their importance,[23] a sentiment echoed two generations later by W F Cobb, assistant secretary of the English Church Union: 'The most correct ritual will fail of its end if it disturbs the peace of a devout congregation and gives occasion for the mischievous activity of that most odious of social parasites, the professional agitator'.[24] But the sad truth is that priests did force Catholic liturgy upon parishioners with the same high-handedness with which some of them stuck to the letter of the law and refused burial to unbaptised dissenters.[25] Early Tractarians like Bennett, and even more their brash juniors, overestimated the speed with which people could arrive at an understanding of Catholic worship, believing that Catholic principle was deeply embedded in Anglican forms – if somewhat overlaid. They spoke almost as if one generation would be sufficient to bring about a transformation.[26] This was dangerously deceptive.

Furthermore, as the ritualist movement developed, it showed more and more signs of eclecticism, throwing up characters as preposterous and confusing as Father Ignatius of Llanthony and Father George Nugee. These were what Newman called 'improper Tractarians' or the 'gilt gingerbread school'. The eclecticism, of course, did not go entirely without a species of justification. Nugee, a man so wealthy that he could afford to be a law unto himself, argued that his borrowings from Rome were all in the interests of reunion.[27] Yet the most striking fact about this development is not the particular arguments advanced for this or that usage, but the bifurcation of the movement into two distinct personality types: on the one hand the flamboyant, lineage-conscious, campaigning, restless type; on the other the reserved, austere, self-effacing, witnessing type. These psychological profiles were neatly matched by corresponding liturgical tendencies. The one gravitated to glamour – what William Gresley called the 'gaiety and glitter' of Roman ceremonial – while the other gravitated to the almost nude and penitential. Nugee's chapel at St Austin's Priory in New Kent Road well represents the first, the old chapel of the Cowley Fathers at Oxford the second. The one, phenomenologically speaking, shaded off into the underworld of *episcopi vagantes*, which is always conscious of 'style', even when worshipping in back rooms and garages. The other, in its complete lack of self-consciousness and its identification with the self-emptying of Christ, shaded off into the peculiar austerity of Orthodox monasticism.[28] This dependence of public liturgy on private personality was not a healthy sign. Contemporary critics intuited it correctly, although they took their inferences too far.

Tractarian leaders found it impossible – even had they whole-heartedly wished – to discourage those who always crave 'some new thing'.[29] To some extent, they became the victims of their own original self-effacingness in the hands of a minority of neurotics. Had not Pusey said: 'We the clergy had taught the truth; the people said "Set it before our eyes"?'[30] Moreover, the tendency among younger ritualists to encourage the laity to expect ever new emotional sensations fell into the trap, foreseen by Newman in his sermons at St. Mary's, of excitement being seen as the ordinary state of mind.[31] It was simply a re-run of the basic revivalist illusion. There was something distinctly unhealthy, though no more so then evangelical sermon-sampling of an earlier generation, in the floods of people from far and wide into new ultramontane churches at Clerkenwell or Southwark, areas previously unknown for 'Catholic' worship. Many ritualist clergy abetted such goings-on. Bishop Beckwith of Alabama spoke of one priest who, he said, was 'not a humble-minded man, but has much of that defiance of authority in him which characterises those gentlemen who make a speciality of being Catholic'.[32] Ironically, more moderate and responsible Tractarian clergy, like Nugent Wade, found themselves morally blackmailed by those used to more extreme variety. In Wade's case, the blackmailer was Mother Harriett Monsell of Clewer. 'Surely, my dear Mrs Monsell', wrote Wade, in some exasperation at her demands for the reserved sacrament, 'in your great zeal for your own views, conscientiously held, you have allowed yourself for a moment to forget that I too have a conscience, and am the responsible person having cure of souls in the parish.'[33]

It is not then surprising that a moderate like Vernon Staley should have been worried at the time of the Archbishops' Hearings on Incense in 1899 at how often 'the proclamation and acceptance of Catholic truth' had not 'kept pace with the advance of ceremonial'.[34] Accompanying this imbalance was an increasing casuistry by Tractarian clergy to justify their liturgical practices in face of episcopal disapproval. 'The real extremists', wrote Bishop Edward Talbot of Rochester to Archbishop Frederick Temple in 1899, 'seem to me to get more and more technical. It's like epicycles in the Ptolemaic astronomy. And this must alienate and offend plain folk'.[35] Preaching at the consecration of Frederick Burgess as Bishop of Long Island in 1902, Bishop W C Doane of Albany warned that when worthwhile accessories of worship so absorbed minds that 'the one effort of the minister and the one test of soundness in his ministry' turned largely on such minutiae, then there was an absence of wholeness. He cited the issue of reservation, which was also worrying Talbot, as such an imbalance.[36]

And this brings us to a key litmus-test of liturgical renewal: sensitivity to the condition of Christ's poor. When the movement began, the field was wide open for a total service to the poor. In London, neither the Free Churches nor, for the most part, Roman Catholics showed much concern. (In the area of Regent's Park and Somers Town where the first Anglican sisterhood was established, there were only some French Roman Catholic sisters concerned with the education of wealthy girls.) When the Anglican sisterhoods moved into such areas – the Park Village Sisters, the Mission Sisters of St Peter, the Sisters of the Poor, the Sisters of the Church – they could, and did, bring a concern to be in the midst of the derelict, and also a rich liturgical life. They were followed by mission priests like Father Lowder, who offended about equally, and probably co-ordinately, by their ceremonial, and by their insistence on seeing the 'image of Divine Royalty in the most dirt-encrusted coins of a derelict humanity'. Lowder was convinced that his ritualism in no way patronised or trivialised the poor, but gave them back their human dignity.[37] Each new liturgical innovation could be seen to serve a practical function. Thus Henry Scott Holland saw reservation as essential in poor parishes where the slums contained a great many sick and infirm.[38]

The most eloquent expounder of what might be termed revolutionary liturgy was undoubtedly Robert Dolling. Only the Blessed Sacrament, he averred, could drag slum-dwellers out of their death-agony. His ideal was that each parish should be a 'common roof-tree ... the centre of social righteousness in the whole district'. He had no time for prim writers to the *Church Times* who objected to a waif munching an apple in the hallowed precincts of St Paul's. He so offended one member of the Confraternity of the Blessed Sacrament by his attitude that his critic blamed a drought in East London on Dolling's appointment to St Saviour's. He was unrepentant. In a retreat address to the clergy of Chicago, a city which, he noted, has as many wretchedly destitute as did London, he declared that their ministry was both a seraphic intercession before the throne of grace, and a humble service to men. The two aspects were inseparable: the seraph's live coal made the unclean clean.[39] Chicago's own bishop, William McLaren, had earlier warned that if the mission of the Anglican Communion was to be achieved, it must substitute for 'stained glass gentility, the richer ornament of a serious evangelism' capable of applying apostolic truth to all the problems of the age.[40]

How far were the slum missions real? Charles Morley, a visitor to St Augustine's, off Commercial Road, in 1909, pictured to his *Pall Mall Magazine* readers a poor congregation spell-bound by the soft lights on the altar, the low grave voice and reverent movements of the priest, so contrasted with the stupefying roar of the streets and the sordidness of their daily lives. 'Ah! who can say what misty notions of the hereafter glimmer in their souls, not even Father Richard ...'[41] Indeed, how can one evaluate their responses? One can say that efforts by working men to organise in defence of Catholic liturgy were not a notable success. The Church of England Working Men's Society, formed in 1876 under the auspices of the English Church Union on the basis of a committee to defend Father Mackonochie of St Alban's, Holborn, against the Public Worship Regulation Act, expended its energies in legal contestation with the evangelical Church Association. In the view of K S Inglis, to the extent that working people attended Mackonochie's church, it was likely to be for what they could get out of him in political action rather than because they saw the connection he was making between the iconic presence of the Church in their midst, and their dignity as children of God.[42] It has been rare indeed for the Church to be anything to the majority of people, of whatever class, but a vehicle for gaining their secular ends, and the Tractarians were not especially foolish in this regard.

It seems implausible to explain Tractarian failure in evangelism in terms merely of their preoccupation with defending themselves against legal persecution.[43] John Davies, in his essay in this volume, has noted how in South Africa the different strands in Anglican Catholicism have been able to pull together against secular trends in the name of 'Catholic order', but not when it has been a question of Catholic witness to a disordered society.

This suggests that commitment to 'Catholic order' has a dimension missing. Even in terms of a self-conscious 'voluntary option within the mainstream' (Davies), Anglican Catholicism in England contrived to develop a 'pressure to be loyal to the ceremonial features as such', scarcely less fierce and insensitive than among some Orthodox of the western diaspora. Notwithstanding the progressive division of Tractarians into the camps of 'English Use' and 'Western Use', it may be said of the movement as a whole that it revealed, in true pharisaic fashion, greater facility in handling merely technical matters of rubric than in presenting the whole liturgical icon of God to the people of God in a meaningful fashion. In this they were more Anglican than Catholic, for it had been a characteristic of Anglicanism long before the Oxford Movement. The Revd E C Baldwin, seemingly a High Churchman rather than an out-and-out Anglo-Catholic, confessed to the Keble College conference on ritual in 1904: 'I have always been a frightfully strict rubrician, and it has worried me to feel the difficulty of keeping all the rubrics'. And what illustration did he give? Whether it is lawful for a parish priest to refuse communion to a person who has not sent in his name the day before! Baldwin wisely remarked: 'If you try that with agricultural labourers, you will lessen the number of communicants. Some of them cannot write, and would be too nervous'. Another participant in the Keble Conference raised a similar legalistic problem over the rule requiring four or at least three communicants for the Eucharist to be celebrated. One year he got up and found fourteen inches of snow on the ground. He went to his church, expecting to find no one there, but one man was present, a coal heaver who could not always get to church. Would anyone have turned him away? the speaker asked. To their credit, many shouted 'No!'[44]

If such niceties could still be discussed by 'moderate' High Churchmen, we should not be surprised to find the extremists splitting hairs over whether the Book of Common Prayer was anything more than an English 'Paroissen' (that is, a vague guide to practice rather than a definitive framework), and fighting tooth and nail for minute mediaeval observances 'which might be tolerable were they devised for men whose sole work was to be "religious", who had few external interests and no duties to those without as far as worship was concerned', but which were 'altogether a burden and a distraction' when imposed on men and women living in the world 'merely to please the ecclesiastical doctrinaire'.[45]

Tractarian innovations, brought in in such a legalistic spirit, without advantage of continuity or regulatory principle, had inevitably the effect of unbalancing people's devotions. For instance, by pushing extra-liturgical devotion to the Blessed Sacrament, Tractarians of the second and third generation filled worshippers' whole horizon with an all-or-nothing. The tabernacle, wrote Father Alfred Kelly, 'gives us a supernatural presence which necessarily by excess of light darkens its surroundings. We cannot give it a divided allegiance. The special aspects of the faith which it suggests claim the whole of our attention. If we force ourselves to think of other aspects of the faith, we think of them in spite of, rather than by the help of, that presence'. Kelly suggested that the eastern tradition might have had sound reasons for treating the reserved sacrament with no outward marks of worship at all.[46] Certainly those Anglo-Catholics such as Charles Gore, who had pioneered the thoroughly incarnational theology of which the Orthodox liturgy is a standing witness, were deeply unhappy about the divisive issue of reservation. And yet the juggernaut rolled on, driven by its own species of daemon.[47]

One modern liturgist has singled out, as a debit against Tractarianism, the way it made frequent communion into an 'extra' devotion by its emphasis on non-communicating High Masses, which in turn made the sacramental life look like an 'ascetic ideal' rather than an objective fact in the midst of all. The various extra-liturgical devotions then slotted into place as simple stimuli to private prayer. The very frequency of celebrations of Mass blurred the distinction between Sunday liturgy and weekday Office, inevitably downgrading the latter. So the Anglo-Catholic faithful were torn between a corporate worship in which incarnation was swamped by law, and a network of private devotions which took them right back to the individualistic impasse of Evangelicalism.[48] This individualism predominated in spite of the liturgical words, if only because the whole system of Tractarianism was congregational and sectarian. The Roman Newman saw the way things were going in 1850, and imagined a Tractarian priest saying to himself: 'I am doing good in my parish and in my place . . Sunday comes round once a week; the bell rings, the congregation is met, and the service is performed . . . What care I for the Privy Council or the Archbishop while I can preach and catechise as before? I can . . . tell my people about the primitive bishops and martyrs, and about the grace of the sacraments, and the power of the Church . . ; and I can say my hours, or use my edition of Roman Devotions . . . and take confessions if they are offered . . '.[49] In the formative years, when the cohesion of Catholic parishes was being built up, this priestly individualism encouraged individualism of devotion among parishioners also. Later, when monolithic Catholic parishes had emerged from the fray, this individualistic piety remained, and was to prove a major obstacle to later liturgical renewal.

It was, of course, possible for a pastor influenced by the Oxford Movement to teach a thoroughly incarnational view of liturgy without recourse to Tractarian polemics. The Hebrew scholar T L Kingsbury, for instance, was clearly indebted to a study of Keble's *Eucharistic Adoration* and Pusey's *Eirenicon* as well as to Liddon's 1866 Bampton Lectures, but he eschewed party controversy, concentrating on what was common to all ancient liturgical forms -- the confession of the Undivided Trinity, looking to the Second Coming, the atoning work of Christ, passing in heart and mind into the eternal Sanctuary.[50] Yet to do this, one had to stand back somewhat from the Movement from which one had learnt, and not be involved in its manic course. One who did this was Charles Plomer Hopkins, founder of the Order of St Paul,[51] another was Charles Grafton, second Bishop of Fond du Lac and spiritual son of the great ascetic R M Benson. For Grafton, the sacraments were the new creation's secret force.[52] Another was the Irish Bishop of Edinburgh, John Dowden, who jumped into the middle of the ritual polemics of the 1890s with a study of the Prayer Book which avoided all the current issues and emphasised historical connections, continuity, and what Keble had described in his advertisement to *The Christian Year* as 'a sober standard of feeling in matters of practical religion'.[53]

These writers all represent that penitential option for simplicity in ceremonial in church. Some have strangely found it 'soothing',[54] and a contemporary extremist who went to Rome to satisfy his stronger passion, John Bernard Dalgairns, dismissed it as gloomy novatianism. Massey Shepherd waxed scornful of its fake 'correctness' of taste in architecture and furnishings.[55] But its visual preference for white walls contrasted with richly coloured but not too dense stained glass and discreet use of gilding (the 'Ninian Comper' style), was neither effete nor gloomy, and very far from fake. It has that 'joyous simplicity' which A M Allchin finds genuine in Shaker furnishings when contrasted with much neo-Gothic and neo-Baroque. It answers to the nature of an icon, disclosing the *logoi*.[56] Admittedly this 'English' style had its hidden limitations for later liturgical renewal - riddel posts around the altar, for example, making anything other than eastward position impossible. But compared with unquestioning and often illogical imitation of all that contemporary Rome did (including the saying of Epistle, Gospel and Pax with back to the people!), it had some integrity.[57]

Perhaps the 'activists', having lost their way, should have gone back to their starting point, and from there stepped out in a new direction. What ought that to have been? Bishop Dowden, as a young man, wrote, with typically Irish ardour, to his brother Edward that he felt the need of a spirituality with more power than the beautiful but static tradition of Keble. 'There is not', he wrote, 'enough taking of heaven by violence for me in its spirit of prayer.' There was more to the *sursum corda*, he felt, than classical Tractarians imagined. Keble had been the victim of a perhaps satanic temptation when he feared 'winding himself too high', and Dowden feared that this weakness in Keble would be visited on the next generation in spiritual impotence.[58] Dowden was an admirer of Edward Irving, and it is intriguing to apply his strictures in terms of the critique of Anglicanism made by that highly liturgical and charismatic heir to Irving's ministry, the 'Apostles' Fellowship' or 'Catholic Apostolic Church', which was making the final refinements on its liturgy when Dowden wrote to his brother. Dowden was not alone in his impatience with both the old and the new Tractarians. We find signs of it too in Henry Scott Holland, founder of the Christian Social Union, for whom, even as a young man, the Orthodox image of the Eucharistic presence as 'fire in the coal' made most sense.[59]

The situation of a thoughtful disciple of the old Tractarians at the end of the century could be a sad and lonely one as he contemplated the firebrands, the bishops, the Church Association, and the special court set up by the Public Worship Regulation Act, all locked in senseless combat while the population at large was becoming more and more indifferent to the gospel. The theologian J J Lias of St David's College, Lampeter, writing in 1898 to Bishop John Wordsworth of Salisbury, said he felt that there was no longer an old Tractarian party conscious of the importance of 'moral influence'. The devotion of the first generation had been swamped by the 'febrile energy' and 'mere sentimentalism' of the 'advanced men'. He doubted if his own writings would be read because the younger clergy had no time for anything but 'the penny church newspapers'. He looked to Wordsworth among the bishops as the only hope. Lias' ideal from the previous generation was Christopher Wordsworth, Dean of Westminster and Bishop of Lincoln. Christopher had been 'at once Catholic and Anglican', and had not felt that his Catholicism made him look coolly on the post-Reformation history of the Church of England. Writing in 1903, to Ulrich Vernon Herford, who, from an initial Unitarianism, had seen the deficiencies of the later Oxford Movement and turned to the Eastern tradition, Lias bewailed the failure of his life's work for true 'Catholic consent'. Historical continuity and not theory, incorporation into Christ in Holy Communion through the incorporation into the life of the Spirit – these were the only sure foundations of Catholicity. Lias disliked the small-mindedness of the ritualists, and this combined with his deepening sense of isolation was turning him against all dogmatics in a somewhat unhealthy way.[60]

Yet charismatic signs of growth were never entirely absent. Lias may have given up the struggle, but men like John Wordsworth, W E Collins, the saintly Bishop of Gibraltar, and George Howard Wilkinson, Bishop of Truro and then of St Andrew's, showed the deeper stream of sacramental awareness. Peter Anson compared Wilkinson's relationship with Mother Julian, foundress of the Community of the Epiphany, to that between St Francis de Sales and St Jeanne de Chantal. Yet Wilkinson was thoroughly Anglican and not at all exotic: his reverence was combined with deliberate recollection.[61] (The records of the Catholic Apostolic Church, incidentally, show that Wilkinson received the 'sealing' unto the Lord's return at Apostles' hands.)

However, these were exceptions, and by 1899 it could be argued that liturgical chaos was worse than in the Church's 'darkest hour of erastian servility and Protestant apathy and misrule'.[62] Those Church leaders who set their deepest thoughts to paper in private correspondence were generally sick at heart. Dowden and others of like temper were fearfully reconciled to the inevitability of Prayer Book reform.[63] But the breakdown of the Fulham Conference of 1900 over so basic an issue as the link between Jesus' death and his ongoing life-in-Trinity in the Church bode very ill for a resolution of more nitty-gritty issues of liturgy.[64]

There were too many like C F G Turner who, appalled at the strife over what should be the unity of the body, were inclined to take refuge in the plea that the Church of England's position was so peculiar that it was unreasonable to press to liturgical conclusions the great theological issues of east and west, and so urged a policy of live-and-let-live for the sake of the vast numbers of people who were ignorant of, or indifferent to, the great underlying doctrines.[65] The compassion was obvious, but it was no real way out of the dilemma, and its gradual adoption by an episcopate tired of fighting was to create still further grounds for conflict in the 20th century.

In the early years of this century there was what Oliver Quick called 'a great though largely silent crisis' in English Christianity.[66] Quick was thinking chiefly in intellectual terms, but his thesis extended much more widely. Noticeable more after the experiences of the First World War, it was already visible to some during the Edwardian period, and it involved a kind of spiritual vacuum left by the ebb of some 70 years of violently forensic religious life, in which certainties had been born up by the immediacy of controversy. At the intellectual level, claimed Quick, there was a fearless but intelligent experimentation in verifying doctrine on a scale not seen before. Many churchmen were not so prepared to dogmatise, which may explain why one writer, replying to the private circulation of Vernon Herford's *Evangelical Catholic Catechism* in 1902, noted of the number of pseudonyms quoted in the citation of opinions in the advertisement: 'I should say there are many Nicodemuses among your friends'. Another of Herford's correspondents wrote that 'the true grounds of unity were to be sought in the ordinances and institutions of religion apart altogether from any theory explaining them'.[67]

From the standpoint of the Catholic movement in the Church of England, this slide of opinion was serious. It had grown on the soil of intense certainties and combativeness. Now the spirit of Puritan rejection was receding, and there was a general breakdown of the idea of form in life – by which one Anglo-Catholic, writing during the Second World War, felt able to explain not only the decline in public behaviour at bus stops but the decline in the notion of public worship as a pattern of the coming Kingdom.[68] At the height of the ritual riots it may have been true that the incidentals of the trouble facing Tractarian clergy had only a tenuous connection with Puritanism, but the master-minds behind the riots had certainly been spiritual and theological Puritans. Now, in the 20th century, there were much stronger signs of a general inability to see ceremonial as a means of distancing from the particular and momentary. People tended to see Catholic ceremonial as faintly ridiculous, while no longer experiencing a burning sense of its being blasphemous. At the same time, young people were less docile and so less likely than their parents to continue attending church if they found worship meaningless.[69]

It may not be too fanciful to detect in Edwardian Anglo-Catholicism a certain flatness arising out of this malaise, the flatness of the new suburbia of 'endless reduplications of Acacia Villas and Magnolia Avenues' (Roger Lloyd), the flatness of a new class of *petite bourgeoisie*: sedentary, unadventurous, unreflective, respectable, private. If partisanship was becoming a dirty word in the population at large, it was likely to be so also among those whose fathers and grandfathers had identified their unpopular religious stance with the notion of constant battle. Those now pushing to the top of the Church – men like Hensley Henson and Randall Davidson – were likely to discourage partisanship of any kind as a quality in candidates for ministry. The Royal Commission on Worship in 1906 symbolically recognised this change, and distanced itself from the old Judicial Committee of the Privy Council and the Parliament of 1874 by admitting that the standards of worship which had been enforced were 'too narrow' for the present generation.

Roger Lloyd states bluntly that at this date both Anglo-Catholicism and Evangelicalism had shot their respective controversial bolts, and had nothing to put up against the new 'synthetic' theology.[70] Horton Davies takes a similar view.[71] At the time, Bishop John Wordsworth in a work on Holy Communion provided a confirmatory insight.[72] C E Osborne, the biographer of Father Dolling, saw a 'deep, strenuous spirit' being replaced by a shallower, more diffuse spirit, with traces of the trivial. We have already seen that a tendency to the trivial was built into the movement after the first generation. It may be said that that tendency now at last had all the encouragement of a sea-change in social *mores* – *mores* reflected in literature by such writers as Henry James and Arnold Bennett, and in the changing popular magazines and the shape of the daily papers after the revolution of Lord Northcliffe.

During his very long episcopate in London, Winnington-Ingram's cooling off of respect for the Anglo-Catholic clergy probably reflects this decline.[73] Conscious of their weakening base, the clergy made desperate attempts to paper over the cracks in the movement and produce a single Catholic front. That these efforts were unsuccessful can be seeen in the refusal of some Anglo-Catholic clergy to sign the declaration to the Archbishop of Canterbury in July 1903. This failure led to another attempt at unity in the Keble College conference of January 1904 which asked what it meant to call the Church of England Catholic – something which all previous Anglo-Catholics had thought to be axiomatic. Several members had nightmare fears of resolutions meaning very little, and there was also an awareness, reflected by the president, Dean Strong of Oxford, that dogma conveyed little without practice. Bishop W E Collins' magisterial address gave scant encouragment to those who still hankered for certainties of 'English Use' or 'Western Use'. You had to start with a conception of the Catholic Church, said Collins, and then say that any usage authorised by proper authority in any part of it had the 'full sanction of the Catholic Church' because it had the full sanction of a valid authority within it. And in any case, the sacramental reality rested on something wider and deeper than any particular usages. A missionary bishop, Louis George Milne, late of Bombay, threw another spanner into the works by saying that it was disastrous in practice, incompatible with history, and false in principle to put details of public worship or the obligations implied by them on a level with the great principles of Christian faith or church order. A less exalted figure, the Revd F C Kempson, pleaded with the majority who signed the Declaration of 1903 to try to understand the minority who did not, and not treat them as recalcitrants. These were serious men, and it was only fair to credit them with standing for something real. The conference was given a timely warning of what Rome had just done in denying to the cathedral chapters of eleven dioceses the right of free episcopal elections. It was rumoured that Rome was already beginning to legislate the length and pattern of chasubles. The implication was clear: steer clear of witch hunts and fanaticisms, for that was playing Rome's game.[74]

If we move to the Farnham Conference on Reservation in 1925, we see another temperate, listening event, remarkable for the participation of Evangelicals. There was even a distinctly 'Eastern Orthodox' witness from that notorious Broad Churchman, B H Streeter! Was this the charismatic new beginning, the recognition that the old coin of controversy over the 'real presence' was devalued, the wakening to the dynamic of 'real coming' or 'real meeting' or even 'real puissance'? Was this the moment to grasp that old conception of the eternal sacrifice into which each liturgical act was 'inserted', the moment to move forward in one concrete piece of Prayer Book revision, and commemorate not only the death and passion but also the mighty resurrection and glorious ascension? Even St John Damascene and Khomiakov found a place in the discussion, and Bishop Gore, true to his incarnational vision, warned that the issue of reservation was not, in the experience of Orthodox tradition, the whole issue on which the *Shekinha* of God among his people should pivot. Yet, even in this most generous of conferences, the old daemon persisted in the prickly paper by that doyen of Anglo-Catholic liturgists, Darwell Stone.[75]

That echo of battles long ago was symbolic of the situation on the ground. For if we ask what difference new theological perspectives were making to liturgical life in the parishes, the answer must be very little. Darwell Stone's insistence on carrying the banner of all those who had fought the good fight for reservation and extra-liturgical devotion since the 1860s was more representative of parochial Catholicism than the majority of the papers delivered at the Keble and Farnham conferences. The endemic congregationalism of the Oxford Movement really became rampant in the first three decades of the 20th century. Even 'Anglo-Catholic' became a word of abuse with some who wanted to know nothing of the Church of England beyond their parish privacy.[76] Percy Dearmer, almost prophesying this trend in his *Parson's Handbook*, accepted it wearily as the 'inevitable outcome of a period of transition and confusion'. He rather saw his handbook, perhaps naively, as a help towards remedying the confusion and lawlessness as well as the vulgarity, which he imagined were due simply to a lack of liturgical knowledge among the clergy. Since scholars had settled the main points beyond dispute, it was simply a question of disseminating that knowledge. 'The mind of the Prayer Book', he declared, was to simplify rites and ceremonies without detracting from their grace, significance or richness. The clergy now knew, and should act accordingly.[77]

In retrospect it can be seen that Dearmer's whole strategy was faulty. Not only did he ignore the social dynamics and the personality types in 'advanced' Anglo-Catholicism, but he tried to turn selected rubrics into law, which carried no conviction to those not already attracted to his style of worship.[78] Moderates among the clergy may have benefited from his example at St. Mary's, Primrose Hill. The advanced men ignored him, or turned him into an Aunt Sally to vent their spleen upon. When he died in 1936, a typical representative of that school, Father Herbert Hamilton Maughan of Brighton wrote beneath a notice of the interment of his ashes in Westminster Abbey, pasted into his diary: 'The accuser of our brethren is cast down. Apocalypse XII.10'. For someone like Father E E Kilburn, who had introduced the Latin Missal, Rituale, Vesperale, and *Westminster Hymnal* into St Saviour's, Hoxton, Dearmer belonged to another planet.[79] His earnest socialist aesthetics made not a dint in the commercial Romanism of those who subscribed to the publications of the Society of SS Peter and Paul, and who bought their ecclesiastical necessaries in Vanpules or Burns and Oates. Having failed to make any impression on the bishops – despite the legends, Winnington-Ingram was compassionate rather than supportive – and nettled by the vocal, if no longer representative, anti-ritualist campaigns of Kensit, the extremists were not interested in any advice.[80] Serious Evangelicals found them abrasive.[81] There was certainly an element of spitefulness in the way Hamilton Maughan recorded his own anti-Kensit demonstration at Hitchin in the deep February snows of 1909.[82]

Maughan's diaries form an object lesson in the hermetic world of the 'Western' riters. Roman practice for him was always 'proper', at its best 'gorgeous'. 'I said Evensong', he records on one occasion, 'and then thurified – with the new thurible – at Vespers of the Blessed Sacrament; it was a great success, and Ridgeway was awfully pleased with the thurible – which is indeed a little beauty.' (Maughan was then at St Augustine's, Queen's Gate, and Ridgeway was his long-suffering vicar.) 'I called on the Vicar', he wrote on another occasion, '. . . persuading him not to kneel for the confession at High Mass, which is a great strain.' On another occasion he was criticised and did not take it well. 'Mason, who was celebrant, had the cheek to tell me not to hold his chasuble at the censing of the altar as "it's only done at High Mass". I raged, but said nothing . . .' Maughan got a schoolboyish delight in springing Roman practices on incongruous or unfamiliar occasions. He and Langford James, he boasted, both behaved 'very badly' in St Paul's Cathedral at the Gregorian Festival of 1917, wearing their birettas during the psalms and motet. The other clergy, he liked to think, were 'ashamed out of their timidity' by such boldness. When assistant chaplain of Ellesmere School, he decided with the new chaplain one Saturday night to introduce birettas 'at once'. 'Think of birettas in Ellesmere College Chapel!' He referred on one occasion to 'all our festival war-paint', and there was not a touch of irony or self-mockery in the remark.[83]

We may laugh at such juvenile foibles, which lasted well into his 40s, but they go hand in hand with a contempt for the greater part, not only of the Church of England, but even of the Anglo-Catholic wing of it. He 'hated' Matins because it was 'Anglican'. If he had to be at a Eucharist of the 'central school' he would write in his diary about making a 'great effort of imagination to believe it was the Mass' or that he had received communion. He even wrote a tract in imitation of the 18th-Century Non-juror Leslie's *Dialogues* with a view to converting 'mere' High Churchmen into 'Catholics'. He abhorred the devotees of the Sarum Rite. Visiting that great centre of Anglo-Catholicism in South London, St John's, Upper Norwood, in July 1918, he said it had become 'a sarum crank-shop and quite hopeless'. Of St Barnabas, Woodford, he wrote: 'It had been an "English" place, and still has "bed-posts" and only two candles; but its present priests are sound Romans, wear birettas in the sacristy and cottas in church, and all the servers are sound and hate the Dearmerite humbug'.

He would obtain childish satisfaction from celebrating a Roman Mass at an English altar. If a badly sung Mass was celebrated by one not of his school, such as Father Pennington, it was no matter for surprise if the miscreant was 'not a Catholic'. St Cyprian's, Clarence Gate, that gem of Anglo-Catholic piety, was 'that dreadful "English" church'. Englishness for Maughan was a taint, a virus, something to be disinfected. To pray for 'our holy father Benedict' in the liturgy was 'most edifying'. He enjoyed the patronal festival at St Mary-le-Strand because it was 'altogether . . . very Mariolatrous' and 'Popish'.[84]

Nor was there lacking that social exclusiveness and political indifference which one might expect from Maughan's outlook. He was fond of donning his best cassock and silver buckled shoes ('full canonicals' as he put it) to dine out on his 'best form'. On the other hand, he showed no interest in the General Strike or the Depression except in so far as they affected his stocks and shares.[85]

Hamilton Maughan may have been a caricature of extreme Anglo-Catholicism in the first three decades of the century, but a glance at clergy advertisements in the *Church Times* in the same period, with their stress on 'full Catholic privileges', suggests that he was not that much of a caricature, and that the clerical pen portraits in the novels of Shane Leslie and Compton Mackenzie were not that far off the mark. The present writer met many ordinands of that ilk in the Oxford of the 1950s. There was a world, an increasingly fashionable world, in which parish guilds and fraternities became more and more a law unto themselves, obscuring even the nature of the parish as a 'congregation of faithful men', in which even the few associations which had been founded for promoting lay evangelism in the earlier years of the Catholic movement gradually declined into mere devotional clubs. It was the nadir of Tractarianism.

In uncomfortable, often embarrassed, symbiosis with that world was a 'full Catholicism' which had settled down into the practicalities of evangelism. This was the world of Henry Scott Holland and of J S L Burn of All Saints, Middlesborough. Burn made an early promise, having introduced a High Mass at 9 am, to ease the burden of fasting, and to keep 11 am sacred for Morning Prayer and sermon for those whose 'digestion could stand no stronger fare'. By 1908 the congregation at that later service had dwindled to one family, but Burn kept his vow.[86]

Clergy who belonged to this strain were becoming uneasily aware after World War I that, in a world in which the non-British parts of the Anglican Communion were coming to have an increasing importance, the old arguments for 'Western rite' and 'English use' were ceasing to have any meaning. On a visit to Britain, Bishop Frank Weston of Zanzibar could celebrate the Kikuyu Mass in a parish church. In Africa and Asia, the Prayer Book was up for radical revision. What point was there any longer in standing on the idea that the Church of England was, for liturgical purposes, but two provinces of the Western Church accidentally detached from the Western Patriarchate? And the nationalism of the Sarum riters also began to look pretty silly.[87] The lonely plea of one in 1899 that the fundamental Catholic principle of worship was 'the great principle of obedience to the custom and law' of the corporate body within the wider Church of which he was a member, took on new force. Some priests came to see that, although to recite the Roman Canon *sotto voce* might have given them personally a feeling of being united with the Church of past and present, it was injudicious in that it gave rise to the impression that such additions were necessary to 'the completeness of the great Eucharistic act'. There was an ascetic good to be gained from forgoing all this in order to be the better able to bear the 'restless and undisciplined temper of the modern age'.[88] This was the period when the elderly Bishop Gore could publish his *Anglo-Catholicism Today* (1925). One chapter was entitled 'Some necessary modifications'. And it was with an eye to Anglo-Catholics of this outlook that Archbishop Davidson sought for a representative Anglo-Catholic to raise to the episcopate, and found the great liturgical scholar, Father Walter Frere of Mirfield.[89]

The glimmer of social criticism which had sparked among the slum priests of the second and third generation, but failed to take alight, now came to have more appeal to a sobered generation. Scott Holland in 1917, the darkest year of war, warned that taking the food, feeding on the glory, and giving nothing out for suffering humanity because of a tradition of piety taken up with little subjective books of devotion, was a travesty of Catholicism. He had a horror of anything which might intensify the 'religion of the sacristy' and hold the worshipper 'entranced within the shrine'. 'Everything that we know', he said, about the Eucharistic presence is energy, movement, action. Woe to those who, sitting in comfort in devotion to the Reserved Sacrament, took the precious gift out of its living environment, and made it passive, portable and quiescent.[90] At the Anglo-Catholic Congress of 1923, Frank Weston pointed to the connection between liturgy and service to the poor:

> 'You have your Mass, you have your altars, you have begun to get your tabernacles . . . Now go out into the highways and hedges and look for Jesus in the ragged and the naked, in the oppressed and the sweated, in those who have lost hope, and in those who are struggling to make good. Look for Jesus in *them*; and when you have found him, gird yourself with his towel of fellowship and wash his feet in the person of his brethren.'[91]

We find Kenneth Kirk, in his more academic terms, in the Bampton Lectures for 1928 (*The Vision of God*), arguing that the end of man required an unselfish spirit of worship, a facing up to one's own follies and the needs of one's neighbour. Without that, there could be no vision of God. In his address on 'Truth' to the Oxford Movement Centenary Conference in 1933, Kirk linked the sacramental character of the Church, its social mission, and the development of personal holiness as co-ordinate rediscoveries of the movement.[92] The old slum priests' compassion for the poor, and their view of perpetual Reservation and confession as a salve for poverty, persisted in the ministry of the Papalist E E Kilburn of St Saviour's, Hoxton.[93] More typical of the new mood were the dialogue sermons at St Matthew's, Bethnal Green. This was the period too of the work of Father Potter of Peckham, and of the Franciscan Society of the Divine Compassion. But it would be hard not to give pride of place to the Community of the Resurrection, whose mother church at Mirfield always reminded Peter Anson of how the first Christians occupied themselves continually with the Apostles' doctrine, fellowship, breaking of bread, and prayers – and won favour with the people. The key to Mirfield's success in wedding liturgy and service to the people was surely the tradition of incarnational theology inherited from their founder, Charles Gore. This propelled it into a powerful synthesis – one which Archbishop Davidson questioned was possible – of individual liberty and corporate authority.[94] And this must also have had its effect in the shift, noted by Dom Anselm Hughes, in fashions of church music, away from the subjective and sentimental towards 'a more robust and objective emphasis in worship'.[95]

The feeling around the turn of the century – given an appearance of reality in 1906 by the Royal Commission of Worship – that Prayer Book reform was inevitable, was frozen, partly by the First World War, and during the period of inertia extremism of the type described above flourished in a totally unreal atmosphere. The 1920 Lambeth Conference opened the sluices sufficiently for a liturgical commission to produce for the bishops the notorious book of 1927. It has been argued that the debacle of 1927–28 opened the way for practical liturgical renewal and greater congregational participation.[96] This was not an immediate, nor even a very direct, consequence of the 'Deposited Book', which, for all its modest virtues, was winked at by the bishops in defiance of a Parliamentary majority, more as a device for releasing the pressures of clerical insubordination and arrogating to themselves an appearance of liberality than with a view to opening up the spirit of worship. But to the extent that it showed that the idea of reaching common worship by some degree of experiment under episcopal guidance was 'not an extravagant exercise of faith', it may be said to have set in motion, or at any rate liberated, factors which led to the embodiment of the Parish and People movement.[97]

Did the attempts of 1927 and 1928 favour the Catholic movement? Conservative Evangelicals certainly thought so, and the Bishop of Norwich said so. They may have been 'Catholic' by eliminating explicit alternatives to the Catholic position on some points, but the spirit of vague optionalism which permeated the Alternative Book – even down to its optional title! – was alien to the *sensus fidelium* on which Catholicism, whether of the older Tractarians or of the advanced guard, was predicated. It was far less constructively Catholic than was the newly disestablished and hyper-evangelical Church of Ireland when it revised its Prayer Book in the 1870s.

The equivocal nature of the operation was clear in the parliamentary debates which led to its rejection, in which spokesmen for the book contrived to say in quick succession that the changes were both insignificant and urgently necessary. Anglo-Catholic opponents of the book were so concerned with particulars that they failed to notice the deep underlying assumption behind the exercise that the Church of England did not, and could not, have true *sobornost* even in worship, but was what its Roman critics had always claimed it to be – a mere marriage of convenience.[98] Evangelicals, and even politicians and lawyers scarcely involved such as Sir John Simons, could see clearly that if some of the permissive things were valid, then they demanded total assent from the Church and not simply permission.[99] The fact that this was never faced up to left the Catholic party vulnerable to the charge of dishonesty. One Evangelical Fellow of the Royal Historical Society, who was a stickler for the 'facts', began to wonder in the wake of 1928 whether 'the exercise of ordinary faculties' was anything but a waste of time in the Church of England, and felt that the Catholic party had surreptitiously 'gutted' the Church.[100] Largely because of this attitude from Evangelicals, the public debate over the 1927 and 1928 Prayer Books led to a revival of many of the old polemical attitudes which had fallen somewhat flat with the new century. Charity was not helped by a declaration by more than 2000 Catholic priests which appeared in the *Church Times* on 28 May 1928.[101] The extent of Catholic defensiveness can be seen in the tactic by which the Anglo-Catholic Congress of 1933 sought to stave off Kensitite trouble-making by complying at the public High Masses with the Prayer Book rubric regarding the minimum number of communicants. 'Five stalwart men, duly fasting, made their communion, and no unseemliness occurred', wrote S C Carpenter. But the unseemliness was there in the deviousness of the ruse, and in the insistence on flouting all sound modern liturgical scholarship, including that of Mersch and Pius Parsch, for the sake of maintaining a very recent Anglo-Catholic tradition for which clergy had been prepared to go to gaol. This was an illogicality shortly to be brought to the surface by Father Gabriel Hebert of Kelham in his clarion call for a truly 'parish communion'.[102]

Hebert was saddened by the 'shrunken form' of fellowship in the Anglo-Catholic High Mass, and looked enviously at the way in which the early Church divided the functions of worship among as many people as possible, including all the faithful exchanging the Peace. He associated the lack of common celebration with the popular image of the Church as the pillar of the established order. The true dynamic of the Church at worship was being restrained from contact with the life of men and women in society. 'The Church has indeed the key to the street. Too often she seems inclined to use it to lock herself in.' The answer was to rediscover the meaning of intercession, especially on behalf of church members who felt themselves compromised as members of the eucharistic community by the immoral conditions imposed on them by their daily work. To achieve this it was essential to escape from the mindset of neo-scholasticism in which Anglo-Catholicism had become trapped, and to see that faith and dogma were not synonymous. The Creed was a charter of freedom, not of constraint. Hebert associated himself with the Orthodox liturgical spirit, but he also looked wistfully to the neglected example of F D Maurice, whose path the Oxford Movement had neglected at its peril. Hebert summed up his understanding of liturgy thus:

> 'We are looking for the interpretation and embodiment of God's meaning for our life and for the world. We men pose our problems and ask our questions. The answer is in God and in God's will in Christ and His saving work, and, somehow, in the Body of Christ which is His Church. All that we have said hitherto points us to seek in the worship of the Church the clearest expression of what the Church really is. The Christian liturgy . . . is a kind of meeting point, in which all the elements of the Church are seen in their right perspective. Scriptures and creeds hold a central place in the liturgy, their liturgical use shows that the true meaning of dogma is seen in the setting of worship. The personal religion of the individual soul is here seen in its true setting, when the individual takes his place in the life of the Body.'[103]

Hebert avoided the arid sociological speculation of many Anglican writers between the wars, centring his model of liturgy on the dynamic of *kerygma*, and drawing social consequences and implications from that. At a time also when psychology was being drawn into discussion of worship in the wake of William James and Evelyn Underhill – witness, for instance, Donald MacKinnon's paper to the Malvern Conference in 1941 – Hebert, like Dom Gregory Dix, was plotting the ways in which ritual change preceded and led into social change, social deprivation being, as it were, a function of sacramental disorder. In some ways this was a belated discovery of what the Catholic Apostolic Church had intuited about the priority of sacramental health or decay over irreversible social malfunction a century earlier.[104]

At the same time as the pioneer liturgical work of Hebert and Dix, Father Basil Jellicoe was beginning to experiment pragmatically along the same lines in Somers Town. Christ in the Holy Sacrifice of the Altar was, for Jellicoe, the same Christ who suffered in the daily horrors in the LMS flats. Both the eucharistic space and the flat space were alike the venue for battle between Christ and the powers of darkness. It was for him a special agony to celebrate at the altar with this awareness combined with the sheer weight of his experience of social deprivation.[105]

The new breakthrough of priests like Jellicoe was timely, for the break-up of inner city neighbourhoods was threatening to make it impossible for old-style Anglo-Catholic churches to sustain anything like a viable worship-ping community. This process can be observed in an advanced stage in R H T Thompson's sociological analysis of one inner Birmingham parish in 1957. The parish was making valiant efforts to hold its own in the absence of a real neighbourhood constituency.[106] Such stranded parishes were turning into 'gathered' congregations, often drawing on catchment areas so wide that large aspects of the *koinonia* of the traditional congre-gation were absent or greatly weakened. Their liturgical and devotional practices were very much at the mercy of changes in social *mores* rather than rooted in a spiritual consensus. For instance, as masses for the dead increased as the century advanced, it had more to do with the uncontrolled grief of thousands who had lost relatives in wars than with any deepening of the Catholic doctrine of the Communion of Saints, or even less the sacrificial doctrine of the Mass. So, enervated by sociological change which no longer responded to the sacramental in the old ways, the 'traditional' Anglo-Catholic party was now incapable of addressing itself even to the efforts of the official ecclesiastical machine to modify details of worship. Witness their failure in the 1940s to block the reconstruction of the lectionary for the sake of casual churchgoers, an action which distorted the whole purpose of the lectionary as a way of ensuring a proper *lectio continua*, and encouraged the trend to the particularising of worship in terms of momentary preoccupations.[107]

To all this chaos Hebert and Jellicoe, in their vastly different ways, addressed themselves. Hebert was open to a far wider range of theological insights than the ritualists would have permitted themselves, Jellicoe felt free to take liberties on rubrical matters for the sake of translating to the people the heart of the matter in a way which really touched their blighted lives. On the one hand, there was the need to uphold the things that could not be shaken, and liturgy was a sign of this; on the other hand, it was equally necessary to convey to people used to thinking of worship as essentially static that liturgy was not simply the passive illumination that early Tractarians had implicitly taught, but was a source of life, capable of changing things. William Temple's influence in all this should not be overlooked. It was from him that at least one young Catholic priest learned that 'isolated, fragmented worship, existing in a world of its own, is not worship'. Temple, in company with more traditional Anglo-Catholics like the young Eric Mascall, pursued the 'purity of the real' in the new Industrial Christian Fellowship. One of the aims of the ICF was to face the challenge of the rejection of all worship by young people as they left home for the 'modern economic maelstrom' with its apparent lack of a need for essential forms, and to recover for them, without resort to the artificial religiosity of the old ritualism, the sense that liturgy was a 'recall to life'. Many who could not be called 'Catholic' were responding at this time to the need for renewal in worship. What distinguished the Catholic contribution from that of the central churchmen or the liberal Evangelicals was that they saw that renewal was not a matter for making worship self-consciously didactic, but was an actual re-ordering of an earthly life, disrupted by sin, and a rendering of it back to God in praise and thanksgiving.[108]

The single most important movement to arise out of this new awareness was undoubtedly the Parish and People, or Parish Communion movement. Although Hebert was its guiding light, it must be remembered that efforts to downplay non-communicating High Masses, and to see the Eucharist as a true communion of the people, go back to the beginning of the century in the North-East and even further in the West Midlands. What Hebert did was to provide a coherent apologia for such practical efforts in the widest of ecumenical terms, taking account of much modern Roman Catholic thought in Europe such as that of Emil Mersch, Pius Parsch, Anselme Robeyns and Ildefons Herwegen. It was an unknown priest who planted in Hebert's mind the idea of producing the volume of essays which appeared in 1937 as *The Parish Communion*. This priest wanted to see the promotion of parish communion followed by parish breakfast, not as something which 'works well', but as a vision of the nature of the Church as the Body of Christ. Numbers as such did not matter. Any achievement of the goal must be a real embodiment and foretaste of that *koinonia* for lack of which the world perished.[109]

There have been those who have argued that the movement which gave substance to Hebert's two books, *Liturgy and Society* and *The Parish Communion*, arose not so much from theological imperative as from a belated response to inevitable social change – growth of mass democracy, universal suffrage, universal education. This no doubt makes sense in terms of 'pure' sociological theory, but it runs counter to everything we know about the most active promoters of the movement. Hebert defined the Parish Communion in 1937 as the Sunday assembly of the Christian community for worship of God in the Holy Eucharist: not one worship among many, but *the* worship. The issue at stake for him was 'the growth of priest and people in grace'. Indeed, all the contributors to *The Parish Communion* were at one in this, and conscious of the sacraments as shared means of grace. To the extent that the earlier stages of the Oxford Movement had left Baptism isolated as a private event, that sacrament as much as the Eucharist needed to be made an event of fellowship in fidelity to the primitive witness that Baptism was the 'sacrament of churchmanship'. Father Henry de Candole reminded his readers of Father Benson's assertion that, had the Oxford Movement at its inception paid as much attention to Baptism as it did to the Eucharist, churchmanship after two generations would have been better understood than it was. Given this context, the rediscovery of the Parish Communion was a rediscovery of the Church, understood as *koinonia* rather than corporation.

> 'As it is by the calling and grace of God alone that we are Christians, and in Him we are one as members of his Church, so in proportion as we put the Sacrament and the Communion in the centre of our worship, we shall thereby be brought to an understanding of one another far deeper than any that can be attained by Round Table Conferences.'

Thus wrote Hebert, for whom the whole gospel of salvation was set forth in the liturgy so that people might be brought face to face with the real meaning of things, and so live as people redeemed by God in fellowship with one another. His notion of the Eucharist as a hallowing and transforming of daily life and work, the central part of the 'work of God in its entirety', was akin to the intuition of the Catholic Apostolic fellowship a century earlier. It was also faithful to the pre-Nicene image, expressed in the Didache, of the bread scattered on the mountains being gathered up by Christ for the salvation of the world.[110]

So the Parish Communion movement spoke of the need for a holy priest to live visibly among the people. The clergy must not be defensive towards their people. 'We who preach', warned Canon M R Newbold of Chester, 'cannot remind ourselves too often that we speak in the bosom of a sacred family. We are not like John the Baptist, confronting a generation of vipers.' If liturgy was a redeeming thing, it was the prayer of a redeemed race, priests and people alike.[111]

Another way in which the Parish Communion movement echoed the earlier liturgical renewal of the Catholic Apostolic Church was in its sharp sense of eschatological urgency. The priest who cared for the Kingdom, said Canon J F Lovel Southam of Chester, must be 'oppressed with a sense of urgency' which was able to overcome frustration and impotence when he was beaten to his knees together with his people. Not all his people, of course, would have an equal awareness of the issues at stake. There needed to be a process of sifting, of 'calling out' of people to be 'the soul of the Church'. Only such a remnant could seed an understanding of corporate living in the wider body by re-experiencing for the whole the sacrament of initiation through the 'love of the brethren'. There was much that was rotten in the Church of England, claimed Hebert, and this must be 'purged out by the fire of tribulation'. In the meantime it was imperative that those who were sensitive to the signs of the times should 'stablish the things that remain' so that when the hour came they might stand firm. This was pure Catholic Apostolic prophecy in a progressive Anglican movement, and also a presage of the seeding idea of charismatic renewal.[112]

All this was geared to gospel priorities. It was no mere *ad hoc* reaction to those social changes which threatened the continuance of traditional forms of worship. The proponents of the movement were aware of these forces.[113] But a Parish Communion stalwart, Kenneth Packard, could say in 1963: 'I value Parish and People for its maxim, 'Being the Church, not Going to Church'.[114] The movement fixed its eyes on the model of the first apostolic community, and when someone, baffled by the whole thing, said to Henry de Candole that it was 'all Greek' to him, de Candole replied: 'Anyway, it's New Testament Greek!'.[115] This radical archaism gave it a certain freedom in its attitude to theological terms which had become shibboleths to the ritualists, such as 'sacrifice', 'pleading' and 'blessing'. In this way it sought to embrace Catholic and Evangelical without selling any pass.

The *Church Times*, appraising the first ten years of Parish and People, held it to have been largely responsible for the renewed sense of connection between liturgy (corporate worship) and liturgical action (application of worship to the world), and consequently for a reduction in parochial mindedness. De Candole suggested that this had been brought about not by a pressure group but by a pervasive influence.[116] Like every movement, its membership ran down over the years. By 1963, its paid-up membership of some 15,000 was heavily weighted on the side of the middle-aged and elderly. The fact that it was still merely an influence, that it had no more transformed the Church of England than had the original Oxford Movement, led within the movement itself to a certain instinctive conservatism, and among the younger generation to an impatience to try other organs and means to precipitate rapid change. The smaller and more radical Keble Conference Group, numbering the newly notorious author of *Honest to God*, John Robinson, among its members, pressed heavily upon the older organisation. The Anglican-Methodist Report, the Paul Report, the Toronto Pan-Anglican Congress all provided an unnerving context in which Parish and People had to ask itself if there was any longer justification for its existence. Canon Eric James was extremely gloomy. The Church of England was not corporately waking up. What use would it be if committees provided an 'efficient' but 'irrelevant' Church? In the event,

Parish and People collapsed suddenly during the debate on the Anglican-Methodist proposals in 1968. What succeeded it, from a merger with the old Keble Group, finally to be named One for Christian Renewal, was heavily politicised, so that, as in the wider ecumenical movement, traditional concerns with liturgy played a smaller part. The looked-for 'new forms of Christian presence in the world' could quite well have little to do with liturgy.[117]

It was a sad and muted end to something which had so sparkled with hope and life when Gabriel Hebert first gave it his blessing. Perhaps the promoters of the Parish Communion had not thought liturgical principles through sufficiently. Convinced that by doing what they felt was pastorally right in a given situation, they would learn to extrapolate from the particular to the general, they fell into the unconscious Pelagianism about which Michael Ramsey warned in his *Durham Essays*, especially in relation to 'over-acting' the Offertory procession. Perhaps also they too gratefully grasped at any signs of support without asking how far it might be due to quite adventitious factors, such as the stopping up of outlets of energy in Christian housing schemes. (Roger Lloyd attributes the phenomenal development of the movement on Tyneside to this factor.) Perhaps they even fell victim to the easy motive of refilling the emptying churches without thinking too much about the absolute priority of a sense of gathering and choosing, even if it were only a remnant.[118] But if in some respects they were not as sensitive as they might have been to the Orthodox admonition 'Holy things for holy persons', they did nevertheless keep alive in pockets the need for an inward sense of silence before God in any liturgical renewal. In this, and in the innovation of liturgical 'leader' – a primitive form of deacon's ministry – they were indebted to Hebert's interest in the Greek Orthodox Zoe Movement which was seeking the same renewed sense of community.[119]

The demise of Parish and People left a vacuum at a time when British society was torn between outward security and quiet inward despair. There was a need, as David Edwards wrote in an early study, for honesty about the roots of worship and corporate discipline. Yet the impending age of extensive liturgical rewriting was heralded by unpromising *angst* over infant baptism – a legacy maybe of the Tractarians' failure to face an issue which was burning even in 1833 – and over the meaning of holy order. Committee minds were loosened up for the task of rewriting hallowed texts by a certain currency of linguistic symbolism in the philosophy of the 1950s which gave an exciting sense of fluidity to what had formerly been felt to be as secure as the Bank of England or the Houses of Parliament. A landmark in the permeation of this feeling among those who would be responsible for Series 2 and 3 and the Alternative Services Book was Basil Moss's paper to the Parish and People conference of 1962 on 'the dialogue of redemption'. It pointed to the creative character of liturgy especially the liturgy of the word, in the 'mutuality of *koinonia*'.[120] There was also a sudden panic at the realisation that the old liturgical forms were meaningless to most people simply because of the collapse of knowledge of the Bible. This was felt both by Evangelicals and by Catholics, and in a sense it helped to soften the edges of old ceremonial conflicts, at least on the level of what S C Clark called 'parochial methods'.[121] Greater subtlety in the analysis of literary forms in the 1960s enabled Anglicans of differing churchmanships to agree that the 1662 Canon could equally be taken in either a Zwinglian sense or as a near magical formula with the implication, first seen by A C Headlam in 1927, that something more primitive and more 'eastern' might be preferable to cut through the ambiguity.[122]

In all this it cannot be said that the Catholic wing of the Church played a particularly outstanding role. Although at earlier stages of liturgical renewal they had been paralysed of initiative, the Evangelicals were catapulted into renewal by their South India experience, and thereafter played a vital role, especially through the work of Colin Buchanan.[123] Indeed a cynic might say that the whole Catholic movement was sliding into confusion and compromise in every area, liturgical, theological and moral, in the '60s and '70s, evidenced in the work of such figures as Norman Pittenger, Denis Nineham and Harry Williams. If so, the slide was a subtle philosophical one, difficult to pin down. Certainly, for some consciously conservative Catholics, the constancy and durability of liturgy became a more pressing concern as signs of massive revision revealed themselves in an unsettling and bewildering context. Colin Dunlop, Dean of Lincoln, wrote as early as 1953 that if a workman found a new set of tools at his bench every morning, his progress in his craft would be slow. Liturgy, he held, was a perennial corrective to the itch to make worship relevant and partial. Its function was to confront worshippers with eternal verities and place them 'upon the everlasting hills' where they could better realise that their thoughts were not God's thoughts nor their ways His ways. 'The value of a liturgy lies especially in its contrasts, in its theological light and shade, and in its vast horizons, in the presence within it of "things new and old".' Dunlop was worried by the increasing tendency to use liturgy as an instrument of evangelism, a practice which worked according to the law of diminishing returns.[124] Impatient with endless inquests on alternative parish strategies, David Paton thought that Anglicans would never see their way liturgically until they allowed their understanding to be controlled by the 'faithful corporate anamnesis of our redemption in the tremendous climaxes of Holy Week which led the early Church to locate Christian initiation between Good Friday and Easter Sunday'.[125] It was insufficient to treat the parish meeting as an 'essential middle term' between the Eucharist and service in the world. This recalls David Peck's pleas, almost twenty years earlier, that there was a nexus between Christian community and the very elements of the Eucharist which was itself prophetic and representative of the true relation of men to the created order.[126] Such radical simplicity cut right to the root of the formal differences between Catholic and Evangelical. S C Clark, in a modest eirenicon in 1961, wrote that the difference between simple and grand, which might make sense in terms of parish *vis-a-vis* cathedral worship, had inexcusably become a test of party. Converts being prepared for admission to the Church found this not commendable comprehension but confusion. 'It is not enough', wrote Fr Clark, 'for the Anglican Church to be both "Catholic" and "Evangelical" if this means that we have "two Churches under one roof" . . .'[127] One way of breaking loose from this double-think and bringing the traditions of churchmanship closer together was to see, as the early Church saw, *leitourgia* as mission (*Romans* 15:16; *Philippians* 2:17). But to do this, the Prayer Book did need to be seriously recast, for the 1662 book was seriously lacking in reference to mission, and had encouraged an introspective pietism often worse even than Roman Catholic pietism. John Robinson's two books *On Being the Church in the World* and *Liturgy Coming to Life* helped to prepare Catholics for a drastically simple revision of the Prayer Book, following upon the English translations in the 1950s of the publications of the parish of St Severin in Paris, and the Abbe Michonneau's *Revolution in a City Parish*.

For the greater part of its history, the Oxford Movement worked painfully towards the attainment of a liturgical ideal which, once attained, would be as normative as the followers of Archbishop Lefebvre see the Tridentine Mass to be. That they sometimes became confused about the details of that ideal, and even fell into factionalism over it, does not alter the fact that such was their ultimate ideal. The experience of this century, especially since 1928, has forced Anglican Catholics to accept, to some degree, the logic of Evelyn Underhill's argument that worship is conditioned by, if not subject to, the laws of change as an inseparable part of the life of sense.[128] They have been made aware, as Roman Catholics (for the most part) have been made aware, that liturgy is not simply something done for them, but is a co-working with God so that they may effectively do His will. As St Leo the Great put it, 'We must carry out in deeds what we celebrate in mystery'.[129] This is now much more widely appreciated than it was a generation ago. What is not so clearly realised – and here the Orthodox have something pertinent to say to the Anglican situation – is that liturgical growth according to the mind and will of God requires not merely a concurrence of individual goodwills, but an actual *koinonia* which does not need to resort to merely verbal expedients to secure agreed use. True consensus is not a leveller down or even simply a leveller up.[130] It implies breakthrough to an understanding that none of the participants had previously thought of as even a key-hole, let alone a key. To take but one example: the endless arguments between Catholic and Evangelical revisers over whether additional eucharistic elements should be consecrated by repetition of the Words of Institution or by words of thanksgiving have perhaps only been papered over. A true resolution might be found elsewhere, in the Orthodox conception of liturgical action.

For the moment there seems to be, in the midst of liturgical revision from the top, a considerable degree of grass-roots oscillation between the transcendent and the immanent in people's attitude to worship, an uncertainty as to whether salvation or social consciousness stands at the heart of the whole thing.[131] There are some who are afraid that the total complex of standing for communion, discouragement of genuflexion, and a general dis-emphasis on sin and atonement are a sign of an unspoken assumption that all things are possible, and no holds are barred for modern man.[132] There may be some ground for this fear. Yet there is so much in the new rites which is essential to the early Christian sense of awe and dependence, and which must surely work its way into people's subconscious, even if, as J R Halliburton has warned, there is need for some instruction in order that they may have their full conscious effect.[133] That instruction could benefit from the study of Orthodox worship, as Gabriel Hebert, building on the liturgical researches of Walter Frere, saw in the 1930s.[134] In particular, worshippers would benefit from an instructional filling-out of the somewhat staccato prayers of the new rites from the more discursive Orthodox responds which instruct in the very act of worship.[135] For it is essential, as J L Houlden argued in an essay on Series 3, that people not only think they have grasped the faith, but also have a sense that the faith has grasped them.[136] Prayer, said Henry Vaughan three centuries ago, is 'the world in tune', and *koinonia* is not merely a superficial togetherness but inner wholeness, integrity, the essence of things.[137]

That, after all, was what the first Tractarians were aiming at.

References

1 In David Martin and Peter Mullen (eds), *No Alternative: The Prayer Book Controversy* (Oxford, 1981), p 3.

2 W H Mackean, *The Eucharistic Doctrine of the Oxford Movement* (London 1933) pp 28–29. William Cobbett doubted that no more than one in a thousand communicated more than once in his life unless he was over 60, but this seems not to be borne out by the statistics. His other assumption, that not one in a thousand under the age of 30 had any knowledge of the faith, is probably more accurate. See *Cobbett's Legacy to the Parsons . . . In Six Letters* (London, 1869).

3 G W E Russell, *A Short History of the Evangelical Movement* (London, 1915), pp 122–4, 137.

4 See the Revd J B Douglas to Bishop Benjamin Whipple of Minnesota, 19 March 1869, Whipple Papers P823/6, Minnesota Historical Society.

5 W J E Bennett, *The Principles of the Book of Common Prayer Considered* (London, 1845), p xi.
6 Letter dated 16 February 1849 in the Phillpotts Papers ED/11/42, Exeter Cathedral Library.
7 See Newman's sermon 'Self-denial the test of religious earnestness' in *Parochial and Plain Sermons.*
8 E W Benson, *God's Board* (London, 1904), pp 90, 133. Collins first told his story in a paper to the Church Historical Society and repeated it at the Keble Conference on Ritual in 1904. See *The Declaration of the Clergy on Ritual* (London, 1904), p 25.
9 Benson, *op cit.* pp 180–1, 207–8, 219–20.
10 E B Pusey, *Letter to the Bishop of London* (London, 1851), p 259; F W Faber, *A Churchman's Politics in Disturbed Times* (London, 1840), p 17.
11 Memorandum in Phillpotts Papers ED/11/76.
12 Massey Hamilton Shepherd Jr. *The Reform of Liturgical Worship: Perspectives and Prospects* (New York, 1961), p 15.
13 Whitehouse, *Twentieth Annual Address to the Diocesan Convention of Illinois* (Chicago, 1871), pp 32–3.
14 Cf A C Headlam, *The Church of England* (London, 1924), pp 86–9, 103. Although there was much sense in Bishop Samuel Wilberforce's comments on the formation of ordinands at Cuddesdon in his day, there lurked behind them this same exaggerated cult of masculinity. See John Newton, *Search for a Saint* (London, 1977), pp 37–8, 45–6. Dean Stanley, anxious about 'excited females' going into hysterics at ritual riots, noted as significant an occasion at St George's-in-the-East when one female clapped her hands on the appearance of the preacher in a black gown, and shouted 'Thank God! It's black!' Perhaps what passed through his mind was the thought that even women prefer their men to be masculine.
15 Whitehouse, *Seventeenth Annual Address to the Diocesan Convention of Illinois* (Chicago, 1868).
16 E Abbott and Lewis Campbell, *The Life and Letters of Benjamin Jowett* (London, 1897), I, p 381.
17 Cf R M Benson, *The Followers of the Lamb: a Series of Meditations* (London, 1900), p 18.
18 Dieter Voll, *Catholic Evangelicalism: The Acceptance of Evangelical Traditions by the Oxford Movement During the Second Half of the Nineteenth Century* (London, 1963), p 25.
19 Peter F Anson, *The Call of the Cloister* (London, 1955), p 231; *The Life and Letters of W J Butler* (London, 1898), p 154.
20 H L Stewart, *A Century of Anglo-Catholicism* (London, 1929), p 257.
21 F W Faber, *The Ancient Things of the Catholic Church in England* (London, 1840) pp 17–18.
22 Hook to Pusey, 24 September 1841, Pusey House MSS.
23 W J E Bennett, *op cit*, p xiii.
24 In Robert Linklater (ed), *True Limits of Ritual in the Church* (London, 1988), p 217. John Wilde, Vicar of St Saviour's, Leeds, expressed himself in similar vein (*ibid*, p 121).
25 For the worst instance see Ronald Fletcher, *The Akenham Burial Case* (London, 1974).
26 Bennett, *op cit*, pp xiv–xv.
27 *Report of the Royal Commission on Ritual* (London, 1867), p 93.
28 Anson, *op cit*, pp 79–81, 91–102. There was undoubtedly a political dimension too. The lace cotta brigade tended on balance to be politically conservative or 'neutral' (i e politically indifferent); the other camp, with Mirfield, St Mary's, Primrose Hill, and Thaxted, in the van moved with assurance into socialism. But here the distinction was not quite so sharp.

29 Cf Charles Booth, *Life and Labour of the People of London*, 3rd Series (London, 1902), I, p 184.
30 One genuine and surprisingly early case of the laity forcing the pace of liturgical change was at St George's-in-the-East under Bryan King in the late 1850s. But Henry Arnott, Rector of Beckenham, later claimed that in the 'great majority of instances', requests for more advanced ritual were urged again and again on parish priests before changes were finally adopted. Cf Linklater, *op cit*, pp 125–6.
31 Newman, *Parochial and Plain Sermons*, I, p 263. Cf his *Lectures on Justification* written when he was a Roman Catholic (3rd edn, 1874).
32 Beckwith to Whipple, 8 April 1878, Whipple Papers, p823/13.
33 Wade to Harriett Monsell, 22 December 1870, Wade Papers, Pusey House.
34 Vernon Staley, *The Ceremonial of the English Church* (4th edn, London, 1918), p 23.
35 Talbot to Temple, 25 August 1899, Temple Papers, vol 29ff, 178–9, Lambeth Palace Library.
36 Sermon preached by the Right Revd William Croswell Doane, DD, LLD, Bishop of Albany, at the Consecration of the Revd Frederick Burgess, DD, as Bishop of Long Island (Boston, 1902), pp 10–11.
37 Horton Davies, *Worship and Theology in England from Newman to Martineau 1850–1900* (Princeton and London, 1962), pp 123–4; E A Down in N P Williams (ed), *Northern Catholicism*(London, 1933), pp 282–3.
38 Article in *The Commonwealth*, June 1900.
39 Robert Dolling, *Ten Years in a Portsmouth Slum* (London, 1896), p 198; C E Osborne, *The Life of Father Dolling* (London, 1903), pp 227, 242.
40 William McLaren, *The Triumph and Failure of the Church* (Marqueete, 1896), p 20.
41 Charles Morley, *London at Prayer* (London, 1909), p 160.
42 K S Inglis, *Churches and the Working Classes in Victorian England* (London, 1963), pp 48ff.
43 Cf C P S Clarke, *The Oxford Movement and After* (London, 1932), p 284.
44 *The Declaration of the Clergy on Ritual* (1904), pp 117–8, 182.
45 This was debated at length in the *Church Times* in May 1896. See C F G Turner's caustic comment in Linklater, *op cit*, pp 78–82. See also the comments of W F Cobb, *ibid*, pp 215–6.
46 Alfred Kelly, *The Cultus of the Sacramental Presence in the Eucharist and in the Reserved Sacrament* (London, 1920), pp 137–8. Kelly argued further that the notion of Christ's presence in extra-liturgical devotion logically rendered the Eucharist unnecessary except as an occasional necessity to replace consecrated hosts. Cf W H Mackean, *op cit*, p 217.
47 For a belated Roman Catholic comment on this danger see Cipriano Vagaggino, OSB, *The Flesh: Instrument of Salvation* (New York, 1969), p 124. Cf E W Benson, *op cit*, pp 50–1.
48 Massey Shepherd, *op cit*, p 20.
49 Cf Newman's *Difficulties of Anglicans* (1850), pp 123–4.
50 T L Kingsbury, *Spiritual Sacrifice and Holy Communion* (Cambridge, 1900), pp 113–8.
51 Hopkins to Herford, 24 January 1903, Herford Papers, vol 4ff, 51–53. Archives of the Orthodox Church of the British Isles.
52 Charles Grafton, *The Living Temple of Christ's Church and the Two Witnesses of the Word Written and the Sacraments: a Consecration Sermon* (Milwaukee, 1891), pp 16ff.
53 John Dowden, *The Workmanship of the Prayer Book in its Literary and Liturgical Aspects* (London, 1899), pp 6–9.
54 Thus Peter Anson, *op cit*, p 257 n 2.
55 Dalgairns, *The Holy Communion, Its Philosophy, Theology and Practice*

(Dublin and London, 1861), p 241; Massey Shepherd, *op cit*, p 23.

56 In A M Allchin (ed), *Sacrament and Image: Essays in the Christian Understanding of Man* (London, 1967), p 10.

57 Cf D E W Harrison and Michael C Sansom, *Worship in the Church of England* (London, 1982), p 72; Henry Arnott in Linklater, *op cit*, pp 137–8.

58 Letters in the National Library of Scotland.

59 Stephen Paget (ed), *Henry Scott Holland: Memoir and Letters* (London, 1921) p 21. For a later instance Scott Holland's intuitive approach to the Eucharist see p 161.

60 Lias to Wordsworth, 5 May 1890 and 19 September 1898 in Lambeth MS. 2911 f 190v and 2912 ff 13–16v; Lias to Herford, 18 August 1903, Herford Papers, vol 1, ff 103–4v, Archives of the Orthodox Church of the British Isles.

61 Anson, *op cit*, pp 458–9; G P H Pawson, CR, *Edward Keble Talbot: Community and his Friends* (London, 1954), pp 29, 32–33.

62 C F G Turner in Linklater, *op cit*, pp 56–9, 70.

63 John Dowden, *op cit*, pp 4–5.

64 See Frank Woods' comment as chairman of the 1925 Farnham Conference in the report of that conference entitled *Reservation*, p 51.

65 In Linklater, *op cit*, pp 50–1.

66 O C Quick, *The Christian Sacraments* (London, 1927), p vii.

67 E C Blewett to Vernon Herford, 10 October 1902, Herford Papers, vol 1, ff 128v–9; the Revd F E Powell (Vicar of St James, Warrington) to Herford, n d (1902), *ibid*, vol 1, ff 29–30. See also W H Fremantle, Dean of Ripon, to Herford, 3 September 1903, *ibid*, vol 1, ff 120–121v. Father Ignatius of Llanthony told Mar Julius Alvarez of Colombo in 1899 that he wanted to enter into communion with him because people like Fremantle were allowed to propagate their rationalist heresies without even a whimper of protest from the English Church Union. Cf Ignatius Lync to Mar Julius, March 1899, printed in *The Western Mail*, 20 July 1899.

68 David G. Peck, *Living Worship* (London, 1944), pp 11ff.

69 Francis Underhill in N P Williams (ed), *Northern Catholicism* (London, 1933), pp 289ff.

70 Roger Lloyd, *The Church of England in the Twentieth Century*, vol 1 (London, 1946), p 44; vol 2 (London, 1954), pp 9, 58–60, 76–7.

71 Horton Davies, *op cit*, pp 121–2.

72 John Wordsworth, *The Holy Communion* (2nd revised edn, London, 1901), p 171.

73 S C Carpenter, *Winnington-Ingram* (London, 1949), p 196.

74 *The Declaration of Clergy . . op cit*, pp 68, 96, 119. W E Collins gave short shrift at the conference to extreme clergy who, by manipulating the idea of the Church of England as two provinces of the Church Catholic, avoided facing the fact that the Church of England had a 'real life and character' of its own which it was dangerous to tamper with. 'The man who is unable to discern and recognise this', he said, 'may understand many things: he may be able to study logic; he may be able to understand mechanics in a perfunctory and wooden sort of way; he may even be able to study law; but at least let him keep his profane hands off the study of history, and Church history above all, for he has shown himself incapable of understanding what it means.' (p 28).

75 *Reservation, Report of a Conference* (London, 1926), pp 5–6, 42–4, 52–3, 67–8. Gore, in his remarks, was drawing directly on a book review which had appeared in the *Revue Benedictine* for January of that year. This Roman Catholic article, in his view, revealed the weaknesses in the official Roman position on reservation. E G Selwyn stressed the vital importance of the quality of teaching, whatever the particular practice advocated. If such a standard as he had in mind were achieved, then it

would be possible to say that Anglo-Catholics were wrong in speaking of devotion to the Reserved Sacrament as a necessary protection of the doctrine of the Real Presence, and that Evangelicals were wrong in speaking of that devotion as mere superstition and magic. For Evangelical talk about 'magic' was on a par with the insensitive language used by some Anglo-Catholics about churches without reservation being 'empty churches'. Both attitudes were essentially sacrilegious, but, in the absence of proper instruction, both were understandable. The real issue, said Selwyn, resided at the level of ascetic, and not sacramental, theology. It ought to be made the object not of legal ruling or theological contestation but of prayerful synodal consideration. He advocated the addresses of Bishop Garbett of Southwark to his clergy as breathing precisely this atmosphere (*ibid*, pp 85–6, 89–90).

76 Anselm Hughes, OSB, *The Rivers of the Flood* (London, 1961), p 95.

77 Percy Dearmer, *The Parson's Handbook* (6th edn, London, 1907), pp 1, 7, 45. The Revd H E Hall, Vicar of St Benet's and All Saints, Kentish Town, wrote, in the same year as Dearmer's first edition, in much the same terms, of two essential Catholic principles in Prayer Book worship: simplicity of form, and complicity of the people. This was conducive both to deep personal piety and to a corporate sense of sacred action. The ritualists' double tendency to omit the exhortations to penitence, and to introduce variable elements of the Roman liturgy into the action, had the effect of obscuring the form, and weakening this double effect. See Robert Linklater (ed), *True Limits of Ritual in the Church* (London, 1899), pp 221–2.

78 Hughes, *op cit*, p 49. In some quarters, *The Parson's Handbook* was derided as 'British Museum religion'.

79 S C Carpenter, *op cit*, pp 170–5.

80 Dearmer wrote fiercely: 'A modern preacher often stands in a sweated pulpit, wearing a sweated surplice over a cassock that was not produced under faith conditions, and holding a sweated book in one hand, with the other he points to the machine-made cross at the jerry-built altar, and appeals to the sacred principles of mutual sacrifice and love'. *The Parson's Handbook, op cit*, pp 4–5.

81 Roger Lloyd, *op cit*, 1, p 123.

82 F G Llewellin, *Anglo-Catholicism* (*A Review*) (London, n d), p 25.
For Hamilton Maughan's comments on the Kensitite demonstrations at Hitchin, see his diary for 12-16 February 1909, presently in the author's possession. On the 16th he recorded, with typical childishness: 'Today the Kensites leave Hitchin after their five days' campaign, during which I am proud to think they have been greatly harassed and worried – and all through little me!'

83 Hamilton Maughan, diary, 1 October 1910, 2 March 1911, 25 January 1913, 20 September 1914, 25 April 1917, 11 June 1917, 11 June 1917, 30 September 1917.

84 *ibid*, 3 January 1909, 9 July 1918, 17 March, 21 September, 21 December 1919. 25 April, 25 July, 31 October 1920, 28 May, 3 July, 25 October 1921, 18 October 1925, 1 July 1933.

85 *ibid*, 7 February, 10 March, 10 June 1910.

86 Hughes, *op cit*, p 33. Scott Holland itched to have a full Requiem Mass for the fallen in the South African War, but held back for fear of using that 'awful moment' to make a point for the 'Catholic movement'. The memorial service which he did have was framed 'on Catholic lines'. Cf Stephen Paget, *op cit*, p 147.

87 Hughes, *op cit*, pp 49ff.

88 C F G Turner, in Linklater, *op cit*, pp 68–9, 92–3.

89 Hughes, *op cit*, pp 70–3.

90 *Commonwealth*, March 1917.

91 H Maynard Smith, *Frank Weston, Bishop of Zanzibar* (London, 1926), p 302.
92 K E Kirk, *The Vision of God* (London, 1928), pp 444ff. Cf *ibid*, pp 65–7.
93 Carpenter, *op cit*, p 143.
94 Anson, *op cit*, p 131.
95 Hughes, *op cit*, p 143.
96 Harrison and Sansom, *op cit*, p 74.
97 C P S Clarke, *The Oxford Movement and After* (London, 1932), p 283. Ironically, as the new book was being proposed to Parliament, Vernon Herford brought out a new edition of his *Liturgy of Sarapion*, after twelve years of experimental use in his Evangelical Catholic Church in Oxford. This did not go without notice in one Oxford paper, which described Herford's liturgy as a document designed 'to meet the needs of all sections of the Christian Church'. This has not yet been said of any Anglican revision!
98 H L Stewart, *A Century of Anglo-Catholicism* (London, 1929), p 322.
99 Sir John Simon, a lapsed Congregationalist, had had no intention of intervening in the debate, until his legal mind detected inconsistencies which offended his moral sense.
100 Llewellin, *op cit*, pp 23, 105.
101 *ibid*, pp 18–9.
102 Carpenter, *op cit*, p 195.
103 A G Herbert, *Liturgy and Society* (London, 1935), pp 75, 102–3, 165, 171, 176, 182, 195, 203–4, 211.
104 *ibid*, p xii.
105 Roger Lloyd, *op cit*, pp 11, 117ff.
106 R H T Thompson, *The Church's Understanding of Itself* (London, 1957), *passim*.
107 Peck, *op cit*, pp 15–6.
108 Hebert, *Liturgy and Society, op cit* p 7; Peck, *op cit*, p 26, citing Temple's *The Social Significance of Worship* (Industrial Christian Fellowship), and pp 53ff and 84–7. The phil-Orthodox Fr Patrick Hankey of Little St Mary's, Cambridge, complained of most Anglican faithful: 'In effect they are saying: "Since corporate prayer is at times unavoidable, let it be as little distracting as possible." This suggested that the task of living in communion with one's fellows was not particularly difficult or important, and that the final vision of God was to be like 'a private view of an exhibition of pictures'. Such a view repelled Hankey, suggesting as it did a completely disembodied notion of man's destiny. Common life, he held, was the offering of bodies and physical environment as a living sacrifice. Canon Newbolt of Chester concurred with this. 'It is quite certain', he wrote, 'that unless we can bring our people back to the true spirit of corporate worship in the Body of Christ, no development of mystical religion, in which the faithful Christian draws near to God *solus cum solo*, is going to convert the nation. We must teach people to pray in unison in Church, not as unrelated units each seeking God in quiet and silence'. Hebert (ed), *The Parish Communion* (London, 1937), pp 153, 212. Hebert's own position was predicated on the idea of mystery as 'substance', the total reality of Jesus Christ. In working this out in the context of modern society, he drew heavily on Gibson Winter's *The Suburban Captivity of the Churches*, seeing the failure of so many people to grasp this nature of mystery as being rooted in the disintegration of the family as the matrix in which people discovered their personhood and vocation. This had encouraged routinisation of worship.
109 *The Parish Communion*, p ix.
110 *ibid*, pp 4, 6, 11, 13, 20ff, 236–9, 303–8.
111 *ibid*, pp 211–2, 214–5.

112 *ibid*, pp 21, 168–9, 172, 175. One interesting way of bringing out the principles of the Parish Communion movement which was never followed up was the exposition of the Prayer Book as an enactment of the Book of Revelation by Stacy Waddy of the SPG in his *The Drama of the Eucharist* (1935). Waddy was seeking to show the nexus between liturgy and life via the immediate prophetic experience of the early Church in John the Divine. The Prayer Book, like Revelation, he said, was a 'marching book', but Anglicans had lost their way, recognising only a few isolated familiar words of direction on the processional banners. In order to recover the totality of vision, they had to realise the necessary worship-faculty to see in the Spirit, with a view constantly to the Kingdom and the coming Lord. With this perspective, the whole shape of the liturgy would fall into place and worshippers would once again be urgent, knowing that the Lord might come at any time. True worship could never be the product of committees of scholars, for it was always part of the 'worshipping host of heaven and of the dead'. This could often be better grasped in the simple worship of pioneer communities than in sophisticated urban churches. (pp 9–11, 23, 47, 49).

113 F R Fairbairn and F M Downton in *The Parish Communion*, p 257.

114 Peter J Jagger, *A History of the Parish and People, Movement* (Leighton Buzzard, 1978), p 70.

115 *ibid*, p 71; David M Paton (ed), *The Parish Communion Today*. Report of the 1962 Conference of Parish and People (London, 1962), p 7.

116 Jagger, *op cit*, pp 6, 53.

117 *ibid*, pp 80, 95, 116.

118 A M Ramsey, *Durham Essays and Addresses* (London, 1956), p 18; Roger Lloyd, *op cit*, pp 11, 205; W S Baker in *The Parish Communion*, pp 285–6; Jagger, *op cit*, p 102.

119 *The Parish Communion*, p 14. Cf pp 177, 274ff. For the influence of the ideas of the Zoe Movement see *ibid*, pp 29, 142.

120 David L Edwards, *Not Angels but Anglicans* (London, 1958), pp 86ff; Paton, *op cit*, pp 22–49.

121 Colin Dunlop, *Anglican Public Worship* (London, 1953), pp 42–4, 59–60, 72, 124; S C Clark, *Unity, Uniformity and the English Church* (London, 1961), p 6.

122 Ronald Jasper, *Arthur Caley Headlam: Life and Letters of a Bishop* (London, 1960), pp 183–4.

123 Cf. Colin Buchanan (ed) *Modern Anglican Liturgies* (London, 1968), pp 5–6; Gregory Dix, OSB, *The Shape of the Liturgy* (London, 1944), p 720.

124 Dunlop, *op cit*, pp 11–12, 35–9.

125 Paton, *op cit*, p 133.

126 Peck, *op cit*, p 44.

127 S C Clark, *op cit*, p 5.

128 In H M Relton (ed), *The New Prayer Book* (London, 1927), pp 49–50.

129 Michael J Richards, *The Liturgy in England* (London, 1966), p 54.

130 Cf R C D Jasper (ed), *The Eucharist Today: Studies in Series 3* (London, 1974), pp 16, 18.

131 Ann Bond in David Martin and Peter Mullen (eds), *op cit*, p 129.

132 Margaret Doody and Rachel Trickett in *ibid*, p 62.

133 Cf R C D Jasper, *op cit*, pp 120, 165.

134 Hebert, *Liturgy and Society, op cit*, p 213 and elsewhere.

135 'Caroline Adams'. *The Prayer Book Pattern: A Consideration* (London, 1957), p 167.

136 J L Houlden in R C D Jasper, *op cit*, p 169.

137 George Florovsky, 'Sobornost: the Catholicity of the Church' in E L Mascall (ed), *The Church: an Anglo-Russian Symposium* (London, 1934), p 56.

8 Parishes and People

Roger Arguile

> 'Belonging is all. A community of Christians means a community of persons who call themselves Christians, and a person who wishes to belong to such a community is a Christan. It is presumptuous to look for any special qualities in such a community; this is to forget our complete dependence on the Word of God (in Christ Jesus). God declared that he would create a spiritual community and we cannot question this decree. The great point is that its distinguishing attributes are spiritual – i e imperceptible.'[1]

One of the outworkings of the Catholic Revival of the last century was a revival of parish life. A high doctrine of the Church, if it is to have any cash value, must work itself out in the life of the parishes. The 'slum priest' became legendary: Father Dolling at Landport, Stewart Headlam in Bethnal Green, Charles Lowder, John Groser, and many others established in the mind of the Church a picture of Anglo-Catholic concern for the poor, and of churches lightening up the lives of the poor with the glories of liturgy and the hope of the transformation of the world. High doctrine, splendid liturgy, and social concern were, it seemed, combined.

In fact, it is not clear how often there was such a combination. There was more talk than action. The Guild of St Matthew was always minute, and even the much vaguer and more genteel Christian Social Union never rose to more than 6000 in membership. The talk was wide-ranging: the just wage, the system of property renting, housing, infant mortality, industrial conditions. In 1913 Scott Holland, writing to the Church Congress in Birmingham, commented that 'the whole world has become Christian Social Union now'.[2] In 1926 Archbishop Davidson attempted to intervene on behalf of the miners in the General Strike – as Bishop Westcott had done in Durham in 1882 – but much of the concern was at a distance. All clergy had to be graduates until after the turn of the century, and this in practice meant Oxbridge. Most of them had a moneyed background, whether commercial or aristocratic. The setting up of the Cavendish Club in London is symptomatic of the approach: it was an ordinary London club with the usual amenities, but for those who undertook social welfare work! Bishop Frank Weston compared the good intentions of the missionaries in Africa with the church social workers in the English slums. Both, he claimed, were unconsciously patronising those whom they sought to serve.[3] So the Church remained 'content to be at heart a country Church, administering parishes from large vicarages, a gentleman's Church with a married clergy, and a ministry entered as a profession, not merely a vocation'.[4] Those who entered the slums did not necessarily stay very long, and those who did sometimes introduced a liturgy that was as much eccentric and esoteric as splendid.

There was too the ever-present danger of withdrawal into the church building. The religious orders represented this danger very well. Pusey had spoken of the need for a college of clergy in large town parishes, and in 1844 he spoke, on the setting up of the Park Village Community, of 'the need to visit the sick in their homes, to visit hospitals and workhouses or prisons, to feed, clothe and instruct destitute children, to give shelter to distressed women of good character'.[5] The Devonport Sisters of Mercy were set up to meet parochial needs, the Convent of the Holy Name was set up at St Peter's, Vauxhall, the Sisters of the Church began at St Augustine's, Kilburn, while, among men, the Society of the Divine Compassion began at Plaistow. But as time went on, almost all withdrew into the cloister and the country: Ascot, Malvern, London Colney.

On the other hand, the practical leadership of the movement was largely from the bottom. In spite of the high principles of Catholicism, since bishops did not know what to do with rebellious priests and religious orders, and since the Church as a whole still clung to the trappings of privilege, it was bound to be so. Some priests took a grim pride in the knowledge that they would be forced to remain in the slums for the rest of their ministries, and would never get preferment. Temple, once a socialist, was made Primate. Men like Basil Jellicoe influenced housing policy by their work. But if ever there was a danger that the Church might effect the conversion of English society and the ending of class exploitation, it did not materialise. The slums and the urban deserts became publicly owned, the influence of the Church lessened as membership fell. Baptisms, confirmations, Easter communions, ordinations all lessened in number: in places, only the dead were still claimed by the Church.[6]

After the Second World War, the Church of England lost its optimism, and came increasingly to concern itself with internal matters: the reorganisation of parochial structures, the revision of the liturgy, the improvement of pay and conditions of the clergy, and new patterns of ministry.

The Organised Church

The immediate rush of ordinands from the services soon declined, and the work of pastoral reorganisation was, to a great extent, intended to offset the fall in numbers of clergy by the grouping together of rural parishes and by attempts to provide clergy with more satisfying jobs. Rural clergy might have found their life-style pleasant, but by the 1960s the departure of urban clergy for secular jobs in the state welfare services and elsewhere was becoming alarming. Inner city parishes were becoming depopulated, and their churches were often impossible to maintain. In many cases it was the old slum Catholic parish which was axed, for its local people were gone, and it relied for support on an eclectic congregation. Daughter churches, which had been provided for the new residential sprawls, were hard to staff and hard to work; their buildings were humble, and their curates often inexperienced. Yet new developments and new towns called for a rapid response. So team and group methods of working, first developed in rural Norfolk, grew quickly, especially after the Pastoral Measure of 1968. In 1974 in the Diocese of Lichfield there was one team; by 1982 there were 18 either in being or in process of formation. Teams were often ecumenical, whatever the law said, and eventually Local Ecumenical Projects became a means of sanctioning such operations. The initiative, first suggested by Pusey, for colleges of clergy took over a hundred years to be officially accepted, and when it was accepted, it was based on quite different principles. The Company of Mission Priests were celibate and committed to a monastic ideal; the new teams which were emerging often consisted of married men inspired by social work and management principles. Their masters in the dioceses saw teams as a means of getting reluctant clergy to work where otherwise they would not. Moreover, the decline in numbers of curates made it seem necessary to offer them quick promotion. Even so, expecting showers and bidets in their vicarages, many men preferred to stay in the south and in the countryside. Even the imposition of quotas after the Sheffield Report did not produce commitment. A man was expected to do a few years of hard labour before being rewarded with an 'easier' parish. Pastoral reorganisation has also involved the alteration of parish boundaries, so that the parish constitutes a community. Unfortunately, nobody talked with the architects and planners of the featureless streets of St Helier, Trafford Park and Blakenall Heath about what communities are.

The ethos of ministry too has changed. Now it is much more a matter of going to a parish, doing a job, and then leaving after five years or so.

'Good men' tend to stay no longer than that. No longer will they be left in a parish for 30 years or more. The power to suspend has been used to facilitate short stays. Concepts which had their origin in the production of goods and services, and which had already penetrated nursing and the social services, have become widely used in the Church. Objectives are set to make the 'task' seem more feasible, supposing (as all planners do) that the key factors for achieving the objective are within one's control. This encourages the setting of narrow objectives or the avoidance of monitoring. Meanwhile, in the absence of substantive doctrinal pronouncements, consensus is backed by a vague and occasionally cynical Biblicism.

The fall in the number of clergy had been a cause of concern for over a century, and the loss of confidence in the parochial structure has produced a number of other proposals. Sector ministers, industrial chaplains, town centre ministers are sent to be where others work, ministering to this factory, that leisure complex or shopping centre, or some international airport. The urban parish, whose streets are dormitories which are no longer the focus they once were for urban men and women, has become intractable, not to be compared with the village it aped. And the priesthood has come to be associated with a spurious professionalism. There never was any intention that sector ministries would cover every factory, every social meeting place or travel terminus, and provide it with a worshipping community. The atmosphere in many of them is not conducive to the training of lay leadership. The fruit of the exercise is largely the news it brings back to the Church. Moreover, it is not clear why such clericalisation is necessary at all. If lay people can be trained for parish tasks such as baptism visiting and marriage counselling, they could surely be trained to be Christians to their workmates.

To a certain degree this has been done. Auxiliary Pastoral Ministers, as they were first called, were intended to do two things: to 'help out' on Sundays and in their spare time, and to minister during the week to the 'real world' of which the full-time clergy were supposed to be ignorant. Often there was an assumption that all ministries must be concentrated in priesthood, though this need not, and should not, be so. Another problem is that APMs, or Non-Stipendiary Ministers, have so far tended to come from professional classes and not from down-town parishes. So suburban parishes become silted up with 'part-time priests' while the inner city parishes starve.

Two movements can be detected. One is to put the professionals into places where people work and play, while the other is to replace them in the parishes. Thus in some dioceses there are proposals to create Locally Ordained Ministers, each one chosen from the congregation, to be ordained and serve the parishes in which they live, and with no certainty that they will have a ministry if they move. The idea is an old one. Father Herbert

Kelly advocated a 'handcart ministry' at the beginning of the century. Drawn from within a congregation, a 'farmer priest', he felt, would not foster the dependence of the congregation, which he saw as a destructive force in the life of the Church.[7] Kelly envisaged such men as replacing, or simply being supplemented by, the stipendiary priest, and he believed that the system would work only if the class system were diminished and the country became more democratic. The modern proposals are more modest. Class divisions have altered but not diminished, and there are many areas of public housing and demolition areas in which the local church is often feeble, sometimes divided by fear, feeling itself 'not good enough' to have the services of clergy who choose to work where the going is easier. Sometimes the priest in such an area becomes a lone missionary, often cut off from his parishioners, strangely friendless in a parish of thousands. The style of parish life certainly needs to alter if dependence is not to be encouraged, but the urban parish is not a village. Find a teacher or social worker or accountant who will move in, or a potential leader who does not feel the desire to move out. The problems of the urban parish go very deep, and will not be cured by organisation, by the use of volunteers or professionals. The virtue of the LOM is that he may free stipendiary priests to live and learn the life of the city – if, indeed, we are training the right men to go there.

Again, the organised Church has been concerned with bringing itself up to date liturgically. Liturgy is something that the local church should be good at. Priests may waver at working in mean streets, may dominate their flocks, and may have no feeling for prophecy, but the glory of God expressed in the splendid liturgy should surely be their forte. The process which led to the publication of the Alternative Service Book began with the liturgical chaos propagated in part by the ritualists, and continued with the thinking of the Liturgical Movement. From their different perspectives, such men as Dom Gregory Dix and Father Kelly wished to restore the Eucharist to the centre of worshipping life, and make it express the life of the local community. What was produced was a compromise, a sort of '*missa tombola*', designed to please everybody, and requiring a good deal of dexterity to use. The sacrament of Penance finds no place in it and there is to be an optional leaflet for those who want it, and the offertory, important as an expression of the life of the community, has been omitted.[8] If one looks at the 'world' dimension of the book, the omissions are startling and illuminating. There are no special intentions for work – or the lack of it –, for peace and justice, for times of famine, for racial justice, for those oppressed by war, for the poor or the persecuted. All we have are those for Social Responsibility, for Civic Occasions, and the incredibly vague intentions for use In Time of Trouble and For Peace in the World.

It is not clear how widely the book will be used. Other developments which have come from the evangelical tradition are leading the Church in a quite new direction. 'Non-liturgical services', whose intention is often evangelistic, but which make less demands on the congregation, and exhibit, albeit unconsciously, a marketing approach to worship, are increasingly used to charm people into church.

The last way in which the Church has sought to maintain its life is in the pay and conditions of the clergy. Stipends have become salaries. In the mid-'50s dioceses began to employ entrepreneurs to raise money from the parishes. Alarmed by such naked business methods, which were also costly, they modified the principle in terms of the parable of the Talents: God has given them all so that they ought to give something back to Him. What was originally a statement of eschatological judgment became a piece of Pelagianism. However, something had to be done about the Church's finances. Money which had formerly come from the dead, the historic endowments, had become insufficient, and in any case had led to massive inequalities between dioceses and even parishes. The change from the model of a state Church, subsidised by private charity, and providing spiritual welfare, to that of a Church whose members are responsible for its continued life, was and still is painful. Inflation began to clear away some of the ancient inequalities as more and more parishes had to be augmented, and this was aided by decisions following the Paul Report of 1964.[10] But the business ethic supervened. Rich parishes have to be enabled to flourish in order to pay for poor parishes which can pay little. There has been no radical appraisal of the whole question of the distribution of wealth, but simply a form of taxation. A good deal of bullying and manipulation can be observed in the conduct of campaigns. But commitment cannot be bought, and there is the risk that parishes may be judged on the basis of their profitability. No one talks of 'holding all things common'. It is not even the tithe we need, but the widow's mite.

It would, of course, be wrong to deprecate organisation for what it cannot do. But there is a serious problem where organisation tries to do too much, and without an adequate theological basis. It is certain that we need to be committed to some kind of parish structure, but we need a new understanding of it. We need priests, not managers, who are concerned with pay and conditions of work. We need a restoration of the discipline of prayer and the direction of souls. We need to be unafraid of being unpopular with the authorities, for as long as we side with the technocratic society, we shall not be fulfilling our vocation.

Some models of ministry

In some places the church is still the centre of community life; a tall building set among small ones, attractive for weddings. In some places the priest is still an important figure in the community, and the local church a focus for community celebrations. Processions, religious and secular, gather people together. But such parishes are rare. In many places, badly built imitations of some bygone style decay in city back streets or in rotting centres of communities which no longer exist. Humble brick structures rise scarcely above the sea of houses, or cower beneath tower blocks. Yet here is holy ground, a piece of land whose existence means something to different people. Alan Ecclestone has written of the necessity of 'praying the parish': making all that goes on there to be part of our prayer. How its people relate, how its social life enmeshes their thought, what is assumed or taken for granted, what divides its people, in what ways it is oppressive to some and indulgent to others: prayer over such themes must become as deliberate an act as the way we dispose our bodies and breathing when we endeavour to pray.[11] Is this how we see the parish? Or do we mean the church congregation on offer, among many commodities, religious and secular, seeking to command a share of the decreasing market? Paul Rowntree Clifford has distinguished between those Christians and churches who see salvation as the act of God and of grace, and those who see it as the act of man and of faith: 'the former are concerned with the reconciliation of the whole world, the latter with the saving of individual souls from damnation'.[12] The question is about whether the Church is a beleaguered garrison stretching out hands to restore individuals, or part of a world which belongs to God through creation, redemption and the Kingdom found in unexpected places. Much parish work falls on one side or the other of this divide.

Thus, for instance, on the side of 'the world sets the agenda' was the influential book *The Church for Others*,[13] two reports from the World Council of Churches. It exhibited a confidence in secularisation (which others feared) and saw it as the fruit of the gospel. It spoke of the need for reflection on the situations confronting men and women, of the need for differentiation of ministries and for a variety of groups organised on a functional basis, for the creation of macro-parishes (zones) and for the integration and diversification of structures. It contended that 'the world sets the agenda' for the Church, and it demanded of churches a high degree of flexibility, competence, and organisational expertise. At the other end of the scale, training courses such as those of the Urban Ministry Project in its early days concerned themselves with the opportunities afforded by the new discipline of community work. Churches worked with secular agencies on common concerns. The church on the site of the Croydon airport was styled the Roundshaw Experiment, and its priest concentrated on the building of local community rather than on the establishment of a congregation. Community building was to be achieved by the so-called 'issue strategy': the identification of those problems which might unite the people of a locality, such as lack of play space, amenities, proposals to build a motorway through housing areas, factory pollution, and so on.

Community work, however, had a narrow base. It depended on the availability of resources to meet the needs and wants of a community, and while in new developments and in housing clearance areas it could draw attention to planning failures, the frustrated expectations of those who saw that things were not changing could easily rebound on strangers who could not stay long, and so lead to deeper depression. Yet success might so change the character of an area that the solidarity created out of deprivation would evaporate. Such a model led to the community use of church buildings and to an increased awareness in congregations. But it could also be very clerical. The expertise required for such work was specialised, and the congregation could easily be left behind. It was also often more horizontal than vertical in its theology, often too optimistic about the capacities of human beings. While it might have been undergirded by a sacramental theology, it had in fact a liberal protestant base. It was about doing a job and then going. It is only when one begins to think about what 'community' actually means – in terms of a persistent oral culture, of the skeins of relationship which bind it together, of a collective consciousness – that the method, for all its virtues, is seen as extraordinary. It is true that communities, as unorganised relational entities with a common culture, are rarer now in cities, and some insights and techniques such as community work was able to develop were essential. Their use by priests gave a wider dimension to pastoral thinking in the Church at large. The treason was the failure to remain, the failure to learn obedience by what they suffered. The creation of community is slow and long-term, and the factors are never within one's control. In Leslie Paul's words: 'One of the necessary tasks today is to see the pastoral charge of the Church over against the social patterns and demographic groupings given by history. Their capacity to be darkly and unyieldingly themselves, impervious to argument because they are not decided at the level of argument, tells us that here are positions to be taken by attrition rather than assault'.[14]

One of the problems of urban theology is that much pastoral work today is done against a profoundly non-Christian background. Whether it be community work or the creation of 'basic communities', the response of working-class English folk is much the same. The Christian religion is marginal to their lives. The Church itself remains obdurately middle-class. Its clergy 'compromise with the rulers of this new world, and turn a blind eye to problems they dare not face . . . Their training was geared to a world that had vanished, (and) diverted attention from the aspirations and anxieties of a population compelled to be militant and suspicious'.[15] The work of a few has little impact on this situation.

When we turn to the local congregation, the traditional mould has been 'churchy'. Since liturgy is what the church does well, much pastoral work has used the Sunday service and the occasional offices as a means of enabling the church to grow and live. Thus, for instance, because many people still want their children baptised, a church can use their request as a means of inducting children into Sunday school, and sometimes their parents into church. The growth of restrictive baptismal policies, however, is reflected in the new services, with their increased stress on the element of future commitment required of parents. Wedding preparation may not be so productive since newly-weds often move elsewhere, though funerals will bring the bereaved. Certainly here the church, unlike most other people, is not silenced. Likewise, ministry to the sick, in hospital and at home, is a point of contact. So religion gives comfort in face of the unknown. Ministry to children can also be conducted through schools and the various uniformed organisations. The Baden-Powell groups still hold to their 'duty to God', and it is sometimes possible to use these organisations to fill the church with children and a few of their parents.

Children, the sick, the bereaved: is this the communion of the saints on earth? There is no doubt that such a strategy sometimes works, but it reinforces the view that religion is essentially for children and the dependent. The Church becomes a hospital ship, the spiritual arm of the National Health Service. It may even become like an elderly whore, there to provide what is needed, and with some need to be grateful that it is still called for at all.

Yet the liturgy should be the centre of the Church's life, not simply as a good show to go to, not as a commodity to appeal to the tastes of a leisured public, but as expressive of the life of the community. 'Let its liturgy be splendid and full of meaning. Let each parish make of itself a real community, devoted to the conquest of souls, and united within itself for that single goal.'[16] The Liturgy is to be not only glorious but also expressive. The Parish and People movement, expressed in its local form supremely by Ernest Southcott at Halton, Leeds, sought to make the Offertory a focus of involvement. 'For at this point, representative elements are taken from the "secular" context, and are made ready for the "sacred" '.[17] But if the parish was to be gathered and not divided on Sunday, it was right that all should be involved in its decision making. And so the PCC met once a month, while every other week there was a Parish Meeting for a variety of purposes, some related to parish policy, some to organisations in the church, some to more general questions. And since the parish would not always come to church, the church would be taken to them: meetings in houses for study, meetings to involve the lapsed, ecumenical meetings, meetings to discuss world affairs. House Communions at Halton were meant to involve the lapsed. 'We have seen that baptism for the many and Communion for the few is a contradiction in terms'.[18] The whole operation was very churchy, not very activist, but it involved a far greater number of people than those who actually 'came to church'. Its theses were that people must see the local church being itself, and that in public affairs a few well-informed people could have an influence far beyond their numbers. Southcott recounts how a miner who had never been to church in his life, before three days had elapsed after a Communion service in his house, asked to be prepared for confirmation.[19] Worship must be part of what is being done, thought and discussed by the parish: if it is just what happens on Sundays, it can become merely magic.

Again, the clergy are not the Church. Their control over its life is deadening. Yet there remains, and not only in the Catholic wing of the Church, an unreflective clericalism. To find a genuine distribution of ministry we must look to the Evangelical wing. Following a model in Ephesians, lay elders are now increasingly appointed, and often trained as readers, to supplement, and sometimes to replace the work of the ordained priest. The National Evangelical Anglican Congress declared in 1977: 'Not only must groups of presbyters be recognised in each place, but they, and other members of the congregation, must be adequately trained and retrained to fulfil their ministry'.[20] There is no doubt that, in a parish of 10,000, contact can be made only with a few unless ministry is shared. The pastoral care of the sick, the bereaved, the teaching of parents of children to be baptised, and of engaged couples, are valuable, but they call for such a shared ministry. A cellular structure is essential too for the continued growth in spirituality, although such groups can easily become anarchic, eclectic or introverted. It is easier to discuss 'spiritual' matters unrelated to the affairs of the world, for they are less likely to generate controversy. In this context, the Charismatic movement may have produced as much spiritual arrogance as obedience, penitence or service. Again, lay training is often superficial, concerned with knowledge rather than skills, rarely, if ever, about spiritual growth. Yet Anglican Catholics once talked about spiritual direction, about 'helping souls', and about the development of spiritual resistance to evil. The old rigid systems have broken down, and today 'teachers must be companions on the same journey that we ourselves are making, and . . . their authority derives from their ability to be fellow-travellers, friends and comrades on the journey'.[21] The aim of all direction should be self-direction, but professional guides are useful, and while a director is always helpless before the integrity of another, we need people – not only priests but including them – who have the gifts of discernment. Parish work is not all about marital breakdown, bereavement, sexual conduct and Bible study. There are signs, though few, that once again some thought is being given to the need for spiritual direction, and it is long overdue.[22]

There is also the question of evangelism. In 1945 the Church of England produced a document, *Towards the Conversion of England*. It was a response to the decline in churchgoing, and many of its suggestions were taken up by priests such as Southcott. 'Fellowship', he stressed, 'is the by-product of sharing in a common purpose, and a devotion to a common cause.'[23] The various national missionary 'crusades' were, and still are, taken up by parishes and supported, though Southcott thought little of them. However, the most systematic thinking about parish evangelism has come from the more recent Church Growth movement. Church Growth begins with the principle that the gospel must be preached to all nations. Donald McGavran, its prime mover, observed that one of the limitations on evangelism is the number of churches.[24] Churches only grow numerically to a certain size, whatever the population of the parish, or the size of the church. The number of clergy may marginally increase the numbers of worshippers, but even here the graph flattens off after a certain point.[25] The characteristics of different kinds of groups are studied: the intimate person-to-person discussion group, the large social gathering, the great rally. Their functions are not interchangeable, but each must exist for the Church to grow. Certain kinds of people are more receptive to the local church: young families, newcomers, those requiring the occasional offices. The ways in which congregations may grow are also analysed: from one church to another (transfer growth), from lapse to membership (restoration growth), biological growth, and conversion growth. So far it may seem to be a series of insights and techniques, peppered with a new jargon. Many of the ideas, in fact, have been put into practice by clergy for a long time. Thus levels of commitment are to be divined within the congregation for the selection of lay leaders. Data collection, and the determination of the hierarchy of psychological needs, are part of the portfolio. There is the Engel scale (How far you are from God), and, most worrying of all, the Homogeneous Unit concept (the idea that, since people should not be made to leap cultural barriers, like should preach to like). There seems to be no sense of Christ as the transformer of culture, but rather of Christ above, and working through, culture. Eddie Gibbs writes that 'the Church must neither identify with the Westernising/technological/materialist influence, nor provide a bolthole in which to hide and avoid the challenge of social disruption', but the general impression is of a programme to produce a socially conformist Church, a Church which will not challenge the structures of injustice between cultures, and will perpetuate the divisions within society. What is useful about the Church Growth Movement is that, because it is so explicit, it exposes many of the things which churches have actually been doing for a long time. If one goes for growth in this way, one is likely to want to avoid controversial matters, as one competes with the sects for the receptive folk – the market.

If some people are put off by the raiding of many scientific disciplines, and by the analysis of congregations, others may feel that the approach is too crude. It does not attempt to debate with the secularists, or examine their theses: it ignores them. The questions raised by the natural and human sciences, by historical study and biblical criticism, and even by the injustice and evil in the world, are bypassed in the name of biblical fundamentalism. The kind of Christianity preached has the simple authority of 'what the Bible says'. One detects, as with the sects, an appeal to those who are confused by the plethora of new knowledge, intimidated by the pluralism of life-styles and the decline of traditional morals. A comparison might be made with the growth patterns of Mormons and Jehovah's Witnesses. It is striking that in the United States this is the religion of the Moral Majority, a movement opposed to left-of-centre political ideas in the name of the family and of strict moral standards. But biblical fundamentalism of itself does not lead to such attitudes. Jim Wallis and Ronald Sider are poles apart from the Moral Majority, and this should make one wonder more about the techniques and presuppositions of the movement.

Conclusion

The foundation of our pastoral work in the parish must be an adequate doctrine of creation, and an adequate soteriology. The former calls for a willingness to debate about the impact of new knowledge, and to act together with agencies and organisations which have different ideologies and objectives. And this must imply, negatively, a rejection of fundamentalist Christianity, however attractive its apparent simplicity may be in the short term. It will not wear well, for it is not true. The Bible is the Church's handbook, not its rulebook. Positively, it requires a willingness not to raid new disciplines for whatever aids they can give to the Church, but to engage in discussions about the social and ethical implications of new thought and new technology. There is much to be done. There is a well-documented decline in religious observance. Is it the city which has made people less religious, or our particular ways of ordering urban life? The places in the world where the Church is growing are not the great industrialised nations. Paris, according to Gabriel Le Bras, seemed to have the capacity to change rural practising Catholics into urban non-practising ones. There seems to have been a change of consciousness, a limitation of language to that related to the rational, an alienation of man from nature, a growth of the acquisitive mentality, as well as the fragmentation of the family and the altered character of the class struggle. In the past exploited groups, not initially irreligious, found themselves opposed by those in authority who 'so often appealed to religious values in defence of their own positions'.[27] Now, while this is still true, many of the moderately unsuccessful, seeing no clear divisions, yet confused and resentful, simply opt out. 'The individual finds unifying meaning for his existence in the private sphere, in conscious withdrawal from these enormous institutions and powerful interests which objectively control his existence.'[28] No coherent values are affirmed. Leisure becomes the universal anaesthetic, and when religion succeeds, it often does so by appealing to this desire to opt out, to find certainty in an alternative universe which does not challenge the one in which all, as a matter of fact, actually live. For the most part, the strength of the churches is affected more by the national mood than by the efforts of individual churches and their priests and ministers.[29]

Yet the world belongs to God. People of prayer can see this, and acknowledge the sacramental character of the world. It has in it the potential to reveal God who speaks concretely, even to the non-literate. Catholic spirituality is, and always should be, highly materialistic, restoring, by its liturgy and its life, the significance of the created universe.

If an adequate doctrine of creation is necessary to our strategy, an adequate doctrine of salvation is equally important. Our gospel is vain unless we can say that no one falls outside the realm of Christ's redeeming work except by his or her own fault. Yet there are not only Hindu villagers who have not responded to the gospel, but many English men and women who have been stunted by circumstances, blinded by inherited attitudes, cut off from spiritual light, confused by the manifold evils of the world, who are not committed Christians, and it is not their fault. Surely, 'to find our way into the Church is not the only way of finding salvation here below. We may so live as to make ourselves the men who will both recognise and love the Church, that is, the mystical Christ, when revealed to us in glory; who, recognising it and loving it, will be capable of assimilation to it, through the transforming company of its members – not to say, of its Head'.[30]

The Church must be Christ to the world, must create parables of hope and trust, and participate in them wherever they exist; it must foster that freedom which enables people to choose love. As John Baker has stressed in *The Foolishness of God*: 'We need the moral attitude before belief can become living and real'.[31] People need to see the possibility of improvements in their condition, and the Church needs to be involved in the work of social change and transformation. Otherwise its sacramental life comes to have no relation to the world and constitutes merely some form of private magic. Christians then become spectators rather than witnesses, moral heretics who are open to the response of Christ, 'I never knew you'. Such involvement in the work of change needs to be with a community, not imposed upon it, an involvement of weakness rather than of strength. Ivan Illich describes graphically how the desire to do good on the part of the Roman Catholic Church in South America and among immigrants in New York failed because it was not sensitive to what people and their communities really are.[32]

To prescribe how these things should be done is beyond the scope of an essay. Indeed, much modern thinking has made the fatal error of trying to prescribe systems and programmes for making parishes work. Such ideas are largely misguided. Each parish is different. Some still constitute villages, even in the midst of big cities; communities of fate with a feeling of identity. Others seem to be mere dormitories whose inhabitants belong nowhere and who are apt to choose their religion in much the same way as they choose their squash club. Some contain pockets of abject poverty which are not visible from the arterial roads which carry commuters to work. In some parishes, people move constantly; in others, many have known the place for the whole of their lives. In addition to these differences, there is the danger of ignoring the differences between people, not only culturally but in terms of their personalities. 'Marketing' evangelism will capture the 'joiners', the emotionally insecure. An 'exclusive' product will attract those who wish to opt out of a confusing world. There is, on the other hand, a place for the gregarious and the solitary, the enthusiast and the placid, the doubter and the dogmatic.

However, some general principles for the parish ministry can be stated. First the organised Church needs to ensure that parish boundaries, so far as possible, unite real communities on the ground. That is often not possible, and so there is certainly much to be said for collective working between parishes, whether as legal teams or as informal groupings.

Secondly, there needs to be a much closer relationship between different kinds of parish. It is still a fact that inner city and suburban parishes have little to do with each other, and would have nothing to say to each other if they met. The informing of society about the iniquitous division between the deprived and other sections of the community is one in which local churches should have a key role. The present relationship, via Synods and parish share assessments, is insufficient; it neither makes the better-off parishes aware of the conditions of life of their brothers and sisters, nor commits them to a common cause. How that can be done needs considerable thought, but structures themselves will not produce the commitment.

Thirdly, the local church needs to get out into the streets. It is essential that the life of a congregation should include a shared reflection and prayer with others who live in the streets of the parish. Small groups must be concerned, however, not only with individual piety but with the structure of the community, with the hopes and fears of its people, and their place in the economy of salvation. Hence the Church must resist the growing movement to turn in upon itself, and to regard the community merely as a market to be researched and sold to. Britain is no longer a Christian country, and religious yearnings have become an incoherent and often secret part of people's lives. The appeal only to the few who want to opt out of society is heretical. We need a liturgy which is expressive of the transformation of society, a concern with the pain and oppression of communities, the generation of new forms of religious language which can speak of God to an urban society which has lost its roots in the created order, lost its sense of imaginative wonder and belonging. And, for all its limitations, community work offers a tool for the creation of just those parables of hope which will speak to people.

Fourthly, the Church at large needs to engage in thinking about society, about the meaning of words like 'work' and 'leisure', about the structure of our society and its right ordering. Anglican Catholics were once in the forefront of such thinking, but there is no evidence that the movement of Catholic Renewal is interested in carrying on and developing that tradition.

Fifthly, parish clergy need to stay. The difference between the Locally Ordained Minister (LOM) and the Stipendiary Careerist Manager (SCM) is marked and largely unnoticed. The former is expected to stay, the latter to be mobile. Stipendiary clergy, who come largely from the middle classes, need to stay in their parishes long enough to learn, from their failures as well as their successes, to become enmeshed in the life of the community, going far beyond guilt and a social conscience. Incarnation is the model which should guide our thinking. Of course, something must be said on the other side about the danger of losing one's vision, of not appreciating the ways in which a community has changed, of creating dependence, or of becoming oneself dependent on the parish. But, in spite of the Paul Report, these are not the only problems.[33] There is a vast difference between the rootlessness of the mobile who have no commitment to a place, and the religious sense that 'we have here no continuing city'.

Sixthly, we need to reaffirm the notion of priesthood. Priesthood is not a matter of being an organiser, and it cannot be divorced from the priesthood of all believers in a congregation. Distribution of ministries within a local church is essential. But priests need to be 'walking sacraments',[34] men who must be what others may be, foci of responsible communities of faith, holy men who will enable others to be holy. If there can be found preachers, spiritual guides, teachers and counsellors within a congregation, well and good: the priest remains as celebrant of the Eucharist and confessor, a symbol of unity and reconciliation. There are wrong principles of order, based on class and power: that does not in any way detract from the need for holy order.

Seventhly, the Church must return to the idea of holiness. It is essential to the authenticity of our faith that Christians are seen as apprentices, souls on a journey. There should be something special about being a Christian for all to see. We need a return to the use of spiritual directors, and a rediscovery of the principles involved in such direction. But such holiness is inextricably related to the transformation of society. Struggle and contemplation belong together.

Finally, the task of the Church is apologetic, but that must never mean apologising. To each generation the gospel must be worked out anew, and the organised Church must be subservient to that task, not the other way round. If, because the Church is critical of the organised state, of the industrial machine, and of prevailing assumptions and attitudes, it becomes unpopular, so be it. Albert Camus once said that the world was waiting for the Church to stand by what it spoke of, to 'speak, speak up clearly, and pay up personally'. We need to take note.

References

1 Celia Green, *The Human Eunuch* (Hamish Hamilton, 1969), p 73.
2 Quoted in E R Norman, *Church and Society in England 1770–1970* (Oxford, 1971), p 221.
3 H Maynard Smith, *Frank Bishop of Zanzibar* (London, 1926), p 262, quoted in Norman, *op cit*, p 23.
4 F W Bussell, *The National Church and Social Crisis, or The Churchman's Attitude to Political Panaceas* (London, 1978), p 8, quoted in Norman, *op cit*, p 233.
5 A M Allchin, *The Silent Rebellion* (London, 1968), pp 57–62.
6 B R Wilson, *Religion in Secular Society* (Penguin, 1966), ch 1; Leslie Paul, *The Deployment and Payment of the Clergy* ('The Paul Report') (CIO, 1964, ch 1.
7 Quoted in Vincent Strudwick, 'Local Ordained Ministry: Yesterday's Case for Tomorrow's Church, *Theology*, May 1981, p 172ff.
8 cf *The Parish Communion*, ed A G Hebert (SPCK, 1937), Essay by W S Baker: 'The offertory procession' restores the act of offering to its true importance and marks it as the foundation of the whole eucharistic action', p 277. Opinion has moved since those heady days of that movement and there has been a reaction. However, on the charge of Pelagianism see F Hastings Smyth, *Manhood into God*, (Round Table Press, New York), pp 219–20. On the need for renewed thinking about the question see J L Houlden in *Thinking about the Eucharist* (Essays by members of the Archbishop's Commission on Christian Doctrine) (SCM, 1972), p 96: '. . how else can man come before God except in the attitude of sacrifice and with the intention to offer all? The question is, how ought this to be articulated in relation to the eucharist?'
9 cf the Intentions provided in the Ordo Missae.
10 (CIO, 1964), p 15.
11 *A Staircase for Silence*, (DLT, 1977), p 69.
12 *Now is the Time* (Collins, 1970), pp 41–3.
13 WCC, 1968.
14 *The Paul Report*, (CIO, 1964), p 15.
15 Alan Ecclestone, *op cit*, p 73.
16 Abbe Michonneau, *Revolution in a City Parish*, quoted in E W Southcott, *The Parish comes Alive* (Mowbray, 1956), p 19.
17 Southcott, *op cit*, pp 37–8.
18 *op cit*, p 60.
19 *op cit*, p 81.
20 *The Nottingham Statement* (Falcon, 1977), p 34.
21 Alistair V Campbell, *Rediscovering Pastoral Care* (DLT, 1981), p 5.
22 See, for instance, Kenneth Leech, *Soul Friend* (Sheldon, 1977).
23 *op cit*, p 45.

24 *The Bridges of God* (World Dominion, 1955) and *How Churches Grow* (New York, Friendship Press, 1959) were the first books on the subject; the most comprehensive is *Understanding Church Growth* (Eerdmans, Grand Rapids, Michigan, 1970).
25 David Wasdell, *Let My People Grow* (Urban Church Project Workpaper No 1, 1974).
26 *I believe in Church Growth* (Hodder and Stoughton, 1981), p 208; the book gives a history of the movement and is intended as a primer for parishes.
27 S S Acquaviva, *The Decline of the Sacred in Industrial Society* (Blackwell, 1979), p 137.
28 J Frejtag and K Ozaki, *Nominal Christianity: Studies of Church and People in Hamburg*, p 53.
29 *Church and Churchgoers* (OUP, 1978).
30 A M Farrer, *Love Almighty and Ills Unlimited* (Collins, 1962), p 127.
31 (DLT, 1970), p 327.
32 *Celebration of Awareness* (Penguin Education, 1973), ch 3. This book contains some of the most creative thinking about the future of the church.
33 *op cit*, p 173. It is one thing to move men who have begun to 'sit down on the job', quite another to move men merely to provide some kind of career structure. The result of that is to move 'good' men too often and to leave the mediocre where they are, a classic example of the working of the Peter principle.
34 A M Farrer, *A Celebration of Faith* (Hodder and Stoughton, 1970), p 108.

9 Anglo-Catholicism and the Women's Movement

Eleanor McLaughlin

> 'At first sight all the rationality . . . is on the side of the innovator. We have discovered in one profession after another that women can do very well all sorts of things which were once supposed to be in the power of men alone. No one among us who dislikes the proposal is maintaining that women are less capable than men of piety, zeal, learning, and whatever else seems necessary for the pastoral office. What then except prejudice begotten by tradition forbids us to draw on the huge reserves which would pour into the priesthood if women were here, as in so many other professions, put on the same footing as men? And against this flood of commonsense, the opposers (many of them women) can produce at first nothing but an inarticulate distaste, a sense of discomfort which they themselves find it hard to analyse.'[1]

I begin this essay on Anglo-Catholicism and the women's movement with this rather dated comment from C S Lewis because it raises issues which will be addressed here: rationality, changes in relation between the sexes, tradition, 'inarticulate distaste'. Also, Lewis' comment is personal, as will be these reflections. This essay will be personal because it was my Catholic faith and a vocation to the priesthood which gave impetus and focus to the historical research that lies behind what I have to say in summary here.

I write as a Yankee, that is an American born, raised and educated in Boston, but of working-class English immigrant parentage. An Anglican by birth, I became a Catholic Anglican by intellectual and spiritual attraction through the books in my foster-father's library. He is a priest, and the parish in which I grew up was typically Massachusetts 'Broad Church'. My Catholicism was deepened by my studies of mediaeval mysticism in the University and a long career as a professor of mediaeval church history. I may have more in common with fourteenth-century Anglican piety than with the Tractarians, whose nineteenth-century version of the middle ages I find wanting. You will not be presented here with an historical overview or theological analysis of Anglo-Catholicism as it took shape in the seventeenth or the nineteenth century or as it exists in a variety of forms in the United States today. Certainly I cannot address Anglo-Catholicism in Great Britain, for I am woefully ignorant of the English Church – I wish more English Church-people would admit that about us! Furthermore, good authorities tell me that Anglo-Catholicism in England is no longer a 'movement' unless it be defined in terms of what it fears! What I shall do is simply stated: a setting forth of the historical, spiritual, and theological reflections I went through to convince myself in the light of Scripture, Tradition, and Right Reason, that it is possible for a Catholic Anglican who is a woman to be a priest in Christ's Holy Catholic Church. This process was nothing more nor less than the results of the pressure of a vocation on my intellectual and spiritual integrity as a Catholic Christian. Further than this statement of mere possibility, I will suggest that it is necessary for Catholic Christianity to open its ordained ministry to women appropriately called and tested, as well as men, if Catholicity is to be preserved as a living and prophetic note of the Church. This argument is grounded in an analysis of modernity, not in its invitation, but in its threat to Catholicism. To meet that threat and challenge, only a change in the tradition can preserve Tradition.

The second partner in this dialogue is the women's movement. How difficult it is to give a British audience a just sense of what that means, theologically, sociologically, and for the psyche of the American people and the churches and synagogues of this vast and varied land. A few names, a few books and articles travel across the Atlantic, but from conversations with English visitors, I get the impression that only the outrageous is remarked. Perhaps this is because we Americans are expected to be true to our revolutionary beginnings. There are, to be sure, 'post-Christian' feminists, such as Mary Daly, but there is also, for example, a large Evangelical Woman's Caucus whose biblical orthodoxy is impeccable. Even more important is the vast majority of Christian women who simply feel empowered in their sense of themselves as made in the image of God as they see sisters on vestries, as delegates to General Convention, and above all, at the altar as Presider, Celebrant, Shepherd, and Preacher of the Word amidst the People of God.

Except for the very far left who reject all institutions, or turn to what they imagine to be ancient pagan female mysteries, [2] virtually all women within the Church found the ordination issue to be the key to the 'woman question'. The reason for this is a matter both of sensibility and, theology. The sensibility came to me suddenly one cold, rainy All Saints Day before the altar in a poor urban parish in Cambridge, Massachusetts where a deacon, a woman, presided at a deacon's mass. When she came to the Great Thanksgiving, she had to stop. She had been a deacon then five years, and had been a pastor ten years before that. I stared at the polychrome Christus Rex above the altar and fought down the question, if the Revd Elsa Walberg cannot be for me an image of the Great High Priest, how can either of us, or any woman, participate in the saving death of my Lord Jesus Christ? On that dark November morning, the ordination of women became a matter of my humanity and my salvation.

Theology historically confirms that sensibility, for the tradition has forbidden women ordination from the age of the Fathers on the grounds that the female sex is physiologically, and therefore morally and spiritually, deficient to the human norm, the male.[3] Only as a woman rose above her sex by heroic effort and grace, to become, as it were, a male, was the sanctity possible which Jerome admired in his learned Roman lady friends, vowed to virginity. The tradition of the all-male priesthood is not rooted and grounded in modern Jungian symbolic distinctions between anima and animus or the Vatican Declaration's claim that a woman is incapable of being a natural symbol of the priesthood of Jesus Christ. These are all innovations, modern post-Freudian arguments. The tradition rather assumes the unambiguous physiology of Aristotle, taken into Christian theology by the Fathers and canonised by Thomas Aquinas, that a woman is a defective human being.[4] This point has been amply demonstrated, yet it must be set in the foreground again and again, for it is what the women's movement is all about – not rights, claims, equality, liberation, a piece of the pie, but our common humanity and salvation. What Jesus Christ did not assume he cannot save. I come back to that All Saints' Day deacon's mass. If my sister is so 'other' that she cannot be a priest, then how can I in my 'otherness' be saved? This then is how I understand the Christian 'women's movement', an essentially spiritual yearning led primarily by women but not in its core a women's issue. It is a yearning for a recovered or even a discovered wholeness for women and men in which, perhaps for the first time in Christian history, we can experience and live out the promise of *Galatians* 3:28. By our Baptism we are made one, and taste, even here, that eschatological promise that in Christ and by faith 'There is neither Jew nor Greek, there is neither slave nor free, there is neither male nor female . . .'. This experience of grace promised to us as a pilgrim people does not mean the denial of all human difference, but it does mean the gradual overcoming of that difference, that otherness which understands all women to be daughters of Eve, the gateway of perdition, as Tertullian put it. This call to holiness or wholeness for men and women is thus nothing more nor less than the Catholic vision of sanctification by which the 'male sins' of pride and control and the 'female sins' of passivity and childish irresponsibility are gradually overcome as we move towards a redeemed humanity of strong and gentle women and feeling and effective men. The women's movement is a matter of reclaiming the whole range of human possibility for both women and men.

Now what has Anglo-Catholicism to do with this women's movement which I have defined initially in terms of an anthropology, a moral vision of human nature? It would seem at first that in its origins, the Oxford Movement, stood flat against the liberal currents of the Enlightenment which evoked the hope of renewed humanity without help of God or grace. It is therefore of utmost importance that this vision of a whole human being, capable of the full range of affect and action, whether male or female, women of strength and men of feeling, find its model in the perfect humanity of Jesus Christ and be thus freed of Enlightenment, rationalist and liberal dogmas. It is a Christian anthropology we seek, and that anthropology presupposes and reflects a theology, a doctrine of God. Because the Oxford Movement was a spiritual and a theological reformation as well as an ecclesiological one, it has a vital theological word to say to and with Christian women. That word is, that biology is not destiny and that in Christ, men and women share a common redeemed humanity. Obedience to God frees us from obedience to the slavery of sex-role stereotypes and for a genuine human mutuality. This is an important word, for obedience has been a difficult notion for Christian women, it has been so misused.

My outrageous suggestion is that the ordination of women can be a third Reformation which may enable the Church and specifically Anglo-Catholicism towards a fuller realisation of that sacramentality, the wedding of body and spirit which has been so central to Catholic spirituality from the beginning.

The underlying principles of Anglo-Catholicism as they emerged in the Oxford Movement could be reduced to the following: a respect for Tradition and history as preserver of Catholicity, a particular normativeness given to the first five centuries of the Church, a concern to recover the autonomy and sanctity of the Church over against the world, especially the state and secular society, a respect for ecclesial authority as an expression of the divine nature of the Church. Perhaps encompassing all this was a renewal of spirituality and lived holiness which was expressed through a recovery of sacramentality. Not simply the restoration of eucharistic worship and daily masses, but a sacramental sensibility was rediscovered which included the adoration of God in the beauty of holiness expressed through the physical forms of movement in liturgy and procession, music, incense and splendid art and architecture.[5] The Oxford Movement and its revival of Anglo-Catholicism was an aspect of the larger Romantic reaction against Enlightenment reductionism: in religion, Deism, in ethics, utilitarianism, and in epistemology, positivism, However, I would assert that the reformation which was the Oxford Movement never went far enough, because it failed to recover that aspect of Catholicism which in the pre-Reformation church had been born and carried by women. It failed to recover the full embodied realities symbolled forth by Mary, Mother Jesus, Mother Church. The Oxford Movement and Anglo-Catholicism failed to recover the full catholicity of Anglicanism because it remained resolutely patriarchal, male, androcentric, spiritualised in a narrow even prudish Victorian mode. Anglo-Catholicism to this day is weakened and distracted by this faintly aesthetic, disembodied nineteenth-century gentlemanly manner. At its core lies a body/soul dualism freed of the earthy incarnationalism of mediaeval popular piety. Above all, the Oxford Movement failed to go far enough in its redressing of the losses to English Calvinist Puritanism.

Let me flesh out this argument. Mediaeval Christianity, especially in its piety, was truly incarnational, making Chalcedon real in a way that the vaguely Platonising Church Fathers never dreamed of. The humanity of Jesus from the 12th century onwards became a focus of a piety of desire. Especially the suffering and crucified sacred humanity of Jesus Christ carried and evoked a spirituality of compassion giving expression to the whole gamut of human emotions. Devotion to the Five Sacred Wounds and the wounded side of Jesus elicited metaphors in the poetry and handbooks of devotion of the womb of God and the breasts of Jesus which nourish with water and blood in the sacraments of baptism and eucharist. This piety demonstrates how wide and deep was the experience of the 'motherhood of Jesus', who gives birth to a redeemed creation on the labour bed of the Cross.[6] The motherhood of God was not a mere fringe devotion found in the writings of, for example, St Clement of Alexandria, St Anselm, Aelred of Rievaulx, and most extensively in the Revelations of Dame Julian of Norwich. The perception that 'God is as truly our mother as he is our father', as Julian wrote, was a deeply felt if not always wholly explicit ground tone of much of mediaeval affective spirituality, having its roots in scripture as well as the Fathers.[7] This rich mixture of female and male imagery and language for the experience of Transcendence was expressed also in the nuptial piety of mediaeval mysticism which called a serious Christian, male and female, to the kiss of the mouth of God, the bridal chamber of union between the soul (feminine) and the Bridegroom Christ. Whether male or female imagery was employed of God or Jesus, the invitation was to intimacy, a homely and loving relationship of love with Jesus our brother, mother, bridegroom, saviour, and child whom we, like Mary, bear into the world.

This, for us, startling mixture of male and female imagery for God and our relationships with God in Jesus Christ was enhanced by the depth of popular and learned devotion to the Blessed Virgin Mary, Queen of Heaven and Mother of God. Not to be forgotten also were the many popular devotions to other female saints, especially that of Mary Magdalene, penitent, mourner at Christ's tomb, joyful first witness to the resurrection, and apostle to the Apostles. The many faces of God were reflected in the many embodiments of holiness, the saints. Not bishops, priests and popes but saints were the real leaders of the mediaeval church. There in the ranks of the holy ones women stood beside men as Lioba with Boniface, apostles to the Germans, of Catherine of Siena, stern pastor to Pope Urban VI, or Christina of the Markyate, giving spiritual direction to her archbishop. The remarkable fact is not so much that of abbesses carrying magisterial authority which many women have been so excited to discover,[8] but the fact of a society in which that which counted was not magisterium so much as holiness. Women and men were publically and institutionally on the same footing with respect to holiness in the Pre-Reformation church. What happens when the models of popular devotion shift in the sixteenth century from Saints' Lives to Lives of Preachers? All of a sudden no women are present! So in the recently revised calendar of the American Episcopal Church no woman is commemorated who lived after the fifteenth century. Curious.

Finally, this imaging of God which was feminine as well as masculine in the Pre-Reformation church, and of the incarnated image of God in the saints, had its impact on how men and women thought and felt and perceived themselves as human beings. What we not refer to as 'feminine' virtues, traits, modes, were not as today privatised and assigned to biological females. The cultivation of the 'gift of tears' was a spirituality addressed to both sexes, and monks and friars were called by their abbots and superiors to be mothers and nurturers. Religious women, despite the world's disapproval, acted with force and power, emboldened by their full 'manhood' in Christ.[9] The equivalence of women and men was secure and institutionalised in the piety so rich in female and male images of the holy and in the public structures of the religious life, the nursery of holiness.

It is not too much to claim that most of this spirituality was lost to the Protestant Reformation and what was left, as in the poetry and works of devotion of the Caroline Divines, fell victim to the cold swift winds of the Enlightenment. The theology and philosophy which justified female subordination and an understanding of human nature as normatively male inherited from patristic and mediaeval authorities survived the Reformation virtually unscathed. A Protestant authority has remarked that one of Calvin's signal contributions to Christian theology was the recovery of the Fatherhood of God after its long eclipse under the 'perversions' of mediaeval Catholic piety.[10] Indeed, the Fatherhood of God was celebrated in

Puritan piety and in the new sacralisation of the family, the 'little Commonwealth', where the father presided over religious nurture and instruction. The vocation of vowed virginity, with its symbolisation of transcendence, was lost to Protestant women. Women would serve God now as wives and mothers in accord with their biological destiny.

Alongside this sociological revolution, the substitution of the natural family for the religious life as the focus of spiritual nurture, was a theological shift in which was lost the Catholic balance between God's love and judgment, pity and majesty. So also the Catholic spirituality of desire and union bestowed in sacrament and acts of devotion faded before a spirituality of justification by faith alone, unmediated amongst the left wing of the Reformation such as the Quakers, or mediated by the bare Word, stripped of sacrament or icon in the rational Zwinglian liturgies of English Calvinism. The God of Puritanism, although not necessarily so intended by John Calvin, felt something like the enlightened absolute monarchs of Early Modern Europe in his transcendent, predestining majesty and otherness. The 'motherhood of God', of the Blessed Virgin, of the Church was lost to a faith which was balanced away from nurture and immanence towards the less sensual and more rational didacticism of much Puritan worship and confident display of God's acceptance in the often profitable work of a Christian vocation in the world. The loss of the feminine was a concomitant of this shift in an understanding of God and how God relates to His creatures, most especially in the loss of a sacramental world view and the physicality of the devotions which embody a sacramental religion. It is not simply that the Blessed Mother, St Catherine and St Brigette and St Frideswide, as well as all the religious orders, are gone. Far more serious for the integrity of an incarnational Catholic Christianity is the virtual denial of God's use of the physical creation to convey grace and the Transcendent. The disappearance of the feminine from the realm of the holy was the sign and result of this 'reformation', the attack on physicality in worship as 'vain superstition'.[11]

The Enlightenment completed, or was even in part an effect, of this theological revolution as it moved in its theory of knowledge from the nominalism which shaped the Protestant Reformers to the rationalism and empiricism of seventeenth- and eighteenth-century science and philosophy. These gave no place for truth claims to a sacramental world view. Symbol and metaphor, the language of liturgical action and poetry and feeling, were the language of women and children, not of the world of men, science and politics. It is natural that the Tractarians, unconsciously resisting this privatisation and even feminisation of Catholic religion, would attempt to reclaim Catholic epistemologies and sacramentality in a virile and robust fashion, for now the real world has been defined as the world of men, separate from the domestic feeling world of pious women.[12]

What had been held together in mediaeval Catholicism, faith, and reason, feeling and logic, female and male images for the divine – see, for a glorious example, the prayers of St Anselm[13] – had by the nineteenth century fallen almost wholly apart.

My argument, if you have followed this shorthand of historical analysis without much of the documentation I could bring to support it, is simple. Like my Tractarian ancestors, I am fundamentally hostile to certain aspects of modernity and its now discredited Liberal philosophical underpinnings. Specifically, the inadequacy of post-enlightenment theories of knowledge which, in their sharp dichotomy of subject and object, undercut a way of knowing and being that reflects the true nature of reality as sacramental and co-inherent, known by the 'second naivety' of intuition or participation that a few men and many women have been able to cultivate in the face of modern educational assumptions.[14] To preach the Catholic faith, to hold to Catholic tradition today, without recognising that we speak and act out in worship a language which the modern world is hardly equipped to understand, is a fundamental misjudgment of our task as Christian evangelists. It is within this almost desperate sense of the gap between modernity, its notion of reality, and how we as Catholic Christians know reality, that I come back to the women's movement and the ordination of women. Like the Tractarians, I yearn for a renewed celebration and living out of the Catholicity of Anglicanism. This means a recovery of sacramentality, a building up of fully eucharistic communities and an ideal of eucharistic living as a basic paradigm of Christian spirituality. It means a recovery of the Church's sense of herself as a called community distinct from but servant in the world. It means a renewal of the priesthood, turning aside from the false God of professionalism to embrace once again a genuine vision of priest as *alter Christus*, as Archbishop Ramsey expressed it, 'with God, with the people on your heart'. Such a priest is a clown for Christ, always on the fringe, identified with the outcast, taking one's power and authority from the centre, the altar, where we are reborn and remade and transformed into God's own life and Body, repeatedly, joyfully, and without fail. This revival of Catholicity means a renewal of authority and the Christian's sense of the authority of the Church and her own Spirit-based stance against the principalities and powers. From this renewed sense of the authority of Christian witness grounded in Scripture, Tradition, and Right Reason will come a strong and compassionate moral witness to the world in those areas of human life to which the Church has all too feebly spoken – disarmament, abortion, hunger, family violence, and the driving racism and poverty on which our capitalist system thrives. Most encompassing, if the Catholic Tradition is to speak again with power and clarity to our world, it must overcome that crippling dualism inherited from our Christian past which has so often led us into a false religiosity and spiritualism or a false sensuality and worldliness.

Why, you ask, do we have to ordain women to the priesthood to get on with this, the Lord's business? Is not this 'women question' but a distraction from the pressing tasks of Catholic renewal? The answer is simply no, for this renewal is dependent upon a conscious challenge to the epistemology and institutions of modernity which carry this destructive dualism between mind and feeling, body and soul, public and private, rational and intuitive, male and female. This dualism which afflicts all our endeavours has been given the high priestly sanction of the sciences and engrained social habit. Women alone cannot overcome this dualism, nor, for example, save the priesthood from professionalism, although, given the socialisation process, they have a better chance than men. But men and women together can begin that process of resacralising, resymbolising our world, overcoming false dichotomies and living out an ideal of human wholeness/holiness in community, starting with the church. In the middle ages the reality of God's love, mercy, infinite acceptance and righteous judgment, was symbolised by the Mother of God, by Mary Magdalene or John the Beloved Disciple resting on our Lord's bosom, or Peter, ever failing and ever forgiven. Our Catholic pre-Reformation sisters and brothers experienced Jesus in a way that elicited maternal as well as feudal or spousal imagery. All of this was institutionalised by men and women in the religious life which dominated the spiritual, intellectual, cultural, and even political life of an entire civilisation. Today we cannot revive these old forms of devotion or their institutional embodiment to lead us back to that integration of spirit and flesh, mind and feeling which we so need. What we are able to do is to celebrate the central mystery of our faith at a table presided over by women as well as men. It seems a little thing for so vast a task.

I return to C S Lewis. It is not rationality or a freedom from prejudice which calls for the ordination of women. It is precisely that part of him and me and all of you which is inarticulate and which tastes. My experience as a priest now in an Anglo-Catholic parish for two years, and that of my sisters and brothers in the community, is that God is more completely, more fully tasted, and that those Christians who worship where women preside as well as men know themselves more completely as whole people. Their feeling and rational selves, their embodiment in relation to their spirits, their imaged being in God, is touched and enabled as never before. A priest at the altar who is a woman brings back to life the Tradition in its fullness, a loss sustained at the Reformation and deepened by modern rationalism is overcome. What more can I say to my British brothers and sisters in the Faith? 'O taste and see . . .'

References

1 C S Lewis, *Undeceptions*, p 192, cited in M Bruce and G E Duffield, *Why Not? Priesthood and the Ministry of Women* (Marcham Manor Press, Appleford, Abingdon, Berks, 1972), p 6.

2 A broad range of views can be found in C P Christ and J Plaskow, *Womanspirit Rising, A Feminist Reader in Religion* (Harper and Row, 1979).

3 Thomas Aquinas, *Summa Theologica* I 92 1 ad 1: 'Women is said to be a misbegotten male, as being a product outside the purpose of nature considered in the individual case . . .'.

4 For a discussion of this tradition in the Fathers and in the Middle Ages, see articles by R R Ruether and E McLaughlin in R R Ruether (ed), *Religion and Sexism* (Simon and Schuster, New York, 1974).

5 I found no recent book on the Oxford Movement as enlightening as the old essay by Christopher Dawson, *The Spirit of the Oxford Movement* (Sheed and Ward, 1933).

6 I have shown the relationship between devotion to the wounds of Christ, the Sacred Heart, and the nourishing images of the motherhood of Jesus in the Kellogg Lectures given at the Episcopal Divinity School, Massachusetts, February 1978, unpublished.

7 E McLaughlin, 'Christ my Mother, feminine naming and metaphor in mediaeval spirituality', *Nashotah Review* 15 (1975); C W Bynum, *Jesus as Mother, Studies in the Spirituality of the High Middle Ages* (University of California, Berkeley, 1982).

8 Joan Morris, *The Lady Was A Bishop* (New York, 1973).

9 E McLaughlin, 'Women, Power and the Pursuit of Holiness in Mediaeval Christianity' in R Ruether and E McLaughlin, *Women of Spirit* (Simon and Schuster, New York, 1979), pp 100–30.

10 G Nuttall, *The Holy Spirit in Puritan Faith and Experience* (Oxford, 1946), p 63.

11 I have developed this thesis in some detail in the Kellogg Lectures: see above, n 6.

12 See the important discussion of the feminisation of Liberal religion in the United States in Ann Douglas, *The Feminisation of American Culture* (Knopff, New York, 1977).

13 *The Prayers and Meditations of St Anselm*, trans Benedicta Ward, SLG, (Penguin, 1973), p 155: 'Christ my mother, you gather your chickens under your wings . . .'.

14 See the work of Owen Barfield, *Saving the Appearances* (Harcourt, Brace and World, New York, n d).

10 Priesthood and Prophecy: the development of Anglo-Catholic socialism

John Orens

For years *The Rock*, the most ferocious organ of the Evangelical party in the Church of England, had denounced Anglo-Catholic doctrine and worship. But in the spring of 1883 its editors expressed special alarm at 'an alliance utterly inexplicable between the Ritualists and the Revolutionists ... If insurrection should break out in England', they warned, 'it will be due, and largely indeed, to the clerical and other firebrands . . . who are seeking to propagate what they call Christian Socialism'.[1] *The Rock* was not alone in expressing amazement and dismay. Up to our own day few aspects of the Catholic revival in the Church of England have been more controversial than the persistent claim of Christian Socialists that they are the rightful heirs of the Oxford Movement. There is certainly much about Christian Socialism which would have appalled the Tractarians. No comfort for apostles of social change can be found in John Henry Newman's excoriation of 'latitudinarianism, indifferentism, republicanism, and schism', or in John Keble's observation that 'the poor good man . . . need not be mindful of this country from which he is soon to go out, inasmuch as God has prepared for him a better country, that is a heavenly.'[2] Yet the links between the Tractarian and the radicals who called themselves their disciples are real and form a legacy which the Church can ill afford to neglect.

To grasp this point, it is necessary to understand the perilous condition of the English Church on the eve of Keble's historic Assize sermon. Although the Anglican Establishment was not without devoted servants, the 'prevailing religion', in Lord Melbourne's words, was 'cool and indifferent'.[3] Nepotism, pluralism, and simony were rampant. The average incumbent, complained the Baron d'Haussez, 'is one who hoards his emoluments in order to settle his children; who spends his fortune in wagering, in horses, in dogs, sometimes (when he is thoughtless and devoid of foresight) with a mistress . . .'. As for the poor, d'Haussez lamented, they are ignored by their pastor. Their care instead is given over 'to some miserable curate, who for a miserable stipend is obliged to exhibit the virtues and fulfil the duties which his incumbent despises and neglects'.[4] Even the most dedicated clergyman, Dean Church later recalled, was likely to be little more than 'a kindly and respectable person'.[5]

Particularly indicative of the sorry state of the Anglican Establishment was the growing popularity of pew rents which forced the poor to the back of the church, and sometimes out of the church altogether. In the rapidly growing industrial towns the problem was compounded by the absence of even a fraction of the churches needed to serve the working classes.[6] Indeed, one of the most striking characteristics of the early Victorian Church was its attitude towards the poor: a mixture of indifference, fear, and contempt. Social equality had never been an article of the Anglican creed. But it had been axiomatic that the rich have an obligation to look after the needs of their less fortunate neighbours. To say, as Keble did, that 'God has divided the world into rich and poor that there might be the more exercise of charity and patience', was to insist on the sacred and mutual obligations between the social classes.[7]

By 1833 this assumption was being challenged by the new doctrine of individual responsibility taught by political economists and utilitarian philosophers. Poverty, it was now argued, is the result of laziness and improvidence. Along with this harsher view of the poor came a startling reversal in moral theology. Selfishness and greed, hitherto regarded as sins, were now defended as essential aspects of human nature. The contest for riches, wrote Archbishop Sumner, is a boon to the State because it makes citizens more active.[8] Cruder but more direct was the advice of the *Evangelical Magazine*: 'Religion promotes industry, industry gains respect, respect gains recommendation, recommendation gains business, business gains wealth, and thus religion itself naturally leads to prosperity'.[9] Far from offering the Church a true vision of its mission, the apostles of the new wisdom threatened to drive the poor from its doors. How far the clerical disciples of political economy were willing to go is strikingly illustrated by Richard Whately's suggestion to the Poor Law Enquiry Commission 'that all paupers should be tatooed on the foot or some other place' so as to deter them from begging or seeking additional relief. 'Any female receiving relief', the Archbishop of Dublin continued, 'should have her hair cut off' ... 'A good head of hair,' he went to the trouble of calculating, 'will fetch from 5s to 10s, which would be perhaps a fortnights's maintenance.'[10]

To be sure, there were Anglicans who challenged this new and unholy orthodoxy. Prominent among them were Evangelicals who, faithful to the reforming spirit of the eighteenth-century revival, railed against the exploitation of the poor. The factory system, Charlotte Elizabeth Tonna exclaimed, is 'one of the worst and cruellest things ever invented to pamper the rich at the expense of the poor'. A few critics were perceptive enough to realise that there was something inherently wrong about the society growing up around them. Drawing back from a wholesale denunciation of capitalism, Lord Shaftesbury nevertheless declared unhesitatingly that its intellectual justification, political economy, was 'the rubbish of an atheist system'. But although the Evangelicals helped awaken the nation's conscience, they were unable to offer a coherent programme of radical reform to the State, or a theological foundation for social mission to the Church. With their belief in human depravity, they found it difficult to hope for justice on earth. To this fatalism was wedded a theological individualism which compelled them to regard salvation as something offered to men and women one by one.[11] Moreover, Evangelicals were unable to attack the root of so many of the Church's ills: its subservience to the State and the upper classes. Distressed though Shaftesbury and others were by clerical snobbery, they had little conception of the Church as a divine institution. The renewal of the Church, like the renewal of the nation, was a matter of individual conversion. Radical social criticism would have to come from elsewhere.

That it would come from the ranks of the High Church party, Tory in politics and rooted in the rural gentry, seemed equally unlikely. This is not to say that High Churchmen were unmoved by the suffering around them. Their very devotion to a dying social order made them perceptive critics of the new. Like their Evangelical counterparts, High Church critics were convinced that the new gospel of individualism and utilitarianism was profoundly anti-Christian. Modern liberalism, argued Samuel Wilberforce, is 'the Devil's creed, a heartless steam-engine, un-Christian, low . . . utilitarian creed . . . '. In pursuit of 'such miserable comforts as going very fast through the air on a railroad', he warned, liberalism is prepared to 'overturn the Church . . . and worship the very devil if his horns were gold and his tail was a steam engine'.[12] But although they were unencumbered by a Calvinistic fatalism, as were Evangelicals, High Churchmen shied away from the implications of their own criticism. They challenged neither the subordination of the Church to the State nor the secular view of the priesthood as a genteel profession. It was left to the Oxford Movement to shatter these old assumptions and, in so doing, to set the stage for even more radical criticism.

The Oxford Movement began to protest against liberalism. Both Evangelicals and High Churchmen had already denounced the worship of self and wealth enshrined by political economists and utilitarian philosophers. But the Tractarians went still further, attacking as liberalism's most dangerous fruit Erastianism and its corollary: the degradation of the ordained ministry. Undoubtedly there was an element of political expediency in this concern, coming as it did on the heels of Roman Catholic emancipation and the passage of the Reform Act. But from the beginning there was a new tone in the Tractarians' appeals: at once rebellious and penitential. 'I do believe we are corrupt in gain, far more than we know it – and need very awful chastenings,' lamented Newman.[13] The time is coming, Keble warned in his sermon on national apostasy, when the Church will be 'forsaken, degraded, nay trampled upon by the State and people of England'.[14] Shorn of worldly authority, the Church will be compelled to rely not on the rich but on Christ. In the first of the *Tracts for the Times*, Newman struck an even more sombre note. Bleak though it would be for the country, he wrote, 'we could not wish [the bishops] a more blessed termination of their course than the spoiling of their goods and martyrdom'.[15] 'In truth,' he declared later, 'we have had enough ... of mere political religion; which, like a broken reed, has pierced through the hand that leaned upon it.'[16]

To the Tractarians everything hinged on the Church's authority. 'Are we content to be accounted the mere creatures of the State . . . ?' Newman asked. 'Did the State make us?' The questions did not end here. Their new sense of spiritual authority led the Tractarians to challenge the Church's worldly complacency towards the poor. The clergy have been quick to chastise the destitute for their sins, Newman observed acidly, while ignoring those of the rich and powerful. In the first of his contributions to the *Tracts*, Dr Pusey asked wealthy Anglicans to 'only trace out one single item in the mass of human wretchedness, disease, insanity, religious ignorance, and picture to themselves what a Christian people might do, what the primitive Christians would have done, to relieve it . . .'[17] The connection between apostolic authority and caring for the poor was made most tellingly by Henry Manning. By what right, he asked, dared he even enter the homes of the poor? Surely it was not because he was wealthy or well-born. The only answer, he came to realise, was that he was 'a messenger sent from God'.[18]

This was condescending, to be sure. But at times the Tractarians saw more deeply. There is no justification, Hurrell Froude insisted, for the 'gentleman heresy': the odious notion that the priesthood is an occupation for the respectable classes. On the contrary, it is the poor upon whom the Church's survival depends. 'We will have a *vocabularium apostolicum,'* he wrote angrily, 'and I will start with four words: "pampered aristocrats," "resident gentlemen," "smug persons," and "*pauperes Christi*." '[19] More daring still was W G Ward's *The Ideal of a Christian Church*. In this controversial book, remembered today largely for its Roman sympathies, Ward excoriated the Anglican Establishment for its indifference to the plight of the poor. A pure Church, he wrote, 'would with eager and urgent zeal have pleaded, clamoured, threatened in the workers' behalf'. In words which must have scandalised his readers, Ward declared that the Church ought to be 'the poor man's court of justice', just as 'her ordinary condition [should be] one of opposition to those in worldly status'.[20]

The depth of the Tractarians' concern is evident in Pusey's appeal for slum missions. In words startlingly similar to those Percy Widdrington would use more than a half-century later, Pusey wrote that mission priests must 'grapple with our manufacturing system as the Apostles did with the slave system of the ancient world . . . if by God's grace we would wrest from the principalities and powers of evil those portions of his kingdom, of which, while unregarded by the Church, they have been taking full possession'.[21] In this struggle no one can stand aside. 'The cry of the poor reacheth the ear of God . . .,' Pusey warned elsewhere. 'Woe to the man whom the poor shall implead at the Judgment-Seat of Christ. Woe to him, for whom they do not plead.'[22]

These condemnations of injustice were complemented by a leniency toward the foibles of working-class life which shocked most respectable Christians. Moderate drinking, dancing, and card-playing – the objects of Evangelical wrath – were sanctioned by the usually rigorist Apostolicals. John Keble encouraged Sunday evening games at Hursley and abandoned them only after his well-to-do parishioners protested. The audacity of wealthy pietists who rebuked the poor for dancing but saw nothing wrong in decking themselves out in luxurious clothes appalled the Tractarians. During the cholera epidemic of 1831, Newman complained about the 'very presumptuous and hard-hearted' attitude of the rich toward poor drunkards. Temperance advocates, he noted bitterly, 'are puffed up by their sense of superior decency, illumination, etc'.[23]

Some of this leniency reflects the tolerant attitude of the old High Church party. But the Tractarians' incarnational theology played an important part as well. Although the gloominess of Evangelical religion has been exaggerated, by placing the Fall and the Atonement at the centre of their theology Evangelicals were almost inevitably led to be suspicious of pleasure, however innocent, and to emphasise release from the world rather than the world's redemption. The Tractarians, on the other hand, insisted that through incorporation into Christ humanity has been raised to a new dignity. The world itself, they believed, has a sacramental quality.[24]

This was one of the principal points of Pusey's tract on baptism. 'Baptismal Regeneration as connected with the Incarnation of our blessed Lord,' he wrote, 'gives a depth to our Christian existence, an actualness to our union with Christ, a reality to our sonship to God . . . a joyousness amid the subduing of the flesh, an overwhelmingness to the dignity conferred on human nature . . . that to those who retain this truth, the school which abandoned it must needs appear to have sold its birthright.' Pusey never fully understood the social implications of what he said. But at least one of his critics may have stumbled upon them. If baptism can convey grace, asked an angry Evangelical, why not give communion to infants and the unconscious? 'Why not to idiots?'[25] What the Tractarians did see is that a right understanding of the incarnation makes the Evangelical conception of the Church as a society of redeemed individuals untenable. Both grace and salvation, Newman noted, are social. 'The body is not made up of individual Christians,' he wrote, 'but each Christian has been made such in his turn by being taken into the body.'[26]

The most impressive statement of this theology is Robert Isaac Wilberforce's *The Doctrine of the Incarnation of Our Lord Jesus Christ*. Like F D Maurice, Wilberforce argued that the meaning of the incarnation is not that God became man, but rather that He became *the* man, the representative and head of our race, thereby establishing a permanent bond between Himself and humanity. The Church, far from being the ark of the saved, is the means whereby Christ's gifts are extended to the whole race.[27] How this understanding of the incarnation changes our understanding of the poor was drawn out in a remarkable sermon by Pusey. God, he told his congregation, has made the poor 'the visible representatives to the rich of his Only Begotten Son, who, "being rich", for us men and for our salvation, "became poor", who, in *their* earthly lot, exalted our human nature to the union with his divine, gave to it its true surpassing dignity, and now vouchsafes to unite to himself all human miseries, except sin . . .'. The hands of the poor are the hands of Christ. 'You would not knowingly deck your walls with pictures,' Pusey observed grimly, 'while man, the image of God and the representative of Christ, you clothe not; you would not knowingly multiply delicacies upon yourselves, while men, like yourselves, members of Christ, and Christ in them, is an hungered.'[28]

The Tractarians dreamed of a popular Catholic revival which would drive away Erastianism, Protestantism, liberalism, and 'all erroneous and strange doctrine contrary to God's word'. In place of the comfortable Establishment there would stand the Bride of Christ, the haven of the poor and lowly. But their efforts went unnoticed by the great mass of the English people. The Oxford scholars conducted no campaigns to evangelise the poor, nor did they look with favour on the nascent democratic and socialist movements. For all their theological daring and sympathy for the poor, the Tractarians shared the common belief that the gulf between rich and poor could be bridged only by charity. Legislation against the worst abuses of the factory system was all well and good, but for the Tractarians, as for the Evangelicals, an end to suffering lay beyond the grave. Even the joys of Heaven were not assured. The unregenerate, the Oxford Movement taught, are doomed to everlasting damnation.

The one High Church theologian who recognised the full extent of the crisis facing the Church was Frederick Denison Maurice. Soon, he warned in 1853, the established order in both Church and State will hear the awful cry: 'Cut it down. Why cumbreth it the ground?'. No amount of careful theologising or Sabbatarian piety can avert the sentence. Only 'earnest repentance for the sins individual and national, for the sins of the people and the sins of the priest, which have kept us from feeling for one another and caring for one another, which have made our rest godless, and our work godless', offers hope for peace. Indeed, he wrote, it is only by such repentance that 'all the blessed testimonies of Scripture concerning the Son of man and the Son of God' can be understood.[29] Like the Tractarians, whose early stirrings he had supported, Maurice insisted that the Church must recover its faith. But whereas the Tractarians were reluctant to follow where their theology led, Maurice dug down to the foundations of the Catholic faith, convinced that belief and justice are inextricably bound together.

Maurice began, as did the Tractarians, with the doctrine of the Incarnation. Long before Robert Wilberforce, Maurice had argued that the significance of the Incarnation is that God became not merely a man, but Man. In so doing, He joined the whole race to Himself. Where the Tractarians erred, he believed, was in not taking this glorification of human nature seriously enough. It was Pusey's tract on baptism which most pained him. Maurice had no difficulty with Pusey's almost ecstatic language about baptismal regeneration. What alarmed him was Pusey's suggestion that the bond between God and His children can be severed by post-baptismal sin, and the effect of this teaching on the poor. 'Where is the minister of Christ in London, Birmingham, or Manchester, whom such a doctrine, heartily and inwardly maintained, would not drive to madness?' he asked. What gospel can he preach? 'Of all the thousands whom he addresses, he cannot venture to believe that there are ten who, in Dr Pusey's sense, retain their baptismal purity. All he can do,' Maurice noted bitterly, '. . . is to tell wretched creatures, who spend eighteen hours out of twenty-four in close factories and bitter toil . . . that if they spent the remaining six in prayer – he need not add fasting – they may possibly be saved. How can we insult God and torment man with such mockery'?[30]

Maurice maintained forcefully that both rich and poor share in the common redemption of humanity. Christ, he wrote, did not die and rise again 'to give a few proud Philosophers or . . . ascetical Pharisees some high notions about the powers of the soul and the meanness of the body'. No, Christ 'entered into the state of the lowest beggar, of the poorest, stupidest, wickedest wretch whom that Philosopher or that Pharisee can trample upon', in order that He might 'redeem the humanity which Philosophers,

Pharisees, beggars, and harlots share together'.[31] It was this deep and consistent incarnationalism which underlay Maurice's social theology. Convinced that human beings, created in the image of the triune God and knit together in Christ, are members one of another, Maurice insisted that our life with God cannot be considered apart from our relations with our neighbours. Our family life, our politics, our economics are all sacred. It is impossible, he argued, to lead a Christian life apart from the divine society which God has ordained for the human race.[32]

To be sure, Maurice proved to be one of the most cautious members of the Christian Socialist circle which began to meet in 1848. But to concentrate on his political timidity is to miss the theological revolution which he began. Not only did he deepen the incarnational and sacramental theology of the High Church school; to it he joined the doctrine of the Kingdom of God. It was this, more than anything else, which transformed what had been a conservative faith into a potentially revolutionary one. The Kingdom of God, Maurice taught, is not a ghostly place reserved for the elect after death. It is an already present reality destined to supplant the kingdoms of this world and to be enjoyed by the whole human race. The task of the Church, therefore, is to proclaim the divine order against which all societies are to be judged. Thus Maurice could insist, as the Tractarians could not, that 'a true socialism is the necessary result of a social Christianity'.[33]

By 1850, when Maurice made this startling pronouncement, the Evangelical passion for social reform had been largely exhausted. The Broad Church party as well was unable to repudiate Erastianism or to develop its own social theology. Christian Socialists and Anglo-Catholics alone seemed capable of challenging the comfortable indifference of the Anglican Establishment. Sharing, as they did, a common theological heritage, it is not surprising that members of the two movements – particularly Charles Kingsley and John Malcolm Ludlow among the Christian Socialists, and Henry Manning among the Tractarians – made tentative efforts to draw closer together.[34] But their hopes were premature and came to naught. Maurice regarded the Anglo-Catholic understanding of post-baptismal sin and belief in everlasting damnation as anathema. Anglo-Catholics, for their part, regarded Maurice as woolly-minded and even heretical. So irreconcilable were their views on everlasting damnation that both Maurice and Pusey concluded that they worshipped different Gods.[35] Yet despite these differences, some members of the most advanced party of Anglo-Catholics – the ritualists – soon found themselves echoing Christian Socialist positions.

Contrary to legend, by the 1860s, many ritualists had found comfortable livings.[36] But others, driven by their sense of priestly vocation, took positions in the neglected slum parishes of the great industrial cities. They were pastors, not politicians, and their principal goal, like that of the early Evangelicals, was to bring the masses to Christ. But, like the Evangelicals before them, they were compelled to protest against the exploitation of their parishioners by slum-lords and sweatshop owners. The persecution which they suffered at the hands of Protestant mobs and their own bishops only increased the ritualists' radicalism. Their anger, it is true, was often aroused by disputes over ceremonial minutiae. But the ritualists were convinced that liturgy and social justice were somehow related. In this they were strongly supported by their parishioners. When A H Mackonochie was suspended from his duties at St Alban's Holborn, a protest delegation told Archbishop Tait that ritualism was 'a working-man's question'. 'When the working classes . . . become aware of the way in which their heritage in Church matters is being attacked', the startled prelate was warned, 'they will rise up, and the Church of England, as an established Church, will fall.'[37]

Mackonochie himself identified his enemies as 'the Bishops and the Upper Middle Classes in Church and State. In fact the Chief Priests with the Scribes and Pharisees'.[38] Among the new religious orders for women there was a similar insistence that the Catholic cause was also the cause of the poor. 'I feel,' wrote Mother Emily Ayckbown, the foundress of the Community of the Sisters of the Church, 'as if I could pray God to raise up some prophet among us, to enter ... warm and scented drawing-rooms, crying Woe! Woe! to such as sit unconcerned while the poor die in body and souls around them.'[39] More radical still was Arthur Stanton, Mackonochie's curate, who described himself as 'politically socialistic, in faith papistical, in Church policy a thorough-going Nonconformist'.[40]

Anglo-Catholicism was taking on a new and even revolutionary cast. But with a few exceptions, the slum ritualists still eschewed politics and held themselves aloof from both Christian Socialists and the secular Left. Before they could embrace political radicalism, their theology needed to be reformulated in the light of Maurice's broad incarnationalism and prophetic understanding of the Kingdom. It was this task which was undertaken by Stewart Headlam, the father of the modern Christian Socialist movement. Headlam was a thorough-going Maurician. His explanation of baptismal regeneration, his belief that the Incarnation hallows every human faculty and concern, and his insistence that the Kingdom of God is to come on earth, all bear the mark of Maurice's teaching.[41] Indeed, it was only 'from an earnest desire to apply [Maurice's] principles and teachings to our times', Headlam wrote in 1878, 'that I have reached conclusions which some will regard as sacerdotal'.[42] But although he revered Maurice, Headlam clearly believed that his master's theology was incomplete.

If the Incarnation is the foundation of theology, and the union between

God and humanity in Christ is the first principle of Christian anthropology, he argued, there can be no peace with those who deny these truths. Unlike Maurice, who sought to embrace both Protestantism and Catholicism, Headlam insisted that Catholic theology alone is consistent with Christian humanism. Similarly, Headlam was far more outspoken about the centrality of the Eucharist than Maurice had been. The Eucharist, he argued, shows forth the just and loving God who took our flesh upon Himself, thereby uniting the world to Himself. Thus, the Mass is both a social sacrament and a witness against the Manicheanism which Maurice had so vigorously denounced. With this insistence on the importance of Catholic faith and worship there came a heightened emphasis on the necessity of right doctrine. Although sympathetic with the doubts of working-class secularists, Headlam had none of Maurice's grudging toleration of theological liberalism. Like the Tractarians, from whom he differed in many ways, Headlam believed that there can be no Christianity without 'definite doctrines'.[43]

So convinced was Headlam of this that in later years he was forced to lecture his fellow-Christian Socialists about the need to put first things first. Far better an old-fashioned pedant teaching sound doctrinal theology, he told them, than a priest 'whose passion for socialism is fed by his own enthusiasm'.[44] Appeals to mere principle, his friend Thomas Hancock pointed out, are of no avail. 'We may proclaim to all men that they are brothers in the name of love or in the name of Right,' Hancock wrote, 'but this will no more enable them to be brotherly, to forgive their enemies in the 19th century than it did in the first century. Unless we have already been made brothers . . . we cannot be made so in Love's or Right's or anything else's name.'[45] Not surprisingly, Headlam insisted that Christian Socialists preserve their separate identity. 'We have our own weapons in our armoury,' he reminded the Young Turks in the Guild of St Matthew, 'the Sacraments, the Priesthood, the Church's doctrines, the Church's catechism.'[46]

Headlam, then, did more than clothe Maurice's theology in Anglo-Catholic garb. He deepened its Catholicism and, in so doing, made it a far more potent instrument of social criticism. He also set afoot a transformation of Anglo-Catholicism itself. As a student at Cambridge, Headlam once recalled, he had gone to hear Pusey preach and was sadly disappointed. All the great man talked about was death and the imminence of death, whereas what concerned Headlam was 'life and the living of it more abundantly'.[47] This world-weariness, Headlam was convinced, was the result of the Tractarians' failure to perceive the consequences of the doctrine of the Incarnation. Here, he taught a generation of Anglo-Catholics, Maurice is the wiser guide. Only when the redemption of our whole nature is recognised, he argued, will sceptics, the oppressed, the young, and ordinary people 'again crowd our altars, dispelling that gloom and doubt of introspection, that worship of the Bible, that individualistic commercial religion which is summed up in the word Protestantism'.[48]

Headlam's innovations were political as well as theological. Drawing the obvious conclusions from his faith and from his experience as a parish priest in East London, Headlam rejected Maurice's belief in class co-operation. The poor must demand their rights, he insisted, and struggle to abolish the class system itself.[49] 'In the light of the Incarnation the present contrast between rich and poor cannot be justified for a moment,' Headlam thundered; 'in the light of the Incarnation the social revolution, in the plain meaning of the words, is justified, nay demanded.'[50] The secular Left, he declared, is doing the work which the Church has neglected. As Thomas Hancock observed, the banner of Christ was now in the hands of the socialists.[51] Yet even while throwing himself into the struggle for secular reform, Headlam retained his critical faculties. He voiced concern about the sectarianism of his secular comrades and their faith in the bureaucratic State. What most troubled him was the possibility that young idealists would settle for material prosperity rather than the heavenly city. Headlam repeated tirelessly that no programme – not even Henry George's Single Tax, in which he had almost unbounded confidence – can replace the gospel. 'We exist not only to bring about the economic revolution,' he told the Guild of St Matthew, 'but to maintain and where necessary to revive the great institution of the Church . . . ' for the Church alone is the divine society founded to struggle against evil and usher in the Kingdom of God.[52]

By drawing together the two great schools of Anglican sacramental and social theology, and by allying himself with the secular Left, Headlam set the tone of Christian Socialism up to the Second World War. This is not to say that Headlam was solely responsible for this synthesis. Other Anglo-Catholics were reaching similar conclusions, albeit with Headlam's persistent prodding. The most prominent of these radical Catholics were Charles Gore and Henry Scott Holland, the founders of the Christian Social Union and the leaders of the liberal Catholic circle at Oxford which produced the controversial *Lux Mundi* essays in 1889. The relation between the essays and the concerns of the Christian Social Union was not coincidental. As in Headlam's case, it was sacramental religion which was the foundation of radical politics. Indeed, although the *Lux Mundi* writers owed more to the Tractarians and even Hegel than they did to Maurice – both Gore and Holland has been students of T H Green – their theology was remarkably similar to Headlam's broad incarnationalism.[53]

The only significant difference between Gore and Holland on the one hand, and Headlam on the other, is that the former were less likely to leap into the political fray, or to pass from statements about brotherhood to appeals for social revolution. In part this was a reflection of their greater intellectual sophistication. More important was the desire to win for the Christian Social Union as broad a membership as possible. This had the unfortunate effect of watering down both the Union's politics and its Catholic theology. But it also enabled the Union to become the principal instrument for disseminating Catholic social thought in the Church of England and elsewhere in the Anglican communion. Theology too played a part in the caution of the Union's leadership. Gore, in particular, although he fully shared Headlam's incarnationalism, warned that we remain fallen creatures. The pursuit of social reform, he counselled, must be tempered by repentance and recognition of the limits of what can be accomplished by the State.[54] Even Scott Holland, who almost matched Headlam in exuberance, thought there was a need for a measure of Tractarian, even Puritan, austerity. 'We preach Art; we preach Literature; we preach the Brotherhood of Man,' he complained. 'We sometimes wonder where sin has got to . . . what has happened to the doctrine of the Fall; whether we need remember the old language about Judgment and Hell.'[55]

But whatever their disagreements, Headlam, Gore, Holland, and their friends shared the same faith and the same vision. In them the theological and political struggle which began with the Oxford Movement and the early Christian Socialists bore its finest fruit. Indeed, through the labours of this third generation of Anglo-Catholic radicals, by the turn of the century the Church of England had all but endorsed a vague form of Christian Socialism.[56] Yet at the very moment when they were emerging from the wilderness, Anglo-Catholic radicals were deeply troubled. From the beginning, they had assumed that it was the Church which would eventually lead the fight for social justice. Awaken the Church, Headlam had argued, and working-class radicals will flock to its banner and hail Christ as their emancipator. The Christian Social Union's bold proclamation that 'Christian Law [is] the ultimate authority to rule social practice' was based on the same assumption.[57] But the workers did not come, trusting in the secular Left rather than in the Church.

Faced with this grave challenge, younger members of the Guild of St Matthew and the Christian Social Union demanded unreserved suport for the secular socialist movement. Only in this way, they argued, could Christian Socialists be effective and allay the suspicions of the very class they hoped to serve. The choice is simple, William Temple declared: socialism or heresy.[58]. But once these Young Turks organised the Church Socialist League in 1906, they discovered that the most important questions facing them were theological rather than political. Was their goal to win the nation to socialism, the Church to socialism, or socialists to the Church? If Christian Socialists shared the same goals as their secular comrades, what was the relevance of a theology which assumed the primacy of the Church and the necessity of orthodox doctrine? Could the Kingdom of God be ushered in by act of Parliament? Was Christianity nothing more than 'the religion of which socialism is the practice'?

Not surprisingly, former members of the Guild of St Matthew were most troubled by these questions. Without denying the need for unalloyed socialism, they objectied to being 'tied to the chariot of the Labour party'.[59] More alarming was the League's failure to commit itself to what they regarded as the only foundation for its work: orthodox and sacramental doctrine. In recalling their comrades to the legacy of Maurice and the Tractarians, disenchanted Anglo-Catholics faced their own dilemma: how to hold fast to the faith without severing their ties to the broader socialist movement. For the time guild socialism seemed to be the solution. As propounded by J N Figgis and Arthur J Penty, guild socialism was a thoroughly Christian theory which guaranteed both the rights of the Church and the individual – long a concern of Anglo-Catholics – while assuring working-class control of industry. The popularity of similar ideas, such as distributivism and syndicalism elsewhere on the Left, heightened Anglican interest in the guild system. Unfortunately, after the outbreak of the First World War the guild movement lost what little influence it had among socialists, and was abandoned by most of its proponents.

The choices facing radical Anglo-Catholics by 1918 were particularly painful. The war, which had shattered the facile optimism of Christians and secularists alike, had all but destroyed the Church Socialist League and the Christian Social Union. There was still a host of socialist clergy and lay people. But much of the old prophetic fire and theological acuity was gone. Some joined the Industrial Christian Fellowship which, for all its good work, was never clear as to its goals. Some joined the non-denominational Society of Socialist Christians, which was formally affiliated with the Labour party. Others repented of their youthful enthusiasm. 'Our need,' wrote William Temple, 'is for steady, gradual, yet perceptible conservative reform.'[60] But there were those who remained faithful to the radical Catholicism championed by Stewart Headlam. From their ranks two men emerged who challenged the retreat from the vision of the early years of Anglo-Catholic social protest.

Percy Widdrington had been one of the disaffected members of the Guild of St Matthew who had helped found the Church Socialist League. But he was never comfortable with the league's doctrinal laxity and its early ties to the Labour party. Like Headlam, Widdrington believed that the secular Left was abandoning the cause of socialism for the simpler goal of a bureaucratic welfare State. At the same time, Christian Socialists, either because they had abandoned Catholic doctrine or because they feared offending their secular comrades, were unable to criticise this change in direction. If the vision which had animated the Anglican radicals of the nineteenth century were to be maintained, if indeed the dreams of the early labour movement were to be realised, there would have to be a return to first theological principles. Once they were recovered, the hard work would follow of developing a Christian sociology to guide the Church in making economic and political decisions.[61]

Just how radical a task this would be became evident in 1921, when Widdrington and his friends produced their manifesto: a volume of essays entitled *The Return of Christendom*.[62] Theologically, the book hearkened back to Headlam, Gore, and Holland. In his brilliant contribution, Lionel Thornton reasserted the necessity of Catholic doctrine for the right re-ordering of society. Only a full understanding of the social character of the sacraments, and whole-hearted devotion to the incarnate Lord, Thornton wrote, can reveal the Church's mission. 'If God Incarnate lived as a poor man and worked in a carpenter's shop,' he argued, as had generations of Anglo-Catholic radicals, 'and if the Manhood in which He did these things suffered death for all and is now on the throne of Heaven; then it is a blasphemous insult to that Manhood to treat any man's liberty as an indifferent thing on grounds of class or colour.' If Christ's incarnation sanctifies every human being, 'then the present social order is an open denial of Christ; for it condemns the majority of mankind to be economic slaves ministering to the selfishness of the minority. To acquiesce in it,' Thornton concluded solemnly, 'is to crucify Christ afresh.'[63]

The reason so many Anglo-Catholics were unable to see this, the essayist believed, is that these otherwise orthodox Anglicans had lost sight of the Kingdom of God. It is 'the vision of the Kingdom of God to be realised on earth', Thornton had told the Anglo-Catholic Congress a year earlier, 'which we must recover at all costs'.[64] This point was made most forcefully by Widdrington. Once the Kingdom of God is restored to its proper place as 'the regulative principle of theology', he wrote excitedly, once the Body of Christ is 'aflame with the faith of the Kingdom', the Church 'will be compelled to adopt towards our industrial system the same attitude which our missionaries take towards the social order of heathendom. It will then challenge the Industrial World as it challenged the forces of Roman Imperialism in the days of the persecution'. The consequences will be awesome, Widdrington insisted: 'a Reformation in comparison to which the Reformation of the sixteenth century will seem a small thing'.[65]

But although the essayists' principles were radical, their politics were cautious. The greatest evil of industrial capitalism, they believed, is not poverty but the degradation of the human spirit. A false and exaggerated individualism has torn apart the bonds which make social life possible. Labour and property have been degraded from means of self-expression to mere instruments for the accumulation of wealth. This being the case, they argued, neither collectivism nor communism offers any hope of change, for both are interested in little more than who should profit from the industrial machine. 'Only the conception of Christendom,' Maurice Reckitt wrote, 'the clear vision of a society in which the free activities of men are gathered together to create a social order which can be offered as a gift to the glory of God' can inspire a continuation of the crusade begun by socialism.[66]

None of the contributors to *The Return of Christendom* advocated making peace with capitalism or retreating into political passivity. No reader of the book, no one familiar with the work of the League for the Kingdom of God, which Widdrington established in 1923, or that of the Christendom Group, the League's intellectual nucleus and eventual successor, can fail to be impressed by the determination of Widdrington and his friends to overturn the existing social order. But they believed that to lose sight of the principles of Christian society in order to gain some political advantage was too high a price to pay. This, indeed, is the root of their much-criticised mediaevalism. Whatever its failings, they argued, mediaeval society was animated by a Christian vision. Justice, not profit, was the highest economic good. Production was intended to meet human needs, rather than men and women being reduced to the level of being mere hands. Moreover, mediaeval society was a rich community of communities, rather than a homogeneous order governed by an ominpotent State.

This idealised portrait of life in the Middle Ages was offered as a way of criticising the present, not as a clarion call to return to the past. Nevertheless, there was a faintly antiquarian air to much of the Christendom Group's work. This was heightened by the Group's exaggerated confidence, based in part on its neo-Thomist view of natural law, in the ability of theology to determine social policy. This dogmatism, joined as it was to suspicion of much modern social thought and a scholastic distrust of banks, left the Group prey to all sorts of dubious schemes, particularly the 'social credit' theories of Major C H Douglas, which held that most of the world's ills could be cured by a direct assault on 'finance capital'.[67] But even this economic fallacy was partially redeemed by a theological insight. When money is the centre of economic life it becomes an idol.

By preserving the theological heritage of the nineteenth-century Christian Socialist movement and applying it to the problems of the modern state, Widdrington and his friends offered direction to those Anglo-Catholics eager to do battle with capitalism yet disenchanted with socialism. But this very refusal to take sides in the day-to-day political struggle between Left and Right kept the Christendom Group from exercising much influence outside the small world of Anglo-Catholic intellectuals. For ardent spirits impatient with discussions of Christian sociology, there was another home: the Catholic Crusade organised in 1912 by one of the most remarkable personalities of the twentieth-century Church, Conrad Noel.

Like Widdrington, Noel was one of the young radicals in the Guild of St Matthew who had rallied to the Church Socialist League only to be disillusioned by its vague theology and unimaginative politics. But whereas Widdrington called for theological renewal, Noel demanded revolution. Even more than Headlam, Noel loved to shock middle-class churchgoers. There was certainly something deliberately outrageous about the Catholic Crusade's determination 'to shatter the British Empire and all Empires to bits . . . to break up the present world and make a new in the power of the outlaw of Galilee'.[68] But behind Noel's extravagant prose there lay the deeply-held conviction that the Christian Socialist movement, and the Church itself, had no future unless they took part in the great struggle to overthrow capitalism and usher in the Kingdom of God.

Noel's theology was rooted in the Maurician Catholicism which had inspired Christian Socialists since Stewart Headlam. Like all of Maurice's disciples, Noel insisted that the Incarnation hallows human nature and all our earthly concerns. 'God is *perpetually* "intruding" himself into this world, and is himself its very substance,' he wrote. 'Every wayside flower is a sacrament of his Body and Blood, and every human heroism a Revelation. This,' Noel proclaimed, 'is the Catholic Faith, which except a man believe faithfully, without doubt he will shrivel into mean and narrow death'. It is because these things are so, because the Holy Spirit dwells within us, that 'those who defraud men's bodies of proper nourishment and proper rest' are guilty of the most awful sacrilege.[69] The Church's principal responsibility, therefore, is not the teaching of spiritual truths. It is the proclamation of the coming of the new world order, God's co-operative commonwealth, here on earth.

Where Noel differed from his predecessors was in his radically democratic conception of the Church. The union between God and the human race in Christ, he believed, means that the Holy Spirit is sacramentally present in humanity as a whole. Everyone, not just the ordained or believers, is a priest. The Church's authority does not rest on revelations given to a hierarchy, but on the presence of God's Spirit in the congregation of all His faithful people.[70] To this extraordinary confidence in the working of God through ordinary men and women, Christians and unbelievers alike, Noel joined an almost apocalyptic urgency about the building of God's kingdom. The political consequences of his theology are obvious. Having identified the longings of oppressed humanity with the work of the Holy Spirit, Noel had no doubts about the righteousness of the socialist cause. He had no more fondness for the Labour party than did Widdrington. But the answer to Fabian collectivism, he argued, is to plunge further to the Left. Nevertheless, Noel was careful not to allow politics to supplant the faith. Heresy, he believed, is the greatest enemy of socialism. Indeed, he wrote, nothing is more important than that revolutionaries learn 'that all that is eternal in their plans is inspired by God's Eternal Plan, and sealed by the blood of the Lamb slain from the foundation of the world . . .'[71]

A brilliant and sensitive liturgist, Noel made Thaxted church a Christian Socialist shrine. Even those chary of his politics flocked to the tiny Essex village to catch a glimpse of the vision embodied in the glorious Easter Mass. But for all his ardour and genius, Noel was no more able to solve the problems faced by radical Anglo-Catholics than was Widdrington. Noel insisted on Catholic orthodoxy, yet much of his own theology was highly idiosyncratic. Not surprisingly, friends and critics alike were never sure what he meant by Catholicism. Noel's politics were even more eccentric. Convinced that nothing less than revolution could lay the foundation of the Kingdom of God, Noel became an ardent Leninist and, for a time, an apologist for Stalin. The effect on the Catholic Crusade was disastrous. Isolated from all but a small segment of the socialist movement, Christian or secular, the Crusade was torn apart by the factionalism endemic among friends of the Soviet Union in the 1930s. Moreover, despite his support for the Soviet regime, Noel was never a Marxist. Indeed, his vision of a new world order was much closer to the Christendom Group's distinctly mediaeval utopia than it was to the industrial state being constructed by the authorities in Moscow. To even sympathetic outsiders, the Crusade's politics must have seemed utopian and even a bit ludicrous. It is little wonder that the Order of the Church Militant, which Noel had organised to take the place of the Catholic Crusade, disappeared soon after his death in 1942.

Had the collapse of the Catholic Crusade been an isolated incident, it could be blamed solely on Noel's impatient zeal. But by the end of the Second World War the entire Anglo-Catholic Left was a mere shadow of its former self. The Christendom Group lingered on for a time; there were plenty of veterans of the Catholic Crusade about. But the heady day of campaigns to 'build Jerusalem in England's green and pleasant land' were past. In part, the Anglo-Catholic Left, like the Christian Socialist movement as a whole, was a victim of its own success. Both Church and State had been awakened to their social responsibilities to an extent which would have been unthinkable a century earlier. After the primacy of William Temple and the reforms of the Atlee government, Anglicans could be forgiven for thinking that the great battles lay in the past.

But success alone does not explain the virtual disappearance of the Anglo-Catholic Left. Neither the welfare state nor Temple's cautious proposals fulfilled the dreams of the Christian Socialist movement, as

Temple himself would have been the first to admit.[72] In fact, the Anglo-Catholic Left had been ailing for some time. Confronted by a host of secular movements for social reform, all of them unpalatable to one degree or another, Anglo-Catholics lost confidence in their secular comrades and in their own ability to influence events. They had all believed that the future hinged on the eventual conversion of the socialist movement to the Catholic faith. Now that there was no prospect of that happening, talk of a Catholic crusade or the restoration of Christendom seemed quaint at best.

Anglo-Catholic socialists were further afflicted by their own theological and ecclesiastical parochialism. That secular radicals were doing God's work, however imperfectly, had been an article of faith since Headlam's day. But there was equally strong agreement that any religion other than Anglo-Catholicism leads to reaction. Against Protestantism in particular, the Anglo-Catholic Left launched countless polemics. The results were as sad as they were predictable. Radical Protestants, both Anglicans and Dessenters, whose co-operation was vital for the Christian Socialist cause, were reluctant to support the efforts of those who regarded them as misguided heretics.[73] This narrowness even affected relations between Anglo-Catholics and the secular Left. Convinced that what others saw dimly they perceived clearly – God's plan for human society – Anglo-Catholics were often impatient with both the day-to-day concerns of the labour movement and the fine points of economic theory. Thus, they tended to leap directly from moral theology to politics, advocating programmes which, whatever their merits, could hardly accomplish all that their proponents claimed. It is no coincidence that Headlam, Widdrington and Noel all placed undue confidence in eccentric schemes: the Single Tax, social credit, and Bolshevism. Nor is it surprising that working-class politicians, many of whom came from Dissenting families, regarded these unusual programmes as further evidence of the unreliability of parsons.

Born at a time when it was possible to see in a reformed Church of England the herald of the age to come, the Christian Socialist movement, particularly its Anglo-Catholic wing, was ill-equipped to deal with the problems of a thoroughly secularised society. Had its expectations been more modest, the Anglo-Catholic Left would have led an easier, if less eventful, life. But although aspects of its Tractarian and Maurician heritage need to be revised or perhaps even rejected, the main body of Anglo-Catholic social theology stands as an enduring monument to the pioneers of our faith. They taught the necessity of right doctrine, without which Christian Socialists would be doomed to pursue one fad after another. Salvation, they insisted, is not a matter of individuals being brought into a right relationship with God, but rather is the process whereby redeemed humanity is restored to wholeness in Christ and His Church. Tractarians and Christian Socialists alike reminded the Church that it was to the poor and the oppressed that Christ especially came. Yet they also warned against the kind of unreflecting activism which has always attracted liberal clerics. The priest is no more a social worker than he is an ordained gentleman. Prayer is his principal responsibility from which all else flows.

Even in political matters, there is much we can learn from the Anglo-Catholic Left. What the Christian prays and labours for, its adherents recognised, is more than social reform: it is the Kingdom of God. No programme, no ideology, therefore, has more than secondary value. In waging war against capitalism, they warned, the rights of individuals and communities must be respected. The bureaucratic State is not the heavenly city. In an era of tyrannies, the vision of a decentralised and co-operative commonwealth has lost none of its relevance. Nor, confronted as we are by the joyless puritanism of conservative sects and joyless hedonism of mass culture, has Headlam's sacramental materialism.

Above all, the Anglo-Catholic Left reminds us that our hopes are grounded in the awesome truth that God took our human nature upon himself. At the Anglo-Catholic Congress of 1923 Frank Weston, the Bishop of Zanzibar and a veteran of the Guild of St Matthew, made this point eloquently. What England needs to learn, he told the assembly, 'is that Christ is found amid matter – Spirit through matter – God in flesh, God in the Sacrament'. But to give lip-service to this principle is not to grasp its meaning. 'I say to you, and I say it to you with all the earnest-bess that I have,' he pleaded with conservative Anglo-Catholics, 'that if you are prepared to fight for Jesus in his Blessed Sacrament, then you have got to come out from before your Tabernacle and walk, with Christ present mystically in you, out into the streets of this country, and find the same Jesus in the people of your cities and your villages.' To claim to worship Jesus in the Sacrament while ignoring Jesus in his sweated children in the slums, Weston warned, is sheer madness.[74]

The battles which the Tractarians and ritualists fought on behalf of Catholic worship have been largely won, Weston noted. The Mass, the altar, even the tabernacle are widely tolerated. 'Now,' he counselled, 'go out into the highways and hedges where not even the Bishops will try and hinder you. Go out and look for Jesus in the ragged, in the naked, and in the oppressed and sweated, in those who have lost hope, in those who are struggling to make good. Look for Jesus. And when you see him, gird yourselves with his towel and try to wash his feet.[75]

In this simple appeal, Weston summed up nearly a century of Anglo-Catholic social protest. It is, indeed, what Maurice and Pusey preached to the unbelieving Victorian Church. Despite their differences, Tractarians and Christian Socialists worshipped the same God after all. Much has happened since the first stirrings of rebellion more than a century-and-a-half ago. We cannot embrace the parochialism of the Anglo-Catholic Left, nor its clericalism, nor its political panacea. But we can keep the same faith, serve the same incarnate Lord, and pray for the same heavenly kingdom of righteousness and peace on earth.

References

1 Maurice B Reckitt, *Maurice to Temple: A Century of the Social Movement in the Church of England* (Faber and Faber, London, 1946), p 122.
2 *The Letters and Diaries of John Henry Newman*, ed Ian Ker and Thomas Gornall, vol 2 (Clarendon Press, Oxford, 1979), p 130; John Keble, *Sermons, Occasional and Parochial* (John Parker, Oxford, 1868), p 147.
3 Owen Chadwick, *The Victorian Church*, 2 vols (Oxford University Press, New York, 1966, 1970), 1:107.
4 Baron d'Haussez, *Great Britain in 1833*, 2 vols (Richard Bentley, London, 1833), 1.264.
5 R W Church, *The Oxford Movement: Twelve Years, 1833–1845*, ed Geoffrey Best (University of Chicago Press, Chicago and London, 1970), pp 10–11.
6 This is not to say that the urban poor would have flocked to church had there been a building nearby. The failure of Bishop Blomfield's church expansion programme is a case in point. See Richard Allen Soloway, *Prelates and People: Ecclesiastical Social Thought in England, 1783–1852* (Routledge & Kegan Paul, London; University of Toronto Press, Toronto, 1969), p 307.
7 Keble, p 174.
8 Soloway, pp 110–1.
9 E R Norman, *Church and Society in England, 1770–1970* (Clarendon Press, Oxford, 1976), p 33.
10 Soloway, pp 162–3.
11 J Douglas Holladay, 'Nineteenth-Century Evangelical Activism' *Historical Magazine of the Protestant Episcopal Church*, 50 (March, 1882), pp 64–6, 69, 75.
12 Soloway, p 260.
13 *Letters and Diaries*, 2:130.
14 John Keble, *National Apostasy* (Mowbray, London, 1931), p 14.
15 *Tracts for the Times*, 5 vols (F & J Rivington, London, 1840–2), 1:no 1, 'Thoughts on the Ministerial Commission', p 1.
16 John Henry Newman, *Lectures on the Prophetical Office of the Church*, 2nd ed (J G & F Rivington, London, J H Parker, Oxford, 1838), p 13.
17 *Tracts* 1. No 2, 'The Catholic Church', p 1; No 18, 'Thoughts on the Benefits of the System of Fasting', p 14.
18 David Newsome, *The Wilberforces and Henry Manning: The Parting of Friends* (The Belknap Press of Harvard University Press, Cambridge, 1966), p 203.
19 *Remains of the Late Reverend Richard Hurrell Froude*, 2 vols (J G & F Rivington, Derby, 1839), 1: xxxi.
20 W G Ward, *The Ideal of a Christian Church* (John Toovey, London, 1844), pp 31–2, 50.
21 Edward Bouverie Pusey, *The Councils of the Church from the Council of Jerusalem to the Council of Constantinople* (F Rivington, Oxford, 1857) pp 4–5, cited in Bernard Kent Markwell, 'The Seed-Time', unpublished paper, p 6.
22 *Idem, University Sermons*, 4 vols (Joseph Parker, Oxford, 1872–79), 2:386
23 *Letters and Diaries*, 3: 55.

24 See Alf Hardelin, *The Tractarian Understanding of the Eucharist* (University of Uppsala Press, Uppsala, 1965), pp 62–4; Stephen Prickett, *Romanticism and Religion. The Tradition of Coleridge and Wordsworth in the Victorian Church* (Cambridge University Press, Cambridge, pp 104–15.

25 *Tracts*, 2: No 67, 'Scriptural Views of Holy Baptism', pp 12–13; 4: No 82, 'Letters to a Magazine on the Subject of Dr Pusey's Tract on Baptism', p iv.

26 Hardelin, p 75.

27 See *ibid*, pp 84–5 for a summary of Wilberforce's book, and Newsome, p 374. On the similarities between Wilberforce and the Christian Socialists see John E Booty, *The Church in History* (Seabury Press, New York, 1979), p 125.

28 Pusey, *University Sermons*, 2: 28, 28. Oddly enough, Paul A Welsby writes: 'This sermon illustrates the Tractarian's lack of social concern. Welsby, ed *Sermons and Society: An Anglican Anthology* (Penguin, Harmondsworth and Baltimore, 1970), p 270.

29 Frederick Denison Maurice, *Sermons on the Sabbath Day, on the Character of the Warrior, and on the Interpretations of History* (John W Parker and Son, London, 1853), pp 76–7.

30 *Idem, Kingdom of Christ*, 2 vols (1838 ed), 1: 97, cited in Alec R Vidler, *F D Maurice and Company* (SCM Press, London, 1959), p 97.

31 *Idem, The Prayer Book* (James Clarke & Co, London, 1966), p 200.

32 *Idem, Social Morality* (Macmillan, London, 1872), p 20.

33 *Idem, Tracts on Christian Socialism, No 1: Dialogue between Somebody (A Person of Respectability) and Nobody (the Author)* (n pub, London, 1850), p 8.

34 See the *Christian Socialist*, 14 June 1851, pp 257–9; N C Masterman, *John Malcolm Ludlow: The Builder of Christian Socialism* (Cambridge University Press, Cambridge, 1963), pp 125–9.

35 *The Life of Frederick Denison Maurice*, ed Frederick Maurice, 2 vols (Macmilland and Co, London, 1884), 2: 465–8. See also Henry Parry Liddon, *Life of Edward Bouverie Pusey*, ed J O Johnston and R F Wilson, 4 vols (Longmans, Green, and Co, London, 1893-97), 4: 54–61.

36 See James Bentley, *Ritualism and Politics in Victorian Britain* (Oxford University Press, Oxford, 1978), p 4; and Chadwick, 2: 317.

37 Michael Reynolds, *Martyr of Ritualism: Fr Mackonochie of Saint Alban's, Holborn* (Faber and Faber, London, 1965), pp 190–1.

38 S C Carpenter, *Church and People, 1789–1889* (SPCK, London, 1933), p 244.

39 A M Allchin, *The Silent Rebellion* (SCM Press, London, 1958), p 207. See also Markwell, pp 9–15.

40 Desmond Bowen, *The Idea of the Victorian Church* (McGill University Press, Montreal, 1968), p 300.

41 See John Richard Orens, 'Christ, Communism, and Chorus Girls: a Reassessment of Stewart Headlam', *Historical Magazine of the Protestant Episcopal Church*, 49 (September 1980), pp 234–40.

42 Stewart D Headlam, *Priestcraft and Progress* (John Hodges, London, 1878), p vi.

43 See *idem, The Need for Tangible Sacraments and Definite Doctrines* (n pub, London, 1892?).

44 *Ibid.*

45 Stephen Yeo, 'Thomas Hancock: The Banner of Christ in the Hands of the Socialists', in *For Christ and the People*, ed Maurice B Reckitt (SPCK, London, 1968), p 30.

46 *Church Reformer*, October 1895, pp 219–20.

47 F G Bettany, *Stewart Headlam: A Biography* (John Murray, London, 1926), p 22.

48 Stewart D Headlam, *The Laws of Eternal Life* (Frederick Verinder, London, 1888), p 52.

49 See *idem, Priestcraft*, p 64: *The Church Catechism and the Emancipation of Labour* (G Palmer, London, 1875), p 3.
50 *Church Reformer*, November 1890, p 245.
51 See Thomas Hancock, *The Banner of Christ in the Hands of the Socialists* (Foulger & Co, London, 1887).
52 *Church Reformer*, October 1890, p 200; Headlam, *Meaning of the Mass*, p 59.
53 Apart from *Lux Mundi* itself (11th ed Thomas Whittaker, New York, n d), especially the essays by Gore, Holland, and Francis Paget, the most impressive statement of this theology is Gore's *The Incarnation of the Son of God*, 2nd ed (John Murray, London, 1896). Some of Maurice's ideas were undoubtedly transmitted to Gore through B F Westcott.
54 See Charles Gore, *Christ and Society* (George Allen & Unwin, London, 1928), pp 54, 139.
55 Henry Scott Holland, 'The Anti-Puritan League', *Commonwealth*, 11 (November 1906), pp 259–61. Headlam himself sometimes raised similar questions. See e g, *Church Reformer*, January 1894, p 6.
56 See John Richard Orens, 'Politics and the Kingdom: The Legacy of the Anglican Left', *Anglican Theological Review*, 53 (January 1981), p 31.
57 Peter d'A Jones, *The Christian Socialist Revival, 1877–1914* (Princeton University Press, Princeton, 1968), p 177.
58 Joseph Fletcher, *William Temple, Twentieth-Century Christian* (Seabury Press, New York, 1963), p 180.
59 David O Wagner, *The Church of England and Social Reform since 1854* (Columbia University Press, New York, 1930), p 273. The phrase is Percy Widdrington's.
60 William Temple, *Essays on Christian Politics and Kindred Subjects* (Longmans, Green, and Co, London, 1927), p 65.
61 The term 'christian sociology' has a misleadingly academic air to it, as some Christian sociologists readily admitted. See e g, Maurice B Reckitt, *Faith and Society* (Longmans, Green, and Co, London, 1932), p 76.
62 P E T Widdrington et al, *The Return of Christendom* (Macmillan, New York, 1922). Charles Gore wrote the introduction but did not identify himself with the essayist's views. The epilogue was one of G K Chesterton's last works as an Anglican.
63 L S Thornton, 'The Necessity of Catholic Dogma', in *ibid*, pp 55–77. See especially pp 61–3, 65, 75.
64 Lionel Thornton, 'The Kingdom of God', in *Report of the Anglo-Catholic Congress* (SPCK, London, 1920), p 61.
65 P E T Widdrington, 'The Return of the Kingdom of God', in Widdrington *et al*, pp 102, 106–7.
66 Maurice B Reckitt, 'The Idea of Christendom in Relation to Modern Society', in *ibid*, p 26.
67 See Reckitt in Widdrington *et al*, p 27; *idem*, 'The Moralisation of Property' in *ibid*, pp 168–77; and A J Carlyle, 'The Mediaeval Theory of Social Order' in *ibid*, pp 111–20. Reckitt even likened Douglass to Einstein, Eddington and Keynes. See Maurice B Reckitt, *Religion in Social Action* (John Heritage, the Unicorn Press, London, 1937), p 149.
68 Reg Groves, ed, *The Catholic Crusade, 1918–1936* (Archive, London, 1970), p 9. This is the text of the Crusade manifesto. John Groser, a Crusade priest, aptly descrined the manifesto as 'a bit unbalanced, but still pretty splendid . . .' William Purcell, 'Birth of a Rebel', in *John Groser, East London Priest*, ed Kenneth Brill (Mowbray, London and Oxford, 1971), p 14.
69 Robert Woodifield, 'Conrad Noel, Catholic Crusader', in *For Christ and the People*, p 155. Reg Groves, *Conrad Noel and the Thaxted Movement* (Merlin Press, London, 1978), p 85.

70 See Woodifield, p 160.

71 Groves, *Catholic Crusade*, p 14.

72 Temple's politics were extraordinarily elusive. There is some merit in Stanley Evans' complaint that Temple had sanctified the welfare state (see Kenneth Leech, 'The Christian Left in Britain, 1850–1950', in *Agenda for Prophets: Towards a Politcal Theology for Britain*, ed Rex Ambler and David Haslam, (Bowerdean Press, London, 1980) p 68). But although his programme for reform was cautious see his *Christianity and Social Order* (Penguin, London, 1942; reprint ed (Shepheard-Walwyn and SPCK, London, 1976), both his theology and his social ethics were a good deal more radical. Ronald Preston's introduction to *Christianity and Social Order* is helpful on this question, as is Robert Craig, *Social Concern in the Thought of William Temple* (Victor Gollancz, London, 1963).

73 The most extraordinary example of this often well-meaning insistence on Anglo-Catholic orthodoxy is Frederic Hasting Smyth's contention that the Anglican Church was destined dialectically to usher in the coming international socialist order. See Smyth and David Hecht, *Western Christianity's Whence and Whither* (Oratory of St Mary and St Michael, Cambridge, Mass, 1948). Smyth, an American admirer of Conrad Noel and founder of the Society of the Catholic Commonwealth, later repented of this argument.

74 Frank Weston, 'Our Present Duty', in *Report of the Anglo-Catholic Congress of 1923* (Society of SS Peter and Paul, London, 1923), pp 85–6. It is ironic that the doctrine of the incarnation, which Anglo-Catholic socialists have regarded as the charter of social equality, has been used by otherwise radical theologians to justify barring women from ordination to the priesthood.

75 *Ibid*, p 86.

11 The Catholic Movement for Export

John Davies

Most of our contributions in this book focus on England, and rightly so. The Catholic movement within Anglicanism, the movement which we trace back to the Assize Sermon, was developed within England in response to English needs. It was of its place and of its day.

For instance, the Catholic movement developed at the same time as the growth of mass society. Vast number of people moved into cities; traditional skills and roots were lost, membership of tribe and family became weaker. Romantic individualism came in as a remedy, for those who were socially and intellectually mobile. One's identity, if one had any at all, came to depend on one's individual achievement or attitude rather than on one's tribe. Otherwise one was probably only a statistic, or a member of the 'problem' class. The Catholic movement was one of many responses to all this. It had, and it has, peculiar advantages as such a response: it combines a social message with an individual opportunity. In its message, it has stressed the values of corporate membership and the image of the Body of Christ. It has appealed to the old tradition of national religious corporateness, particularly in its glorification of Catholic mediaeval England, and it taught us to prize our belief in the Communion of Saints. At the same time, the actual experience of being an Anglo-Catholic has been to affirm one's individuality. Like many of my age, I first labelled myself as an Anglo-Catholic at about the time when I became aware of being treated as a piece of human beef, designated as a conscripted aircraftman with a seven-digit number. It was a way of saying, Here, look at me, I'm different, I'm not just one of the mindless mass labelled 'C of E' – but also I'm not one of those who have to make themselves conspicuous on parade when the Warrant Officer calls out 'Fall out, the Roman Catholics and Jews'.

In England, therefore Anglican Catholicism has been serving a particular purpose. It has been providing a voluntary option within the mainstream, a way of being non-conformist without being Nonconformist. Although the same social conditions applied elsewhere in Britain, ecclesiastically it was England that gave Anglican Catholicism its particular niche, as an opportunity to be a minority within the establishment, to be different within the convention. One effect of this is still noticeable within the major cities, that gradations between churches of this tradition are of considerable identificational importance: churches distinguish themselves from each other not on the basis of the area they serve but in terms of their style within a range of conventions. And a further effect of this is that again there can be a curious dislocation between the message and the experience. The message – and one of the most glorious qualities of the Catholic movement is that it puts this message at the top of its agenda – is that our God is a God who changes things, changes bread into Body, changes sinners into saints, changes society into the Kingdom of Heaven. The experience of belonging within the Catholic movement, however, can enrol the ordinary member into a conspiracy against change; we go around trying to find a Church which suits us, and end up wishing that we could find a god who suits us.

Along with so many other elements in English culture, Anglican Catholicism has been exported. And, as in the case of other exporting enterprises, we have to ask, In whose interests? Fast, energy-intensive motor-cars are exported from the industrialised nations to other areas of the world: they are useless without expensive highways, so capital development is shaped by the demands of the wealthy minority who possess cars, and the gap between possessors and non-possessors is widened. This is similar to the critique which Julius Nyerere has for so long been urging against the educational conventions which we have been exporting. What about our religious exports?

Certainly we have to acknowledge that, in its exported form, Anglican Catholicism has become a different thing, serving different purposes and having different effects. The movement has been developed and transmitted very largely by priests; the sacrificial ideal of Catholicism inspired many priests to go overseas from Britain to transmit and commend Catholicism as they valued it and to strengthen it institutionally. Priests in England were grasped by the attraction of this unconvention, and went overseas to establish it as the convention. In many cases, they succeeded in forming an environment overseas which was impossible even to aim at in England; they developed a church in which their understanding of Anglicanism was uncompromised, unqualified, and unquestioned.

For instance, we can compare the Eucharistic liturgies that were developed in different parts of the Anglican Communion in, roughly speaking, the second quarter of this century. In England, and in the British Isles as a whole, any priest who wanted to celebrate according to the full details of the 'Western' convention had to make all sorts of additions, alterations and, to some extent, defiances to the authorised rites: in some areas overseas, the designers of the rites have been able to commit the church to the complete 'Western' convention as the only authorised form. This is to be seen, for example, in the Anglican liturgies for such totally different areas as Korea, Mozambique, and Madagascar. These areas have nothing special in common in terms of language, culture, or religious attitude. It is not their Korean-ness or Mozambique-ness or Madagascar-ness that makes their liturgies similar: the one thing they have in common is their distance from mainstream Englishness, their lack of need to take any notice of an English colonial presence.

I have no authority to comment on Anglicanism world-wide. My own experience outside Britain is limited to Southern Africa, and for the remainder of this contribution I will concentrate on that area. But I do this without much apology. I cannot make a world-wide trip to describe Anglican Catholicism in all its many presences in Africa, Asia and the Americas. But I hope to show that South Africa is a particularly revealing area within which to observe and evaluate Anglican Catholicism in an exported form.

In South Africa, the most significant formative feature in the historical position of the Anglican Church is that, within a unitary structure, it has had to hold together two commitments, viz the chaplaincy to the expatriate colonial inheritance and the mission to the indigenous population. The South African experience is virtually unique. In no other colonised country has there been such a large minority of expatriate residents. And no other South African Church, apart from the Methodists, has had such large proportions of membership from both sections of the population. Churches of the Reformed tradition have, on the whole, devised totally distinct structures to serve the two commitments. This remains true of the Dutch Reformed churches and the other Afrikaans-medium churches: it was true also of the Presbyterian churches until relatively recently. The Roman Catholic Church certainly has a unitary structure but does not have the Anglican Church's long history of involvement with the white communities, and the Lutheran Church has never had a substantial white membership. Even Methodism has not had as clear a tradition as Anglicanism concerning the essentially unitary character of the Church's structure. This is not to say that Anglicanism's unitary character is obvious to all; far from it. There are Anglican churches which, to all intents and purposes, are as 'whites only' as any Dutch Reformed Church. There are Anglican churches built on sites which they have been allocated by the municipal authorities only on condition that the congregation shall consist of whites only. There are many Anglican churches which are virtually inaccessible to whites and so are black only. But Anglicans properly do not speak of black churches and white churches but only the churches in black areas and in white areas. And at the supra-congregational level, there remains only one structure, under one bishop and one archdeacon in any one place. Many church members are almost completely unaware of the significance of this: but it is a matter of immense importance to the minority who do exercise a ministry in both sections of the population, and they tend to be the people in the public eye, who speak in the name of the Church. The position of leadership, as always, separates the leaders from the members: but it also adds a range of experience, in this instance, which most ordinary members do not have and which many ordinary members might not particularly want. And this is one of the reasons for the peculiar responsibility of those who hold positions high in the leadership-structure of the Anglican Church in South Africa.

At the congregational level, it is in practice necessary to speak of white Anglicanism and black Anglicanism. We must note that this is an imposed classification; 'whiteness' and 'blackness', in South African terms, are political, not biological terms. Whites are those who are classified as white by those who have the power to determine the classification, which they do in the interests of their own group: and blacks are those who are classified as black. Although a more complex classification is possible, indeed traditional, the effect of generations of law and custom has been to reduce the groups to two, 'white' and 'non-white'. Rightly rejecting a nomenclature which describes people in terms of what they are not, the 'non-whites' have been tending in recent years to call themselves corporately 'black', including those who would, according to the more complex classification, be called 'coloured' and 'Asian'. And, on the whole, Anglican custom and terminology has fitted into this simple classification: 'coloured' and 'Indian' work have been put into the same bag as 'African' work.

If we examine the contribution of the Catholic movement within Anglicanism, we will find that, whether we like it or not, it also fits into this pattern.

The whole of the Province of Southern Africa has been very strongly influenced by the Catholic movement. The Province includes Mozambique, which has a quite distinct and special history, but otherwise the style of the Anglican tradition is fairly homogeneous, whether we are considering the Republic and Namibia or the old High Commission territories of Lesotho and Swaziland. With a few exceptions, located in the white urban areas, South African Anglicanism outwardly and obviously testifies to its indebtedness to the Catholic movement.

But this Catholic-ness has to be evaluated according to its historical causation and influence, and this is different in the different population groups.

In the white areas, the Catholic tradition has had an obvious effect in that almost all church buildings have most of the normal insignia of that tradition – lights, vestments, eucharistic music, etc. This is conventional Anglicanism, the mildly Catholic majority. A minority, in the cities, take it further, with the full High Mass, statues and other more specialised practice. This minority serves some of the same needs as its counterpart in England. it is a minority option, a way of being a bit unconventional within the convention. Within this more definitely Catholic minority, there are two types. First there are some priests and congregations who see Catholicism as a kind of conservatism which can be used to justify and bless 'conservatism' as that word is normally understood in South Africa. They would agree with Archbishop Lefevbre that Catholicism has to fight against everything to do with socialism or communism; they would have a lot of sympathy for the efforts of the South African Defence Force. The God who is worshipped is the God who will save South Africa from change, unrest and anarchy. Secondly, within this more consciously Catholic minority, there are those who see Catholicism as a true conservatism which is in business to expose and attack the false and destructive conservatism which the privileged invent as a disguise for self-interest. They take the fulness of Catholicism as their starting point, and on it they base their critique of everything that conceals or denies the reality of the Body of Christ. This is the Catholicism of Reeves, Huddleston, de Blank and ffrench-Beytagh – all people who have been strongly committed to, and indeed fussy about, Catholic order and Catholic practice. They are people whose Catholic commitment has made them used to being in a minority, and who operate with a fair degree of consecrated aggressiveness. This category is, of course, much larger than the 'big names' that I have mentioned; although it includes many conspicuous people, it is certainly not confined to church leaders or to priests. There are many lay people who follow Catholic practice, make their confessions and so on, who have been led to this practice by their admiration for the public stand made by some of the conspicuous people of this type, and have realised and adopted the spiritual disciplines which sustained that public stand. There is a kind of subversive orthodoxy in this inheritance which has an emotional and intellectual appeal and an inner consistency; and it is not invalidated by the discovery that one's model may turn out to be a person who is capable of ambition or pettiness or plain stupidity. This is the second category within the group of more consciously Catholic whites. It is obviously more conspicuous than the other, partly because it makes its home in those city-centre church buildings, notably some cathedrals, where a racially inclusive – and therefore 'catholic' – congregation is a live reality; whether it is actually more numerous than the other category is very doubtful.

In any evaluation of Anglican Catholicism, one has to ask, has it worked? How does one answer? If in terms of self-propagation, then this tradition has done fairly well in the South African white communities. The total percentage of the white population calling themselves Anglican has been slightly decreasing for several years, and this may perhaps be due to a certain monochromeness: but Catholicism, in some form, has been established as the convention, among white Anglicans, in a way which has no counterpart in England. Has it made its members enthusiastic for its ideals? This is much more difficult to answer. My own judgment is that, for most white people who attend churches within the majority, mildly Catholic, Anglican convention, their social, religious and spiritual attitudes would be very little different if they were attending a church in a 'High Matins' tradition. They hear references to such things as fasting and confession, but not with any great impact. The more self-conscious Anglo-Catholic minority is ambiguous, divided into two categories: these will unite with each other over against the more woolly, secular-minded types when there is an internal ecclesiastical issue which for them raises questions of catholic order; and they divide sharply on issues concerning the witness of catholic conviction within a disordered society. So, in matters of public debate, you have to choose your issue and your allies with some care!

In recent years, the picture has been further complicated by the development of the charismatic movement. As a white phenomenon, this has had its biggest impact in congregations where there has been a mildly conventional rather than a self-conscious Catholicism. It has offered another minority option, which has appealed to those who have been alienated from Catholicism either because of Catholicism's ritual and authoritarianism or by its association with political commitment. From being a new unconvention, it has moved quickly into being a new convention. Numerically, it is important among whites and may well fall into a pattern of convention and alternative, rather similar to that which Catholicism has developed. The most important judgment must be concerning the difference which it makes to the contribution of the Church in society. At this point, compared to Catholicism even at its most ambiguous, it seems to have little to show for itself.

In the black communities the pattern has been different in many ways. There is no need for minority options within black Anglicanism: Anglicanism is itself a minority option, and one's Anglican identity says nothing about one's country of origin, one's overseas tribe. Anglicanism as shared with blacks is almost universally an Anglicanism which has much more than a few Catholic trimmings: it is the full-scale Anglican Catholicism of the High Mass, regular confession, paschal ceremonies, and so on. This kind of Catholicism is taken for granted. Even in churches which cannot provide three Sacred Ministers – and it is common enough in the rural areas for communicants to see their solitary priest only monthly or quarterly – there is still plenty of incense, with dried mealie cobs serving the purpose of charcoal. This is the convention, and there is no need for much variety or alternative within the convention. So there is no interest in the subtle gradations which make up the identificational language of some whites. There is much less pressure to be loyal to the ceremonial features as such. Africans tend to slip in and out of different religious styles with much less sense of compromising their religious or aesthetic taste. As Bishop Alphaeus Zulu remarked, 'We blacks don't need a charismatic *movement*, we've always been charismatic'. Catholic elements and evangelical elements and charismatic elements flow together and get jumbled up in a way which would disturb the stronger identificational sensitivities of whites. The correct ritual will be followed as dictated by the authorities, at a wedding, for instance, but all sorts of unauthorised ceremonies will be fitted in, such as the providing of a role-badge for the best man – to wit, a clothes-brush – or the using of motor-horns instead of bells.

Humanly speaking, religion is one of several devices which we have invented to tell us who we are different to. It is not likely to have a wide appeal unless it can tell us whom to hate and perhaps whom to kill. This needs gives boundaries and definition to religion's badges and language. White Anglicans have a need to know who they are different from; the answer is, quite often, other white Anglicans. African Anglicans, in the areas I know best, need most of all to distinguish themselves from Zionists. Anglo-Catholics have, for a variety of reasons, tried to foster the practise of total immersion, at least for adult baptism; some churches of this tradition, in Britain and South Africa, have been furnished with full-scale baptisteries for this purpose. In Tanzania, where, in the old UMCA dioceses, the Anglican traditon is very similar to that of South African black Anglicans, adult baptims have been performed in the river. In South Africa, this is unheard of; I once made a staged photograph of a river baptism for an instructional pamphlet on Christian initiation – it killed the pamphlet's chances of credibility! Zionists baptise in the river, so we don't, even though we know theoretically that we should. But Tanzania doesn't have Zionists.

So we have to ask again, about the Anglican Catholic contribution among blacks: has it worked? In terms of self-propagation, yes; it has worked reasonably well. It has an appeal which makes some impact and sense, which I will return to. Has it worked in terms of commanding its ideals, in terms of representing the claims of God's Kingdom and inspiring people to sacrifice for them? It has provided criteria, points by which Church and society can be judged. To many black Anglicans, it has been quite important that the kind of Anglicanism practised by the whites that have stood up for social justice – Reeves and ffrench-Beytagh and so on –

is the kind of Anglicanism that they as blacks are used to, rather than the vaguer kind mostly practised in the white suburbs. The fuller version of Catholic practice has gone along with a sharper concern for the sufferings of blacks: the fact that it has also gone along with a total disinterest in the sufferings of blacks is easy to ignore. But, among blacks, this kind of Anglicanism is the convention. No black Anglican can express creativity or rebellion or independence by identifying herself as an Anglo-Catholic. It is quite worthwhile for a pastor to encourage a young white South African to get enthusiastic even for the mere externalities of Anglo-Catholicism, because in good hands this enthusiasm will lead him to a much deeper vision of what God is about than the traditions of most white parents and their parishioners. But the effect of encouraging a young black to be enthusiastic about Catholic practice as such will almost certainly be to encourage a finicky preoccupation with things that can act as a frosted-glass screen against the real world. The creativity and independence of a young black Anglican will almost certainly have to include some reaction against the Anglo-Catholic tradition. People like Steve Biko tend to have drawn what they can from that tradition and seek to grow into something wider. The important point remains, however, that this tradition has supplied criteria. Very probably these criteria will be used in judgment on the tradition itself, but this is the inevitable risk of any honourable educational enterprise.

What has been the appeal of Anglican Catholicism? Why has its contribution been received? We must acknowledge, first of all, that this tradition has no monopoly of Christian treasures. Most of the main Christian traditions, except Orthodoxy, have consciously undertaken missionary endeavour in South Africa, and I would not suggest that Anglican Catholicism has been more successful than others. But it has offered a distinct emphasis, and this has spoken to people and found favour and drawn them closer to God's purposes.

Firstly, it has been a tradition which has laid great emphasis on visibility. Africa is pragmatic, not metaphysical; in Africa, a thing is more real if it is visible, touchable, and effective than if it is universal, mental and abstract. A form of Christianity which takes incarnation seriously speaks and registers. Incarnation is a gospel, not an embarrassment. Christ present in the sacrament, Christ present in the community, Christ present in the person of the priest – all this has made converting and sanctifying sense. If this has been at the expense of other sensitivities to Christ's presence – and I think that reverence for the priest has been at the expense of reverence for the ordinary sister and brother – this has been a failure to follow the logic through, rather than a failure in the basic emphasis. Catholicism has well stressed the gospel in terms of the visible body. The most powerful weapon in Catholicism's armoury of imagery in the struggle against injustice is the doctrine of the Body of Christ. There has been nothing radical or intellectually daring about this: the South African situation has required Catholicism to be thoroughly conservative and oppose the novel nonsense of upstart racism with a traditional orthodoxy which insists that there must be a visible fellowship of believers and that Christian love must be acted out in visible terms. South African apartheid ideology is Eutychian. It says that the love and fellowship of Christian belief is a spiritual reality and need not be visible in structure or meeting. People can be in a holy relation of common belief while remaining in separate churches and while cut off from each other by vast differences of power and privilege. An incarnational faith will insist that this is reversing the gospel; instead of representing a word that becomes flesh it is removing people from flesh into a world only of words. The doctrine of the Body of Christ insists that the love of God must continue to be embodied, made visible, verifiable, even structured. This has been the central message of the Catholic tradition, and it has been received with enthusiasm by blacks – who of course go on to ask us to show the evidence for our witness! But even when we are criticised, we are criticised functionally, we are criticised because we fail to fulfil our ideals, whereas apartheid is criticised fundamentally; it is criticised because it fulfils its ideals only too well.

Secondly, Catholicism appeals because it has an instinct for the operation of symbols. It uses visuals and action. It is not concerned only to get words right (although the Catholicism of the monoglot English has often been very preoccupied with this); it is concerned that meaning should be conveyed by as wide a range of communication as possible. So Catholicism speaks to people by its use of rites of passage and sacraments of healing. This is important anywhere: it is particularly important in the polyglot context of so much South African society. My first work with Africans was in a mining area. The Anglican congregation in the mine compound was drawn from all over Central and Southern Africa. Hymns were announced in six languages, the sermon was heard in four languages; the eucharist was communicated in one language, the language of the eucharistic act. At this point, observe that in contrast to Latin Catholicism, Anglican Catholicism has also a long tradition of linguistic Catholicism. Anglican Catholics have been as keen as any Protestants on using the language of the people: the difference has been that they have stressed that the vernacular should be used for the tools for worship, the liturgy, and not just for the Bible.

Thirdly, Catholicism has taken doctrine seriously. Doubtless, it has often satisfied itself with getting people to learn the dogmatic formulae by rote; it has come into Africa powerfully, confident in the universal meaningfulness of its symbols; it has imposed a 'classroom religion'.

But also, in its insistence upon the importance of doctrine, it has treated Africans as intellectually competent people; unlike so many other elements in the landscape, it has not let them off with anything second-rate. It may have mystified and dominated them, but it has not despised them. And there are some elements in Catholic doctrine which are of great importance, in which contact can be made with an African world view to an extent which the missionaries could not have realised at first. The most obvious of these is the doctrine of the Communion of Saints: and, even more important, because it is more Christologically central, is the doctrine of the descent of Christ into Hell. Most central of all, a Church which truly insists on the doctrine of the Trinity will, if it is patient, discover that Africa, can not only receive it but renew it in a fresh disclosure. The doctrine of the Trinity is, in part, an account of how, at the heart of things, the power-principle is subordinated to the community-principle, and how the shared properties of personhood are related to the distinct and unique features of individuality. The doctrine of the Trinity also affirms that there is mediation and indirectness even in the very nature of God. It would be valuable, for instance, to have a truly African mind to comment on the community models which are implied in the dispute concerning the filioque. Issues of this sort are home ground within African community life, much more so than in western society, with its assumptions and conventions concerning the operation of power in management, land-tenure and education. Recent South African Black Theology has been developing the words and theories for the necessary theological analysis, but the fundamental values concerned have been at work for a long time. However crudely the doctrines may have been taught, when they are given in their traditional fullness there are lures and links and barbs within them which have caught people's minds in a way that a reduced version would not have done.

Fourthly, Catholicism has offered a specific programme for the healing of guilt. Again, there has been a real danger of 'classroom religion' – the priest tells the penitent what actions are sinful and the penitent tells the priest that these are the things she has been doing. This may be miles away from what the old Prayer Book meant when it said the the penitent should 'open his grief', which means putting one's felt guilt into words, not just the guilt which one has been instructed to have. None the less, in spite of all the dangers of formality and subservience to authority, the Catholic provision for sacramental absolution has been accepted and valued – partly because it is an alternative to mere legalism, which is perhaps the biggest disease in African Christianity. It stands for the belief that badness is not a fundamental property of creation but is a blemish or deformity which can be healed. This is an important point of contact when the Church is seeking to meet a culture which is, as Africa is on the whole, world-affirming. In spite of the common allegations that Christianity came into Africa destroying indigenous culture and making the people feel purely bad about their past, we can see in, for instance, the immensely sensitive approach of Bishop Lucas of Masasi, that a truly Catholic gospel will seek to affirm that which is creative in a culture and to destroy only that which is destructive.

The two most serious accusations about Anglican Catholicism – and indeed against most forms of Christianity – in Southern Africa are that it is a white man's gospel and that it has the effect of disabling and supressing the ordinary church member. Clearly, there is some truth in both charges. Just as Calvinism is vulnerable to being taken over as an instrument of separation, Catholicism can be co-opted into an unconscious imperialism. Its stress on unity can work out as a conformity based on the presuppositions of those who happen to have power. And this is, inevitably, disabling. The church-member is made to feel that he has only very limited ability to be an agent of Christ and has to depend all the time on the specialist priest – who may visit the church only very infrequently. These dangers are obvious, and very serious. But they can be overcome, and we shall realise that they are being overcome when the exported Catholicism flows back towards its source-area with independent perceptions and creative disturbances. What influences can we in Britain hope for?

Firstly, I offer my opinion that the Anglican Provinces outside the Church of England (including those of the other nations in Britain) have more in common with each other than any of them has with the Church of England. The Church of England can take itself for granted in a way that Anglicanism elsewhere cannot. In all the little books for series 2 and series 3, one had to look rather hard in the small print to discover the Church which authorised them. And I have learned to recognise the kind of saddened expression which one receives when one states that one is leaving the Church of England – even if only to join the Anglican Church in an adjacent province! But the Church of England is becoming more like the non-established provinces, rather than the other way round. It has less of a monopoly of being the 'mainstream' than it used to have. In the religious department of the royal celebration in 1977, the Church of England could operate on its own: in 1981, the other Churches were treated as part of the establishment. English Anglicanism is itself becoming a minority among other minorities, and therefore the identificational reasons for being an English Anglo-Catholic are declining. Anglican Catholicism in England will not have to be judged by its ability to provide an alternative within the establishment for those who desire it, nor even by its power to steer the whole establishment in its preferred direction. It will be judged in a manner more similar to the manner by which it has been judged outside England, by its ability to be a creative minority within society as a whole, not by domestic self-propagation but by the integrity of its total contribution.

Secondly, English Anglicanism has, in the past, been fairly unsuccessful in relating to the less powerful language-groups and cultural groups in Britain. It has lived for too long as if only one language and one accent were fit for serious use. This now is especially a problem for the Church of England, because in other areas of Britain disestablishment has relaxed this bondage to the most powerful culture. English Anglicanism is, therefore, out of practice in relating to minority cultures, and has found itself ill-equipped to cope with the sudden increase in the variety of cultures which have recently come to stay in its area. Here the experience and instinct of non-English Anglicanism should be of great service to the Church of England. And particularly, Anglican Catholicism which has been through a non-English experience should have much to offer. There are many possibilities, of which I select just one as an example. Racism is an identificational disease: it is ancestor-consciousness gone neurotic. It calls for real healing, not mere denunciation. The Catholic doctrine of the communion of saints enables us to take our ancestral identities seriously. A Christianity which fails to teach this doctrine can do little about our racial, national, or tribal consciousness except tell us to grow out of it, be ashamed of it, or suppress it. Catholicism can recognise that our racial consciousness is indeed part of our created nature: but it also insists that in Christ's descent to Hell he has healed the antagonisms which made our ancestors enemies of each other, and that the Christian altar is the meeting place of all the human race, living and departed, in all their ancestral identities. Christ enables racial enemies to meet as neighbours; the Church is the place where people of different cultures meet their one Lord, because the Church stands for the destruction of those patterns of injustice which elevate one group into a supposed superiority over another. This is the kind of appropriation of traditional Catholic doctrine which Anglican Catholicism outside England has developed, to meet the needs of a non-English situation. It shows that there is a real task ahead for Anglican Catholicism to do in England, if it can be renewed by its comrades in discipleship from outside its borders.

12 Monastic Witness: a personal view

Aelred Stubbs CR

Then

My dear friend,' wrote Dr Pusey to Mr Newman early in the morning of Trinity Sunday 1841, 'a young lady, who is very grateful for your teaching, is purposing today to take a vow of holy celibacy . . . and hopes to receive the Holy Communion . . . It was wished that you should know it and remember her. You will know her by her being dressed in white with an ivory cross . . .'[1] With this religious profession of Miss Marian Hughes the monastic life may be reckoned to have returned to the Church of England after an interval of three hundred years. The ideal of the monastic life had never died out, but 'it was not until evangelical social concern for the spiritual and physical needs of a growing population caught up in the turmoil of the Industrial Revolution became juxtaposed with Tractarian spirituality that conditions which proved favourable for the foundation of a stable Religious Community were created in the Church of England'.[2]

The first community, founded at Park Village West in Easter Week 1845, is an apt illustration of this historical judgment. Founded through the untiring labours of Dr Pusey, it also owed its existence to the patronage of an influential committee, chaired by Lord John Manners (a leading member of the Young England Group), which had desired a sisterhood which 'living under a religious rule, would engage in some work of mercy as visiting the poor and sick in their own homes, visiting hospitals, workhouses and prisons, feeding, clothing and instructing destitute children, and assisting in burying the dead'.[3] But if this committee envisaged religious communities as a real political possibility until the storm broke over the 'Puseyites' after Newman's secession to the Church of Rome, the reaction of John Keble was more characteristic of that quiet High Church spirit which was the real backbone of the Oxford Movement. He wrote to Pusey that he feared that 'being so few . . . they may easily think too much of themselves and be made too much of'.[4]

Besides this propitious conjunction of circumstances, there was a third factor, whose theological significance has not often been observed – the generally oppressive conditions under which unmarried gentlewomen lived at the time. The most famous of them, who at one time looked longingly in the direction of the Roman Catholic Sisters of Charity, but who in the end found another route of escape, was Florence Nightingale. In a private note of 1851 she wrote: 'Women don't consider themselves as human beings at all. There is absolutely no God, no country, no duty to them at all, except family . . . I have known a good deal of convents. And of course everyone has talked of the petty grinding tyranny of a good English family. And the only alleviation is that the tyrannised submits with a heart full of affection'.[5] So liberating proved the power of grace in the new monastic communities that J M Neale, who founded the Society of St Margaret at East Grinstead in 1855, found in his little community that complete identification of the Christian community with the life of Christ, which the Tractarians believed to be the real goal of the Church.[6] Not surprisingly, they were persecuted by the Church.

Between 1845 and 1870 some 25 sisterhoods were founded, some of them owing their origin to a remarkable priest-founder – Carter of Clewer, Butler of Wantage, to name only two besides Neale. Only one men's community founded at that time took enduring root in the Church of England – the Society of St John the Evangelist, founded at Cowley in 1866 by the Revd Richard Meux Benson, the one undoubted spiritual giant in the Anglican revival of the monastic life. From the beginning there was a determination towards two goals, both of which are significant in a consideration of Anglican monastic witness. First was a desire for life vows. This met with rigid opposition, even from the one diocesan Bishop who was a strong advocate for the sisterhoods, Samuel Wilberforce, of Oxford, and even from some of the priest-founders. But the women persevered. A breakthrough came when Father Benson secured the agreement of Bishop Wilberforce to the first members of the Cowley community taking a life vow from the beginning; and by about 1883 the taking of life vows could be said to be 'almost universally prevalent'. This making over of the whole life to God, which has always been an element in monastic vocation, was a powerful, if largely hidden, factor in its witness to the liberating power of Christ.

Secondly, there was a determination that the life to be lived would be both apostolic and monastic, a life of contemplation and of action. This has remained a special characteristic of the mainstream of Anglican community life, to the admiration of many Roman Catholic observers. For example, after recording how the rule of Neale's Society of St Margaret was closely modelled on the first rule of the Visitation, a recent biographer of St Jeanne-Francoise de Chantal continues: 'the spirit and achievement of this sisterhood, the whole history of its later development along lines laid down by a remarkable founder, illustrates in a striking way how St Francis' [de Sales] original idea of a real compromise between contemplation and action can be put into effect and adapted to English attitudes'.[7] We may compare with this comment of an external observer the words of Mother Kate of Haggerston. Writing towards the end of her long life about the early days at East Grinstead, she speaks of the 'breadth and large-mindedness' of Neale's foundation – 'a sort of what we nowadays call Christian Socialism'.[8] So persistent in the Anglican monastic revival has been this determination towards the so-called 'mixed' life of contemplation and action that the same balance may be observed in the American Episcopalian Community of the Holy Spirit, a teaching order established as recently as 1952.

But although the Anglican monastic revival owed much for its inspiration to the social conditions of the time, both in regard to the oppressed status of gentlewomen, and to the appalling conditions of the urban and rural poor, it has to be admitted that few of the Tractarians – Neale, a Cambridge man, was an exception – had a positive theological vision of the political and social regeneration of society in their approach to strictly non-religious questions. A M Allchin cites F D Maurice's criticism that 'they opposed to the spirit of the age, not so much the Spirit of God, but the spirit of an earlier century'.[9] From Cambridge, however, influenced by Maurice, came a group of men who were impressed by the social implications of monasticism – E W Benson, later Archbishop of Canterbury, J B Lightfoot, and B F Westcott, successively Bishops of Durham. 'We all "saw visions" as is the privilege of young men,' Westcott wrote later of their undergraduate years, 'and those visions were of monastic orders.' The vision remained with Westcott all his life, and was closely related by him to the needs of the age. 'History teaches us,' he preached to the boys at Harrow on October 25th 1868, 'that social evils must be met by social organisations.' After reviewing the contribution in their own times of such monastic founders as Antony of Egypt, Benedict, Francis of Assisi and Ignatius Loyola, he continued: 'nothing from old times will meet our exigencies. We want a rule which shall answer to the complexity of our own age'.[10] Although Westcott himself believed that these 'exigencies' and 'complexity' demanded the family rather than the celibate individual as the unit, this sermon sowed a seed in the heart of one boy who heard it, a seed which bore fruit nearly a quarter of a century later in Charles Gore's founding of the Community of the Resurrection. From the beginning this Community took as its model the description of the earliest church in *Acts* 2:42 and 4:32; and there can be no doubt that it was their own experience of the *koinonia* which led many of the early brethren to 'appear on Labour platforms, even to declare themselves Socialists –

at a time when the title was one of opprobrium in the minds of many Church people'.[11]

Another man, contemporary with Gore, who was influenced by F D Maurice, was H H Kelly, founder of the Society of the Sacred Mission. Alike at Kelham and at Mirfield were founded theological colleges for the training of men who would otherwise not have been able to afford to be ordained in the Church of England. Nothing has done more than this practical expression of Christian socialism to broaden the social base of the Church of England during the 20th century.[12] The third men's community to spring from the last decade of the 19th century was the Society of the Divine Compassion. Of Franciscan inspiration, it practised from the beginning a real identification with the poor of London's East End. In 1906 one of its number, Father William Sirr, marched at the head of a large procession of unemployed men into the heart of fashionable London to protest against the unendurable conditions in which they were forced to live.

Less than ten years later the same priest was seeking a life of monastic seclusion. His Society, which had supported him in his protest march, failed to perceive the connection. Father Benson (of whom the young William had been a disciple) would have understood: and it was his Society which provided the setting at Cowley in which this monastic vocation could be nourished, thus making possible the revival of the enclosed life of prayer for men in the English Church. As in the original revival, the women had already led the way, many of the contemplative communities which today are relatively well-known having begun in obscurity and, often, in real hardship during the first two decades of the 20th century. As with Father William, so with more than one of the women's enclosed communities, it was the service of Christ in his poor that drew these women deeper and deeper into the life of prayer.[13] There seems to be, in the monastic vocation, this integral connection.

Only the briefest mention can be made here of the revival and development of religious communities in other parts of the Anglican Communion. The Episcopal Church in the United States has had its own long history in this area since 1852, when an ex-Lutheran priest founded a sisterhood modelled on the lines of the deaconesses of Kaiserswerth. In countries such as Canada, South Africa, Australia and New Zealand there were autonomous foundations, again deriving their inspiration from the Oxford Movement. Also, in many parts of what was then the British Empire, there were overseas houses of English communities, most of them engaged in 'missionary' work. In some cases 'native' communities were established under the wing of a 'mother', for example, in Tanganyika (as it was called at that time) the Community of St Mary of Nazareth and Calvary was formed under the Community of the Sacred Passion. Truly indigenous communities, however, reflecting the virile Christian faith of a non-European culture, were rare – with one notable exception. Retatasiv, the Melanesian Brotherhood, was founded in 1925 by Ini Kopuria, a policeman, as an evangelistic lay movement. Annual or triennial promises are made: to remain unmarried, to receive no pay, and to obey the spiritual direction of the Bishop. In 1960 there were 74 who had made this temporary but renewable promise, with many more in training, and in their work of evangelism they had moved out from Melanesia as far as the highlands of New Guinea.[14] There is also a small Community of the Holy Fire at Gokwe in Zimbabwe, founded by an African priest, and dedicated to spiritual healing, but it is as yet too early to tell whether this community will survive.

Now

The fifty years since the celebration of the centenary of the Oxford Movement have been, as far as religious communities in the Church of England are concerned, years first of consolidation and even – particularly for the contemplative orders after World War 2 – of growth; and of a measure of incorporation into the structures of the Church. The Advisory Council for Religious Communities was established in 1935, and there are now four representatives of communities on the General Synod. But since the early 1960s the whole climate of monastic life in the Church of England has altered so radically that the last twenty-five years seem to embrace changes which make 1958 nearer by far to 1933 than to this year of grace. There has been a 'shaking of the foundations', as a result of which monastic witness in the Church of England today is modest and hidden.

After their meeting at Canterbury in May 1982 the Permanent Ecumenical Consultation of Religious issued a Statement in which they contrasted the relationship to the Church of Roman Catholic religious ('. . . integral, even necessary to the Church's full expression') with that of Anglicans, who are described as being '. . . few, and less formally incorporated in their Church's structure'.[15] It is possible to raise an Anglican eyebrow over the Consultation's claim for the Roman Catholic orders to be 'necessary to the Church's full expression' without arguing with their assessment of the Anglicans' position. It is a modest one indeed.

Monastic witness is an ecumenical witness. Since Vatican 2 we have a quite new sense of sharing a common vocation with our Roman Catholic brothers and sisters in religion. To quote again from the May 1982 Statement: 'Religious of the two Churches . . . are an effective sign of the unity they are called to promote . . . This promotion is an integral part of our life and mission'. The present Pope has expressed this by the personal audience which he granted to a group of Anglican Religious Superiors a few years ago, and by the special warmth with which he greeted the Anglican participants in the Mass for Religious which he celebrated at Roehampton during his visit to England in 1982. Our brothers and sisters of the Roman obedience, with their traditions going back, in the case of the Benedictines in particular, to the very roots of English and European history, appreciate more warmly today the Anglicans as bearers of that life-giving Christian tradition which has been one of the shaping factors in the society in which all our communities, Roman and Anglican alike, are called to minister and witness. Particularly they value the determination of our mainstream communities to maintain a 'mixed' life of contemplation and action, with, as a visible sign of that determination, the universal Anglican practice of the corporate recitation of the Office.[16] Whatever the peculiar values of, for example, the Jesuit tradition, particularly in the fields of directed retreats and of spiritual direction, they wish us to hold on to the far older, deeper, and – in England – more pervasive Benedictine and Augustinian traditions of common life and common prayer. We are accepted as part of the Western Church. The unity we already enjoy is a unity effected by Baptism. Our own specific unity is defined by the working out of our baptismal promise in a shared religious vocation, the special costingness and joy of travelling together along this road to the 'End without end'.

Anglicans have, at least since the time of Lancelot Andrewes' *Preces Privatae*, acknowledged a particular ecumenical vocation and responsibility; and this was reaffirmed by the Tractarians. Amongst early founders of sisterhoods, J M Neale had a special feeling for the Eastern Orthodox Church, and was affirmed by some of them as understanding them 'from within'.[17] This affinity of Anglicanism and Orthodoxy now has a special monastic significance from the revival – 'one of the less expected characteristics of our time'[18] – of the solitary life in our Church (as also in the Roman Catholic Church). Although the then Abbot Primate of the Benedictine Congregation, speaking 'off the cuff' at a large gathering of Anglican religious in 1974, gave it as his opinion that 75 per cent of the 'hermits' he had encountered were 'phoney', he also said that the other 25 per cent were 'pure gold': gold tried in the furnace of affliction. This most primitive form of monastic life is once more so firmly established in our Church that the latest edition of the Directory devotes three pages to its consideration. The considerable Orthodox monastic presence in England today, the fact that in 1982 the first English-born Orthodox monk (Dr Kallistos Ware, monk of the monastery of St John on Patmos) was consecrated bishop – these are indications of the recovery in our time of links with the unbroken tradition descending from the Fathers (and Mothers) of the Egyptian deserts of the fourth century.[19]

Exigencies of space forbid more than a mention of the revival of religious communities in continental Protestantism, but it may be pointed out that when, in 1934, Bonhoeffer was planning the seminary which afterwards took shape at Finkenwalde ('young theologians ought now to be trained throughout in conventual seminaries where the pure doctrine, the Sermon on the Mount and worship are taken seriously as they never are . . . at university'), he visited, among other places, Mirfield and Kelham, not only with regard to methods of training for the Ministry, but also to investigate models of the *vita communis* which he wished to establish, and about which he later wrote in *Life Together*.[20] Amongst these continental communities the best known is, of course, Taize. But of all of them these words in the Directory are applicable: 'As often happens, the first generation of such new foundations seems to be given a special grace. We have much indeed to learn from their example'.[21]

But the special ecumenical responsibility of Anglican religious communities is not only to religious of other ecclesial communions: it is also to be a sign of unity in our own Church. One of the four representatives of the religious communities in the General Synod has told how displeased some members of the so-called 'Catholic party' have been to note that the religious can never be relied on to vote as 'Catholics'. But the communities belong to the whole Church, not to any sect within it. From the beginning of the revival one can discern 'evangelical' as well as 'Catholic' influences. This is not surprising, seeing that the religious life is an evangelical response to an evangelical call. 'Jesus, looking upon him, loved him . . .' 'She has done what she could . . .' The Franciscans notably have always made an appeal to a very wide spectrum in the Church of England. This, together with the attractiveness of Franciscan simplicity in an affluent society, and the fact that the community is predominantly lay, may account for the fact that since World War 2 it has far outstripped the older men's communities, and now has houses in many different parts of the world. From the Evangelical tradition in the Church of England some forty years ago sprang up also a little community of singular attractiveness with a twofold purpose: to live together in a spirit of Christian charity, and to minister to the needs of exhausted missionaries on leave. St Julian's has much to teach the older communities about the practice of the common life, and it offers a specially English example of monastic hospitality.[22] Nor should we forget the popular Evangelical communities at Lee Abbey and Scargill.

It is impossible in an essay of this scope to do more than allude to the mushrooming during the past decade of so-called 'basic Christian communities'[23] – not to be confused with the 'base communities' which are playing a vital and heroic part in the renewal of the Roman Catholic Church in Latin America and in the liberation struggle there. But specific mention at least must be made, in connection with the internal ecumenical responsibilities and opportunities open to 'traditional' religious communities, of the appearance on the scene of communities which have sprung out of the Charismatic renewal movement. One such community is located at Whatcombe in Dorset, another at Post Green in the same county. Whatcombe consists of married families as well as unmarried men and women, some of whom make a semi-permanent commitment, while others are more temporary. The community runs the large house as a residential centre for parish and other renewal conferences.[24] It is also interesting to learn that a number of those who have found renewal through this Pentecostal type of Christian life and worship subsequently find they want to commit themselves in a more permanent way through becoming Oblates or Tertiaries of a 'traditional' community, or through actually joining such a community.

The foregoing paragraphs may give the impression that Anglicans are somehow at the centre of a monastic ecumenical network. Such is neither the intention nor the case. Rather, by the faithfulness of their corporate and personal witness to the dying and rising of Jesus, religious communities have the freedom to witness to that unity of all the baptised that is already ours, and to make their own modest contribution to the recovery of that visible unity which is our Lord's urgent desire – not for the Church's sake, but so that God's Kingdom may be proclaimed with a single heart and voice. The ecumenical task of the religious communities leads them above all into the largely hidden dimension of prayer. Just as the task of the theologian, according to F D Maurice, is to dig, so the religious has to dig so deep into the life of prayer that he or she bears living witness to the unity of all the baptised, indeed of all humanity, in the one Christ.

It is to that hidden witness of prayer that we now turn. There has been a remarkable revival of interest in prayer, and particularly in contemplative prayer, in the Church in the last few years. The person of Mother Julian, the 14th-century anchoress and mystic, is symbolic of this revival. With reason she has been called the greatest of all English theologians. 'Julian Groups' have been started all over the country in recent years. Something, though not nearly enough, is now being done at some theological colleges to equip ordinands for what is arguably the most important task in their ministry: to teach the faithful to pray. This cannot be done unless the man himself not only knows how to pray but is praying, wants to pray better, and is profoundly convinced that nothing is more important than this.

There is a hunger for God. It drives thousands of the young half-way across the world to India and the Far East, seeking a reality they think they cannot find in the West. It would be glib to say that the West is spiritually bankrupt, but that there is a spiritual crisis no thinking person would deny. What do the Anglican religious communities have to offer in this witness of prayer? First, a witness of stability and perseverance, places where 'prayer has been valid', where silence and solitude are treasured, not selfishly, but as precious gifts to be made available to those who will value them too. Of women's communities, whose active works have been taken over by state agencies, or have had to be given up because the resources were no longer available, many have found a new sphere of work in the running of retreat houses, and in the training of retreat givers and spiritual directors. Liturgical renewal has enabled some of the larger houses to revitalise their corporate worship in Office and Eucharist. There is strength in siting a retreat house so that the retreatants can participate in a community's ordered worship.

There is a revival of Plainsong. The communities' Consultative Council has produced an excellent Anglican Office Book. Some communities can welcome guests to share in the celebration of the Paschal Mystery, the centre of the Christian year. Even if there may still be some 'unscrambling' of the tradition to be done – for the founders of a century and more ago drew their inspiration from a number of conflicting sources, patristic, mediaeval, post-Tridentine, and 19th-century France – yet now, as in the past, there is a continuing witness of perseverance, faithfulness and the humility and wisdom of experience which makes religious communities a valuable asset to Christian men and women in turning more deeply to God in prayer. At the very least, monasteries and convents can provide that traditional hospitality, especially to the casualties of modern society who are most often its most sensitive and potentially valuable members, where they can find healing and a new direction.

Deeper still is the hidden witness of intercession, most particularly of hermits and enclosed communities, but also experienced as a burden of love laid on all religious. Not that this most Christian kind of prayer is a preserve of religious. Perhaps the most eloquent plea since the time of Charles Williams for all Christians to be burden-bearers in this work of intercession is to be found in Alan Ecclestone's *Yes to God*. Ecclestone is a married priest who served all his long parish ministry in an industrial city, was for many years a member of the Communist Party, and, through his *Prism* pamphlet *On Praying* has done much to help ordinary people to begin to pray again.[25] But religious communities provide continuity. It would, for example, be hard to overestimate what many hard-pressed Christians and non-Christians in South Africa feel they owe to the life of prayer undertaken by one small women's community at the heart of the evil situation there. They are a kind of convenanted sign that God cares.

And . . .

Monastic witness is, of its very nature, a witness to the Kingdom of God, that is, it is a witness to something beyond itself, beyond even the visible

Church, while integrally a part of that Church. It is a witness to the Kingdom which has come in the birth, life, death and resurrection of our Lord Jesus Christ, and is to be consummated in his final coming. It is a witness to the final state of affairs. There are three things to be said about this monastic witness. Firstly, it is, of its nature, risky. Secondly, it is a corporate witness. Thirdly, it is a witness to the essential incompleteness of our human life as we experience it here and now. 'Il faut parier,' said Pascal. 'One has to make a bet.' Religious are those who stake their whole lives on the story having a happy ending. They are supported in their gamble by the memory of those who have made the same bet in the past, who, even if they were mistaken, lived lives of courage, generosity and compassion, who were filled with a kind of gaiety that seems somehow enviable and desirable. It is a bet on the truth of the resurrection of the Lord Jesus. And the bet has to be one's whole life: that is part of the game. Instinctively, those women who offered themselves 140 years ago knew this. Discretion is a virtue of fundamental import in the ascetic life, but in this matter the religious throws discretion to the winds and himself overboard. 'Once you've made your oblation, I don't see that it matters much when you die' was a saying of Raymond Raynes, CR, who certainly lived every minute of his life to the full. There is a recklessness about monastic witness, present in every form, and evident in the three-fold vow of celibacy, poverty and obedience.

Celibacy is a vow, that is, primarily a prayer, not only to be delivered from 'the tyranny of genitality' (the phrase is that of a modern Dominican) but far more profoundly to be set free to love in the mode of the Kingdom, a love by which, in its perfection, one can give the whole of one's self to the other, whoever the other may be. It is a prayer for grace to do this, and a promise to try to order the rest of one's life in conformity with the grace given. Poverty is a vow not so much to be delivered from the selfishness symbolised in the possessive pronoun 'mine', as to be made progressively aware that, by this act of dispossession, all the riches of the Kingdom are yours – 'and you are Christ's, and Christ is God's' – (1 *Cor* 3:23). Obedience is a vow to be delivered from enslavement to the false self into 'the glorious freedom of the children of God' (*Romans* 8:21).

Obedience: authority. And so to the second point about monastic witness to the Kingdom of God: that it is a corporate witness. The Church of England has always had a problem about authority, and about a sense of corporateness. Interestingly, the recent publication of the Doctrine Commission is sub-titled 'the corporate nature of faith'.[26] One would hope that here the monastic community could make a modest witness to a corporate faith lived out in community. But it is a broken witness. Near the beginning of the 20th century Archbishop Randall Davidson, then Visitor to the young Community of the Resurrection, said of its

Rule: 'It seems to me that you are trying to combine two incompatibles – individual liberty and corporate authority'. To this a young brother, later to be superior, replied: 'But is it not precisely that difficult essay that the Church of England has been attempting for the last four hundred years? If not, what has it been trying?'[27] But that exchange took place within a shared background of common values, values moreover which had not, at that time, been explicitly rejected by a good part of the Church, or by the greater part of society. Today the insistence on the exercise of individual liberty, or rather of the quest for 'personal fulfilment' and 'authenticity' leads, or if indulged would lead, to a community of Stylites. 'Where do you go from the top of a thirty-foot pole?'[28] There is only one reason for obeying, and that is a desire to be conformed to Christ crucified and risen. And obedience today is seen much more as a mutual courtesy of attention: to listen, to remain open, flexible. And all this in the dark. Certainly it is a broken witness which monastic communities give. Certainly it is possible for the individual monk or nun to live a kind of split life, in which the exterior witness is one thing, and the life lived in community is altogether something different. In this time, when we experience the love of God as wrath and absence, what would you expect?

For, finally, monastic witness to the Kingdom of God is a witness to our radical incompleteness, and that is a very unpopular witness in this closed world. To the writer, the accidental death of Thomas Merton, electrocuted by a fan while taking a shower in his Bangkok hotel in December 1968, is as good a symbol as one could hope to find of contemporary monastic witness. For a humanist, it was a tragic accident. But for his fellow-monks (though they, of course, experienced the sharpest grief and shock, for he was a beloved brother), it was, ultimately, a very good joke, a divine joke in fact: God's 'Yes' to his servant. Absurd, and funny, and oddly satisfactory.

References

1 The letter is cited in H P Liddon, *Life of Pusey*, vol 3, p 10.

2 *Anglican Religious Communities: a Directory of Principles and Practice* (3rd edition, SLG Press, Oxford, 1978). Subsequently cited as 'Directory'.

3 Liddon, *op cit*.

4 Quoted in A M Allchin, *The Silent Rebellion* (SCM Press, 1958), p 63. This is the best account of the revival of the Religious Life in the Church of England in the 19th century, and I have drawn heavily on it in the first part of this essay.

5 Cited in C Woodham Smith, *Florence Nightingale* (Fontana, 1968), p 74.

6 Allchin, *op cit*, p 112.

7 E A Stopp, *Madame de Chantal: portrait of a saint* (Faber, 1962), p 209.

8 Quoted in A G Lough, *The Influence of John Mason Neale* (SPCK, 1962), p 67.

9 Allchin, *op cit*, p 218.

10 *ibid*, pp 219ff.

11 E K Talbot, CR, quoted in P F Anson, *The Call of the Cloister* (SPCK, 1964).

12 It is only right to recall that Butler of Wantage, even in 1845, had seen the need for a religious community of men for the training of ordinands, and for raising the whole standard of clerical life. (Allchin, pp 185ff). Also, of course, the Evangelicals had, as long ago as 1767, tried to make provision for 'poor and pious' men to be enabled to train for the ministry. Cf H E Hopkins, *Charles Simeon of Cambridge* (Hodder, 1977), pp 86ff.
13 See, for example, Sister Felicity Mary, SPB, *Mother Millicent Mary, SPB* (Macmillan, 1968).
14 See Howard A Johnson, *Global Odyssey* (Harper and Row, 1963), pp 308ff.
15 The full text of the Statement was published in *Signum*, October 1982.
16 It is hard to resist the conclusion that the strongest strand of monastic continuity between the 16th-century dissolution, and the 19th-century revival, is found in the Book of Common Prayer's provision for the daily public recitation of Morning and Evening Prayer – and this despite the fact that the Reformers' intention was anything but to perpetuate the monastic office!
17 See especially A G Lough, *op cit*, chapter 10.
18 Directory, p 44.
19 In the autumn of 1975 a conference was held at St David's in Wales on the solitary life in which representatives of the Roman Catholic, Orthodox, Congregational and Anglican traditions took part. The proceedings were published in *Solitude and Communion* (ed A M Allchin, SLG Press, 1977). The Statement made at the end of the conference is published in the Directory, p 44.
20 See E Bethge, *Dietrich Bonhoeffer* (Collins, 1970), pp 334ff.
21 Directory, p 55.
22 See M Potts, *St Julian's: an experiment in two continents* (SCM, 1968), and J H Oldham, *Florence Allshorn and the Story of St Julian's* (Hodder, 1974).
23 See David Clark, *Basic Christian Communities* (Institute of Socio-Religious Studies, Liverpool, 1978).
24 The story of this community's origins and of its early problems and joys is told in John Gunstone, *The Beginnings of Whatcombe: an experience of community* (Hodder, 1976).
25 Alan Ecclestone, *Yes to God* (Darton, Longman and Todd, 1975). The Prism pamphlet was reprinted in Eric James (ed) *Spirituality for Today.*
26 *Believing in the Church* (SPCK, 1981).
27 Quoted in Nicholas Mosley, *The Life of Raymond Raynes* (Faith Press, 1961), p 36.
28 Zen saying, quoted in Thomas Merton, 'Marxism and Monastic Perspectives', in The *Asian Journal of Thomas Merton* (Sheldon, 1974), pp 338ff.

13 The Oxford Movement: A Case of Cultural Distortion?

Valerie Pitt

Faith, it is claimed, is a state of initiate knowledge, a condition analagous to marriage in which lovers, in this case the creature and the Creator, come by covenant and commitment to 'know' each other in a continuing relationship. The theologians also say that the condition is of grace, sometimes of spectacular grace,

> 'Whether at once, as once at a crash Paul
> Or as Austin, a lingering-out sweet skill,'

a ravishing of will and perception, prissily effective, justifying and so forth, but so detached from ordinary social and moral experience that it seems to belong to a para-universe, alongside but secret from the normal world. This is misleading. The phenomena of conversion are not faith but, precisely, phenomena: surface manifestations of states of being running deep into the unseen strata of personality. For faith does, indeed, have the characteristics of marriage. Its commitments, though personal, are never private: the forms it takes and its consequences are corporate, locked into the customary life of particular societies, more especially the churches in which it is nourished, and the secular and civil communities in which they subsist. Besides, believing, that is the acts and responses of a life of faith over time, like being married, build into the believer's psyche conditions of perception and moral sensitivity which are not apart from, but integral to, his or her social existence and will, for good or evil, alter its quality. Faith belongs, that is, to what Raymond Williams calls our 'structures of feeling', the matrices created by our social and personal history for the most deeply personal of our experiences. Spiritual writers know this well enough – when they attend to it. St Augustine, for instance, set out in *The Confessions* to enquire about the modelling of his soul, to display to the glory of God the processes by which Christian structures came to be built into a sceptical late Roman mind: his own. Unfortunately, his rhetorician's instincts were carried away by the drama of it all: he doesn't engage our attention for the subtleties of his analysis but for the excitement of his experience. Just so, when we're caught by the long-running saga of the Oxford Movement, with its splendid settings and its charismatic caste, we don't attend to the cultural matrix of the Movement, nor to its re-making in the minds of those early and indeed, pre-Victorian actors. That's a pity, for that reconstruction of our Church's culture did not stop at the frontiers of that Oxford set. The faith of the Oxford Fathers has the character of a sub-culture within the Church of England but, more than that, it consolidated, at the wrong moment, and partly modified, the character of the Church itself.

That is what makes it significant. The Movement gave a hagiographical glamour even to its lesser leaders, like Marriot or Isaac Williams, as though each were a bright particular star. That won't do. Many of them were distinguished by talent and certainly by devotion, and the Movement had the luck to include two of the really towering Victorian Eminences, Newman and Gladstone, but then, theirs was a very remarkable generation. Keble himself was born in 1792, that is a year later than Michael Faraday and in the same year as the younger Herschel and Shelley. And the years between 1792 and 1815 which bred Pusey, Froude, Rogers, Church and so on, also fathered Keats and Carlyle, John Stuart Mill, Darwin, Disraeli and Isambard Kingdom Brunel, to say nothing of Tennyson, Browning and Dickens. How any of them will stand up to the light of the Great Doom who shall say, but any lesser comparison scarcely justifies Church's claim that his Oxford friends were the salt of their generation. They were not, in fact – and always excepting Newman – creative theologians. The future of theology lay not with them but, if anything, with the German professors who so shocked Pusey in the 1820s. Nor, though disciplined in their spiritual lives, and even virtuous, were all of them entirely admirable as human beings. Froude was a domestic bully with a streak of cruelty, Manning a manipulator of his own mind as well as other people's lives, Pusey was neurotically scrupulous and entirely wanting in common sense. Even Newman, as Austin Farrer said, 'was such an uncheerful codger'. All of them were notably ungenerous, as in the matter of Arnold's salvation or the prosecution of Jowett, to their opponents. All the same, as a group they re-dug and realigned the channels by which future generations of the Church of England were to receive the life of faith. It was not an accidental achievement. they meant to do it – not that is, to do what they actually did, which was to re-create the forms of the Church's culture, but to recover it to what they believed was its true and Catholic being.

What they achieved is generally considered to be a 'good thing'. It is the purpose of this essay to murmur a qualification to that, to suggest that, like all conservative revolutionaries, they attempted to force a living, growing society into dream patterns and that, in that attempt, they distorted the common life of the Church and accentuated its alienation from modern secular society. That's not to say that theirs were not real achievements. It is the conventional wisdom – and it is wisdom – that the 'Movement' 'saved' the Church of England though from what dangers is not always made clear. The Divines who made the Movement knew, or thought they knew: Erastianism, Liberalism and German Biblical speculation. In their search for effective weapon systems against the first of these enemies they recovered for Anglicanism at least one great prize: the vision of the Church itself, terrible as an army with banners, stretching rank on rank across the shores of Time and Eternity. That sense of their Church's coinherence with the Christian past and with its Lord, *sobornost, koinonia, Catholicity*, the thing for which the sober Churchman had no word in 1825, was not then, as it is now, grained into the thoughts and feelings of the instructed Anglican. 'We now hear' said a Regency Divine, 'not a breath about the Church, by and by those who live to see it will hear nothing else.' It was the Oxford Movement which brought this about and it is the consensus that, though the awareness of Christian Community in Christ did not (how should it?) contain the advancing tides of secularism at least it provided the Church with a sea wall, the sense of its own true identity as the Divine Society and of its relationship with other Churches. Paradoxically, no Oxford Movement, no ecumenism. There needs to be a sense of what the Church is and is meant to be before its members can be shocked by its divisions.

However, the definitely cultural change which the Movement made in Anglicanism was in the practice of religion, that is in rite, in devotion and in ascesis. That's often mistaken for changes in the appearance of religion – the substitution of the episcopal mitre for the episcopal wig for instance. And it was the trivia which attracted the fuss: not surprisingly, for the feel and fit of religious practice is symbiotic with personal belief: the paraphernalia of what happens in Church sustains its structure and quality in the worshipper. Hence the genuine outrage felt about flowers or candles on Dr Pusey's altar and some of the absurder identifications of the 'Catholic Cause' with liturgical flounces of one kind and another. It is usual to argue, of course, that that 'sort of thing' was neither the fault nor the merit of the original Tractarians who were supposed to be notably conservative in their ecclesiological practice, hardly willing to shift a box pew or alter the cut of a surplice. That is to mistake the nature of the change the Movement brought about in English religion – for the candles and incense and the wearing of various items of decorative, ecclesiastical gear were merely incidental to a shift in attitudes to worship. All religious revival deepens, as a matter of course, the practice of personal devotion: personal and family prayers, bible reading, the keeping of Sunday and the practice of careful self examination were the marks of the 'serious' in the Evangelical revival. And of course such changes are formative in personal culture. What the Tractarians did was, strictly, to build on all that: by example and precept, by insisting on the cleric's duty to read the daily office publicly, and on the regular celebration of the Holy Communion; by placing very great emphasis on baptismal regeneration and on the significance of Confirmation they locked the deepening of personal devotion into the sacramental life of the sacramental community of the Church. Moreover, by their researches into past spirituality and by the revival of the Religious Life they grounded personal devotion and personal prayer in Tradition. That was not necessarily, I shall suggest, a useful development. Yet, after all the polemic and the excesses the change is felt to be a good thing. The Holy Communion is as a matter of course celebrated in Churches of all shades much more frequently and more certainly as the central act of the Church's being. It is even felt, though the latest revisions may leave some doubt that the conviction is universal, that it ought to be decently conducted and aesthetically pleasing. By culture, if not by conviction, most of the Church of England assumes in its worship a sacramental community.

There was a price for all that. There is a sermon of Newman's which Owen Chadwick quotes in *The Mind of the Oxford Movement*, one of his most eloquent Anglican sermons which reveals the cost only too clearly. The presence of the visible Church, Newman says, the people, the ministry, the sacraments, are 'spells' (his word, not mine) to bring us all into the company of the Church Invisible, armies of saints and angels, legions of the holy dead, all swept into a passion of unity and worship - that is where real life is: 'The Church is not in time or place, but in the region of spirits'. The sermon itself is, even on the printed page, spell-binding, uncomfortably and unconsciously reminiscent of the language and imagery of magic. Given probably in St Mary the Virgin, in the incantations of that famous silver voice, it must have carried the preacher's congregation out of itself into a daze of glory. And sheer unreality. Once one lifts one's eyes from the page and the spell is broken one is aware that the man has enchanted himself into dispensing not merely the clumsy encumbrances of this world, but with the awkward solidities of the Visible Church itself, or at the least that he has set its true life outide time in a pure otherness of being. Just so the Tractarian vision of the spiritual life, even of the sacramental life, has a certain abstraction. It withdraws the people of God into a world apart (the region of spirits Newman says), a bubble world, sheltered by an iridiscent glass of exquisite feeling from the common demands of ordinary life. That we will explore a little later. For as the means by which a culture modifies itself may well determine the nature of change, there is a prior problem. We have to consider how a handful of dons and

and country clergymen could, even with the aid of a magical eloquence, stir such seismic disturbances in so venerably settled an institution as the Established Church.

One answer lies in the social and cultural situation of the 1820s and '30s: it could be argued that then no institution was venerably settled. For the Movement was itself, of course, a reaction against the imminence of other changes in the Church's fabric and the way it worked was determined by conditions already present in the inherited attitudes of the Church and the personal culture of a post-Romantic generation. The Tractarians believed that they were going back in history to secure their Church's truth against the forces of liberalism and reform. What they meant by the Church's truth was, at least in the case of Keble, and probably of Froude and Pusey, that formation in the faith which they had received in their own High Church and High Tory families and parishes. Keble is especially important here since, more than anyone else, his kind of devotion formed the mood, the cultural atmosphere of Tractarianism in its earliest phase and it was not susceptible to reason. For Keble's conservatism was ingrained and it belonged to a remoter past than the conservatism of his own generation. Even Wellington, and certainly Peel, were held to have betrayed, in the matter of Catholic Emancipation, political morality and the Church's inheritance. These attitudes were deeply influential and still lie, hidden and distorting, in the subsoil of our own experience of the Church's understanding of society. We will return to that.

Yet any comparison of the Tractarians and Tory High Churchmen of a previous generation, say William Law, or Dr. Johnson, reveals that between them there is a great gulf fixed. It is the gulf between imagination nurtured on Dryden and Addison and Pope and those nourished, if one may call it nourished, on Scott and Byron, Gothic Romance and Mackenzie's *The Man of Feeling*. It is misleading to label the cast of mind of the Tractarian generation 'Romantic': Romanticism is a complex and difficult phrase in European civilisation involving, among other things, a sense of revolutionary power in the human mind – not an awareness especially common in Victorian Churchmen of any stamp. What concerns us here is, happily, a simpler, more superficial manifestation of the Romantic Movement: I mean in the propensity of the Victorian leisured classes to seek a refined pleasure in their own feelings and sensibilities. They sought occasion for the indulgence in the contemplation of nature and antiquity and, of course, in art and literature, but more especially in the working of their own emotions, in passionate loves and friendships and in all the raptures and languors of religion. The Tractarians were not exempt from all this: they were addicted, like everyone else to the contemporary taste for melancholy and literary thrill. Isaac Williams repented his taste, at Harrow, for the pleasures and poison of Byron, but Pusey showed no particular sign of regretting his feel for what he calls the extreme force and beauty of Byron's poetry. Keble, in an extravagant phrase, says that he never lifted a work of Scott's without reverence – which, when one remembers that he meant not the novels but *The Lady of the Lake* and *Marmion*, does not entirely reveal a sense of proportion. As for their religion – the Tractarians are supposed to practise 'Reserve', that is to show a special constraint in reaction to Evangelical excesses, a gentlemanly fastidiousness in the faith. Yet their letters and diaries and the reminiscences of their friends and admirers show that as a group they were deeply emotional, minutely introspective, and only too ready to enter into lengthy correspondences with each other at the breath of a doubt or a problem. So Thomas Arnold wrote to Keble about his scruples on the Trinity; Keble wrote on to John Coleridge saying that he would sooner have Arnold's doubts than other's certainties. And so on. And as for the letters about Newman's inner states – they are endless. The fact is, though one isn't supposed to say it, the Oxford Fathers evidently expected life and religion to be conducted in a state of high sensibility which might well have gratified Miss Marianne Dashwood. In their generation and those immediately following, that was a major asset in promoting the views of and diffusing the ethos of their Movement.

For what originally carried the Movement into the country was not its formal propaganda, but a kind of miasmic infection, a high fever of religious feeling which spread outwards from Oxford. Oxford then, after all, was a nursery of the Anglican ministry and that nursery existed, during the Tractarian years, in a state of abnormal, carefully cultivated religious excitement. Year after year those putative parish priests, the makers of English Church life until the 1880s, were engaged in, or were the spectators of, a protracted communal love affair with religion and religious personalities. The very language the histories and the memoirs use to describe the Tractarian heroes – 'light', 'bright low laugh', 'sweetness', 'charm', 'silver voice' and so on – is the language of heightened erotic perception: 'O She (or in this case He) doth teach the torches to burn bright.'

One minor effect of all that is the Anglican tendency to expect of, or ascribe to, their Church's leaders, a charisma even when they haven't got it. Yet the intensity of feeling then was not entirely a matter of personal charisma, even Newman's. What intoxicated them all was what they believed to be the deliciousness of God, or, if that sounds too strong a brew, of religion itself. Apart from that the opponents and the protagonists of the Movement put on between them a kind of continuous 'Happening', Theology and Ecclesiastical Politics as Instant Theatre. If nothing else was happening there was Newman's own weekly performance, his glide to his pulpit in St Mary the Virgin, and what by all accounts was a superb dramatic management of beautiful voice and striking message. But there was usually something else happening, an endless seethe of incidents and characters for common room gossip and the great set piece confrontations like the scene in the Sheldonian when the Proctors vetoed the motion for the condemnation of Tract 90. What is more, the more susceptible young men – and some young women (for there were wives and sisters and female friends about the place) – were encouraged, especially by Dr Pusey, into an over-excited attention to their own spiritual health. It is not known how much academic work actually got done under these conditions.

What did develop in these conditions was the fatal Anglican habit of directing the energies of the devout into self cultivation and controversy. Newman complains, somewhere, that the tendency of religious novels was to foster 'the religious affections' apart from religious practice. Its a fair observation, but it may be turned on to the man himself and his friends. Religious practice and religious affection defined their life and being, sequestered it day by day from any experience of the cold common world. In its origins in Oxford and, with honourable exceptions, later in its parishes and religious houses, the Catholic Revival in the Church of England was privileged and peripheral, self absorbed to the point of gross ignorance about anything which might distract the devout from that other life and world of light on which the Church had, as Newman said in his sermon, opened the portals. The point may be illustrated dramatically, if a thought unfairly, by bringing together two situations parallel in time. In 1844 the continuous Oxford drama was rising to its climax: Newman was at Littlemore worrying about the safety of his soul which his audience waited hushed for his decision. In 1844, unconcerned with, and probably ignorant of all that, Engels was writing *The Condition of the Working Class in England*. It is worth asking whether what Keble called Newman's *agonia* was quite in order, in terms of the dignity of great suffering, of the more sordid, pitiful agonies that Engels observed in the back slums of Manchester, but that is not the issue. What is, is that to all intents and purposes the Tractarians did not notice them. Even when, as a Roman Catholic priest, Newman came to live in an industrial city, what disturbed him about the teeming thousands about him was not their hunger, or bad housing, or want of the common amenities, but their godless state. He might, nobly, tell the Monsignori that people in Birmingham had souls no less than the inhabitants of Rome: it might have been something if he had also expected them to have bread and boots and education. Now the ungodly Engels did notice and he was not alone. It was precisely during the Tractarian years that a whole tribe of Statistical Societies and interested private persons, Peter Gaskell for instance, and Kay Shuttleworth, added their observations on the conditions of the working class to the immense body of information and analysis collected in the Reports of the Poor Law Commission, the Factory Commission, the Commission on Handloom Weavers and all the other official enquiries. Nor was concern about the 'Manufacturing Population' confined to the users of Blue Books. *Oliver Twist* appeared in serial parts in 1838 and '39, *Past and Present* in 1843, *Sybil or the Two Nations* in 1845 and *Mary Barton* in 1847. The educated Victorian had 'the Condition of England question' on his mind. So did those more directly concerned. The crisis period for the Tractarians, the end of the 1830s, the beginning of the '40s, was the period of the Chartist agitations, of the Irish famine and the debate about the Corn Laws:

> 'Slowly comes a hungry people, like a lion creeping nigher,
> Glares at one that winks and nods behind a slowly dying fire . . .'

The Tractarians were otherwise engaged: they either could not or would not attend to all that – to what Carlyle might have called the great fact of Manchester, that is Manchester as Engels used it, as an outward and visible sign of seismic upheaval in the geology of English society.

That is not to argue that the Oxford fathers and their followers did not care about the sufferings of the poor: just that they made no attempt at all to understand what was happening about them. It was *de rigueur* in those circles to undertake or to promote and finance what we should now call health visiting and social work with the old (and honourable) intention of serving Christ in the bodies of his suffering children. Often, their efforts were heroic: they would give themselves, for instance, tirelessly to the nursing of cholera victims 'with a Prayerbook in one hand and a bottle of Cholera medicine in the other'. However, it was an ignorant heroism: cholera yields to neither. The disease, brought from India in the 1830s, is water-borne, a slum disease, epidemic in Victorian England because of the vile conditions into which its cities had fallen. Long-term, the bodies of Christ's poor were less well served by the devoted nursing of Miss Sellon's nuns than they were by the *Report on the Sanitary Conditions of the Labouring Poor* and the invention of the glazed ceramic sewerage pipe. So, unless we suppose (one has heard something near that view) that the divine purpose includes epidemic cholera, typhus, diphtheria and all the other evils of living in a back slum, it does seem that the energetic Victorian habit of social enquiry and administrative action was as certainly 'of God' as the revival of the Religious Orders.

Given a proper theology of creation or of the incarnation that is how we would regard it. The Tractarians however, unlike their fellow-Churchmen, excluded themselves from all that. Lord Shaftesbury (then Lord Ashley) and Bishop Blomfield served on the secular Commissions; the Oxford men (the mere thought is bewildering) did not. It was not that they had no interest in social justice; they hadn't, but then neither had anyone else. It took a long time for the notion that he himself and his class were possibly over-privileged to creep into the conscience of the Christian gentleman and justice, in any sense which implied a less unequal relationship between the orders of society, was never a prime concern either of the utilitarian or the philanthropic reformers. Apart from the Chartists and Engels, there is little in the mid century interest in social arrangements to suggest that new wine should be decanted into a new bottle. Those reformers, however, at least understood that the situation was new and that it warranted new approaches and attitudes. The Tractarians did not care; all that concerned them in the state of the nation was the welfare of the Church. All their considerable intellectual power and spiritual energy was directed towards 'the region of spirits' and, if possible, into sustaining the framework of a past age, or even restoring it so that the Church could still support the gates into that world. Otherwise, they simply stood aside from what was happening.

Their attitude was perhaps in its origins at least partly geographical. R W Church remarks, in his history of the Movement, that it took some of its character from Oxford itself:

> 'The scene of Methodism had been English villages and country towns, the moors of Cornwall and the collieries of Bristol, at length London fashionable chapels. The scene of this new movement was as like as it could be in our modern world to a Greek *polis*, or an Italian self-centred city of the Middle Ages. Oxford stood by itself in its meadows by the rivers, having its relations with all England, but, like its sister at Cambridge, living a life of its own, unlike that of any other spot in England, with its privileged powers, and exemptions from the general law, with its special mode of government and police, its usages and tastes and traditions, and even costume, which the rest of England looked at from the outside . . .'

Indeed, when they were all young dons in 1820, even the railways were not, and the place was so quiet in the Long Vacation that grass grew between the cobbles in the High. Manchester might just as well have been the Galapagos Islands. Moreover, the remote, enclosed relationships of the Senior Common Rooms were continued, and if anything intensified, when the young dons resigned their fellowships for marriage and the world. Some of the laymen, John Coleridge and Frederick Rogers for instance, established themselves in London professions, the clerics, however, withdrew to country livings and the limited circle of domestic life in a small parish. The cosiness and intensity of Tractarian family life, cultured, religious, deeply concerned for the souls and bodies of delicate wives and sisters and children, was itself a barrier against the wider awareness of the world. Besides, though the villages of England were much troubled by the pull of the chapel, the country parson was at least shielded from the immediate awareness of massive city populations not attending their parish church. Yet, having made as much allowance as possible for all that, it remains the case that the general Tractarian indifference to the 'Condition of England question' was willed and deliberate.

For the Tractarians were as capable as anyone else of following the debate: indeed, by the end of the 'forties, moved by a closer experience and perception of the Revolutions of 1848, Church himself had begun to find a different more 'Liberal' view of what was happening to the world. And after all Blue Books were as available as books of devotion. It is not even as if even remote villages were idyllically removed from the troubles of the age – even Keble (though it is not clear that he did anything about it) was moved to some distress by the effect of the new Poor Law on his parishioners. He was, too, obliged, when his father's curate, to encounter machine breaking rioters in the village of Coln St Aldwyn. It is symptomatic that the rioters put up a Methodist lay preacher to answer him, and that he himself put the 'evil' down to the fact that his father was not resident in the parish. Pastoral presence in fact was a means of keeping one's parishioners peaceable no matter what their grievances. The attitude, of course, is profoundly political and not unusual. It wasn't only Keble who consiously or unconsciously looked to religion as a cure-all for social ills. Carlyle saw the healing of the nations in an adherence to the Everlasting Yea, Pugin in a return to the organic unity of Catholic Society, Thomas Arnold in a widening of the boundaries of Establishment so as to compass all varieties of Christian belief except Roman Catholicism. We must not, however, suppose that Keble was concerned in any way with the alleviation of social ills; religion to him was essentially an Other Worldly phenomenon . . . it gave us grace for duty and to endure troubles to the end rather than to seek for social justice. The fact is that the man had no sense of justice in political matters and scarcely any in religious affairs. And, since his mind was formative in the Movement, that was disastrous.

The flaw begins to be apparent in the Assize Sermon itself. The occasion of Keble's declaration, the Bill for the suppression of the Irish bishoprics, was in any case preposterously inappropriate for a denunciation of National Apostasy. There could be no political sense, let alone justice, in insisting that the Catholic and Presbyterian Irish should pay for the maintenance of an English Episcopal Church. It is, too, difficult not to be contemptuous of the Movement's perception of Apostacy in the Government's presumed interference with the Church's property rights (in the income of the bishoprics). It would not have been unreasonable to enquire what they thought the gospel was about. All the same, the Sermon and the first of the Tracts indicate that Keble was aware – and so were his friends – that there was a shift, apparently, in the immemorial condition of England: that there was a crumbling, in experience – and after Catholic Emancipation, in Law – of the Tudor-Restoration fiction that the Established Church and the political nation are and ought to be alternate phases of the same thing. They, however, saw that shift (again not unusually) in terms of institutional relationships between the Government and the Church Politic, and show no sense at all of the social causes of social phenomena. They certainly did not realise that the crumbling was a sympton of a profounder change, a loosening of coherence between the orders of society which Disraeli saw in the emergence of 'two nations' and Tennyson in the slow dangerous advance of a hungry people. Keble's view is very simple: the nation's state being one of apostasy the only thing for it is to repent. If it did not, he at least viewed the possibility, even the desirability, of disestablishment with equanimity. For, as he said, after the Gorham judgment, 'If the Church of England were to fail altogether, yet it would be found in my parish'.

It is the sort of statement which made the man a hero to Anglicans of his own generation and later. And it is an insistence on isolation, on a fortress mentality. Was it, we may ask with hindsight, an adequate Christian witness for that generation? Was it within the purpose of God that these Oxford 'leaders of the people' should cut themselves off from the intellectual and political developments of their time in defence of the integrity of the Church? Of course there were exceptions: above all there was Gladstone – but Gladstone is an illuminating anomaly. As a young man, a High Tory, he was of course acceptable to the Oxford men: when he accepted an invitation to join Palmerston's cabinet and so declared himself a Liberal, he lost, as Peel had done, the Movement's trust and so his seat for the University of Oxford. Liberalism of party or of philosophy was a real rock of offence. It was infidelity, and like all infidelity deliberate sin. It is extraordinary the lengths to which the older Tractarians went in this matter. Pusey and Keble tied themselves into knots of conscience about subscribing to an Oxford Memorial to Thomas Arnold, though Keble was Arnold's closest friend as an undergraduate and godfather to his son, Matthew. There are other vignettes in the biographies. Newman, for instance, refused to review Carlyle's *The French Revolution* because he feared that the writer was an infidel, Keble reads *In Memoriam* years after it was published but fears he must lay it aside because of the Laureate's religious views. This kind of thing was not simple eccentricity; it is symptomatic in the Tractarians of the older generation of a shying from any encounter with the consciousness of their own generation. For Tennyson and Carlyle were both sensitive to the pitch of genius to the quality of their own time, possessed with the imagination of the old order changing and an intuition of what that meant in direct human experience. Carlyle's imagination of history happening, irritating as it must be for sober orthodox historians, enlivened his first readers with the sense of what revolution really is. *The French Revolution*, infidel or not, carries – no it creates – an awareness of the terror behind Terror, the great sweep of history, embodied in the Paris mobs, bearing away the obsolescent, rotten structures and institutions which could no longer contain or sustain the energies of society. As for Tennyson, in his apprehension an awareness of the undertow on secure order and meaning was cosmic:

> 'But I should turn mine ears and hear
> The moaning of the homeless sea,
> The sound of streams that swift or slow
> Draw down Aeonian hills and sow
> The dust of continents to be.'

These writers whom the Tractarians were so wary of reading display a heightened consciousness of the conditions of their own times when everything, it seemed, was shifting and changing.

> 'The old order changeth, yielding place to new
> And God fulfils himself in many ways . . .'

Newman who was near enough to genius to have a genius's intuition of the *Weltanschauung*, felt something of this, but always in terms of shadows and the 'encircling gloom' and fled to the security of Rome. Keble behaved all his life as if the supposition that God fulfils Himself in any ways except those approved in his family circle were simply a temptation, and gave the same advice, impartially, to those drawn to doubt the Athanasian Creed and those attracted by Rome: 'Ignore it'; 'Do something practical'; 'Stay where you are'.

The dominant ethos of an age so constantly growing and changing (that is not the ethos most widely accepted but the one which, on hindsight is seen to be formative) had to be Liberalism and its practical achievement was the modern democratic state and the pluralist society. John Stuart Mill notes that liberty of thought is both a concomitant and a necessary condition of societies in states of transition since no new consensus can emerge without experiments in opinion. Marxists, pejoratively, but really making Mill's point in another way, associate nineteenth century ideals of individual liberty with the transition from landed aristocracy to bourgeois capitalism. Transitions in social order and institutions do not in fact happen without violent revolution unless there is space in society for free thought and action, even anarchy, and certainly not if the past is permitted to constrain the energies of the present. The Tractarians could not (there was something in their formation and psychology which prevented it) tolerate the feel of that give and space within their society. They had been conditioned to an ideology of hierarchy and a god-given order:

> 'The Apostle . . . giving instruction to public societies, requireth that all things be orderly done. Order can have no place in things, unless it be settled amongst the persons that shall by office be conversant about them. And if things or persons be ordered, this doth imply, that they are distinguished by degrees. For order is a gradual disposition.
>
> 'The whole world consisting of parts so many, so different, is by this only thing upheld; he that framed them hath set them in order. *Yea, the very Deity itself both keepeth and requireth forever this to be kept as a law that wheresoever there is a coagmentation of many, that the lowest be knit to the highest by that which being interjacent may cause each to cleave unto other, and so all continue one.'*

That is Hooker's version of the official ideology (still unrepudiated) of the Church of England: *Let every soul be subject to the Higher Powers*. It's all there, after all, in the *Book of Common Prayer* and the *Book of Homilies*. When Keble put his stick round the shoulders of rude boys in his parish who did not raise their caps to the vicar he was re-inforcing the principles of subordination and deference they ought to have taken in with the mother's milk of the Catechism – The Tractarians, we must remember, were very enthusiastic about Catechism:

> 'My duty towards my neighbour is . . . to honour and obey the king and all that are put in authority under him . . . *to order myself lowly and reverently to all my betters* . . . Not to covet or desire other men's goods, but to learn and labour truly to get mine own living, and to do my duty in that state of life to which it shall please God to call me.'

Keble, of course, was especially stiff-necked; it is startling, at least to us, to find that he half rebukes Hooker (in the Preface to his edition of Hooker's *Works*) as a Liberal fellow-traveller because that upright Divine suggests, or seems to suggest, in Book VIII of the *Laws of Ecclesiastical Polity*, that government should have the consent of the governed: not the mandate, which is of God, but merely the consent. It is not for the people to veto the Lord's anointed; that was Oliver's crime, that was the error that brought in Dutch William and dispossessed the nonjuring Divines. Keble's attitudes in fact are fundamentally nonjuring. The link of civil and ecclesiastical power in England gave a specially sacred character to secular arrangements so long as Church and State had each their defined position; when that is lost – well – one withdraws. None of the others was quite as certain in himself of this as Keble was – but he left his ambience in the feel of the Movement.

The principle of subordination and deference was and is profoundly 'political' rather than theological; it is perhaps the paradigmatic ruling class ideology, and extremely useful both in Tudor and in Victorian England. It was not, however, entirely suitable for a society painfully and necessarily developing democratic forms and egalitarian attitudes. There's no question but that it did place the Church in England on the wrong side of a developing nation, and still does. No one would now argue the principle of deference in Christian assemblies, but in unconscious attitudes in its approach to questions of 'law and order', in the insufferable paternalism of its approach to working people and to women, in its assumption of a normative role in the moral life of the nation, the Church (and Churchmen) demonstrate that the principle is still live in their Christian culture. One cannot put that down entirely to Tractarian influence. What the Tractarians did was to reinforce and to ensure, given their obsession with the forms of authority, that the Church did not, ever, question or criticise its hierarchical assumptions. There was something more. Even in the reign of Victoria the notion of an hierarchical order in society was a matter of political culture rather than serious political discussion. The highest of High Tories was unlikely to argue the Divine Right of Queen Victoria and even the principle of subordination had mutated in line with economic change:

> 'The *rich* man in his castle
> The *poor* man at his gate
> God made them high and lowly
> And ordered their estate.'

That popular version, unlike the classic statements in Hooker and the Prayer Book, associated degree not with office or function but with wealth: it is plutocratic where the original ideology was aristocratic. The shift is interesting and allows the second and third generation of the Catholic Movement the luxury of a social witness which does not touch the social establishments in which the Church itself is embodied. The exploitation of working men and women as merely 'hands', the inequalities between the very rich and very poor which belonged to the entrepreneurial ethic, attracted a generous indignation but it had the very curious effect of turning the Catholic mind back to a vision of the organic society (as Demant or Eliot's *Idea of a Christian Society*, or Sir Walter Moberley or even William Temple) not markedly different from Hooker's or Keble's. That kind of speculation is now out of fashion, except in one highly interesting case: the extraordinary arguments which are adduced to assure the public (which doesn't understand a word of it) that it would be unnatural, against the God-given structures of the universe, for women to be ordained. But the way in which the shadowy forms of obsolete, fossilised hierarchies are sustained in the Church of England by Catholic thinking would be a study in itself. The frame of mind it creates does permit a passionate care for social justice but it is constantly thrown by any notion of equality; it cannot always conceive that in any society justice implies that everyone should count for one and no one for more than one – not the sovereign, nor the bishop, nor 'leaders' of any kind – and that goes for intellectual and economic, as well as religious and political, life. Social passion may turn an Anglican Catholic towards Socialism or even to revolutionary Marxism (another vision of the 'coagmentation of many'), but rarely to anarchism or a seriously radical critique of social institutions, and *never* to Republicanism.

The major effect of all this, however, was and is in the Church's vision of itself. The Tractarians disliked Liberalism but they could not stop it; people went on electing reforming governments, writing heretical books, finding their way through the slow evolution of generations to secular democracy. So the Tractarians were nicely hoist, and hoist the rest of us with their own high Toryism. Ironically, what faced them was Cranmer's dilemma, not Sancroft's. You preach indeed that every soul should be subject to the Higher Powers. What happens if the Higher Powers turns out to be Mary Tudor or Lord John Russell, and the truth in not in them? Keble sent to John Coleridge for books on the relation of Church and State, but over a century and a half since then that issue was fudged; the Church of England has not decided that there is a difference between the Divine Society and the political nation. It has, all the same, given a great deal of attention to its own nature and there were moments, especially during the secessions, when the Tractarians found, with great simplicity, that it was their experience of the sacramental life in their own Communion which confirmed for them the authenticity of their Church. The young widow of Guy de Morville in *The Heir of Redclyffe* writes: 'I believe in the Communion of the Saints' on her husband's gravestone 'Because I should like, too, for these Italians to see the stranger has the same creed as themselves'. Unfortunately, this recognition that the Church of England had a reality and a unity in its immediate and eternal life did not inform the controversies. Had it done so we might have derived some insight from a discussion of the nature of the Church, that 'blessed company of all faithful people', in terms of its people and not its institutions, but that is not the way the High Tory mind works. There was no way in which men conditioned to notions of order, of office and function, could consider or would have considered, the being of any corporate body except in terms of jurisdictions, powers and rights. Almost the first words of the Movement, in the first Tract was Newman's fatal directive to the clergy to 'magnify' their office. He might have said 'romanticise it'; it is certainly worth considering how much trouble might have been saved for everybody if Newman had not conceived a kind of mystique of Apostolicity for very ordinary men. But of course for all of the ultimate right, the ultimate authority was Apostolic, reaching back into the mists of time to guarantee a present office and jurisdiction. Authority lay in history.

Now, it is in their use of history that the Tractarians and their successors were most wildly fantastical in the patterning they imposed on the Church. In the second generation of the Catholic movement, that sober and great historian Canon Stubbs, sitting on the Ecclesiastical Courts Commission, endeavoured to persuade its lawyers to look beyond the Reformation Statutes to establish the normative practice of the Church of England across its long, and not merely its recent, history. That was defensive practice, in that case against the protestant predilections of an Erastian Parliament and the Judicial Committee of the Privy Council. It could also be defensive against Roman claims, somehow to present the Church of England as having an identity continuous from before the coming of St Augustine to the present day, so bypassing both the Pope and the Reformers. And before that, of course, there was the Church in antiquity, the Apostolic Church to which the Tractarians made their definite appeal and which provided the proper test for the fidelity of doctrine and practice. 'I maintain' said William Palmer, 'that Christians cannot possibly admit that any doctrine established by universal tradition can be otherwise than DIVINELY, INFALLIBLY, TRUE.' It is, in practice, extremely difficult to determine what doctrine can be established by universal tradition but still that view gives the past a terrifying veto on the present. For what the Church is, and more importantly, what the truth is, is defined by what has been.

The fallacy in that approach to history is that it is, simply, a-historical. What has happened in the past – because, so to speak, time and change have flowed on and away from it – has the appearance of certainty and invulnerability. That, however, is merely an appearance; past events and beliefs may be fixed, like still frames from an old movie; history is and was the movie itself. In its nature it is moving, fluid, unfixed from moment to moment; its dimension is Time, not an unchanging world of eternal realities. The attempt to dam its flow, so as to turn a moment or a period, like the Apostolic age, into a still surface in which 'the truth' is reflected, must distort our understanding not only of the present but of the past itself. The Monophysites, for instance, were not as they appeared to Newman's appalled imagination, prefigurations of Tudor Reformers, certainly not of Victorian Anglicans. And in fact there is, and there is still, a theological blindness about the Divine Creativity in the 'Catholic' (Anglican or Roman) raking of the past for the orthodoxies of the present for God does fulfil himself in many ways – but the consideration of that belongs to another discussion. The more obvious consequences of using history in the Tractarian way, as a guarantee of orthodoxy and authority is that history ceases to be history, a living moving thing, and becomes myth. There always was that danger for the Tractarians, given their addiction to romantic sensibility and the work of Sir Walter Scott, and the further, unavoided risk that all too soon myth would transmute into fantasy.

It is, of course, commonplace that nineteenth-century Europe mined its past for myths. The Middles Ages yielded archetypes for French Catholic Conservatism, German national pride, English Socialism and a variety of other philosophies. Myths, too, are always more powerful than arguments. Newman, for instance, was a much sharper, silkier controversialist than Kingsley: in the quarrel between them the *Apologia Pro Vita Sua* (itself a kind of myth) was a weapon of genius; it clean swept Kingsley out of the fight -- for the moment. For, in the long run, Kingsley had the best of Newman: his real case, his profound English suspicion of the mere foreignness of Roman Catholicism was sustained in the imagination of his times by the success of *Westward Ho!*. He was lucky in his material; the age of Elizabeth and the defeat of the Armada were already paradigmatic for Englishness, his myth was half formed in the history. The Tractarians had no such luck: the first Elizabeth was too suspiciously Erastian for their purposes; there was no sweet Anglican alliance between the Queen and her bishops as there was between Charles I and Laud. *That* was their preferred material; though they drew, like everyone else, on the Middle Ages, the Caroline age, its personalities, its devotion, its politics and theology, was an historical mine for the Oxford Fathers. It was too serious, of course, to find its shaping in novels though Miss Yonge's heroines, always indicators of Tractarian feeling, were found in tears before the portrait of the Martyr King. No; here rite expresses myth. The Oxford Catholic defined himself by devotion to and the cult observance of Charles the Martyr. And also by his hatreds: his hostility to Cromwell and Milton in particular. These were sometimes intemperately or absurdly expressed. Keble, for instance, exiled Richard Cromwell's monument from Hursley Church, Frederick Faber boasted that he had (an unlikely story) nearly persuaded Wordsworth (Wordsworth!) to abandon his admiration of Milton. Now this is all typical of the Tractarians: Kingsley spoke straight to the muddled sense of English identity in his period; they, for all their searching for continuity with the past, found the one mythological fantasy least in tune with their own times. For the nineteenth century was, after the Reform Bill of 1832, the archetypal age of Parliamentary government and the growth of democratic systems. Its affinities were scarcely with Charles and his monarchical stance. The point is best made by Faber's absurdity. Wordsworth, like other Romantic poets, identified Milton as a link between the power of poetry and the cause of liberty: the author not only of *Paradise Lost* but of the *Areopagitica*. Yes, he did defend regicide, but in pamphlets significantly titled the 'Defence of the English People' who still have no great admiration or love for Charles I. That King is a figure, indeed, not so much admired as pitied and his myth had no energy or attractiveness for the Victorians except in a kind of glamorous sadness. The Martyr's cult, in fact, was unreal, drawing its adherents into a world, a fantasy world, like that of King Arthur, alien to that of their bustling contemporaries.

That, of course, is what happens when individuals or groups of individuals refuse to acknowledge the 'now' with which they are blessed or cursed. They make an escape world and it is sterile. It is only too easy to illustrate the continuance of fantasy, in some ways a continuance of the Oxford histrionics, in the permutations and personalities of the Movement. The Religious Communities were blessed, for instance, with a kind of mediaeval archness. The mother house of Miss Sellon's Sisterhood, designed, without a fee, by the admirable Mr Butterfield, in the approved Gothic manner, included a Community Room called the *Sheepfold*. The Lady Superior's room was called *Rest*. The nuns, poor dears, were given titles like Deane Amelia, Child Humbleine (Sister Lucy Watkins), Sister Fridswida and the Eldress Phoebe. The idiom and manner persisted. Certainly when I was a young woman, and for all I know still, the loo in one of the more prestigious Retreat Houses was chastely decorated with appropriate passages from the *Canticle of the Sun*, a whimsy which reveals perhaps the profound cause of all this. It is a fastidiousness about ordinary life, a need to elevate it by setting its activities, especially those of a 'lower nature' in an atmosphere of religious refinement. Much the same trait is obvious in the long line of 'Catholic' eccentrics (beginning, in fact, with Faber), Hawker of Morwenstowe, Joseph Lyne (Fr Ignatius), Fr Hope Patten, perhaps even Conrad Noel and a dozen others, all of them creators of worlds within the Church which were and are totally artificial and alien to an English and modern way of life. Noel's Thaxted has a shrine for John Ball, Hope Patten's Walsingham one for Charles the Martyr: both are hopelessly – though Thaxted is beautiful and Walsingham is not – unhelpful to any Christian consciousness framed by a world in which neither peasants nor autocratic monarchs are exactly at the centre of things. Walsingham illustrates the problem, or rather the sheer wrenching of religion away from common life. For if ever there was an example of fantasy it must be pilgrimage to a modern copy of a mediaeval imitation of what, that is the Holy House of Loretto – can only have been a fraud in the first place. No doubt the mediaeval pilgrim was able to 'kneel where prayer has been valid' but this generation is not, by five hundred years or so of historical learning and science, mediaeval. There is no way in which anyone from archbishops to university dons to middle-aged ladies on a holy parish outing can go on pilgrimage to Walsingham without setting aside, in the interests of devotional feeling, that consciousness of the real world which the pilgrim ordinarily shares with his or her contemporaries. He or she has come to an invented world, a fantasy, to pray. How is he or she not to identify Christian prayer with that fantastical existence, and so distort it?

It is difficult to fathom how a Movement nourished on William Law, George Herbert and the sober beauty of the *Book of Common Prayer* can have left this legacy of devotional bric-a-brac and the other debris cluttering Anglo-Catholic attics. But it is the most unfortunate of its legacies, for in fact the Movement forced the great grace of its devotion, its revival of spirituality, into the matrices of this fantasy life which was often tawdry, and is, very often, psychologically dangerous. And it cannot be put down to the Movement's followers for the twist and distortion which it represents comes out of the histrionics, the extravagant sensibilities of those extraordinary years in Oxford. Some indeed may be especially traced to the particular emotionalism of Dr Pusey's character. The real fault is that the Tractarians unconsciously, made religion a life substitute rather than a life revealer, not a way into the splendours of the visible world but a way out. That habit of mind is fixed in us still and ultimately it is destructive of religion itself.

ADDRESSING THE CULTURE

14 Oxford, Thaxted and World Poverty

Charles Elliott

'Sex' says David Jenkins in a celebrated *Theology* editorial, 'stirs up us Christians. Poverty does not.'[1] Almost the reverse might have been said about Dr Pusey and his colleagues in Oxford when the Tracts were launched. Although it is sometimes said that the Oxford Movement had no interest in social ethics, Pusey at least would have been surprised at such an allegation. However pale his social ethics by contrast with those of Maurice, Headlam and even of Gore, they cannot simply be dismissed.

For Pusey was deeply offended by the mass poverty that marked the late 1830s and 1840s, and perhaps even more so by the sheer squalor and ugliness of much of urban Britain as he knew. His was not a reaction based on a generalised benevolence: rather it stemmed directly from his reading of the Greek Fathers, his understanding of the nature of the Church and, in a rather less well worked out way, his emphasis on the universality of God's love and redemptive purpose. If the shrillness of his appeals to the middle-class Anglicans who heard him embarrasses us by its overtones of condescension and paternalism, the depth of his conviction and the example he set with the application of his own personal wealth need not. In this sense, the ghost of Pusey still haunts the Anglican subconscious.

For it is, of course, true that Pusey interpreted the social crises of his day as a need for greater generosity by the relatively wealthy, rather than as an invitation to diagnose the nature of industrial capitalism and speculate on its replacement. Historians, as different and as distinguished as Carpenter and Orens, have tended to compare the original Oxford Fathers with the later emergence of a more radical strain of thinking around such figures as Headlam and Noel – to the greater disadvantage of the former.[2] That is surely to read history backwards. Pusey deserves greater recognition than he usually receives not only for the passion of his concern, but for the way in which he linked new developments in theology with concern for the poor. The relevant contrast is less with Headlam and Noel than with

Wesley, Wilberforce and Hamilton on the one hand; and with the Liberal-Whigs, usually Nonconformists, who, intoxicated alike by advances in the physical and social sciences, took it that the laws of political economy were the laws of God: a proposition that the Unitarian Thom tried to prove in the *Christian Teacher*.[3]

The implications of that equation can be seen only in the light of an appreciation of the economics of Malthus, Mill and Ricardo. In their own different models, each showed that there was an inevitable tendency for the distribution of income to become more unequal. Wages would not rise above the subsistence level and any surplus, a term more associated with Marxist thinking but implicit in the earlier classical economists, would be acquired by the owners of land or capital. The demand that the poor put up with their lot was thus, at least in its best expression, not a matter of bourgeois heartlessness but of a conviction that it was both intellectually impossible and theologically improper to expect anything else – another ghost that has not been laid as completely as liberal opinion would like to imagine.

There were powerful conservative forces operating on Pusey and, indeed, on all churchmen – Tractarian, High or Evangelical. Pusey, Newman and most other Tractarians were first and foremost theologians. If they were secondarily moral philosophers, they were well insulated from both the technicalities of the debate about the Corn Laws (the major fighting-ground of economists of the day) and from the awkward business of determining economic policy. While it is too trite to write them off as incarcerated in the ivory towers of Oxford, it is fair comment that none actually had to deal with the complexity of economic life at a time when both that complexity itself and the intellectual appreciation of it were growing exponentially: a position which many moral theologians of today will readily recognise.

Second, it is worth remembering that the Tractarians were almost literally fighting for their lives for the fifteen years that followed 1833. They had their own agenda and, if that agenda seems to us, from our historical perpective, bizarre, esoteric and sometimes absurd, that may say more about the failures of our historical imagination than the failure of their moral insights.

Third, the fear of Chartism, however exaggerated it now seems from where we stand in history, was real and it is as cheap as it is unhistorical to minimise that fear. Peterloo and later 1848 were profoundly shocking incidents which made many sensitive Christians ask whether the expression of mass discontent was really in the best interests of the poor. There was a strong body of Church opinion, neither ignorant of the suffering of the urban poor nor uncommitted to its mitigation, that held that it was not. The lust to protect the poor from themselves is not confined to the second half of the twentieth century – or to Anglican reactions to S Africa.

As is well-known, these three constraints loosened over the next 60 years. Maurice, to some extent, Headlam to a greater extent and Noel perhaps to the greatest degree of all, did know what they were talking about at first hand. Although none of them claimed (rightly) any particular expertise in economics, their grappling with the hard facts of economic and political life is of a very different order from that of Pusey. In the same way, although Maurice, Kingsley and Headlam all had their own problems of survival, they were no longer the captives of an agenda set by the terms of another debate. It is important, however, not to over-emphasise the degree to which the later thinkers in the Catholic tradition were able to break out of their own philosophical framework. It is an interesting comment on both theological method and intellectual priorities that *Lux Mundi*, despite its evocative sub-title, came to grips with the hard realities of economic analysis (and that, as it happens, in a rather old-fashioned and flat-footed way, even by the standards of the time) not in the main volume at all but in an appendix – and only two paragraphs at that.[4]

None the less, a few individuals and groups were beginning to progress well beyond Pusey's position and begin to ask questions, not about the voluntary redistribution of income, but about the very nature of the productive process itself. Maurice and the Co-operative Movement; Headlam; the Christian Social Union; and above all, Noel, the Thaxted Movement and the Church Socialist League are the well-known signposts. Crucial for all of these is the doctrine of the Incarnation; and emphasis on the need to derive both ends and means of social policy from the criteria, not of political economy, but of Christian understandings of the nature of man, the nature of society, the nature of human relationships, and the nature of the Kingdom of God.

Yet the truth is that, despite the enormous methodological innovations of *Lux Mundi*, a contribution that in terms of this paper far exceeded that of the Tracts, the number of people standing in the Tractarian tradition and raising questions about the nature of the productive system always remained small. Their influence, such as it was, was felt outside the main lines of Anglican debate (with the possible exception of the Christian Social Union in its heyday) spurned by clergy and laity alike. 'It has been our misfortune to find ourselves in constant opposition to the authorities of the Church,' wrote Widdrington in 1916, 'and we have been out of sympathy with our fellow-Churchmen. We have been driven for fellowship outside rather than inside the Church.'[5] This is not to deny the local significance of parish priests drawing strength from this tradition and re-interpreting the nature of their ministry accordingly. From Hook in Leeds to Garbett in Portsea, the tradition from the Tracts to the Christendom Group made a semi-professional concern in such issues as housing, unemployment, education, sanitation reform and wage-fixing mandatory – and the starting point of that concerns the interests of the poor.

The justification of this historical prologue is that I shall argue in the rest of this paper that, despite innovations in theological method since the Tracts and *Lux Mundi*, the Church of England as a whole and the Catholic tradition within it has lost five elements essential to an adequate reaction to the global mass poverty which is the contemporary analogue of domestic poverty in the 19th century.

Analogously to the previous section, let us start with the appeal to charity, eloquently phrased by Pusey. I take it as incontestable that, for the vast majority of Christians, the normative response to the facts of world poverty are assumed to be of two kinds: first, support of Church-related aid agencies, such as Christian Aid, the Tear Fund or CAFOD; and secondly, (less frequent) support for a more generous British stance on official development assistance as mobilised, for instance, by the Church's Committee of the World Development Movement.

The mobilisation of this charitable response still depends, perhaps to a marginally lower degree than twenty years ago, on an emotional response to horrifying pictures or bare facts. It does not depend upon, and indeed is probably confused by, any kind of social analysis that seeks to determine why so many people are poor or what keeps them poor. Moreover, possibly because there is no serious analysis, the emotional response is attended by, and may even feed upon, vague and inarticulated feelings of guilt – an emotional and spiritual state that reveals, perhaps more clearly than anything else, the sub-Christian level at which the response originates.

To say that is not in any way to decry the work of the aid agencies or to suggest that aid, whether non-governmental or official, is worthless. It is, however, to suggest that in so far as the aid agencies represent an 'official' theological response to world poverty, they have been less than successful in finding and communicating an adequate (much less a genuinely Catholic) mode of Christian action in this area. One is reminded of Ruth Kenyon's rueful comment on the Christian Social Union in its last days: 'We stand just as much as other reformers now for a mere bread-and-butter, gas-and-water movement ... a *Socialisme sans doctrines* ... a philanthropic society'.[6]

It is when we move from the charity-response of 'a philanthropic society' to a more reflective appreciation of the causes of world poverty that we begin to see the consequences of this theological void – and encounter the first of the five elements lost from the tradition. Perhaps the most remarkable demonstration of this has been the enthusiasm with which the Churches in general have greeted the Brandt Report. Whatever else may be said about the Report (and many of its recommendations are entirely sensible in the context of its own analysis), it is clear that it is essentially a reformist document that does not raise questions about the wider facts which the Catholic tradition of social criticism would regard as the proper, indeed inevitable, starting points – the understanding of man and community, the primacy of the claims of the dispossessed, the quality of relationships in production and exchange.

Translated into theological language these are questions about the meaning today of the doctrines of creation and redemption and of the significance of the Eucharist. Now what is both stark and disturbing is the reluctance of Christians to ask questions about the significance of those central theological truths for the kind of global analysis that the Brandt Report half-attempted. Instead, they are anxious to fall in behind a mode of analysis that takes as unquestioned assumptions the moral justification of the capitalist system; the right of rich countries' access to raw materials in the poor countries; a distribution of wealth and income based on average productivity within existing patterns of the control of technology. It is hard to imagine that Headlam, or even Temple would be content with such implicit assumptions – assumptions which they would have found incompatible with their understanding of Incarnation and Eucharist.

It is worth pursuing this point a step further. Most Anglicans can be persuaded of the need for a charitable response (grotesquely inadequate as our response may objectively be); many can be persuaded that reforms to commodity pricing systems, the international monetary system and rules of market access are desirable. Indeed they will lobby Parliament for them in numbers that impress even hard-boiled MPs.

Therein, however, lies the worm in the apple. For it is not difficult to show that these laudable aims, taken *in vacuo*, are inimical to the interests of the less well-off, the economically vulnerable and the occupationally immobile in our own society. Take three examples. First, free trade in manufactures may in the long run be a way of raising real national income in the UK, by freeing resources to produce goods and services in which the UK has a comparative advantage. It does so, however, only by raising both short-term (and how short, one may legitimately ask, will short turn out to be?) problems of unemployment; and long-term problems of redistribution of income. If half the number of workers produce ten times the output in high-productivity industries, that's great for those in employment; but for the rest . . . ?

There is a whole nest of issues here. I shall mention only two. The first is the scale of redistribution of both work and income required in such a situation. The redistribution of work through the shorter working week and earlier retirement may go some way to incorporate more people into the productive system – but it will do little for those most at risk as a result of restructuring of the British economy. They include those who cannot move out of declining areas (especially married women); those who cannot retrain to acquire saleable skills (married women again and older women), those who have been unemployed for a long time during the decline of traditional industries (the chronically unemployed).

The second issue that arises in this connection is the size and taxability of the surplus generated by those new industries. For it is to the revenue produced by taxing them that we have to look to finance the social wage of those not required to work. Assuming such a taxable surplus does appear (and that assumption begs many important questions which cannot be reviewed here), tax rates will have to be very high on those who acquire those surpluses as wages, salaries, rents or dividends. That is the price of redistribution. And without redistribution a smaller high-technology economy is socially unviable – and theologically unacceptable.

Higher and more stable commodity prices are a perfectly legitimate aspiration for the producers; and for the development lobby. When those prices are passed on as higher prices to the consumer, the impact is greater on poor households than on less poor. In that sense, higher commodity prices are a transfer that is costly (in terms of welfare forgone) to the poor. For it is unfortunately true that in the 'Nairobi seventeen' commodities – those of which, from a development standpoint, it is most desirable to stabilise the price – there are many which form a significant proportion of the expenditure of the poor: tea; coffee; cotton. Perhaps more important, a general rise in the real price of commodities – and it is that that is required by the producers – may well contribute to an acceleration of international inflation, though it does not by itself constitute a sufficient condition for such acceleration. Inflation usually has a regressive effect on the distribution of wealth and income, by reducing the real value of debt (and therefore making cheaper the acquisition of assets by those who can borrow) and because some groups are better able to protect themselves than others. In this way justice for producer-countries (which is by no means the same as justice for those who 'mix their labour' in producing commodities) is bought at the expense of increasing injustice for the poor and vulnerable in the UK.

Thirdly, the old gibe that 'aid is a means of transferring welfare from the poor in the UK to the rich in the Third World' has too much truth in it to be dismissed summarily. The overall burden of taxation in the UK is not regressive, though the interaction of taxation and social benefits can produce some remarkably regressive results, the so-called poverty trap. Further, it is not possible to be optimistic that a reduction of taxation would reduce the tax burden on the poor, primarily because most of their taxes are paid through VAT and National Insurance rather than through income tax. It might, however, be true that under anything other than a

Tory Government, a £1bn surplus to the Exchequer resulting from the axeing of the aid programme might be spent, at least in part, on benefits for the poor. While it is not true, then, that the poor pay for aid disproportionately, it could well be true that there is a cost to the poor in terms of benefits forgone. When pleas are made for a larger official aid programme, therefore, we need to be particularly alert that such a programme is not made possible by reducing domestic expenditures to benefit the poor of our own society.

Let me state absolutely clearly that, in my view, it does not follow from these observations that these policies – free trade in manufactures, higher commodity prices, more (and better quality) aid – should be abandoned, a reaction too common on the Left in general and among Trade Union officials in particular. It follows rather that the logic needs to be pressed all the way. A more progressive form of taxation is required both in its own right and because of its global dimension. A more radical response to unemployment – income support, relocation, retraining, psychological support – is required both in its own right and because it makes morally justifiable a proper approach to the global issue. That, however, is not yet within the terms of the debate, on Brandt or on 'development' in general, as it is conducted in the British Churches. We are rather in danger of allowing it to be said that the pressure for more realistic policies on the Third World is essentially a middle-class concern: and that, by allying themselves with that concern, the Churches agitate for changes, the costs of which will be borne most heavily by others. A perspective further removed from Thaxted could hardly be imagined.

The suburban middle-class captivity of the development debate is no less graphically, and more colourfully, displayed in the reaction to the liberation struggle, especially in Southern Africa. Allied with that goes, of course, the British allergy, especially prominent in the Anglican Church, to liberation theology. It is no part of my purpose to enter a detailed apologia for liberation theology (or rather theologies, as to synthesise the various writers is to distort any of them beyond recognition), but in the present context it is relevant to emphasise how far some (but certainly not all) of the tone of liberation theology is consonant with that of the Catholic Socialists – an emphasis on history; on incarnation and redemption; and even (much under-commented on in most British critiques) sanctification. Despite these themes, the impact of people like Guttierez and Bonino has been slight on academic theologians and negligible on the man in the pew. Liberation theology is imperfect and incomplete in many important respects. That does not, however, explain its neglect in Britain – precisely at a time when it might be expected to help Christians understand at least part of the reality (both subjective and objective) of their fellows suffering oppression. Thus, when Cosmas Desmond uses liberation-theology concepts and language in explorations of the South African situation, he is unheard or ignored.[7]

One asks why? Part of the answer, I suspect, is that it is essential to the method of liberation theologians that the social situation, the 'problematic', be analysed by the application of the tools of social science. The tools that are usually used are Marxian, especially the notion of appropriation of surplus value by dominant classes and/or 'core'. It has to be said, unhappily, that some of this analysis is deficient in its own terms, and shows ignorance of the important, and occasionally acrid, debates within Latin American social science. None the less the root of the problem, I suggest, is not that the analysis is open to serious question, but that it is there at all, and in a form and language that speak powerfully of its ideological heritage. If Englishmen are allergic to abstract theorising, Anglicans find Marxian ideas (almost inevitably tagged 'Communist'), bitter to taste, hard to swallow and impossible to digest.[8]

To move to the second lost element in the Catholic socialist tradition, we can be more brief. Even among the tiny handful of theologians and activists who stand, roughly, in the Catholic tradition, there has grown up a gap between activism and theology on the one hand and a sacramental awareness on the other. The Christian Socialists, and perhaps none more so than Noel, saw the Eucharist both as prefiguring a fairer society and as providing the means of nourishment for those involved in creating such a society. '. . . Bread and wine taken in fellowship as a foretaste of that coming world . . . as a means by which they are nourished by His life; and as a stirrup cup to battle'.[9] The Eucharist is no longer a stirrup cup to battle. Spiritualised and etherealised as much by the new Anglican and Roman liturgies – 'let us go forth in peace' – as by the high and dry tradition the Tractarians were reacting against, it has lost too much of the prophetic content that Catholic socialists once found in it.

A rediscovery of the radicalism of the shared bread and cup, a potent symbol of the Gandhian contrast of need and greed, will not by itself break open the prison of individualistic piety which the embourgeoisement of the gospel has built. It would, however, encourage more Christians to glimpse the depth of the *metanoia* to which the celebration of Christ's resurrection commits them – a *metanoia* that demands a turning-out towards the global neighbour. This is something that (a very few) Roman Catholics are discovering. The Commission for International Justice and Peace of England and Wales published in 1980 a restatement of the social implications of the Eucharist that could almost have come from the pen of Noel. In it, David Morland, OSB had this to say: 'In celebrating the Eucharist the Church is not master but servant; it unleashes a power which is not under its control. If it were merely a memorial, the Church could fashion its recollection to suit itself; it could distance Christ and his disturbing history; it could tell the old story without it being about a living and active presence, without it being in a way about itself. Transubstantiation means that the risen Lord is actually present, incarnate, flesh and blood in our world. The presence is dynamic, powerful, transforming. It is the act of a jealous lover who will brook no rivals – the Church as Bride of Christ is no comfortable doctrine – whose will is to shape the community celebrating it into His body, to make it Holy; an instrument here and now of "good news" in the world. This is a painful and costly process but at the same time it is the only way to find true life, genuine hope, true *agape*. It is at once utterly gratuitous and totally demanding. That is what grace is about. It is not a moral achievement, a response to duty or law: it is the reception of a gift, but it is a gift of fire, which burns and purifies those who accept it.'[10] From that to the earlier thought of the Eucharist as 'stirrup cup for battle' is a refreshingly short step.

Third – and no more fashionable among activists – the Catholic tradition fuses prayer and action in a way, and to a depth, that approaches the mystical. Despite the current popularity of Thomas Merton and Daniel Berrigan, both of whom exemplified this fusion, the neglect of a tradition that is fully attested by both Greek and Latin Fathers has reached the point where officials of Church House are scandalised at the suggestion that world poverty is a matter of prayer. That perhaps explains all that needs to be explained of the hollowness and superficiality of much ecclesiastical activism on these, as on other, issues. More significantly, it explains why the debate within the Churches is not substantively different (though qualitatively inferior) to the debate in Parliament, the press or academia. By divorcing activism from prayer and contemplation, we have deprived our energies of a sufficiently deep-seated goal. We protest about cuts in aid – and create the impression that 'aid' could ever be an adequate response. We lobby on the Common Fund and the Integrated Programme on Commodities and allow the inference that controlled exploitation is permissible. We press for improved market access and ignore the conditions under which the imports are produced. Once we separate the contemplative, the mystical, the 'journeying in' from the active, the involved, the 'breaking out'; once, in a word, we drown the silence by the volume of our protest, we make the protest cheap.

Fourth – and in some ways derivative from both the earlier points – it was essential to the Catholic tradition that commitment to 'the politics of the Magnificat' lay at the heart of belief, of faith. It was not an optional extra for those who happened to be 'interested in that kind of thing'. It was what defined faith. 'You are insulting Christ . . . if you do not definitely range yourselves with those who are prepared to drag down the mighty from their seats and exalt the low degree . . . loyalty to the whole tradition [*sic*] of this church is the only loyalty which the Master will accept.'[11] A more modern expression of the same tradition comes from Pannenberg: 'Wherever the message of the imminent Kingdom of God is accepted, God has already come into power and man now has communion with God. The salvation which is Communion with God requires nothing else than to accept the message of the imminent Kingdom of God now'.[12] Or as Cosmas Desmond puts it more pithily: 'To have faith, and to awaken faith, in the coming of the Kingdom means to make God's liberating power real, as Christ did'.[13] It is hard, perhaps, to imagine the revolution that would be wrought on British Anglicanism if this reinterpretation were achieved if faith were identified with liberating action on behalf of the poor and oppressed; if salvation were reinvested with its OT significance and commitment to it was simulataneously renewed in the context of the graces presented in the NT. Nothing perhaps would so quickly and so radically liberate the religious middle classes from the gilded cage in which we so determinedly lock ourselves.

Then the development debate could, as it were, change gear. Instead of reflecting, or being in danger of reflecting, a neo-paternalism that wants vaguely to help without facing the consequences of the kind of change that makes help real rather than rhetorical, we could bind together a radical approach to justice in our own society with a radical approach to justice in the global community.

Fifth and last, the incarnational theology of the Tracts and later the Christian Socialists resulted in a flow, almost a flood, of some of the best priests into the slums. While it is easy to criticise some of their work as attempts at the bourgeoisification of the working class, to do so is to ignore, by the failure of the historical imagination, the depth of the chasm that separated the social classes from which most priests were drawn from the 'urban labouring classes', and the consequent ignorance of the former about the realities of the life of the latter. As a writer in the *Christian Teacher* put it in 1841 'the Home Missions are revealing the habits of a strange people no less dramatically than the Mission in India or elsewhere'. He did not exaggerate. It was not, however, as an exercise in sociological self-education that these men devoted their ministries to work in the slums – slums, incidentally, that it is easy to romanticise. Theirs was a religious purpose, in which social improvement, education, evangelisation, sacramental ministry, and pastoral care were essential components.

It would be distorting the evidence, I believe, to see their ministries as equivalent to the 'identification with the poor' that has become popular, as much as a parrot cry as a rallying cry, in ecumenical circles. If, however, we unpack what can properly be demanded of a typical Anglican congregation by way of such 'identification', then the area of overlap is formidable. It would include, for instance, detailed knowledge of the conditions, life chances, problems, celebrations and ways of coping of the poor; personal acquaintance with some genuinely poor people at a leve! that makes real communication possible; a learned ability to see things, including oneself, from the point of view of the poor; a compassion which may not existentially extend to a physical sharing of suffering but which certainly extends to a shared sense of injustice and outrage or of joy and celebration. Such the Hooks, Wests and Healeys certainly did acquire in their industrial ministries – and in the latter two cases, it was enough to drive them into the Church Socialist League. Doubtless it would not have the same effect on present-day Anglicans, but if it broke down the sense of the poor as external, 'out there', 'them', alien, inferior, then the gospel might be heard.

In conclusion, what parts of the Catholic tradition do we most need to rediscover in the context of a society in which both domestically and internationally the rich impoverish the poor? In doctrine we need to restate – as, interestingly, the Lutherans are beginning to so – not only incarnation but also salvation. In worship we need to develop the social reference of the Eucharist. In ethics we need to be recharged with the vision of the world as it is from the bottom – and as it was created to be from the top. And in spirituality we need to learn afresh the proper integration of contemplation and action.

References

1 *Theology*, July 1980, p 1.
2 J R Orens. 'Politics and the Kingdom: the legacy of the Anglican Left', *Anglican Theological Review*, January 1981, pp 21–41. E C Carpenter, *Church and People 1789–1859*, (SPCK, London), 1959.
3 *Christian Teacher* (1839), pp 280–9.
4 C Gore (ed) *Lux Mundi* (London, 1895) (14th edn), p 385, Appendix 1 for R L Ottley's contribution on Christian ethics.
5 Quoted in R Groves, *Conrad Noel and the Thaxted Movement: an adventure in Christian Socialism* (Merlin Press, London, 1967), p 176.
6 *Ibid*, p 30.
7 Cosmas Desmond, *Christians or Capitalists? Christianity and Politics in South Africa* (Bowerdean Press, London, 1979).
8 For a recent and brilliant reaction to thie refusal to 'take Marx seriously' see N Lash, *A Matter of Hope: A theologian's reflections on the thought of Karl Marx* (Darton, Longman and Todd, London, 1981).
9 Groves, *op cit*, p 195.
10 David Morland, OSB, *Eucharist and Justice* (Catholic Information Service, London, 1980).
11 Groves, *op cit*, p 200.
12 Desmond, *op cit*, p 36.
13 *Ibid*, p 45.

15 Poverty and Theology: towards a renewed understanding

Terry Drummond

Introduction

The problem of poverty in Britain today is one that many people find difficult to take seriously. Most Christians come from reasonably comfortable backgrounds, and find it difficult to face the reality of poverty at home. It is true that most churches are involved in raising money for such bodies as Christian Aid, or Oxfam, and this often leads to a limited understanding of 'Third World Poverty'. But the perception of the problem in the United Kingdom is often less clear, and many Christians will not even accept that there is a problem in their own country.

The problem, however, is not new, for the Church and many Church leaders have wrestled with the need to take seriously the needs of the poor. In the Oxford Movement, it was Pusey who attempted to challenge his contemporaries on this issue and, though he did not reflect a fuller understanding within the Movement, his words are important:

> 'The poor of the Christ are the church's special treasure, and the Gospel is their special property . . . The poor are the wealth, the dowry of the church; they have a sacred character about them; they bring a blessing with them; for they are what Christ, for our sake, made of himself . . .'[1]

It is easy to see the Oxford Movement as a body concerned only with liturgical and theological reform. But there is a limited tradition within its teaching of a concern for the poor and, while the 1830s and 1840s are remembered for the growth of social reform and the beginnings of socialism, the Oxford Fathers are not often included in teaching about the growth of social concern. Yet Bernard Markwell has said of Pusey:

> 'No 19th-century social reformer, to my knowledge, has ever equalled the mystical intensity of Pusey's description of the holiness of the poor . . . His insights are truly revolutionary on the psychological level.'[2]

Pusey's understanding of the place of the poor, in both a practical and spiritual sense, is not central in most teaching on the history of the Oxford Movement, but therein lies the basis for the commitment of those followers who later became the slum priests. The Anglo-Catholic movement is better known for its commitment to liturgy and tradition. But to be fully true to their calling Anglo-Catholics need to rediscover the teaching of Pusey and, in so doing, take seriously the growth of poverty in Britain today. The challenge of poverty demands new policies and renewed understanding of the poor as children of God.

The purpose of this essay is to try to present the facts of poverty and to set them in the light of contemporary theological thinking. My premise is that wealth and material resources in Britain have remained within the confines of a small number of people. This group, who are the most wealthy, see themselves as rightful protectors of wealth, while often taking the view that poverty is no longer a problem and, if it exists at all, is self-inflicted. They will be unable to recognise that their privilege contributes to the continuing existence of the poor. In the words of R H Tawney: '. . . what thoughtful rich people call the problem of poverty, thoughtful poor people call, with equal justice, the problem of riches'.[3]

In the light of biblical and later Church tradition, it must be seen that any discussion of poverty cannot be pursued in isolation and must be seen alongside the question of wealth. Consequently, it must be recognised that to relieve poverty demands a proper use of that wealth. The Church of England as an organisation is wealthy, though its assets are tied up in buildings and other immoveable items, and much of its resources are stretched in sustaining the clergy and the central structures. Yet the origin of the whole Church lies in a man who, according to the Gospels, had little material wealth, and in his teaching called on the wealthy to share all they had.

The issue of wealth and poverty in Britain today is fraught with difficulties. Increasingly, many people live in a middle-income bracket which allows a comfortable life-style without wealth. On the other hand, many fall into poverty through unemployment, low pay and government policies that offer supportive taxation to those in upper income brackets while attempting to reduce benefits to those who are in real need. This can lead to complacency in the middle group and a lack of real concern for the needy.

To rediscover the truth about the poor means treating them not just as statistics in a report, but as real people who have problems caused by circumstances outside their control. Inevitably, this will cause a great disturbance for the affluent who will still claim that the poor should help themselves, or even claim that there are no poor. As Townsend says:

> One of the characteristics of inequality is that many of the people who have most to gain from it are not conscious of it. They want and tend to believe that their privilege is ordained or natural or meritorious, or diminishing and extremely modest; alternatively, that other disprivilege is inevitable or deserved and rather modest.'[4]

The issue seen in this perspective becomes a challenge for Christians to be true to their calling and return to the biblical understanding and teaching of the early Church. A rereading of these sources will show up a real concern for the poor, not just in spirit, but in terms of how they live in society.

The Church's response in history

The Church down the ages has, to some extent, maintained a tradition of caring for the needy, but has done so often as the servant of the State and landowner. The landowner contributed to charity and the Church dispensed the care to those who were seen as most deserving.

The movement towards a more organised response to poverty came in the 19th century with the growth of urbanisation. The movement brought into the cities many of the rural poor, who sought work in the new factories, but had to live in poor housing and squalid areas. The growth of London, in particular, led to the foundation of charities such as Dr Barnardo's, the Salvation Army, and many other philanthropic bodies, often based on Evangelical Christianity. The Clapham Sect, with men such as Lord Shaftesbury, were also key figures in the debate about the need for good working conditions and the need for decent sanitary conditions to alleviate the diseases of their day. All started from a strong Christian base and a commitment to the urban poor.

This same period also saw the beginnings of the movement of some Anglo-Catholic clergy into the areas of poor housing and poverty.

> 'Although most Anglo-Catholic clergy found comfortable livings, others, led by their sense of priestly vocation, ventured into the neglected and poverty-stricken districts of the nation's cities. Left behind were the academic concerns of Oxford and the Tractarian reverence for ecclesiastical authority. In their place the "slum ritualists" brought a rough and simple Catholicism expressed in beautiful, although often eccentric ceremonial, and a pastoral zeal which compelled them to champion the cause of the parishioners against the slum lords, sweat-shop owners, and even bishops.'[5]

Arising out of this movement there was a limited development of a theology that had a concern for the poor, and this can be seen in the work of men like Charles Marson who, in the volume *Vox Clamantium* (The Gospel of the People) published in 1894, wrote an essay entitled 'The Social Teaching of the Early Fathers' in which he presented an argument to show that the poor were a concern of the early Fathers:

> 'Where the Catholic faith is merely latent, there the socialism is less explicit. When the writer is unsound in his orthodoxy, then he is almost sure to favour some form of individualist law or possession. When the writer is sound and saintly, then he is always entirely and unhesitatingly in favour of common holding of goods, of equality of opportunity, of social freedom and even when he is not quite sound, he is always fiercely opposed to covetousness which calls itself enterprise, smartness, natural incentive to extortion, thrift and the like.'[6]

Whether this was written as a serious attempt to assess the Fathers may be questioned, but it is the area of concern in relation to the holding of goods in common that at least challenges poverty and the holding of wealth.

The commitment to find justice for the poor is a small part of the Tractarian tradition of the 1830s which carries on into the post-1914-1918 period. In the clergy who attempted to keep alive the tradition there are many today who look back to men like Fr Groser in East London and Conrad Noel at Thaxted, who in both word and action kept alive the debate on social ethics and the poor.

The commitment to working on these issues is also found in the writing of some of the Catholic thinkers of the 1950s, and it can be especially seen in Puttrill's essay in *Return to Reality*, edited by Stanley Evans:

> 'Wherever love and brotherhood are seen expressed in the sharing of goods, there is *koinonia*. When men live and work unselfishly for a better world, there we see spiritual people, whatever they may call themselves.'[7]

This is Catholic theology based on a commitment to the poor that is not usually found in contemporary thought.

An important step for the Catholic Renewal movement must be a re-assessment of the teaching of Pusey and the later socially active followers of the Oxford Movement who had a commitment to the poor. This commitment was based on a biblical tradition that gave the poor an equal status with other people and based on the Eucharist that opened up the altar to all. In the Eucharist all people are equal; the Church has too easily allowed this central act of witness to become personal and so lose its corporate nature that draws all together.

A major problem in Anglo-Catholic thinking has been a neglect of the Bible and, in particular, the biblical teaching on poverty. This can be contrasted with the renewal in Evangelical circles, where poverty and the

Bible's teaching have become a key issue. This is especially seen in the writings of Ronald Sider in the USA and Bishop David Sheppard in Britain in his new book, *Bias to the Poor*. This renewed thinking has led to the foundation of organisations such as the Evangelical Coalition for Urban Mission and Church Action on Poverty. Their foundation opens up the field to new thought and the poor are put on the agenda – at least for some Christians.

The neglect of the Bible can be rectified, and for a Christian understanding of poverty we need to open up three areas:

1) The Scriptures
2) Christian tradition
3) The present facts of poverty

Out of the information available to us there can be a development of policies that may lead to a political/liberation theology relevant to Britain. A key element will be an active concern for the poor based on the question 'why poverty?' It will also seek to help the poor, not with sympathetic philanthropy, but with a challenge to society to create more just conditions based on the gospel of Jesus. The way forward then lies in looking at three areas and seeking new policies and a theological understanding of material poverty.

The Scriptures

The Bible has many faces, but throughout its many books it shows a constant commitment from God for the poor. From the books of the law through the Prophets to Jesus in the New Testament it is a solidarity with the poor which is seen to be critical of the world's rich and challenges the ownership of wealth. It offers hope and justice to the oppressed and the books are often a challenge to the leaders of the day.

The Old Testament

The Old Testament is the story of the development of a nation from its foundation through its history of nomadic wandering to settlement. Its importance lies in the fact that the people of Israel follow one God whom they interpret as King, and much of their history is based on an understanding of that kingship. In their earliest days this left them as a nation under God's rule, with its law based on this understanding.

The Deuteronomic Law of the Old Testament is the beginning of God's siding with the poor in the form of widows, strangers and orphans:

> 'You must not molest the stranger or oppress him, for you lived as strangers in the land of Egypt. You must not be harsh with the widow, or with the orphan; if you are harsh with them, they will surely cry out to me and be sure that I shall hear their cry.' (*Exodus* 22: 20–23)

It is now suggested that this law was developed to support a classless society (see also *Exodus* 23: 1–12) based on mutual concern which reaches a climax in *Leviticus* (chapters 25–27), where we find the year of Jubilee – a very radical concept which, if followed through to its conclusion, would have led to a society based on a concern for all people, poor and wealthy alike. As Boerma says:

> 'Once every fifty years all slaves have to be freed. Property acquired by anyone has to be returned to the original owner. In that year all debts have to be remitted. Nowadays, we would call these measures structural solutions. They not only take account of the need, but restore just conditions.'[8]

The Jubilee year is important to any understanding of the Old Testament concept of justice, in that it is here that we find a worked-out policy of the people being given a full share of the wealth of the nation. Boerma points out that:

> 'There is no means of telling whether this law was ever enforced or whether it remained simply an ideal requirement. The struggle of the prophets against the great landowners suggests that, in their day at any rate, no such regulation was of general application.'[9]

It remains important to note that the ideal was in existence and, even if it was never actually activated, it was laid down and underpinned the challenge of the prophets in their concern for the poor. Among the criticisms the prophets levelled at the rich was an indictment of their attitudes to land ownership. Originally a shared concept dominated attitudes to the land, with God as the only owner. With settlement the wealthy and powerful took over ownership and began to help the creation of a landless group of peasants. This led to the call of the prophets, who challenged this attitude. In their comments they saw God as the final owner, and this led to their demands for a return to a more just sharing of this resource: 'It is the Lord's possession' (*Joshua* 22:19); 'The Lord's land' (*Hosea* 9:3, *Psalm* 85:2). To understand the Old Testament view of wealth and poverty, God must be seen to be on the side of the poor; reflecting this the law understands Him by giving Divine ownership with a society based on a shared existence. The prophets represent this view, and their demands side directly with the poor and directly challenge the wealthy.

The New Testament

The coming of God in Jesus to be a man is to place the teaching in context of continuing concern for the poor. In the incarnation God comes as the servant and brother to all, not as the ruler. In the Gospels we find Jesus following in the Old Testament tradition of having a firm commitment for the poorest in society. This is clearly seen in Luke who, even before Christ is born, has Mary saying of God: 'He has pulled down Princes from their thrones and exalted the lowly, the hungry he has filled with good things, the rich sent empty away.' (*Luke* 1: 52–53). The Gospel follows this with Jesus declaring himself as a liberator in chapter 4:18, following directly in the tradition of the Jubilee with its year 'of the Lord's favour'. These verses firmly put Jesus in the tradition of the prophets who stand by the poor. In later verses Jesus offers little hope for the rich and presents them with the challenge to give to the poor, or to have no place in Heaven. Earthly wealth offers no hope for inclusion in the future Kingdom, as in the parable of Dives and Lazarus, which suggests that the poor man is raised to Heaven and the rich man is rejected. Miranda says of this particular parable:

> 'At no turn is it insinuated that this rich man was a person of especially depraved habits, or that in order to enrich himself he had committed particular acts of extortion or fraud which other rich persons do not commit. The only thing said of him is that he was rich and lived as if he were rich: "There was a rich man and he clothed himself in scarlet and linen, and daily dined splendidly." (*Luke* 6:19). And, since this is nothing but the story of someone who was punished in torment, the only purpose the parable can have is to tell us why. It would be unforgivably negligent of Christ if, as the experts would have it, he did not tell us why – but he does tell us why; because the man was rich. This is the very title of the parable – "There was a rich man".'[10]

The approach of Jesus seems to have been a return to the early view of the Old Testament and to the prophets with their view that wealth is wrong and the poor must be given the support of the community.

In *Luke* chapter 6: 29–30, 35, Jesus tries to persuade his disciples not to worry about possessions. Where they have two cloaks they are to give one away. In these days he challenges earthly wealth and assets that the Kingdom of God belongs to the poor. All of this would follow as from the Old Testament law, where the oppressed poor are seen as the children of God and under His direct care.

Some will argue that these stories relate to a spiritual poverty and to the lack of a true spirituality, but such an interpretation ignores the teaching throughout the Gospel of Luke that it is the wealthy whom Jesus singles out for criticism, and the poor are seen as those being the closest to God. If wealth is seen as a factor in the creation of poverty, then Luke's Gospel supports an understanding that puts poverty and riches firmly in the teaching of Jesus and from there on to the agenda of Christians.

After the ministry of Jesus as described in the Gospel of Luke, we have in The Acts of the Apostles a Church that experimented with shared wealth, though the Epistles tend to accept the *status quo* and have little to say about the whole area of wealth, with the exception of James, with his commitment to the poor and his warnings for the wealthy:

> 'Now an answer for the rich. Start crying, weep for the miseries that are coming to you. Your wealth is all rotting, your clothes are all eaten up by moths. All your gold and your silver are corroding away and the same corrosion will be your sentence and eat into your body. It was a burning fire that you stored up as treasure for the last days.' (*James* 5: 1–3)

The Church Fathers onwards

The more important developments for the understanding of a commitment to the poor come with the sayings and teachings recorded in the Fathers. For example, John Chrysostom declares:

> 'Tell me how it is that you are rich? From whom did you receive your wealth? And he, whom did he receive it from? From his grand-father you say. From his father. By climbing this genealogical tree you are able to show the justice of this possession? Of course you cannot; rather its beginning and root have come out of injustice.'[11]

Basil the Great continues the tradition:

> 'When someone steals a man's clothing we call him a thief. Should we not give the same name to one who could clothe the naked and does not? The bread in your cupboard belongs to the man who has no shoes; the money which you hoard up belongs to the poor.'[12]

The early Church Fathers had a teaching tradition which follows on the Gospels with statements about the need to accept the poor and, more importantly, to share wealth. This challenge does not seem to have had too much effect, and with the Constantine settlement of the fourth century the Church became part of the government. As with the people of Israel who forgot the poor when they settled in the land of Israel, the early Church lost the teaching on poverty. It is as though once the people of God became settled the will to create wealth and accumulate it for personal gain supersedes a desire to put the poor into a position where they have equality.

From these early beginnings and throughout its history, the Church has created organisations which served the poor and even preached poverty as a gift of God, while at the same time creating and drawing to itself temporal wealth. Its teaching allowed the rich to be philanthropic while keeping their wealth, in direct contradiction to the biblical tradition. The whole concept of shared wealth as found in the Acts of the Apostles was soon lost and, if anything, the opposite occurs, with the Church concerned to serve the rich while giving the poor little more than spiritual support. In its long history, however, groups do appear who seek to reverse such a trend. For example, the Levellers and the Diggers in seventeenth-century England had a professed commitment to greater equality, but they were seen as heretical and suppressed. The reappearance of Christians willing to challenge poverty and related problems that arose with the growth of urbanisation comes in in the 19th century with the wealthy evangelicals who formed the Clapham Sect. Their concern was essentially one of seeking change to the laws that allowed inhuman conditions in factories. Their work later led to the essentially philanthropic work of men like Dr Barnardo and other evangelicals who sought to alleviate the lot of the poor.

The work of these wealthy Christians helped to create a concern for the poor, but did little actually to change the attitudes of Christians who either remained oblivious of the poverty of many of their countrymen, or equally saw the poverty as a result of the way the poor lived, and in that case a judgment.

What is poverty?

A difficulty with any discussion of poverty in contemporary Britain is the common belief that no one needs to be poor today. A report such as Peter Townsend's *Poverty in the United Kingdom*, published in 1979, may be dismissed as a fiction by those who refuse to accept the presence of poverty. The problem becomes one of the difference between an accurate and inaccurate attitude and perception of poverty.

There are also those who are prepared to accept that British society has a problem and may well seek to challenge and change its structures. Their perception will be a response to the analysis of the problem like Townsend's and the figures published in a few government reports, but may also be based on personal experience of poverty as experienced by families. In this area the clergy and church worker who works in a deprived area can bring useful insights to bear. This latter group may well have experience of meeting with people who lack the basic needs for life in contemporary society. These needs are often set by the people around them, but equally it can be a problem of little or no regular wage, poor social security benefits or bad housing.

The groups who suffer poverty will not have sought to live in this way, and yet once at the bottom it is an immense task to break out of the trap. Though many may live in this way, many British people not only ignore the problem, but are actually of the belief that it is self-inflicted, caused by misuse of personal finance, non-payment of debts, too much hire purchase, or being workshy. (This latter attitude continues to persist even with unemployment rising.) In 1977 the EEC published a report on *The Perception of Poverty in Europe*, and the British who were interviewed actually had much harder attitudes to the problem than people from other member states: '43% of the British interviewed attributed poverty and unemployment to the personal defects of the poor and unemployed; in contrast to an average for all the remaining states of 25%.'[13]

This reponse is to be found in the way the press seem to follow up any DHSS fraud and make out of the few cases a major issue, while ignoring the simple fact that actual payments made to a family are not going to cover their living costs. Although fraud is very rare, poverty and an inability to manage on social security are actually increasing problems.

In the 1980s, when we take for granted a welfare State, it can be difficult to imagine that families exist who can fall into financial difficulties and eventual poverty. According to Townsend, using the State standard, they actually compose around 9 per cent of the population, or five million people. The level of poverty is based on a living standard set by the State as a basic minimum for survival, and is set at a level below which no one should fall. The net is set to allow people certain standards, but is certainly below society's accepted norms. It can be argued that the level must be set very low to encourage people to seek to change their standards, but once at the bottom, without the kind of help needed to move out of poverty, it is more and more difficult for people to change their life-style.

The view of definite poverty is a difficult definition to sustain, due to changing expectations even the poor have to base their life style on other people's. In a materialistic society they can see what is available, and most people are influenced to a degree by advertising; the poor are bound to face the need for new goods that are outside their finances. This leads into what has been described as relative deprivation, a definition based on the place of people in society. The poor are poor because they lack the basic material goods and finance that most people consider normal. As John Atherton says: 'Poverty is, therefore, not simply a matter of "hearing the babies cry because they are hungry or cold". It is also about not being able to enjoy life like everyone else. It is about the exclusion of groups from everyday life.'[14] The concept of relative deprivation sees poverty as a problem that is partly dependent on the relationship of an individual or family to others in the community. For example, the annual holiday has in recent years become the norm for many families, including those who in the past would not have had the opportunity. In school many children have the chance of holidays or extra-curricular activities. Where poor families cannot afford these activities society can present a harsh and critical judgment that often ostracises children by presenting them to their classmates as being poor and, as such, carrying the stigma of society.

It may also be said that those who suffer relative deprivation often live in communities that have few facilities, such as health centres, doctors, leisure outlets – other than public houses or bingo halls. They are areas that are often run down and deprived in terms of poor housing. People in these areas are bound to be less healthy and, with the layer upon layer of problems that are added, lead to them feeling inadequate and powerless.

Whom does poverty affect?

The poverty of the 19th century in London, for instance, was a poverty shared by whole communities and, though that does not make it more acceptable, there was at least a shared perception. Today the load is not so easily spread and poverty may be the problem of only a small group in a community, though with increased unemployment this is changing. The problem of poverty today will hit particular groups, for example:

The old-age pensioners
Single-parent families
Large families
The disabled
The unemployed.

In many cases these people will live in council houses with expensive electrical heating. This leads to large bills that cannot be paid, often because families are not used to the idea of having to budget on a quarterly basis. Traditionally, they would have paid by meter and kept above the problem in this way. In their new situation it is only a short time before debt can lead to the electrical supply being disconnected and those most at risk, the young, often in single-parent families, the disabled, having to manage with candles. Such cases are on the increase, due to the continuous cost of electricity and gas, but with no increase in benefit to match. Alongside the deprivation of poor housing there can also be the deprivation of the new council block. With unemployment adding to the numbers who are in poverty, plus cuts in benefit, it is obvious that many people will find it difficult to retain a decent standard of living, and move over the line of survival into poverty. These groups will have to adjust to a level of life that puts them outside society, and this could lead to a two-nation situation, with those who have enough to live on and those in some form of poverty.

How should the Church respond to poverty?

The Church of today needs to give time for working on strategies and policies that arise out of and are based on a theological understanding of poverty. These will take the poor seriously, recognising that British society is based on inequality, and as such rejects the biblical principles referred to above. In the 19th century the response of the Church was based on philanthropy, paternalism and, for some, identification with the poor. These responses said little about the structural causes of poverty. Today, with the facts and information that are available, we are in a position to challenge the causes of poverty and in so doing seek to change society. The good Samaritan bandaged the wounds and paid off the debt, and in British society this is still important. But the task must also be to point out to people that the poor still exist in Britain, showing that this is true because of the way our society is ordered. This leads to a direct challenge on unequal taxation policies and the greed of those who hold wealth at the expense of the poor.

In his book *The Politics of Poverty* David Donnison, ex-chairman of the Supplementary Benefits Commission, argues that poverty is a word we use in three ways. Firstly, to describe destitution, hardship and misery – the conditions described above. This is the area that is found to be covered by the low-paid, those on benefits and the traditional poor. Secondly, there are those who are into the problem of relative deprivation, finding it hard to make ends meet – they cannot compete with neighbours who are on higher incomes. This leads to: 'The third usage poses questions about inequality, exclusion, discrimination, injustice and "relative poverty". If this third concept of poverty is to have a practical and cutting edge, it calls for nothing less than a new morality.'[15] This concept of a new morality is one that Christians must take seriously, and it demands asking questions such as:

What causes poverty?
What can alleviate the problem?
What is the Church doing for the poor?
Is the Church aware of the problems in its own nation?
Is the Church standing on the side of the poor or the rich?

The Christian who worships Sunday by Sunday may say 'What is this to do with me?' The Anglican Catholic who wants a quiet life, or equally who will be involved in the anti-women priest movement or pietistical Catholic renewal may want to ignore the living problem of poverty. But poverty is a problem of people's way of life, and the challenge that was faced up to by some of the clergy of the Oxford Movement is a problem for Christians today. Those clergy took up the challenge of living with the poor, sharing their living conditions based on a morality and theology that demands being part of the community. The priests who lived in those communities were forced to take seriously the issue of poverty and hardship because the people they served were poor! To take Catholic renewal seriously demands that injustice is taken into our thinking as it was for those few priests.

The world Church is taking up these concerns, and in parts of Latin America and South-East Asia there are theologies that arise out of poverty and suffering. In these continents the Church and its theologians are speaking out for the poor, even though this can lead to hardship and oppression. The political theologies of the Third World challenge, in that they present theology as a changing process which grows out of the Bible and people's understanding of what the Bible is actually saying to them. It changes from being a book available just for devotional study to being also a stimulant for recognising a God who, throughout history, stands by the poor.

The liberation theologians offer a theology that lifts up the poor man and gives him worth. The society they seek is based on justice and brotherhood. This may well suggest the form of the new morality that Donnison calls for. It suggests a morality for a society where all have an equal share and poverty is not a problem because no one is condemned to poverty.

This is an ideal, but the liberation theologians at least attempt to explore the possibilities of Jesus as Liberator for the poor and a challenge to the wealthy. It demands that Christians move from a biblical view that is based on a Christian life of personal morality, concerned only with personal ethics, to a morality that is concerned with the whole of life and all people.

A major concern of a morality for today is the use, misuse, redistribution of wealth. The Church is a body to which all are invited, rich and poor. The Gospel tells us that Jesus told the rich man to share his wealth.

To eradicate poverty in Britain there needs to be a direct challenge to the wealthy. We live in a society where 5 per cent of the population own 45 per cent of net assets. This must be challenged. The rich 5 per cent grow richer through the financial system. While they can draw to themselves greater wealth the poor are bound to get poorer, unless there is a change in taxation law to seek to draw some of that wealth back and use it to raise social security benefits. Often the rich are critical of the poor because they have fridges and television sets, which are part and parcel of our consumer society, with the criticism being made by those who will pay out large amounts of money for meals or entertainment.

Governments of the past few years have only exacerbated this situation. They have cut down welfare benefits, not built new homes, and helped to create unemployment that will go up to four million plus in a few years. Those in poverty caused by the lack of equal distribution are going to need to see change, or they will just be part of a widespread discontent. The challenge to poverty demands more, not fewer, hospitals in poor communities, more and higher benefits and higher taxation for the wealthy. For those Christians who would see this as being political, or nothing to do with the Church, they must reread their Gospels, where they will find a challenge to take seriously the need to work for a society based on equal shares, with the wealthy sharing their riches. The Gospels, in so far as they are political, give the poor a fair share, and the direct challenge is presented to the rich.

The task for the Church, and individual Christians, is to look towards developing a commitment to the poor based on the Gospels. The liberation theologians have started the task, and we need similar British endeavours that will move theology out of the academic world into the streets and into the lives of people. The writings of, for example, Jose Miranda on the concept of injustice in the Bible (in *Marx and the Bible* and *Communism in the Bible*) are valuable for a study of the Christian commitment to the poor. Theology in some Third World countries has led to concrete action and given people a will to take on injustice where it is found. A concern to challenge injustice in Britain will be a sign of discipleship for British Christians.

To develop the work demands people who are prepared to change their perception of poverty and accept that there is a problem in society, and that its persistence is a major evil. To seek its eradication may seem like an impossible dream, but we must recognise that to create this kind of society will demand detailed research into wealth, ownership and poverty, but this will lead to strategies to lift up the poor, if, as Leonardo Boff says, 'Jesus affected human beings at their very roots, activating their hope principle and making them dream of the Kingdom, which is not an entirely different world, but this world completely new and renewed.'[16] The hope principle for British Christians will arise out of a willingness to help create a society based on justice, involving equality and the total destruction of the evil that is poverty.

The future of the Church of England may depend on our responses to the poor. They are to be found in the parts of the country where the Church is weakest, the large housing estates and areas of deprivation. The poor were to Jesus the children of God, the prophets saw them as the oppressed, and some of the Anglo-Catholic Fathers took them seriously. We must recognise that the problems will not be solved with an occasional handout from either government or Church. The challenge is as Pusey said: 'Casual almsgiving is not Christian charity, rather, seeking Christ in the poor . . . we must . . . seek them out as we would seek out Christ . . .' This must lead us to radical strategies that are based on facts and figures. This work will show all people the truth of the statement 'the poor are always with you', and in that truth seek to change it to 'the poor no longer exist'.

A new morality such as the one Donnison suggests is possible, and the Church should take up the task of thinking it through with others of like mind. The response in the 19th century was to work alongside the poor.

Our task as Catholic Christians is to present the challenge that seeks change through the gospel that brings change.

References

1 Cited in Owen Chadwick, *The Mind of the Oxford Movement* (A and C Black, 1960), p 227.
2 B K Markwell, 'The Anglican Left: Radical Social Reformers in the Church of England and the Protestant Episcopal Church, 1846–1954' (University of Chicago, Department of History, PhD thesis, 1977), p 60.
3 R H Tawney, 1913. Quoted in *The Wealth Report*, ed Frank Field (London, 1979), p 11.
4 P Townsend, *Poverty in the United Kingdom* (Penguin, London, 1979), p 18.
5 J R Orens, *Politics and the Kingdom* (Jubilee Group, London, 1981), pp 5–6.
6 C Marson, 'The Social Teaching of the Early Fathers', in *Vox Clamantium* (ed A Reid, London, 1894), p 201.
7 J Putterill, 'The Hallmark of Sharing' in *Return to Reality* ed S Evans (London, 1954), p 62.
8 C Boerma, *Rich Man, Poor Man and the Bible* (SCM Press, 1979), p 33.
9 *Ibid*, p 41.
10 J P Miranda, *Communism in the Bible* (SCM Press, 1982), p 23.
11 Quoted in J P Miranda, *Marx and the Bible* (SCM Press, 1977), p 15.
12 J P Miranda, *op cit*, p 12.
13 J R Atherton, *The Poverty Debate and the Churches* (William Temple Foundation, Manchester, 1981), p 18.
14 *Ibid*, p 15.
15 D Donnison, *The Politics of Poverty* (Martin Robertson, Oxford, 1982), p 7.
16 L Boff, *Jesus Christ, Liberator* (Orbis Books, New York, 1978), p 79.

16 Charismatic Renewal, Politics and the Irish Question

Michael Garde

The Oxford Movement began on the Irish question, It was a movement of the Spirit to return to the Catholic origins of the Church of England.

Today, the Charismatic Movement is a similar manifestation of the Spirit. I want to define this movement in relation to politics, and see what hope it yields for the problems of Ireland.

I will do this by looking at two American sources for Charismatic political action, and then apply my conclusions to Ireland. As this is such a vast area, I will consider three expressions of the Charismatic Movement in Ireland.

On the Protestant side, I shall look at the Christian Renewal Centre in Rostrevor; describe a new experiment in interreligious living called the Christian family; and finally the Catholic Renewal Movement.

1 What is the Charismatic Movement?

'Charismatic' is a transliterated term from the Greek *charisma*. The root meaning is, 'a gift or favour, freely and graciously given'.[1] In the New Testament it is especially used to designate special gifts of a non-material sort, bestowed by the grace of God on individual Christians for the benefit of the Christian assembly. In this way, largely, the vitality, leadership and power of the Holy Spirit are directly manifested. It is essentially the exercise of non-institutional, spiritual power, ministry and leadership.

One of the first reactions following the Apostolic period against institutionalism, growing bureaucracy and worldliness (especially moral) in the early Church had been by a charismatic movement known as Montanism. Montanism was a massive reaction in the late second and third century, involving both a fanatical wing (ie 'heretical', which gave its name to the whole movement, from Montanus, the prophet, an alleged incarnation of the Holy Spirit) and a moderate wing (ie 'orthodox', which rejected

Montanus' trances, continued revelation, self-deification and congregational and biblical irresponsibility). The major spokesman for the latter group was Tertullian. As with the heretical wing, the orthodox emphasis was also (1) on prophecy, but prophecy understood as a non-liturgical, non-formal ministry, emphasising edification, exhortation and lay participation, and (2) on holiness of life.

Throughout the history of the Church there have been movements of renewal, like the Anabaptists, Methodism and, more recently in 1906, the Pentecostal Movement and its offshoots. But then, towards the end of the 1950s, a fresh, largely lay, semi-autonomous expression appeared, only partially originating within the older Pentecostal context. It included large numbers of laity and clergy from and remaining within the major denominations, especially Lutheran, Episcopal (Anglican) and Roman Catholic. Finally, yet another wave emerged at the beginning of the '70s, largely associated with the 'Jesus People' movement which also became substantially charismatic in belief, leadership and practice.

An important feature of the Movement has been the experience of gifts or charismata of the Holy Spirit, especially those mentioned by St Paul in 1 *Corinthians* 12: 8–11: the word of wisdom, the word of knowledge, faith, healing, miracles, prophecy, discernment of spirits, speaking in tongues, and the interpretation of tongues. The term, however, has come to have a general application, referring simply to the Movement itself.

The central feature of the Charismatic Movement, as the Roman Catholic scholar Killian McDonnell has pointed out, is not merely the gifts, but 'fullness of life in the Holy Spirit'.[2] The potentiality of the gifts of the Holy Spirit is a matter of constant reckoning in the Charismatic Movement. In every situation one is open to the supernatural activity of God. It is, as Henry P Van Dusen has said in characterising the Pentecostal phenomenon generally, the awareness of 'God present, and God active'.[3]

A 'charismatic' approach to politics may then awaken or call into action gifts of the Holy Spirit in specific situations. But the focus of attention is not upon the gifts as such. It is rather this broader issue of the Holy Spirit's direct involvement in the issues which are approached.

Larry Christenson, in *A Charismatic Approach to Social Action*, says: 'A charismatic approach to social issues is one which is both initiated and carried out in the power of the Holy Spirit – not merely as a theological principle, but as an experienced event. It is distinguished from a rationalistic or pragmatic or so-called commonsense approach, which simply reasons from a general principle to a practical application, with little or no sense of God's active participation in the process. A charismatic approach . . . cannot conclude its enquiry merely by asking, "Is this thing necessary? Is it good?" The prior question must be faced. "Does the Lord initiate this? Is His Spirit the motivating Spirit? Can we confidently expect His supernatural power and resources in this undertaking?" . . . [4] A specific sense of call and direction by the Holy Spirit is at the heart of a charismatic approach to social issues. Lacking that, any action by the Church, no matter how well-intentioned, will lead ultimately to frustration and disillusionment. "Unless the Lord builds the house, those who build it labour in vain." '[5]

2 Two American sources of Charismatic political action

I am taking two sources, not because you can trace a direct relationship between them and Ireland, but because there is a similarity in the one case to what one finds in Ireland, and there is a distant desire yet to be articulated to move in the direction of the other. Also it would be wrong to assume that these two sources do not connect with each other. However, I keep them separate for purposes of description. (1) The first I have already referred to – a study by Larry Christenson.[6] He expressed a deep pessimism about all human projects for social and political change. He is very influenced by the Platonic distinction between primary and secondary aspects of the gospel.

'Two simple facts stand in co-ordinate relation to one another in the New Testament: 1) In the culture of that day there existed no dearth of "problems": famine, starvation, political oppression, repressive institutions, poverty. 2) The primary concern evidenced by the primitive Christian community, living in that culture, was to spread the Good News. Ministering to material needs, even in the case of fellow believers, and much more so in the case of general culture, assumed a decidedly derivative and secondary role. This was not an either/or proposition, but a case of this primarily/that secondarily. This priority arrangement, as the normal order of things, is rooted in the anthropological stance of the New Testament, which views the state of man's soul and spirit as more critical to his real welfare than his immediate material circumstances.'[7]

People are a body/spirit duality, with priority given to the spirit. 'With each person we reach, there must be this dual emphasis. Which means that the opposite question must be posed: "Are we helping this person in the practical needs and issues of his everyday life?" A church which neglects to minister to people's material and practical needs can too easily end up as little more than a Bible study group or, worse, a social club.'[8]

This naturally leads to a downplaying of the political and social. Larry Christenson develops his thesis on the basis of the definitive study by Hans von Campenhausen, *Tradition and Life in the Early Church*: '. . . the crucial interests in the life of early Christianity were plainly of a fundamentally different kind (than those espoused by current social theology – addition by Christenson), and not such as to further any participation in civil and political life. Jesus did not allow the misconception of Himself as a reformer or advocate of a programme, either in the ecclesiastical or political sphere. Jesus called men to God. In current and ephemeral questions He declined to become involved . . . Paul's ethical teaching is wholly defensive in character, with its wish to avoid entanglement and friction with the world, and aiming at social autonomy rather than social integration. In Luke's writings the political innocuousness of Christianity is emphasised over and over again.'[9]

Finally this leads to the following conclusion: 'Jesus' apparent lack of concern for human poverty has often been remarked. Perhaps He was not intimidated by it, being poor Himself. Some of His sayings seem almost to exalt poverty as a surer way into the Kingdom. When some of His followers criticised Mary for expending a whole jar of perfumed ointment on Him, rather than giving the money to the poor, Jesus retorted, "You always have the poor with you" and went on to say that this incident would become a part of preaching the Gospel. The primary concern, as always, is the Gospel, and the people whom it summons together.'[10]

The Hebrew background to this text, which we find in *Deuteronomy* 15:11, points us in a different direction: 'There will always be poor people in the land. Therefore I command you to be open-handed towards your brothers and towards the poor and needy in your land.' Far from endorsing poverty, Jesus recognised the forces that keep the poor poor; in Deuteronomy this recognition is coupled with the exhortation: 'However, there should be no poor among you.' (*Deuteronomy* 15: 4a)

The consequence of Christenson's dualistic emphasis is in the end to deny the material, and therefore to fall into Docetism, and not take the incarnation seriously.

It is clear that reforming society is not the prophetic activity of the Church, but rather the creation of an alternative to the *status quo*. 'Words like "household", "extended family", "Christian community" are heard with increasing frequency in charismatic gatherings, where ten years ago one would more likely have heard about "tongues", "prophecy", "healing", "baptism with the Holy Spirit". Not that these have dropped out of the picture, the frame has been enlarged. The renewal of personal spiritual life has opened the door to a new dimension of corporate Christian experience . . . where Charismatics take up a work of social concern, it is as an expression of a primary commitment to community. Social action operates as a function or expression of the life of the community.'[11]

Community is the hoped way of avoiding the dualism presupposed in this political theory. Though communities are emerging which overcome the dichotomy between the spiritual and the material, this underlying assumption always gives priority to the spiritual over against the material. (2) Let us look at another approach to Charismatic renewal and politics.

This one does not seek to distance itself from every other tradition, but humbly learns from them.[12] It seems to this observer that this emphasis holds out a lot of hope for Ireland, where one of the factors in the conflict is Christianity itself.

'Theologically, evangelicals have abandoned the biblical hope that the kingdom of God breaks into our history, here and now. As one evangelical leader confessed, the kingdom of God is about as natural a part of evangelical conversation as one of those strange names in a Dostoevsky novel. There has been little belief in the kingdom of God as a coming political and social reality, to which the Church is now to be a sign. Cutting away the kingdom of God from the message of Jesus, the evangelical tradition has proclaimed a politically neutral gospel, separating things spiritual from things political. While this separation has broken down in practice – evangelicalism in this century has actually bolstered conservative political forces – it has been maintained in theory.'[13]

This results in a truncated gospel which allows concerns like Northern Ireland, the nuclear arms race, the division between rich and poor, to fall outside the embrace of the gospel. Convictions about politics are private and confidential, and no interrelationship is seen between politics and faith. The exception, of course, are those overt attempts to support right-wing politics with biblical justification.

'The shortcomings of the evangelical heritage, however, have not just been political and social; evangelicalism has been inadequate to provide the long-term spiritual nurture essential to discipleship. Evangelical spirituality has frequently been equated with emotions coming in the wake of a born-again experience. But after six months, a year, or a decade – when the quiet time and the close walk with Jesus stop radiating the same warmth they did in the afterglow of conversion – one is frequently left feeling guilty, isolated and not knowing exactly where to turn. Because evangelical spirituality has been so highly individualistic, there usually has been little experience of the church as a community. What communal sense there is has resulted more from a legalistic separation from the outside world than from the reality of *koinonia* as it is described in the New Testament. Most evangelical worship has been designed to bolster personal piety rather than to nurture the corporate life of Christ's body. Contemporary evangelicalism shows some signs of change at each of these points. New sensitivities to the imperatives of biblical justice can be found, as well as a growth of interest in deeper expression of fellowship. Nevertheless, those who have emerged from the evangelical world toward a more biblically radical understanding of the gospel are looking to other traditions and movements in the Christian Church for the nurturing of their faith. For me, and for countless others on similar journeys, evangelicalism on its own has lacked the resources that are necessary to build and sustain a life of faithful discipleship. True growth never occurs when people are living their lives primarily in reaction to their past. Rather than dwelling upon the deficiencies of an evangelical background, one would do better to dialogue with those currents of theology and contemporary life in the Church which can nurture in us a holistic biblically faithful grasp of the gospel.'[14]

Then Wes Michaelson goes on to describe the sources for the 'holistic' understanding of the gospel:

(1) The Anabaptists

'As a theological and communal tradition, Anabaptism has provided a unique point of identification for many from an evangelical heritage who are taking the call to discipleship seriously in our time. This is because of the pivotal questions which, historically, Anabaptism has asked and attempted to answer:

What does it mean to give our lives according to all the demands of the gospel?

How can our lives be molded consistently by the pattern of Christ's servanthood?

What are the concrete implications of loving our enemies?

How is the Church to live out its life as a called community of God's people?'[15]

(2) The Charismatics

'When many of us began grasping the social, political, and economic meaning of the gospel, we assumed that the charismatic renewal movement was about the last place to turn for nurture and encouragement. Since that movement demonstrated little if any openness toward the prophetic dimensions of the gospel – it was, in fact, a largely reactionary social and political force in society – this mistrust was understandable. But as we understand the starting point for the witness to God's kingdom to be the creation of a faithful people, we began tentatively exploring certain segments of the charismatic movement receptive to the political claims of the gospel. That testing has now matured into bonds of trust, nurture, and mutual edification. The charismatic movement can bring to radical discipleship a deep experience of what it means for the church to be a community, functioning concretely as a dynamic alternative social and spiritual environment. Seasoned charismatics are not obsessed with individualistic gifts; rather, their focus is on the calling of a people, corporately, to be the full expression of Christ's body. Some groups within the charismatic renewal have been moving toward radical political and social understandings of the gospel. In my judgment, this is a crucial event in contemporary church history. Whenever a charismatically-influenced fellowship comes to grasp the meaning of its new life as existing not in and for itself, but for the sake of God's purposes of justice in the world, then it often embraces acts of prophetic witness in an unhesitant and graceful manner. Major currents of the charismatic movement remain closed to such witness, however; they also display styles of rigidly authoritarian leadership, a denial of women of the right to serve in pastoral capacities, and a sometimes implicit, sometimes explicit alliance with the social and political *status quo*. But sweeping stereotypes can no longer be applied to the whole charismatic renewal movement. Many whose Christian radicalism once separated them from charismatics now have found ones among them to be a wellspring of nurture. Those charismatics have helped put flesh on the vision of a biblically radical gospel by spiritually supporting growing fellowships of such believers.'[16]

(3) The Social Justice Activists

'Central to any understanding of faithful discipleship is the biblical imperative to seek fundamental social justice, motivated by God's compassion for those who are impoverished and afflicted. Certain Christians have witnessed to these truths with a compelling clarity and constancy, and they are nurturing all those who have discovered that conversion fo Christ includes a commitment to solidarity with the poor. Third World Christians like Brazilian Archbishop Dom Helder Camara, many black Christians, other voices of prophetic social justice in the American church, liberation theologians, and those who are attempting to integrate their faith with socialism and the insights of Marxism all share a commitment to economic and social justice. These believers know that justice lies at the heart of God's intention for the world, that the Bible gives revolutionary hope to the poor and the oppressed, and that the biblical message condemns the established structures of power and injustice . . . The evangelical tradition remains in desperate need of those streams of the Church which flow from the biblical truth that God is with the oppressed, and that his intention is liberation. The question of how this is to be made historically concrete can be addressed only after we come to a consensus about God's purposes of justice and liberation for all humanity.'[17]

(4) The Contemplatives and the Catholic Left

'There are two tributaries in the Catholic tradition which uniquely feed those called to a radical gospel. The first is the Catholic left, represented in Dorothy Day and the Catholic Worker movement. For decades their faith has propelled them to share their life with the destitute, joining the cause of oppressed workers and struggling to implement a vision of radical social change. The Catholic Worker has felt most at home with their Lord in soup kitchens. Unlike many of their fellow Catholics, they harbour a healthy scepticism about the way social and political power is arranged.

Theirs has been a voice of biblically rooted dissent. It is dissent which bears the stamp of authenticity in living with the poor and for their sake. Throughout the Catholic left, from social reformers like Michael Harrington to prophetic dissenters like Dan Berrigan, a common debt is owed to the Catholic Worker movement. Increasingly, this same debt is acknowledged by many of us whose tradition has been evangelical rather than Catholic, but who have seen in the Catholic Worker's identification with the poor a witness to the gospel marked by a simplicity and purity uncommon in our own upbringing.

'The other nurturing Catholic contribution is the contemplative and monastic tradition of the church. The monastic movement has always professed that seeking the purity of the gospel in our lives required (to use an old Catholic term) spiritual formation. Whenever discipleship has been deepened in the history of the church, it has been acompanied by questions like, "How are we guided and nurtured, both individually and corporately, in that development?" Concern for radical discipleship today which omits any sensitivity to spiritual formation is a grave mistake; it may be radical, but it will not be a call to full discipleship. Those emerging from evangelical backgrounds have frequently discovered its inability to spiritually sustain a pilgrimage of faithful discipleship. The danger, however, is that radical political witness will become the substitute for an authentic spirituality, rather than its fruit. Here the contemplative, monastic tradition has a vital contribution to make. This tradition has the maturity to nourish faith in the midst of darkness – both inward and outward. Through centuries contemplatives have struggled to know the meaning of living as pilgrims in this world, not simply out of a desire to flee it, but because of their thirst to know God, and share in his life.

'It is instructive that Thomas Merton, who secluded himself in the spiritual regimen of a Trappist monastery, was one of the first and most discerning prophetic voices within the church to protest against the war in Indochina. The most vulnerable point in the contemporary movement toward radical discipleship is the need, and often the lack, of an authentic spirituality, one which can sustain a long and arduous struggle, upbuilding life lived in distinct nonconformity with the culture. That such a struggle is our destiny is beyond my doubt. The question is whether we can be nurtured to embrace that struggle not merely with endurance, but rather with celebration, with worship and with joy. This calling necessitates building a vital worship base for our life together as Christ's body. In fact, this renewed life should find its source in such worship. Both individually and communally, those given to a radical following of Jesus will be unable to continue on their journey of faith without feeding the fundamental desire to know God, to do his will, and to be molded by this hunger and thirst for righteousness.'[18]

These two contributions show the different presuppositions that are found in the Charismatic Movement and, as a result the different political strategies entered into. We now move to Ireland and describe three examples of Charismatic renewal. What has been said above will hopefully help us to evaluate the descriptions that follow.

3 The Charismatic Movement in Ireland

Whereas the ecumenical movement has not had much influence in Ireland generally, the Charismatic movement has been able to overcome barriers between Protestants and Catholics more than any other group. This has not resulted from minimising theological differences which are still a major problem, but by avoiding political aspects of the Irish problem. There is a possibility for a political consciousness to develop; the type will depend on the kind of influences that come to bear. One might go as far as to say that unless Christians in Ireland confront the question of the division of Ireland their social relevance will be minimal by the year 2000.

(1) The Christian Renewal Centre in Rostrevor

The Christian Renewal Centre in Rostrevor is one expression of God's reconciling work in this troubled island. The centre has become a beacon of hope for many in a land so often near despair; a light in the darkness that points God's way to peace in Ireland.

Rostrevor is a response to the conflict in Ireland, and an expression of the elusiveness of any human solution. Cecil Kerr, who founded the community together with others, was the Anglican chaplain at Queen's University, Belfast, a conservative Evangelical.

Early in 1973 God spoke to Cecil and Myrtle Kerr about what He was going to do in Ireland. He wanted to establish a place where Christians from all traditions could come together in a spirit of love and prayer and experience His purpose for our land.

At the heart of this work, begun in 1974, is a small community drawn from different traditions witnessing together to the unity which the Spirit gives. Community members may come for a period of a year or more and people are welcomed for shorter periods as temporary members of the community. No one receives a salary, and any money earned outside the community goes towards the work of the centre. Worship and daily prayer together morning and evening are the foundation of their life together. Members are encouraged to be fully involved in the life of their local church in the village of Rostrevor. They have no desire to start another denomination – this would be seen as the last thing Ireland needs.

From this base teams go out to conferences and take part in parish renewal. We can sum up what they are trying to do in Rostrevor with this three-fold vision: To be a place of prayer, renewal and reconciliation. Prayer is seen as undergirding the whole ministry. A constant burden is for peace in Ireland.

Renewal is seen as the greatest need in the Church in Ireland. They have as a result a particular ministry to the clergy of all the churches. There have been some wonderful breakthroughs in people's lives.

Shortly after the centre was started a weekly prayer meeting was begun. At first only a few local people joined the community, and now up to two hundred come every Monday evening for two hours of prayer and praise. Many return on another evening for a Bible study session and Growth in the Spirit seminars.

Finally, it is a place of reconciliation. They see the problem as follows: 'One of the great tragedies in Ireland is the way in which we allow the unfortunate aspects of our history to divide us and to distort our image of one another. We live together yet 5000 miles apart. Ignorance and separation breed fear and bitterness, and enormous walls of division grow. We have found that one of the most urgent needs in Ireland today is to provide opportunities for people not only to meet one another but to be able to pray together'.

In Ireland, one sign of the presence of the Kingdom is the ability for Catholics and Protestants to live and worship together. It is clear that most people associated with Rostrevor tend to view the spiritual as primary, and therefore to relativise the social aspects of life. For this reason they find it harder to take the socio-political aspects of salvation seriously, and would tend to spiritualise power, rather than analyse it. First then one is born again; subsequently certain things follow, ie social, political action, instead of the integration of the personal and social, so that the social area could just as easily be the context of personal faith, and personal faith be related to its practical out-workings. This reveals a basic weakness of Rostrevor which is confusing strategy with the content of the gospel. Because we often come to truth in stages, it is very easy to divide the whole gospel into sections according to our experience.

It is also possible to project all human questions as illusion, and give oneself totally to what one thinks is God, but what is in reality passivity and a-politicism.

Rostrevor, although it does not want to form a new denomination, will have to face up to the reality of an institutional Church which does not want to change. Will becoming a religious order alongside the Church be sufficiently radical in a society dominated by religion? The question may not to be starting another Church, but how then should the new groupings in Ireland relate to each other?

Rostrevor has not taken a position on whether Northern Ireland should join a united Ireland. This issue can so easily be misinterpreted, but one senses a general view emerging. It seems that this issue is dealt with indirectly rather than head-on. In some parishes to bring a Roman Catholic to play a guitar would be a major breakthrough, to talk about a united Ireland would bring the house down. Rather as Protestant forgives Catholic, and vice versa, one gets the impression that Catholics begin really to understand that Unionists (who seek to maintain the union with Britain) cannot be bombed into a united Ireland, and Protestants start to be able to see themselves living in a united Ireland.

As Christians are a minority, it is clear that centres like Rostrevor can only hope that a voluntary reconciliation can lead to a political breakthrough, for if it does not then, as in Zimbabwe, it will come through the barrel of a gun.

The major issue of the divided people of Ireland keeps other concerns like the shape of Christian community and life-style at a distance. But the efforts of Rostrevor are interrelating in God's time to point to a new and better way for Ireland.

(2) The Belfast Christian Family

This is an ecumenical community in Belfast, Northern Ireland, that was set up in mid-1979. Desmond Dick and David Matthews, two of the leaders of this community, had a dream that one day they would see some more concrete expression of the unity God desired for His people and which they had heard so much preached about at the various Charismatic events they attended. Des led a Roman Catholic prayer group in West Belfast that was in the process of members' committing their lives together more. David was the leader of a non-denominational 'house-church' situated in Protestant East Belfast. In 1977 and '78 they developed the relationship between the two groups, bringing their people together for various meetings and social functions. Then, in 1979, they disbanded both groups and formed the Belfast Christian Family under the overall leadership of David Matthews. They use the name 'Family' so as not to use the Catholic term 'community' or the Protestant term 'fellowship'.

At present there are about one hundred people involved in the Family, one third of which are Catholic.

'Charismatic Renewal proved to be the common meeting ground that brought us together. By that time both of us had learnt more of the breadth and scope of God's heart. He was counting far more people as "in" than we had realised. So it was in such a warm atmosphere of love and acceptance that we could hear and heed the call to come together in a more permanent way. Such a move was not without its funny side. Jack, a Protestant, was quite concerned that if Des, as a Catholic, was involved in leadership then Jack would be "submitted" to the Pope. The logic was simple; Des submits to the Pope; Jack submits to Des; Jack submits to the

Pope. We all had a good laugh but Jack was almost serious.

'Strange as it may seem, when we eventually did come together the doctrinal differences were not the major problems to be overcome. That is not to say that we ignored such weighty matters. Our coming together was only initiated after a clear and frank discussion of our "doctrinal" differences. We knew deep inside that, if we were to overcome the barriers that have divided our society for hundreds of years, sentimentality and warm feelings towards each other would not be enough. So the differences were, and still are, openly aired and respected. In reality that means our Catholic brothers and sisters having and maintaining their identity through particular Catholic activities, such as, for example, the mass.

'The local Catholic bishop has also given them his warm support and consent to be part of Belfast Christian Family whose overall leader is a Protestant. Church has been one of our differences. Des and his folk believe that the true Church is essentially the Roman Church and that one day we will all have to join; he adds the rider that it will be so changed by then that we would readily come in. I believe that the Church is yet to be built on the earth and that one day all labels, including "Roman Catholic", will have to be dropped. Meanwhile, we get on with the pragmatics and leave some of the eschatology in God's hands.

'In the current situation in Belfast it is almost impossible for Catholics and Protestants to integrate socially as both live in distinct areas within the city. It is very easy to draw a map of Belfast and accurately pinpoint the different religious localities. Perhaps it should be explained that for a Catholic to be found in a Protestant area or vice versa is a good enough excuse for him to be executed. We borrowed an American idea to help us overcome that obstacle: They call it "bussing". We divide the group up into six or seven social units, composed of Catholic and Protestant members and, using our cars, got to know each other by rotating membership of each group and travelling in and out of each other's localities. I still remember the night we were having a leaders' meeting in Des's house. The two men sitting at the window paled a little, and, as the rest of us stopped talking, we could hear gunfire too! We experienced a little fear but, as one man put it, friends are more important than fear.

'In any other situation a group like ours might not rate a second thought. In Belfast, however, the ordinary is extraordinary. We have committed ourselves to normality in the face of the insanity that is all around us and, God knows, may still be in us. The normality of worshipping the risen Lord, of learning to serve one another and eventually the whole society. It is an interesting coincidence that our present numbers reflect the population percentage of Northern Ireland, ie two-thirds Protestant, one-third Catholic. Maybe one day we will be able to move into one locality and pioneer a new kind of community living in Belfast.

'Where do we go from here? At worst we could fail miserably but even then I for one would be glad we made the attempt rather than sit on the sidelines. There is in this small country of ours a "raging lion seeking whom he may devour". We have discovered that his name is "religious divisiveness" and we, in God's name, are against him and not only in our words and prayers, but in our coming together and staying together. It is a thrill to see our children so easily accept each other and already have an openness of heart and mind that was denied us for so long. Even now there is still a lump in my throat as I think of some of my friends who only a few years ago were one of "them" that "we" didn't mix with. That friendship leaves a good taste in the mouth and a warmth in the heart. We are well aware that the problems of Northern Ireland are far from being solved but if enough of us can live in normality, things can change. Meanwhile, we have taken one small step for mankind but a large leap for Christians in Belfast.'[19]

Here again we see a social reality taking place expressing a highly developed politics of reconciliation. It is implicit, for their explicit view is that 'We are biased and prejudiced to the Kingdom of God. Our real hope is not in *political* or military solutions but in seeing His kingdom come and His will done on earth as it is in heaven'. The social experience is better than the conservative theology. It is only as Charismatics take on a prophetic role and widen their theological perspective that an examination of the Northern Ireland state can take place. At present Catholics and Protestants balance each other's histories, treat them as neutral and do not connect them to the question of justice.

The Charismatic Movement is the Alliance Party at prayer, whereas it should be the Provisional Movement of the Kingdom of God. It has not awoken from the sleep of the *status quo*. It has not yet seen that Christ wants to conquer the forces of the principalities and powers through them. They are to be used to create a new Ireland. Not some heavenly island, but an earthly reality – 'Your Kingdom come on earth'.

(3) The Catholic Charismatic Renewal

Enough has been written about the historical origins of the Catholic Charismatic Renewal in Ireland.[20] The renewal has been in existence in Ireland for about a decade. It followed the classic pattern of personal conversion, the formation of prayer groups and now the development of communities. It seems apparent that the movement has reached a peak and a cross-roads. It has, through the language of the Holy Spirit, been a powerful force to break down barriers between Catholics and Protestants in Ireland. Its strength is also its weakness. It does not seek unity through doctrinal agreement, but by shared experience. However, experience is a hard thing to keep at high pitch. The movement seems to be firmly under hierarchical control, and is in danger of being assimilated like other devotional movements. Many people are happy with the initial release of the Holy Spirit, and in a religious culture like Ireland where religion is so pervasive this is not to be undervalued. But often the deeper questions of justice and politics are rejected. They are too readily influenced by the kind of assumption of our first American example, rather than by the more holistic tradition of social Catholicism. There seems to be a process of re-examination going on among the leadership of the movement which points them in the direction of our second American example. They would readily admit that many in the renewal are into cheap grace and not willing to take on a deeper discipleship. This new approach seems to emanate mainly from those involved with Christian community. At the political level the Catholic Charismatic Movement does not remove the desire for a united Ireland, but provides the spiritual dynamic to make the Republican dream a reality on the one hand, and yet fully enters into the fears of a million Protestants who fear being swamped in a united Ireland on the other.

Conclusion

It is clear that where a dualistic approach to politics is present, the gospel is truncated. A Charismatic approach to politics cannot succeed without taking on other elements. If it is used to answer all questions, it fails, just as weeding is not all there is to gardening. As we in humility open ourselves to different elements of Christian teaching, we are not left with some minimalist Irish stew, but rather with the rich mosaic which integrates the fullness of the gospel.

> 'No round-shouldered pitchers here, no stewards
> To supervise consumption or supplies
> And water locked behind the taps implies
> No expectation of miraculous words.
> But in the bone-shaped womb, like rising yeast,
> Virtue intact is waiting to be shown,
> The consecration wondrous (being their own)
> As when the water reddened at the feast.'[21]

References

1 Arndt-Gingrich, *A Greek-Lexicon of the New Testament and other early Christian Literature* (University of Chicago Press, 1957), p 887.

2 Kilian McDonnell, *Catholic Pentecostalism: Problems in Evaluation* (Dove Publications, Pecos, New Mexico), p 19.

3 Henry P Van Dusen, *Spirit, Son and Father* (Charles Scribners Sons, New York, 1958), pp 18–19.

4 Larry Christenson, *A Charismatic Approach to Social Action* (Lakeland, London), pp 11ff.
5 *Psalm* 127:1.
6 Christenson, *op cit*, pp 11ff.
7 *Ibid*, p 95.
8 *Ibid*, p 96.
9 Hans von Campenhausen, *Tradition and Life in the Early Church* (Fortress Press, Philadelphia, PA, 1968), pp 141, 143, 147, 154.
10 Christenson, *op cit*, pp 49ff; *Mark* 14: 7–9.
11 Christenson, *op cit*, p 113.
12 Wes Michaelson, *What Nurtures Us* (Sojourners, May 1978) (A reprint).
13 *Ibid*, p 1.
14 *Ibid*, pp 1ff.
15 *Ibid*, p 2.
16 *Ibid*, p 2.
17 *Ibid*, p 3.
18 *Ibid*, pp 3ff.
19 David Matthews, *Sins of the Fathers*.
20 Thomas Flynn, *The Charismatic Renewal and the Irish Experience* (Hodder & Stoughton, 1974).
21 Seamus Heaney, 'Cana Revisited'.

17 Hard Times: Catholic theology and the critique of capitalism

Michael Langford

Liberalism in economics

In 1850, Archbishop Richard Whately of Dublin wrote a popular pamphlet in which he hoped to help form the minds of young people, and which was widely circulated by SPCK. In it, Whately argued that 'More harm than good is likely to be done by almost any interference by government with man's money transactions, whether letting or leasing, or buying and selling of any kind'. True freedom, Whately maintained, was 'that every man should be left free to dispose of his own property, his own time, and strength and skill, in whatever way he himself may think fit, provided he does no wrong to his neighbours'. By way of introduction, I want to make three general comments on these words of Whately's.

Firstly, it would be hard to improve upon these words as a summary of the leading moral and philosophical ideas of the classical economic theory of Adam Smith, published in his *Wealth of Nations* in 1779, which ran into many editions. The economist John Maynard Keynes quoted these words of a bishop as evidence of a powerful consensus which had sustained the ideas of individualism and *laissez-faire* for so long, and which Keynes believed was beginning to wane in the 1920s.[1] Keynes went on to challenge this climate in a series of articles in the *Times* during the recession in March 1933, where he proposed the then revolutionary idea that governments could achieve prosperity by becoming involved in the market place, and by 'spending their way out of unemployment'. Keynes attempted, unsuccessfully I believe, to dissociate economics from this pseudo-philosophical background, in order to establish a credible basis for it as a science. However, he continued to acknowledge the importance of political economy, and he recognised that the problem of reconciling individual and corporate interests was not confined to economics. Hitherto, society had been thought to revolve around the workings of the market place, to the extent that even the more philosophically minded almost looked to the businessman to resolve the problem of society. Keynes' modifications virtually shaped the economic policies of Western governments, in practice if not in their theoretical outlook, for the past generation.

Secondly, whilst it would be unusual today to hear a bishop expounding the doctrines of individualism and *laissez-faire* with such clarity and conviction, the attitudes and dispositions advocated by Whately still gain wide acceptance amongst Christians and others, and remain, for example, a major stumbling block in Christian stewardship campaigns, which themselves tend to have more of a commercial than theological ring about them. In addition, in recent years there has been a revival of these ideas in Britain and America under the new name of monetarism, and a discrediting of Keynes' influence.

Finally, Whately's pamphlet was published at the time of the beginning of Christian criticism of capitalism, when Charles Dickens published his bitter attack on England's dark satanic mills and their philosophy, in *Hard Times*. Whately had published lectures on political economy and was active in the political affairs of Ireland which had earlier precipitated the Oxford Movement. At Oxford, Newman had learnt from Whately a high and spiritual view of the Church's mission. But, it will be remembered, Newman and Whately broke over the relationship of faith to reason and reality. It was Newman who wanted to maintain, against liberals like Whately, that at the centre of Christianity is the sacramental principle, a sacramental view of the world, the announcement that the divine gift is bestowed upon man within the material and visible order.

Whately, in his pamphlet of 1850, was advocating liberal views in the fields of personal and public economics. In the rest of this essay I want to open up some areas of contact between theological and economic views of the world, to ask what Newman's sacramental principle might mean to Whately's liberal economics, and to argue that the liberalism of nineteenth-century and present day economics, and the ideas which continue to sustain it, place an adequate Christian view of the world in peril.

The possessive individual

Adam Smith (1723–1790), a close friend of the British empiricist philosoper David Hume, and professor of logic and moral philosophy at Glasgow, was the first to develop a complete system of categories to describe the phenomena of the world of economics in his *Wealth of Nations*. However, in what sense Smith was one of the founding fathers of monetarism, as one British chancellor has described him, and the originator of the ideas of individualism and *laissez-faire*, needs clarification. *Wealth of Nations* is as much a description of what was already taking place as a theoretical prescription. It is more probable that Smith was merely drawing attention to two ideas amongst the values and aspirations of the rising industrial middle classes of the period. Indeed, it would be difficult to imagine how Britain would have been industrialised, in the way it was, without them.

Smith's economic theory is founded upon his belief in the individual who, by pursuing his own interests, helps to bring about and sustain a 'natural' order in society. According to Smith, and his present-day disciple and Nobel Prize Winner Milton Friedman, a man, by pursuing his own interests, frequently promotes the interests of society better than when he really intends to do so. According to this liberal view, any interference in the market place, the mechanism which links the individual with the rest of society, would disturb the 'hidden hand' which guides the actions of the individual towards the common good. As we shall see later, this may be one of the most fascinating and persistent – and dangerous – ideas ever to have been formulated. Let us examine Smith's moral and philosophical outlook in his *Theory of Moral Sentiments,*[2] which he himself acknowledged as the foundation of his *Wealth of Nations*.

The *Theory of Moral Sentiments* is, for the most part, concerned with moral psychology, although Smith does discuss other moral theories. Indeed, for Smith, morality is reducible to the emotion of sympathy tempered by due moderation and propriety. Impartiality is achieved by considering one's own behaviour as someone else's, and virtue consists in propriety (the proper control of the emotions), prudence (the studied pursuit of one's own interest), and benevolence (aiming at the happiness of others). In addition, according to Smith, there is a 'natural' disposition within human nature to sympathise with and emulate the rich, and to recoil from poverty, and on this disposition the social order is founded. Society therefore needs the presence of the rich and powerful in order to mould the passions of the people. Smith defines sloth as the absence of ambition, and avarice as a false perception of the inequalities in society, and of one's place in the natural order.

Consequently, in Smith's social theory, merit and demerit in society are related only to the empirical disposition to admire the rich and spurn poverty. It would, however, be unjust to accuse Smith of an absence of feeling and concern for the poor. For what is missing here is not feeling and concern, but an adequate framework in which to understand fully the plight of the poor, and to relate the individual to the society in which he lives. Smith readily acknowledges that, whilst the disposition to admire riches and spurn poverty is necessary for the social order, it is also the most universal cause of moral corruption.[3] He recognises that the poor and weak are often unjustly accused of vice and folly, that in the superior stations in life flattery and falsehood often prevail over merit and ability, and that the crimes, vices and follies of those most admired may even become fashionable.[4] But he reduces all cases of injustice to those where immediate, material causes can be identified,[5] he restricts the practice of benevolence to family and immediate acquaintances,[6] and there is no sense of the psalmist's view that the poor are caught in snares which ultimately have been laid by other men.[7] In Smith's world view, innocent suffering is statistically insignificant. The idea that large-scale misery might exist simply 'overshadowed his imagination' and '*extinguished* benevolence'.[8] He regarded even the suspicion of a fatherless world, in which the poor were not cared for, as the 'most melancholy of all reflections'.[9]

In Adam Smith's present-day disciple, Milton Friedman, there is a development of the doctrine of the individual.[10] Friedman is deeply suspicious of any social perspectives, which he regards as fictions, and society is nothing more than a collection of individuals related to each other only by the market. Friedman too is disturbed by the existence of poverty, but he extends Smith's doctrine of benevolence to actual criticism of doing good beyond immediate family and friends, and attributes the persistence of poverty to those who break these 'natural' boundaries.[11] The possibility that one man's poverty might be related to another man's self-interest is ruled out *a priori*, since this presupposes a doctrine of the social order, a different doctrine of man, and therefore a completely different economic theory. In any case, Smith observed, man has a remarkable capacity to accommodate himself to his station in life pre-allocated by the Creator, and this capacity is built into 'nature'.[12] Like some of the characters in Dickens' novels, the poor are not real, they do not 'really' exist, for in such a world they are 'naturally' out of sight.

For Smith, the natural human inclination to admire the rich and powerful and recoil from poverty was the foundation of both the moral and social orders. He could find no other disposition within human nature on which to base his moral philosophy, and the possibility of a moral order, independent of the empirical dispositions that are actually found within human nature, was, for him, purely speculative. Since sympathy and propriety were empirical they could be regarded as of divine origin and therefore as an adequate foundation for both morality and society.[13] In Smith's social theory, the social order is the product of the properly managed contents of the psyche on the one hand, and on the other, a structure willed by the Creator. Individuals are related to each other by the market place as owners, workers and consumers. To interfere with this mechanism of the market is to destroy the spontaneous, natural order which arises out of each man pursuing his own interests and trying not to harm his immediate neighbour. Long-term, the end justifies the means as faith in the 'hidden hand' guides the actions of individuals towards the collective good. It is interesting to note that this long-term perspective is also required to justify the modern, scientific theory of monetarism.

Smith, then, finds the only cause of social disorder in avarice, which he defined as a false perception of one's station, resulting from allowing the emotions free reign.[14] Both Smith and Friedman disapprove of meetings of traders to discuss business, as this is against the interests of consumers,[15] defenders of capitalism who do not like competition are chided,[16] and social responsibility in business is cast aside as an aberration since it involves the misuse of other people's money.[17] Both Smith and Friedman have a deep suspicion of the state, and government in general. Indeed, Friedman comes very close to Marx's much misunderstood and misrepresented doctrine of the withering away of the state. Yet in both liberal capitalism and Marxism this doctrine has, paradoxically, led to more government interference of a different kind. Smith died before he was able to publish his sequel to *Moral Sentiments* and *Wealth of Nations*, which was to be on law and order.

Enough has been said to indicate the continued popularity of these liberal ideas, even though individuals may not subscribe to them as a 'theory'. According to these ideas, the world functions on a single, gravitational principle, the private pursuit of self-interest, with the possibility that there might be a God, whose relationship to this world is, however, problematic. In Smith's disciples, and in the industrial world whose outlook and philosophy he helped to shape, man has become the radical individual, an alien in a world he himself has made. Enlightened self-interest, apparently, is enough to explain reality, and the 'world' is co-terminus with the possessive individual. It is easy to see how Marx came to view the religion of such a society as the *locus classicus* of man's self-alienation. Even Marx had more sympathy for the capitalist who, he argued, was more alienated than the worker, and stood in greater need of liberation.

The problem of middle axioms

One of the important contributions that Keynes made to economic theory was his realisation that capitalism was fundamentally flawed. The cycle of 'boom and doom' was evidence of this, and Keynes related this to defects in human self-interest. Supply and demand were not always immediately identical, and demand and need were not necessarily the same either. As an example of this, Keynes referred to the need for housing in the 1930s ('one of the greatest works of man'), and the lack of demand (a slump) in the building industry.[18]

In order to meet these problems Keynes proposed, as it were, a 'middle axiom' approach, the introduction of principles into the economic order to achieve certain altruistic ends, and to mitigate the worst effects of capitalism. These took the form of institutions of a financial, educational and social nature, mid-way between the individual and the state, and a level of government involvement. The 'welfare' principle was substituted for the 'hidden hand'. Modern disciples of Adam Smith sometimes refer to this approach as 'socialism in slow motion'.

Keynes, then, was ready to admit to a defect in capitalism, but was unwilling to call capitalism itself into question. Keynes admired the idealism of Marx but could not understand its popularity, since he found it illogical and dull. Whilst this outright rejection of Marx's departure from capitalism does not in itself constitute a flaw in Keynes, it does reveal a defect in his approach at two levels. First of all, at the theoretical level, his desire to establish a 'neutral' economic science, by seeking to make it politically and morally neutral, led him to pay insufficient attention to this wider context which, in fact, influences economic activity. As we have seen, even monetarism presupposes a wider framework on which it depends for its justification. Keynes wanted to dissociate himself from this liberal context, but his reasons for doing so were pragmatic rather than theoretical, and he saw 'capitalism' as no more than a more or less efficient, neutral economic technique, detached from the total society in which it operated.

In practice, too, the welfare principle has, in fact, been found wanting. Many of the criticisms of the welfare state by monetarists like Friedman are sustainable, and, curiously, parallel Marxist critique of these same institutions. As any priest quickly discovers, health and social services may do fine work, but in reality they are extremely limited in their achievable objectives, are remote from the communities they seek to serve, and they fail to tackle the underlying problems and inequalities of ill-health and social need, which are modern manifestations of the same problems highlighted by men like Charles Dickens and Friedrich Engels, and the Christian socialists in the nineteenth century. Whilst everyone is 'better off' (whatever that may mean), Ordsell in Manchester is still in the same position in relation to the rest of society as it was when Engels documented its problems in his *Condition of the working class in England* in 1845. Moreover, it is becoming clear that the solution to this problem is not simply more welfare, more financial resources, for what has become a growing multi-million pound industry and a major employer. The obvious fact that everyone is better off, and the illusion of twenty-four-hour, cradle-to-grave care, which is sustained by both clients and practitioners, can also become an excuse to avoid the continued existence of poverty. The popular view that no one need suffer today is only an updated version of the Victorian view which blamed the poor for their poverty, a view which was first given its philosophical justification by Adam Smith. Even today, as the Poor Laws become a distant memory, welfare provision still perpetuates the distinction first announced by nineteenth-century Church leaders, that there are poor who deserve to be helped and others who do not, although increasing, permanent unemployment is beginning to impose a crisis of purpose in these services. If there is to be an adequate Christian view of society, it would need not to fall foul of any ideology.

The freedom of the children of God

In conclusion, I want to define two areas where this discussion impinges directly on theology.

The first is concerned with the development of a Christian 'philosophy of life', the way in which Christians arrive at their beliefs of how the world actually functions. 'Capitalism' is not simply pragmatism, a more or less efficient way of managing 'the way things are', a neutral back-cloth against which the individual lives and moves and has his being. Milton Friedman has demonstrated with the clarity and conviction of a bishop that it is a complete world view, a circumscribable system of ideas extending to the whole of public life, whose basic liberal principles of the individual and *laissez-faire* cannot be compromised, at least in theory. The introduction of liberal principles into trade and commerce, education and government, of which Newman spoke so prophetically towards the end of his life, has been completed by Friedman. There is no sector of life which cannot or has not been subjected to what Friedman calls its 'subtlety'.

Perhaps the most serious defect in this world view is its telescoping of reality, reducing it to the single, self-regulating principle of individual self-interest. As Vladimir Lossky once remarked, commenting on the quality of the counselling which Job received from his friends, in such a simplistic and distorted perspective the constantly shifting dimensions of the human, structural, angelic, demonic and divine are welded together. 'God' becomes the 'fate', 'providence', 'fortune' and 'bad luck' spoken of by Adam Smith. Job's friends thought they were defending God against Job's protests and blasphemy, but in reality they were the hyprocritical defenders of the *status quo*, they were seeking to find a legal authority for the current, fallen condition of humanity.[19] In such a cosmology, where the only reality is the individual and his immediate interests, deception and hypocrisy have the upper hand, and this deception is created, not by allowing freedom to the emotions, as Adam Smith claimed, but by their repression and annihilation. In *Hard Times*, Dickens was trying to show how the utilitarian outlook of the industrial world exalted what was alien to human nature and destroyed those very qualities which could transform it. This defective view of reality also imposes a false asceticism which passes the penance down the social order. The factories of Coketown spew out ash over the inhabitants, after the manner of people who do penance for their own sins by putting other people into sackcloth.[20] If the primary mistake in Marxism is that it represents man's self-deification, capitalism, its mirror image, represents the deification of man's lower nature, the sanctification of the present, fallen condition of humanity.

The traditional relationship between Christianity, and the ideas which sustained the growth of capitalism may increasingly be called into question[21] but, at another level, there is a need for the political and social education of the majority of laity and many priests. This education would not encourage them to form up behind the latest political banner and social cause, but enable them to discover the potentially exciting totality of human existence, with its many dimensions and possibilities, and also the way the world has shaped their understanding of existence and even Christianity itself. Ministerial concern with the 'personal' is rarely ministry to the person at all, but ministry to the religious part of the private individual who has been produced by the legacy of nineteenth-century liberalism and the effects of an industrial society. Christian 'freedom' is still equated with this pseudo-philosophical background that the individual is 'free' to think and say and do what he likes within the framework of the law. Christians whose spiritual immaturity leads them into this liberal trap may discover that, in defending what they believe to be the will of God, they are supporting the present sinful condition of man, and defending Satan's claim to unlimited dominion. For there are fallen 'structural realities' as well as individuals. The struggle for the freedom of the children of God is not against other individuals' self-interest, as many Christians seem to practise in their spiritual life, but against the spiritual powers of darkness which rule the world order.[22] Even the simple discovery of this can be liberating. Self-interest, correctly understood, is indeed essential to human nature, but it does need to be distinguished from possessive individualism and the world view this entails.

In addition, the proper autonomy given to human sciences by Vatican I, and by Archbishop William Temple, should be carefully noted.[23] No Christian should have to apologise for wanting his faith to impinge upon areas of life which appear to be the sole concern of secular experts. Religion like politics, is concerned with the whole of life, including public life, or it does not exist. Economic 'techniques' depend for their operation on a wider framework of beliefs and values, ends and means. Even economists have to live in the real world, and no scientific judgment can be made in a moral and political vacuum.

This leads to the second area of dialogue between theological, and social and political world views. Just as the world cannot be reduced to the individual, or a collection of individuals, it cannot be reduced to its social and political dimensions either. The divinity of Adam Smith's *Moral sentiments* is a pseudo-metamorphosis of the divinity of the eighteenth-century deists. His relationship to the world, of that of a clock-maker to a clock, has been transformed into that of the entrepreneur to his workers and machines. Smith never speaks of Jesus Christ, only the 'Creator', the 'Director of the universe'. and there is only one reference to Christianity, and that is where it seems to support his own views.[24] In popular terms this is the persistent belief that there probably is a God, for only a fool would deny it; meanwhile we must try to get on living life in this puzzling world, with its fortune, providence and bad luck, as best we can, with the man Jesus fitting in somewhere in this picture. Perhaps the most important and lasting service Marx gave to the human race was that he risked pointing out what everyone was already beginning to suspect, that such a god does not exist. He is no more than a projection of man's hidden desires and anxieties, his likes and dislikes. As Dickens and others recognised, the god of the industrial revolution was the Great Manufacturer in the sky, the deification of the aspirations of the industrial middle classes who were seeking power from the crown, the Church and the landed gentry, in order to take their new place in history.

The God to whom Adam Smith refers is primarily a Creator, a manufacturer, with some of the positive and negative characteristics of an earthly father. He is a tyrant rather than a King. He can be concerned, compassionate, and providential, but also contrary. According to this theory, the explanation for His capricious activity in the world is the rule of thumb that He 'helps those who help themselves'. The 'god' of Keynes' system and the welfare state, with its substitution of 'welfare' for the 'hidden hand', has more paternal characteristics, and the explanation for the persistence of suffering and poverty is that 'no one need suffer today'. Thus the religion of late industrial society entails an inversion of the divine attribute by asserting that God is first a Creator and then a Father. There is a very ancient problem here which dates back to the formation of the Christian doctrines of the Trinity and incarnation. How does the world actually work, and what is God's relationship to it at any moment in its history and events? Even economics presupposes some answer to these questions, either that there is no God, in the case of Marxism, or, in the case of capitalism, that there probably is a God but his relationship to this world is precarious and puzzling.

Marx's contention that Christianity was the religion peculiar to capitalism, and the question of Marx's atheism and its relationship to his system has been raised afresh in recent years, but there is still no satisfactory conclusion.[25] This state of affairs is likely to continue until the question is taken much more seriously, and until it is realised that the religion that Marx encountered in Britain and elsewhere was hardly distinguishable from atheism with a respectable, religious cover. Marx did not arrive at his atheism out of the blue. He himself remarked on how the established

Church in Britain was ready to entertain atheism whilst clinging tenaciously to its wealth and property. The seeds of Marx's materialistic philosophy he found in the Christianity of his day.[26]

If, as the Oxford Fathers maintained, at the heart of Christianity is a sacramental world view, that the world is a gift by God to man, that from within it God bestows on man the divine nature itself, and that in the incarnation there is a continuity between the orders of creation and redemption, what might this mean in social and political terms? In *Hard Times* Dickens attempts to lift the smokescreen which disguised the arrogant disinterest and false humanitarianism of the nineteenth-century industrial world. It is Stephen, the epitome of the honest worker, who becomes a victim of this world and who discovers the 'incarnate God of the poor'. Our attention is drawn to his direct and penetrating wisdom, and his foolish lack of self-interest, his unconscious lack of concern for 'number one'. In the Incarnation, God reveals Himself to man from below, and not in what man's 'natural dispositions' most admire and aspire to. It is not that the Incarnation involved, primarily, a divine *kenosis* and self-restraint, as though the Incarnation were a divine embarrassment, but rather that Christ's poverty, humiliation, degradation and powerlessness actually manifest the divine richness, majesty, nobility and power in the present world order.[27] It is not that poverty and despair are to be recoiled from, or that welfare is to be heaped upon the poor, as it were, in one way or another to keep them out of sight. At the centre of Christianity is not only the sacramental principle but the experience of suffering, deprivation and poverty. In Christ, poverty and suffering have become the centre of attraction and the means of grace. The tragedy is that Christian civilisation has not discovered this to be the case. The Cross has been found to be a symbol of earthly and political power, rather than a disgrace from which to recoil. In Tolstoy's *Resurrection* the power of Christianity is the political power of the nineteenth-century Russian emperor, yet in the prison cells where men are tortured and beaten hangs an image of the Crucified One. Christian civilisation still lives within the legal categories of the Old Testament. With the friends of Job and the disciples of Adam Smith, it still finds poverty and suffering to be God's judgment on the vices and follies of the poor, rather than God's judgment on the wisdom of this world, and the experience of His mercy and grace.

The Christian life begins and ends in the baptismal life of renunciation and regeneration, in which the individual Christian and the whole Church continually re-enter the desert, the tomb and the Easter mystery with Christ. Part of this struggle is to redirect to God the natural life of man, in his true ownership of things, in the exercise of his creative powers and gifts, and in the control of self-interest and its subordination to the interests of others. To embrace the baptismal life in this way is also to embrace these hard times in the dark night of the soul, where God deprives a man of his inherited views of the world, his ideologies and his false gods. Baptismal renunciation is not just the renouncing of the flesh, but also the devil, the great deceiver of mankind. This is so a man may be truly free, truly detached from the world he has renounced, in order to become more deeply immersed in it to co-operate with God and with other men in its redemption. Any social theory or political economy must face inherent contradictions when the temptation is to dissolve or set in opposition these contradictions.[28] It is the existence and persistence of poverty and suffering which challenge any view of the world with intellectual dishonesty and inconsistency. The unique Christian contribution is that freedom comes from confronting suffering and poverty, and not from retreating from it or attempting to manage it. Yet the perspective required for the human problem of any age is theology. To quote Lossky again:[29]

> 'This struggle which began in the spiritual spheres of the angelic heavens is continued in the earthly cosmos, and in the struggle human freedom is at stake. The spiritual level where this war for the inheritance of the sons of God is waged is more profound than any of the superficial layers of reality which are accessible to analysis by the human sciences. None of the sciences – not psychology, nor sociology, nor economics, not the political sciences – can detect the true origin of the different evils which they observe and attempt to define, in their efforts to exorcise them or at least restrict the damage they do. Even philosophy, though it speaks of the human spirit and uses the terms "person" and "nature", cannot reach the level where the problem of human destiny is posed. The terms which it uses are, for the most part, the result of the decadence and secularisation of theological ideas. Philosophy is never eschatological: its speculation never goes to the furthest extreme, it inevitably transposes into ontology truths which are metaontological. Its field of vision remains on this side of the two abysses which theology alone can name, with fear and trembling: the uncreated abyss of the Life of the Trinity and the abyss of hell which opens up within the freedom of created persons.'

To some this may sound like theological imperialism, yet its perspective contains a genuine recognition of the presence and activity of the incarnate Word in the world. But it also points the Church, and with it the whole world, to the task of discerning spirits, of distinguishing the true God and Father of Jesus Christ from the false gods and idols made by man. To be truly free, to be free of the subtle ideological influences of the world, and from false and partial perspectives, requires an adequate theology, and the personal risk involved in its attainment.

References

1 J M Keynes, *The End of Laissez-Faire* (Hogarth Press, 1926).
2 The edition I have used is, unfortunately, an old one. *Collected Works* (5 vols) 6th ed (London, 1812), vol i.
3 Smith, *op cit*, pp 98–9. For convenience, I have given only the main references so that the basic elements of Smith's argument can be followed.
4 Smith, *op cit*, pp 99, 102, 103.
5 This may be a harsh judgment, but Smith does seem to identify justice with jurisprudence and leave the orphan and widow to God's mercy after death (Smith, *op cit*, pp 155–0).
6 Smith, *op cit*, pp 382ff. Smith, of course, recognises universal benevolence, even beyond one's own country, but this is based on his belief that the Director of the Universe at all times maintains the maximum happiness (p 415).
7 Psalm 10:2. See also the wicked caught in their own snares in Psalm 9:17. The psalms, of course, contain many cries of outrage on behalf of the poor.
8 Smith, *op cit*, p 413.
9 *Ibid.*
10 I havo referred to the following books and articles by Milton Friedman. *Capitalism and freedom* University of Chicago 1962; *An economist's protest* Thomas Horton, New Jersey 1972, which is a collection of popular articles on political economy; and *Free to choose* Penguin 1980.
11 M Friedman, *Capitalism and Freedom* (University of Chicago, 1962), ch 11, 12.
12 Smith, *op cit*, p 251.
13 *Ibid*, pp 559, 571.
14 *Ibid*, pp 270–1.
15 Friedman, *op cit* pp 128–32.
16 *Ibid*, pp 119–33.
17 *Ibid*, pp 133–6, and *An Economist's Protest*, Thomas Horton (1972), pp 177–84.
18 J M Keynes, *The Means to Prosperity* (Macmillan, pamphlet, 1933), pp 5–8. An enlarged version of his articles in the *Times*, March 1933.
19 V Lossky, *In the Image and Likeness of God* (Mowbrays, 1975) p 220.
20 C Dickens, *Hard Times*, Book 3 ch vi.
21 R Preston *Religion and the persistence of capitalism* SCM 1979 discusses the thesis that Christianity provided the religious background to the development of capitalism. The successor to R H Tawney's *Religion and the rise of capitalism* and V A Demant's *Religion and the decline of capitalism*, this book tries to set up some principles of Christian social criticism, and its survey brings Christian social theory up to date.
22 Ephesians 6:12.
23 W Temple, *Christianity and the Social Order* (Penguin, 1956), pp 75–83.
24 Smith, *op cit*, p 294.
25 J P Miranda, *Marx and the Marxists* (SCM, 1980). This is an interesting study by a Latin American theologian, but the discussion is still confined to Marx's humanism, and does not deal specifically with the place of atheism in his thoughts.
26 Marx, *Capital* vol i, preface to the 1st edn. (Penguin, 1976), p 92.
27 John Gaden, 'Incarnation or cross-and-resurrection as the basis of Anglican social action?' in *Crucible* (Oct/Dec 1979), pp 170–8. (The journal of the General Synod Board for Social Responsibility). This article compares the kenotic Christology of Charles Gore with its development in David Jenkins, and discusses the the implications for Anglican social theory.
28 K R Popper *The Open Society and its Enemies* 2 vols Routledge 1966. Chapter 5 discusses the difficulty any social theory must face in distinguishing social convention from 'nature'.
29 Lossky, *op cit*, p 226.

18 Great Expectations: Christian Hope and Marxist Hope

David Nicholls

That the 100th anniversary of the death of Karl Marx coincides with the 150th anniversary of the Oxford Movement is hardly sufficient justification for the inclusion of a chapter on Christianity and Marxism in this volume. Furthermore, the early figures of the Movement were politically conservative and were not generally concerned with the social and economic issues which absorbed the attention of Marx and his associates. Nevertheless the theology of the Oxford Fathers, stressing the social nature of salvation – through Baptism into the Body of Christ – led many of their followers to adopt political positions which invited a dialogue with their Marxist contemporaries. It is not my purpose in this chapter to trace the history of this dialogue. To suggest, however, (as some have done) that it began in England only as an extension of the continental debates of the 1960s is to manifest culpable ignorance.

In this chapter I wish to consider a number of similarities, structural and substantive, between Christian and Marxist understandings of the world and to pinpoint two areas of conflict between them. Any world view wishing to be taken seriously must be able not only to criticise and explain rival views but also to make sense of itself. In Parts two and three of this chapter I attempt an account of how Marxists and Christians understand each other's 'ideology' and also how they explain and justify their own.

I

Looking at Christianity and Marxism from a 'Western' point of view, what perhaps strikes us is the difference between the two. If, however, we were to look at these movements from the standpoint of Asian or African ways of thinking about the world, it would be the similarities which would strike us as most obvious.

History

In the first place they are both concerned with human history. Furthermore, they both see history as manifesting a pattern; not a recurring pattern, but a unique pattern. More important, they both assert that this pattern is significantly affected by the decisions, the actions and the interactions of human beings. They firmly reject fatalism, insisting that human freedom is a real and constructive force in history. Certainly there are limits to this freedom; men make history but they do not make it just as they please. Christianity and Marxism accept the possibility of improvement and progress. 'To live is to change', wrote Newman, 'and to be perfect is to have changed often.' Marxists and Christians agree that man's destiny is to be worked out in history, rather than in an attempt to rise above it.

Materialism

Christianity, like Marxism, is 'materialist' in the very general sense that it denies that the world is simply a figment of the imagination. Neither belief has any room for solipsism. Further, they are materialist in taking the body and its needs seriously. One of the apocryphal writers declared that 'a corruptible body weighs down the immortal soul', but this is hardly a Christian sentiment. The great Christian creeds speak of the resurrection of the body rather than the immortality of the soul (though they do not, of course, deny this idea). Christianity and Marxism are both anti-materialist in another sense of the term. Both reject the idea that material possessions are for men a valid object of ultimate concern. They agree 'a man's life does not consist in the abundance of his possessions'. Throughout his life Marx condemned the way in which capitalism had idolised money. He condemned 'judentum' (a term he used to describe this acquisitive materialism). He exposed the way in which capitalism had reduced the most hallowed relationships to the cash nexus and had made a fetish out of commodities.

Yet both Marxism and Christianity recognise the important role that wealth does in fact play in human relationships and in human history. Marx's materialist conception of history rests on the belief that the ultimately determining factor in history is the economic structure, and that history can be seen as a struggle between classes whose composition is based on the relationship their members bear to the ownership of property. Jesus in turn urged his disciples not to lay up treasure on earth, 'for where your treasure is there will your heart be also'.

Man as a social being

Clearly, if all this is true, then we can expect that both Christianity and Marxism assume that man is a social being, that it is his destiny to live in communities. One speaks of the city of God, of the heavenly Kingdom, the other looks forward to a Communist society in which 'the free development of each is a condition of the free development of all'. If a man's end is to live in communities, his present alienation or estrangement consists essentially in a dislocation of relationships. In his 1844 manuscripts, Marx laid considerable emphasis on the notion of men being alienated from the product of their labour from their fellow-men and from their true selves. There has, of course, been considerable controversy about the role which this concept of alienation plays in Marx's mature writings. The young Marx was very much concerned with the alienating effects of capitalism upon the psychology of the individual worker; later his emphasis was more upon the structural weaknesses of a capitalist system. Nevertheless, he continued to use the term 'alienation' and it can convincingly be argued that his later writings are built upon and assume the position outlined in his early work. The way to overcome alienation is by a change in the economic and social structure, because, although alienation involves a subjective feeling, it has an objective basis. According to Marx, it is properly dealt with by securing changes in the situation rather than by psychotherapy.

Christians have also talked about estrangement or alienation. St Paul told his readers that formerly they were alienated from God, but that they had been reconciled to God through Jesus Christ. The Christian doctrine of original sin asserts that this alienation of man is not simply an individual phenomenon, but that all men are involved in a common fate from birth. Merely being born into the world men find themselves in situations where it is often impossible for them to do good; they frequently find themselves faced by a choice between two or more evils and the very best they can do is to choose the lesser evil. The decisions that others have taken in the past have led to situations in which it is impossible to be good and to do good. The problem is not simply one of individual moral weakness. The doctrine of original sin points to a structural problem in human existence. It is not, therefore, by individual moral effort but by Baptism that salvation or deliverance is possible. Baptism is the symbol of our incorporation into a new society – into a new set of relationships. From then on the Christian is a member of two cities. His alienation, however, will not be completely overcome in the present order of things. This is a point to which I shall return, for we find here a difference, at least in appearance, between Christianity and Marxism. Nevertheless, both Christians and Marxists agree that the human predicament is the consequence of structural defects rather than of individual moral weakness. They agree that the answer to human problems will not be found simply by men being nice to each other, or by their adopting the 'golden rule': 'do to others as you would have them do to you'. They reject the belief of Moral Rearmament that individual conversion and reformation would solve the problems of the world.

A concrete ethic

Christians and Marxists both insist on seeing people in a very specific and concrete historical context, and try to avoid talking about 'man' in the abstract or about human values. Jesus did not tell his disciples to love 'everybody' or 'mankind', he told them to love their neighbour, and gave them a specific and concrete example of what he meant in the story of the good Samaritan. Marx insisted that 'man is not an abstract being sitting outside the world', he is always to be seen in his concrete historical setting. It was partly for this reason that Marx criticised the abstract humanism of Feuerbach. 'The human essence,' wrote Marx in 1845, 'is no abstraction inherent in each single individual. In its reality it is the ensemble of social relations.' The problem of Marxist ethics arising from this rejection of abstract humanism will be considered later.

World views and ideologies

There are two further organic similarities between Christianity and Marxism, but their very similarity leads to a fundamental and irreconcilable conflict between them. In the first place, Marxism, like Christianity, involves a fairly comprehensive world view, or *Weltanschauung*. Marxist assertions, according to Gramsci, imply 'a whole conception of the world, a philosophy'. Neither system of beliefs, however, is totally comprehensive and both are susceptible to reformulation in the language of different philosophical traditions. Christianity has been around longer and has been dressed, more or less elegantly, in a large number of philosophical garbs: Platonism, Aristotelianism, Cartesianism, Hobbist materialism, idealism, existentialism, and so on. Marxism too has been presented in existentialist, humanist, Bergsonian, Hegelian, and in crudely materialist forms. Nevertheless, when Christianity (or indeed Marxism) is presented in terms of the various thought forms mentioned, it radically alters these philosophical systems so that they accommodate its peculiar demands. Christianity and Marxism are both concerned with ultimate questions, making fundamental assertions about the nature and purpose of our life on earth.

This brings me to the second organic similarity between Christianity and Marxism: both are 'ideologies' in the general sense that they are systems of ideas which are closely connected to suggested patterns of action. Neither is simply a description of what is the case. They both have some prescriptive content. Furthermore, the prescriptive element is not something secondary or optional. You do not first accept Marxism or Christianity and then, perhaps, decide to commit yourself to some kind of action in the future. 'Working men of all countries unite!' cried Marx and Engels. 'Repent and be baptised!' urged the apostles. Personal commitment and action are of the very essence of Marxism as well as of Christianity.

They both imply also a dialectical relationship between theory and practice, between knowledge and commitment. As Mao put it:

> 'To discover truth through practice and through practice to verify and develop truth. To start from perceptual knowledge and then, starting from rational knowledge, actively direct revolutionary practice so as to remould the subjective and the objective world. Practice, knowledge, more practice, more knowledge; the cyclical repetition of this pattern to infinity, and with each cycle the elevation of the content of practice and knowledge to a higher level.'

By identifying himself with the revolutionary struggle, the Marxist comes to understand theory better. For the Christian, similarly, faith must be active in love. One Christian writer put the position as follows: religious and moral truths cannot be properly understood unless practised and cannot be practised unless believed, therefore 'unhesitating belief on insufficient evidence is absolutely the only course left for the one who may desire sufficient'. A completely dispassionate approach to Christianity it thus impossible. Marxism and Christianity are different from the natural sciences in this matter, but although they deny that a neutral or unbiased standpoint is possible, and although they refuse to specify in advance the conditions of their falsification, this does not mean that they are in principle unfalsifiable. Nor does it mean that there is no logic of criticism which might lead a disciple to reassess his commitment as a result of reflecting on his experience and to reject his former beliefs as mistaken.

I have, however, suggested that there is a fundamental conflict between Christianity and Marxism. If it is possible to be an Aristotelian and a Christian, why is it not possible to be a Marxist and a Christian? In the first place, it is not possible for a Christian to be an Aristotelian in the strict sense; but Aristotelianism can be modified in such a way that it may be a channel for Christian truth. Marxism is different from Aristotelianism in so far as it demands commitment to action. It may be that the kind of action demanded of Marxists in certain situations might be inconsistent with Christian action.

I once had the opportunity to ask the Dalai Lama about the relationship between Marxism and Buddhism. He said that in many ways they were similar in their understanding of life, but that there are two fundamental differences. In the first place, while Marxists take into account human welfare in a temporal perspective, Buddhists consider all sentient beings in an eternal perspective. Secondly, there are certain means Marxists might use which Buddhists could never sanction. I thought at the time that these are also two points where Christians might find difficulties with Marxism. I shall say a little more about these points below.

II

In these next sections I shall attempt a brief Marxist interpretation of religion, and of Christianity as a religion, and then consider a Marxist critique of Marxism, for any acceptable philsophy must be able to provide a satisfactory explanation of itself. I shall then present a Christian view of Marxism, and, finally, a Christian critique of Christianity.

A Marxist critique of religion

Marxists view religion as a part of ideology, and they see ideology as ultimately dependent on economic relations. Marx himself stated the relationship clearly in 1859:

> 'In the social production of their life, men enter into definite relations that are indispensable and independent of their will, relations of production which correspond to a definite stage of development of productive forces. The sum total of these relations of production constitutes the economic structure of society, the real foundation, on which rises a legal and political superstructure to which correspond certain definite forms of social consciousness. The mode of production of material life conditions the social, political and intellectual life process in general. It is not the consciousness of men that determines their being, but, on the contrary, their social being that determines their consciousness.'

The mode of production thus determines the form of the political, legal and religious institutions in a country and also the ideology that accompanies these institutions. All systems of ideas and all human consciousness are 'interwoven with the material activity and the material intercourse of men' and is to be seen as the product of their material behaviour. Certainly both Marx and Engels insisted that there is an interaction between the superstructure and the economic base and that the former exercises an important influence on historical development in a conservative direction. The legal, political and religious institutions, for example, which developed under feudalism strove to prevent changes taking place in property relations – changes which were called for by new forms of production. Nevertheless, these institutions and ideologies are essentially to be seen as products of a feudal economic system. However much Marxists stress the importance of ideology and consciousness, they are bound to assert that, in the last resort, ideology is the efflux of a particular economic structure. 'The question,' wrote Marx, 'is not what goal is envisaged for the time being by this or that member of the proletariat, or even by the proletariat as a whole. The question is what is the proletariat and what course of action will it be forced historically to take in conformity with its own nature.' We may talk as much as we like about a 'dialectical relationship' between consciousness and material conditions, but for Marxists the latter are basic. This was Marx's principal contribution to the history of thought. Without the insistence on the material base Marx's philosophical position is hardly different from that of Hegel. 'The essence of scientific Marxism,' wrote Lukacs, 'consists, then, in the realisation that the real motor forces of history are independent of man's (psychological) consciousness of them.'

For the Marxist, religion is part of ideology and, like all ideology, can have a significant, though not ultimately determining, effect on historical development (though what this theoretical assertion actually means in concrete historical situations is often difficult to fathom). Furthermore, the dominant religion of a country is, like other aspects of its ideology, the religion of its ruling class. It is therefore to be seen as one of the instruments employed by this class for maintaining property relations as they are, though this is not the only role that religion is thought to play.

In his early writings Marx was particularly concerned with religion. He accepted the basic critique of supernatural religion outlined by Ludwig Feuerbach in *Das Wesen des Christentums* (1841). In this essay Feuerbach maintained that religion is one of the principal sources of man's alienation. Men invent a supernatural being set over against them and they project on to this being all the qualities they feel that they themselves should possess but do not. What is needed is to translate theology into anthropology and psychology and to see that our statements about God are really statements about men as they should be. Feuerbach saw himself as continuing the work which Luther had begun:

> 'The God who is man, the human God, namely, Christ – only this is the God of Protestantism. Protestantism is no longer concerned, as Catholicism is, about what God is in himself, but about what he is for man; it has, therefore, no longer a speculative or contemplative tendency, as is the case in Catholicism. It is no longer theology; it is essentially Christology, that is, religious anthropology.'

Feuerbach's attack on supernaturalism is similar in certain respects to a number of latter-day 'God-is-dead' theologians. Traditional Christian theism, according to Feuerbach,

> 'has long disappeared not only from the reason but also from the life of humanity . . . it is nothing more than a fixed idea that stands in most glaring contradiction to our fire- and life-insurance companies, our railroads and steam engines, our picture galleries, our military and industrial schools, our theatres and scientific museums'.

Marx accepted much of this analysis of religion, though he made a number of adverse criticisms of Feuerbach's thought in his famous *Theses* of 1845. In the first place he emphasised that religion is not the psychological product of some abstract 'man' but is rather a social product taking its form from the concrete historical conditions in which it evolves. Furthermore, Marx insisted that after having reduced religion to anthropology the most important work remained to be done. 'Once the earthly family is discovered to be the secret of the holy family,' he wrote, 'the former must then itself be criticised in theory and revolutionised in practice.'

Religion, for Marx, represents an attempt by men to understand and cope with the world in which they live, providing a 'consolation and justification' for this world. In a famous passage, he wrote: 'Religious suffering is the expression of real suffering and at the same time the protest against real suffering. Religion is the sigh of the oppressed creature, the heart of a heartless world, as it is the soul of soulless circumstances. It is the opium of the people.' While Marx generally assumed that the role of religion in human history is likely to be conservative, there are a number of occasions when it has proved to be a revolutionary or radical force. This fact is, of course, recognised by many Marxists. Karl Kautsky's interest in Thomas Muntzer and Thomas More is an indication of this recognition. Opium is not only a sedative!

Up to this point we have been considering Marx's ideas about the causes and some of the consequences of religion and have said little about Marx's view on the truth of religion. It is fairly clear that Marx could find no use for the concept of God in his attempt to understand human history. Marxists disagree about whether atheism is integral to Marxism, or whether it should be thought of as simply Marx's own personal position and not in any way binding upon Communists. In the past, particularly in the Stalinist era, many Marxists insisted that the only philosophical position compatible with Marxism is a crudely materialistic form of atheism. The classical formulation of this mechanistic materialism is to be found in Bukharin's *Historical Materialism* (1921). The author adopted what Gramsci referred to as an almost 'religious' belief in the reality of an objective external world unrelated to men's perception of it. As we have recently been reminded by Jose Miranda, Marx himself stated that, although he was himself an atheist, he could not speak on behalf of the whole International.

A Marxist critique of Marxism

The Marxist critique of religion is, as we have seen, but part of a more general critique of ideology and of the role played by systems of ideas in human history. Included among these systems would seem to be Marxism itself. How do Marxists account for Marxism? If all knowledge, all consciousness, is the product of a particular set of economic and social relationships at a particular period of history, does the same apply to Marxism itself? Many Marxists, and probably Marx himself, would distinguish between ideology and science. A scientific theory, though it is certainly a system of ideas emerging at a particular period of history, differs from ideology in so far as its assertions may be verified by empirical means. This answer to the question about the status of Marxism itself is unsatisfactory for two reasons. In the first place, this positivist concept of science is untenable. Secondly, Marxism is not to be thought of simply as a descriptive theory, merely outlining and explaining human history. As we have already noted, Marxism also calls for a commitment to revolutionary action, and involves a moral condemnation of capitalism.

How can I say that Marxism involves a moral condemnation of capitalism, when Marx himself wrote, in *The German Ideology:* 'Communists preach no morality at all, they do not put to people that moral demand: "love one another, be not egoists etc." '?

Yet, if Marxists indeed renounce all ethical injunctions, how can they call upon men to unite for the abolishing of capitalism? It is not simply a call to self-interest but a call which may involve considerable hardship and sacrifice on the part of many individuals. It is clear that Marx believed a Communist society to be better than a capitalist society (just as a capitalist society was better than a feudal society). Not merely change but progress takes place in human history. But what is wrong with capitalism, according to Marx? In what sense is Communism a 'higher' stage? Partly in the sense that men under a capitalist system are dehumanised. But in order to talk about men being 'dehumanised', or being unable to manifest and develop their true nature, we must have some conception of true human nature which is distinct from the actual behaviour of concrete human beings as we observe it – a standard from which they at present fall short. Now this humanism, which provides a standard, manifests all the characteristics of an ideology. How is it possible for Marxists to claim some kind of immunity for this ideology which gives it a validity other ideologies, by the mere fact that they are ideologies, cannot claim?

Some contemporary Marxists have recognised the contradiction and have acknowledged Marxist humanism to be clearly ideological. Either they reject Marxist humanism as an aberration of the early Marx or they regretfully accept the need for ideology even among Marxists. If they take the first alternative they are back to the problem of accounting for the prescriptive elements in Marxism; they either opt for some kind of existentialist commitment of an arbitrary kind or they become armchair Marxists denying the very essence of Marxism, which is concerned not merely with understanding but with changing the world; it is a basic assumption of this chapter that Marxism is 'praxis'-oriented. Incidentally, it was amusing some years ago when an eminent Marxist scholar was refused an entry visa to teach in a North American university, presumably on the grounds that he had subversive tendencies. A letter to the government concerned, signed by a large number of academics of a liberal tendency, stated that the person concerned was perfectly harmless and that he would never do anything to disturb the *status quo*! If, on the other hand, Marxist humanism is seen to be an integral part of Marxism, the question arises, for the Marxist, why this particular ideology is exempt from the general critique of ideology developed by Marx. Is this humanism not merely the 'efflux' of a particular economic and social formation which can make no special claims to truth? The attempt by Georg Lucaks to circumvent this problem by suggesting that the proletariat is in some way a universal class, whose ideology can therefore make a special claim to validity, is disingenuous. For one thing, Marxist humanism was not developed by the working class but by middle-class intellectuals, and is clearly part of a tradition stemming through the Enlightenment back to the Renaissance.

The theoretical problem raised for Marxists by the ethical element in a praxis-oriented Marxism is, I think, crucial. Marxism purports to be not only a scientific analysis of what has happened and of what will happen in human history, but also a guide to action. Where does the ethical imperative come from and how is it legitimated? With Marx himself, certainly in his early writings, and I would say also in his mature writings, there is the assumption of a humanist ethic, as recognised by the Dalai Lama. The mainstream of Christian moral theology is also humanist in the sense that Christians generally assume that right conduct will maximise human interest or even happiness in the long run (the eternal perspective), though this humanism has been challenged by James Gustafson in his recent book, *Theology and Ethics*. The theme of man's domination over nature and history is as persistent in Marxist ethics as in Jewish and Christian ethics.

III

A Christian critique of Marxism

'Except the Lord build the house their labour is but lost that build it; except the Lord keep the city, the watchman waketh but in vain', sings the psalmist. It is the assertion by Marxists that salvation will come from the unaided efforts of men – the rejection of divine initiative – which is the main defect of Marxism from a Christian point of view. On this point Christians take a radically anti-humanist stand. While they can welcome the Marxist notion of the free development of each being a condition of the free development of all, and of this goal as being one for which men should strive, Christians insist that this can be reached only by divine action and not in this order of things. We must be careful here, however, for Marxists do not believe in the possibility of achieving this end in the present economic and social order. As we have already noted, the problem for Marxists, as for Christians, is a structural one. Yet the former maintain that this end can be achieved by the unaided efforts of humans through social and political action. The similarity between Christianity and Marxism is underlined by the Haitian Marxist Jacques Roumain. He once told how he had written a life of Jesus the revolutionary for his son, 'because at that time, it was the best means of teaching him respect and love of man, hatred of exploiters, the dignity of poverty, the necessity for the "end of the world" – the world of oppression, of misery, of ignorance'. And yet Christians believe that Marxists are mistaken in converting questions about economic, social and political organisation into questions of 'ultimate concern'. They make the same error as John Stuart Mill made and to which he refers in that famous passage of his *Autobiography*:

> 'it occurred to me to put the question directly to myself: suppose that all your objects in life were realised: that all the changes in institutions and opinions which you are looking forward to, could be completely effected at this very instant: would this be a great joy and happiness to you? And an irrepressible self-consciousness distinctly answered "no!" At this my heart sank within me: the whole foundation on which my life was constructed fell down. All my happiness was to have been found in the continual pursuit of this end. The end had ceased to charm, and how could there ever again be any interest in the means?'

Social reorganisation is, for the Christian, a necessary condition of salvation, but it is not a sufficient condition.

It may be said that this statement of the position implies a supernaturalism and belief in God as a personal (or super-personal) being. The short answer to this is to agree that this is indeed what is assumed and that this is what the great body of Christians believe today and have believed for two thousand years.

The question which then arises is how the action of God in the world relates to human activity. Are Christians saying that part of the work of overthrowing this sinful order and bringing in God's reign is achieved by men and the rest by some kind of supernatural divine action? Some have, indeed, said this. Others have, however, rightly rejected this way of stating the problem. They have pictured God as working through those human actions and natural events which contribute to the coming of His Kingdom. Marxists may ask at this point whether Christians, in asserting this, are merely saying, in mythical form, that they approve of these actions. If this is indeed all that Christians mean then Marxists may well, in applauding the same actions in more prosaic terms, be saying substantially the same thing. If, on the other hand, Christians are making some kind of cognitive claim, Marxists will rightly demand how the alleged divine action is related to human action.

The kind of 'double causation' Christians have in mind may be illustrated in terms of the relationship between the author of a play and the characters who appear in it. While it is undoubtedly true that it is the playwright who decides what each of the characters will do, it is also the case that a good author will ensure that each character acts 'in character'; the action of each can be accounted for in terms of the person he or she has become in the course of the play. The author makes characters who make themselves. Even in the context of the play, there is a difference between characters jumping and being pushed. A good playwright does not bring about the end he desires by imposing it from without – by forcing the characters to behave in a manner which is 'out of character'. He does so by allowing their 'free' actions to contribute to this end in the context of the material situation in which they are living. The question whether there exists a playwright at all may well be debated by the characters, and the point at issue between them is not merely one of differing attitudes but also a difference of cognitive judgment. Theists and atheists disagree; Christians are theists. Marxists are (operationally at least) atheists.

The other issue which the Dalai Lama raised is also relevant for Christians who might have objections to some of the means which Marxists are prepared to use. Marxists are sometimes blamed for believing that 'the end justifies the means', and the most satisfactory reply to this is to the effect that if the ends don't nothing will! In so far as something is considered as a means, it can be justified only by the end to which it is a means. Everyone believes that some ends justify some means. What Christians might question is whether some of the ends posited by Marxists will in fact justify the means which they are prepared to employ and to defend. It is not that Christians are necessarily wedded to an ethic of absolute rules and prohibitions, and are forbidden from taking consequences into account in determining the rightness of an action. Some traditional moral theology would assert that there are certain things a Christian can never do, whatever the consequences of not doing them might be. According to this view it would be wrong, for example, to take 'innocent' life whatever the consequences of not doing so might be; we are not responsible for what happens as a result of our non-actions. This is not an ethical position which I and many Christians share. What then is our objection to Marxism on this count? Perhaps it is a matter of emphasis. Christians will give more weight to moral rules and less to calculations of immediate advantage. In many cases, however, Marxists seem to be more realistic and consistent than Christians, who often want men, for example, to kill without hating.

'We must develop hatred', declared Che Guevara, 'in order to transform man into a machine for killing.' Some Christians who talk blithely about violence fail to face up to the fact that that such violence will be likely to increase the hatred of one group for another. How is it possible to get people to make the sacrifices needed for armed resistance unless they hate their enemies? Yet Christians are bound to love their enemies.

A Christian critique of Christianity

It is a temptation, and one into which many Christian writers fall, to maintain that the history of Christianity, with all its ambiguities, is irrelevant to the truth of the gospel. We sometimes say that it is not that Christianity has been tried and has failed but that it has not been tried at all. Yet for those who believe that the Church is the Body of Christ this is no way forward. Unless we are prepared to distinguish, as some Protestants are, between a visible and an invisible Church, it is impossible to deny that the Church has been, and still is, guilty of some of the most appalling crimes in human history. How is the Christian to make sense of Christianity as a historical phenomenon? How are we to justify the anti-Semitism not just of individual Christians, but of the Church as an institution? How are we to explain the persecution and even torture inflicted not by Christians in their private capacity but by official or semi-official Church bodies? How are we to justify the fact that the Church has frequently sided with the rich and powerful against the poor and oppressed? Christians have often replaced a trinitarian monotheism, univeral in its scope and relevance, by a henotheistic religion which 'makes a finite society whether cultural or religious, the object of trust as well as of loyalty' (H R Niebuhr). In doing so the Church has transformed itself from being a divinely chosen and guided instrument of God's purpose in the world into an end in itself.

All this must be admitted by Christians in dialogue with their critics. Yet they may claim that prophetic voices within the church have always been raised against these evil tendencies. The disruptive presence of the Holy Spirit, calling Christians back to that New Testament vision of the Church as the symbol of God's reign on earth, enables us to claim that the Church contains within itself the seeds of its own salvation.

The Oxford Movement represents a challenge to the idea of the Church as a mere department of state or as the religious side of the nation whose role is to give legitimation and respectability to the ruling classes of its day. The Church has a God-given task of confronting the world in the battle against evil. The stress which such theologians as Newman, Keble, Pusey and Ward place on the holiness and transcendence of God constitutes a potential challenge to all absolute claims on behalf of earthly institutions, including the Church itself, in so far as it falls short of the idea which it represents. Furthermore their emphasis upon supernatural faith provided an incentive for radical changes in the Church of their day. They did not themselves carry over this incentive to the sphere of social and political life; this was the work of their successors in the Anglo-Catholic movement. These men, some of whom are discussed in another essay in this volume, saw faith as a stimulus to political and social action rather than a substitute for it and would have agreed with Tiran Nersoyan that 'the alternative for the exploited has not been belief or struggle, but belief or despair'.

Contributors

Roger Arguile: Team Vicar at St Bertelin's in Stafford Team Ministry.

John Davies: Canon Missioner of St Asaph; author of *Creed and Conflict* and other works, and worked in South Africa for fourteen years.

Terry Drummond: Fieldwork Services Officer of the Church Army.

Charles Elliott: Director of Christian Aid; formerly Professor of Development at the University of Swansea.

Michael Garde: A member of the Mennonite community in Dublin.

Emmett Jarrett: Vicar of St John's, Bowdoin Street, Boston, USA.

Gresham Kirkby: Vicar of St Paul's, Bow Common, London.

Michael Langford: Vicar of St. James, Hartlepool; formerly an industrial chaplain in South Shields.

Kenneth Leech: Race Relations Field Officer at the Church of England's Board for Social Responsibility.

Andrew Louth: Chaplain of Worcester College, Oxford; author of *The Origins of the Christian Mystical Tradition.*

Eleanor McLaughlin: Professor of Church History at Andover Newton Seminary, Massachusetts; Assistant Priest at St John's, Boston; co-editor of *Religion and Sexism, Women of Spirit*, and other works.

David Nicholls: Vicar of Littlemore, Oxford; formerly Lecturer in Politics at the University of the West Indies, Trinidad; author of *The Pluralist State* and other works.

John Orens: Lecturer in History at Boston University; one of the founders of the Jubilee Group in the USA.

Judith Pinnington: Has taught church history in Duquesne University and at the Irish School of Ecumenics; has done extensive research on 19th-century Anglicanism.

Valerie Pitt: Head of the Department of Liberal Studies at Thames Polytechnic in South London.

Aelred Stubbs: A member of the Community of the Resurrection.

Rowan Williams: Lecturer in Divinity at Cambridge University; author of *The Wound of Knowledge* and other works.